BUSINESS PERSC
A LEGAL THEORY OF

Business Persons

A Legal Theory of the Firm

ERIC W. ORTS

OXFORD
UNIVERSITY PRESS

Great Clarendon Street, Oxford, OX2 6DP,
United Kingdom

Oxford University Press is a department of the University of Oxford.
It furthers the University's objective of excellence in research, scholarship,
and education by publishing worldwide. Oxford is a registered trade mark of
Oxford University Press in the UK and in certain other countries

Published in the United States of America by Oxford University Press
198 Madison Avenue, New York, NY 10016, United States of America

British Library Cataloguing in Publication Data
Data available

Library of Congress Cataloging in Publication Data
Data available

ISBN 978–0–19–967091–8 (Hbk.)
ISBN 978–0–19–874646–1 (Pbk.)

For my father, Keith H. Orts, who provided
my first and closest example of a
free and professional "business person"

The clouds part revealing a congregation of bodies
united into one immaterial body, a fictive person
around whom the air is blurred with money, force

from which much harm will come, to whom my welfare
matters nothing. . . .

— Timothy Donnelly, *The Cloud Corporation*
(Wave Books 2010, p. 34)

The world begs for dreamers to set up shop, invent a new product or social technology, and create the kinds of breakthroughs that will bring us together to act responsibly as passengers on this magnificent place we call home. This is truer today than ever before.

— Paul Hawken, *The Ecology of Commerce: A Declaration of Sustainability*
(HarperBusiness, rev. ed. 2010, p. xxiii)

Contents

Preface to the Paperback Edition

In the few years since the publication of the hardcover edition of *Business Persons*, several large-scale developments highlight the continuing salience of some of the book's main themes.

First, we see a hardening in some leading societies in the world—most notably in China and Russia, as well as other bellwethers such as Kenya and Turkey—toward the reassertion of governmental primacy in institutional organization. Strong states, of course, are not going to wither away any time soon. An important prerequisite for various kinds of intermediate-level organizations including business firms and nonprofits, however, is an open structure of governmental regulation that provides the social infrastructure for these institutional persons to be created and maintained. In other words, some version of "the rule of law" is needed.[1] One of the main arguments in *Business Persons* is that legal and governmental respect accorded to business firms matters—not only for the prospects of the firms themselves and their participants, but for civilization generally. I hope to have more to say about the general topic of the relationship between business and government in future work.

Second, we see continuity in a theme emphasized in *Business Persons* regarding the importance of the legal recognition of firms as "entities" with rights and duties. In 2014, the *Hobby Lobby* case decided by the U.S. Supreme Court joined *Citizens United* as a leading illustration of how the attribution of "legal personality" for firms can have large practical consequences.[2] *Hobby Lobby* recognized that a business corporation founded on Christian principles, owned by a close-knit religious family, and operated accordingly (e.g. not open on Sundays, refusing to sell shot glasses, and offering Christian counseling to employees) had religious rights that it could assert as an organizational person. The Court held that companies

---

[1] See Chapters 1, 3, and 5. An implicit argument here is that a healthy institutional environment allowing for the free development and evolution of business firms requires some version of democratic government or at least a version of "the rule of law" that respects organizational autonomy. The retrenchment of regimes in China and Russia on this score reinforces an emerging global historical trend away from democratic government. Larry Diamond, "Facing Up to the Democratic Recession," 26 *Journal of Democracy* 141 (2015) (tracing a reversal of an historical trend toward greater numbers of democracies in the world beginning in 2006); Andrew Jacobs and Chris Buckley, "In China, Civic Groups' Freedom, and Followers, Are Vanishing," *New York Times*, Feb. 27, p. A4 (reporting on a recent crackdown on independent nonprofit organizations). The recession of democracies worldwide follows a previous historical boom of democratic governments in the closing decades of the twentieth century. See Samuel P. Huntington, *The Third Wave: Democratization in the Late Twentieth Century* (University of Oklahoma Press 1991). In 1974, there were only 46 democratic governments in the world accounting for about 30 percent of the total number of nation-states. The succeeding several decades witnessed an historic turn in favor of democratic government, reaching a peak of 119 electoral democracies in 2006 including about 60 percent of the global total. Diamond, op. cit., pp. 141–3 & fig. 1.

[2] *Burwell v. Hobby Lobby Stores, Inc.*, 134 S. Ct. 2751 (2014); *Citizens United v. Federal Election Commission*, 130 S. Ct. 876 (2010). *Citizens United* is discussed at length in Chapter 7.

(specifically Hobby Lobby and other firms with similar characteristics) may raise a religious objection against complying with a federal health care requirement for firms to contribute to insurance for their employees to pay for contraception that a company's owners and managers deemed to function immorally as "abortifacients" (i.e. abortion-causing).[3] My own view is that *Hobby Lobby* was incorrectly decided—not because the Court recognized business firms as a legitimate "persons" with rights, but because the Court once again undertheorized the nature of corporations in a manner similar to treatment accorded to them in *Citizens United*.[4] Companies and their owners may indeed have religious rights, but these should have been balanced against similar rights of Hobby Lobby's 13,000 employees (and another firm's 950 employees).[5] An opposing view is that those in positions of responsibility in cases of a strongly unified ownership and management should have the legal authority to make moral and religious decisions on behalf of their firms.[6] However one judges the wisdom or correctness of the result in *Hobby Lobby* itself, the broader point is that the case exemplifies the continuing critical importance of political, legal, and philosophical debates about the nature of business firms (and other organizations) and correlative conceptions of rights and duties in society. Other related issues include the responsibility of business firms to respect and protect basic human rights (e.g. against genocide and human trafficking) and rights of privacy.[7]

---

[3] *Hobby Lobby*, op. cit., pp. 2759–60, 2764–5, 2785.

[4] Eric Orts, "Theorizing the Firm: Social Ontology in the Supreme Court," 65 *DePaul Law Review* (forthcoming 2015); "Undertheorizing the Corporation Continued: Hobby Lobby and Employees' Rights," The Conglomerate (July 16, 2014), available at http://www.lawblogs.net/go/undertheorizing-the-corporation-continued-hobby-lobby-and-employees-rights. See also my discussion in Chapter 7.

[5] *Hobby Lobby*, op. cit., pp. 2764–5. Similarly to *Citizens United* (see chapter 7), the dissenting opinion also misses the mark in failing to see that the relevant question is "who counts" as participants in a particular businesses. It seems to me that the religious and moral rights of individuals regarding general government health benefits should generally trump religious rights that may otherwise be asserted by firms.

[6] For a cogent argument along these lines, see Amy J. Sepinwall, "Conscience and Complicity: Assessing Pleas for Religious Exemptions after *Hobby Lobby*," 82 *University of Chicago Law Review* (forthcoming 2015).

[7] In one case noted in the hardcover edition of *Business Persons*, the U.S. Supreme Court declined to find jurisdiction to consider whether non-U.S. multinational corporations could be held liable for violations of human rights abroad under the Alien Torts Statute. *Kiobel v. Royal Dutch Petroleum Co.*, 133 S. Ct. 1659 (2013). The case involved corporations based in the U.K. and the Netherlands for actions carried out in Nigeria. The Court refused to consider the Second Circuit's more general argument that "the law of nations does not recognize corporate liability" for human rights violations, potentially leaving the door open for future claims against U.S.-based firms. Id., p. 1663 (citing *Kiobel v. Royal Dutch Petroleum Co.*, 621 F.3d 111 (2d Cir. 2010)). See also Roxanna Altholz, "Chronicle of a Death Foretold: The Future of U.S. Human Rights Litigation Post-*Kiobel*," 102 *California Law Review* 1495 (2014); Doug Cassel, "Suing Americans for Human Rights Torts Overseas: The Supreme Court Leaves the Door Open," 89 *Notre Dame Law Review* 1773 (2014). These kinds of cases also call into question whether international and national laws should change in order to impose responsibility and accountability on firms for complicity in violations of basic human rights of life and security for individuals. See, e.g., Jennifer M. Green, "The Rule of Law at a Crossroad: Enforcing Corporate Responsibility in International Investment Through the Alien Tort Statute," 35 *University of Pennsylvania Journal of International Law* 1085 (2014); Gwynne L. Skinner, "Beyond *Kiobel*: Providing Access to Judicial Remedies for Violations of International Human Rights Norms by Transnational Business in a New (Post-*Kiobel*) World," 46 *Columbia Human Rights Law Review* 158 (2014).

With respect to the complex topic of rights of privacy and business firms, see Eric W. Orts and Amy J. Sepinwall, "Privacy and Organizational Persons," 99 *Minnesota Law Review* 2231 (2015).

A third theme explored in *Business Persons* that has attracted expanding interest concerns the wonderful diversity of the sizes and purposes of business enterprises enabled by the flexible structure of modern organizational law. So-called "social enterprises" and parallels in "socially responsible investing" provide examples of how the changing structures of business may respond to some larger social challenges. Business and consumers may play a larger role than most imagine today in responding to global problems such as climate change and inequalities of wealth.[8] Recent evidence suggests that experiments with benefit corporations and other "hybrid social enterprises" may be accelerating.[9] Some evidence suggests that consumer preferences increasingly favor "sustainable" and "socially responsible" products and services.[10] The number and size of funds following strategies of "social impact investing" is growing.[11] And theoretical treatments are evolving to keep pace.[12]

Looking forward, one can say that the forms and features of "business persons" will continue to play an important part not only in addressing the standard economic problems of the production and consumption of goods and services, but also in dealing with larger moral and environmental concerns on our teeming planet, which is populated by a complex web of organizations as well as people. Getting a handle on the legal levers that influence the management and ownership of "business persons" will therefore remain essential.

---

[8] See, e.g., Eric W. Orts, "Climate Contracts," 29 *Virginia Environmental Law Journal* 197 (2011) (arguing for business to play a role at various levels to address climate change); Michael P. Vandenbergh, "Private Environmental Governance," 99 *Cornell Law Review* 129 (2013) (examining the positive role of business firms in addressing global environmental problems).

[9] I describe "hybrid social enterprise" here in Chapter 5. Although "social enterprise" is not yet clearly conceived as a "hybrid" category in a manner that would allow precise empirical work, some scholars have identified a general historical trend of growth of these alternative forms of enterprise worldwide. See, e.g., Bob Doherty, et al., *Management for Social Enterprise* 3–20 (2009); Janelle A. Kerlin, "A Comparative Analysis of the Global Emergence of Social Enterprise," 21 *Voluntas: International Journal of Voluntary and Nonprofit Organizations* 162 (2010).

[10] For survey evidence (though not always a reliable indicator of actual behavior) that consumers prefer "socially responsible" products, see Markus Kitzmueller and Jay Shimshack, "Economic Perspectives on Corporate Social Responsibility," 50 *Journal of Economic Literature* 51, 51–2 (2012).

[11] According to one estimate by an industry trade group, the growth of "social impact investing" has been accelerating in recent years. Since 2012, funds designated broadly to have "social impact" objectives have increased from 206 to 316 funds worldwide, and corresponding assets under management have grown from $13 billion to $23 billion. Wharton Social Impact Initiative, "Does Social Impact Demand Financial Sacrifice?" (Dec. 23, 2014), available at http://socialimpact.wharton.upenn.edu/impact-story/social-impact-demand-financial-sacrifice/.

[12] See, e.g., Dana Brakman Reiser, "Theorizing Forms for Social Enterprise," 62 *Emory Law Journal* 681 (2013); Wendy K. Smith, et al., "Managing Social-Business Tensions: A Review and Research Agenda for Social Enterprise," 23 *Business Ethics Quarterly* 407 (2013).

Preface to the Original Edition

For the past several decades, theories of the firm have been dominated by the discipline of economics. Even in law schools, economic approaches have informed competing theories that emphasize principal–agent relationships, transaction costs, a "nexus" of contracts, or property rights as central to understanding the nature and purposes of the business enterprise. (I refer to the "firm" and the "business enterprise" as synonymous and interchangeable in this book.)

In many respects, these economic theories of the firm have proven useful. They throw light on some tensions and challenges that arise when managing and governing business enterprises. For example, to the extent that people tend to serve their own self-interests—a well-known universal assumption in neoclassical economics which often holds in the real world—it makes sense to consider how to organize work within a firm to provide strong incentives for its owners, investors, managers, and employees to work together toward the end of sustained profit-making. Positive economic performance of the firm as a whole usually translates into benefits for all of those who contribute to its success.[1]

However, economic theories do not provide an adequate understanding of business firms. There are at least six major reasons for this inadequacy.

First, various economic theories of the firm often conflict with each other. Theories that emphasize "property rights," for example, highlight different aspects of firms than theories that emphasize "transaction costs" or "implicit contracts." Reviewing the disparate theories of the firm within his discipline, the economist Sidney Winter observes:

> Without demeaning the contributions that any of us have made . . . we must acknowledge that the present state is one of incoherence. If we ask, "What does economics have to say about the role of the business firm in a market economy?" the response will be silence followed by an excited babble of significantly conflicting answers—an interesting babble, but a babble nonetheless.[2]

Another assessment of economic theories of the firm concurs. After a review of the large amount of academic literature on the topic, this assessment concludes that "there is still no unified theory of the firm" and observes that "many competing theoretical frameworks coexist, with only partial answers concerning the nature of the firm, its boundaries, and its internal organization."[3] But this situation is not

---

[1] For an accessible introduction to economic theories of the firm, see, e.g., John Roberts, *The Modern Firm: Organizational Design for Performance and Growth* (Oxford University Press 2004).

[2] Sidney G. Winter, "On Coase, Competence, and the Corporation," in *The Nature of the Firm: Origins, Evolution, and Development* (Oliver E. Williamson and Sidney G. Winter eds.) (Oxford University Press 1991), p. 179.

[3] Pierre Garrouste and Stéphane Saussier, "Looking for a Theory of the Firm: Future Challenges," 58 *Journal of Economic Behavior and Organization* 178, 194 (2005).

new. As far back as the 1960s, a survey counted at least twenty-one different "concepts of the firm" in the literature of business and economics.[4]

Several leading economists recognize the need for legal theory to assist in providing an improved conceptual understanding of the firm. Nobel laureates in economics such as Ronald Coase and Oliver Williamson, for example, highlight the importance of legal concepts. Coase's classic article on "The Nature of the Firm" emphasizes legal agency relationships, including the ubiquitous type of agency known as employment.[5] In his Nobel Prize acceptance lecture, Coase observes that "the legal system" has a "profound effect on the working of the economic system and may in certain respects be said to control it."[6] Williamson stresses the importance of legal contracts for the construction of governance arrangements within firms.[7] Another influential economic theorist of the firm, Oliver Hart, focuses on "property rights" as central to the concept of the firm.[8] Property, as well as contracts, describes relationships that are essentially legally defined.

As the chapters of this book will reveal, these economic debates about the nature of the firm examine various pieces of the overall puzzle without a comprehensive view of how the pieces fit together. Only a full-fledged legal theory of the firm can supply the intellectual coherence demanded by these competing and often conflicting economic theories.

Although I do not survey the various modern economic theories of the firm on their own terms here, a primary argument of this book is that a recovery of legal theories can address some of the problems, conflicts, and omissions encountered in many economic theories. In other words, I maintain that answers to some of the most fundamental questions about the firm's "nature," "boundaries," "purposes," and "internal organization" are to be found in the discipline of law rather than economics. Stronger legal foundations will put economics as well as other disciplines in a better position to build and refine their own respective theories of business firms.

A *second reason* that economics is inadequate for a full understanding of the nature of firms is that law is needed to explain the social origins and foundations of firms. Business firms are created and governed through legal institutions. Without law, business firms cannot exist. Law provides the essential social structure of firms because it recognizes them and provides the social rules by which they are both (a)

---

[4] Fritz Machlup, "Theories of the Firm: Marginalist, Behavioral, Managerial," 57 *American Economic Review* 1, 26–8 (1967) (describing ten different theories of the firm in different contexts).

[5] R.H. Coase, "The Nature of the Firm," 4 *Economica* (n.s.) 386 (1937). Almost every anthology of economic theories of the firm includes this article or substantial excerpts from it. See, e.g., *The Economic Nature of the Firm: A Reader* (Randall S. Kroszner and Louis Putterman eds.) (Cambridge University Press, 3rd ed., 2009), pp. 79–95; *The Nature of the Firm*, op. cit., pp. 18–33.

[6] Coase, "The Institutional Structure of Production," 82 *American Economic Review* 713, 717–18 (1992).

[7] See, e.g., Oliver E. Williamson, *The Economic Institutions of Capitalism: Firms, Markets, Relational Contracting* (Free Press 1998).

[8] See Oliver Hart, *Firms, Contracts, and Financial Structure* (Oxford University Press 1995); Oliver Hart and John Moore, "Property Rights and the Nature of the Firm," 98 *Journal of Political Economy* 1119 (1990).

governed and organized internally and (b) treated externally with respect to questions of responsibility and liability for their actions. As explained in Chapters 1 and 2, business firms are artificial entities and "persons" recognized by legal rules within a framework of the evolving cultural traditions of global civilization. The boundaries and social powers of firms are also, to a large extent, legally defined and shaped.

Although lawyers today continue to learn these basic truths and to use them in everyday practice, they are sometimes forgotten by contemporary scholars. Even some legal scholars have been seduced by the false promises and "imperial" claims of economics as a master discipline.[9] Unfortunately, some economists have developed an attitude of "hubris" and "reject . . . anything that . . . does not fit into their own microeconomic theory."[10] And as discussed at various points in this book, the challenge to traditional methods of legal analysis posed by the jurisprudential movement known as law-and-economics has led to a large incursion of economic thinking into the legal field of business organization. My aim here is not to disparage law-and-economics or neoclassical economics as such, but rather to point out their theoretical limitations and the need for a foundational *non-economic* legal perspective for constructing a robust and realistic theory of the firm. One main purpose of this book is to revive a foundational legal understanding of the business firm as a challenge to the primacy that economics has asserted in this field over the last several decades.

A *third reason* for developing a modern legal theory of the firm is that the law allows for the consideration of multiple values in structuring organizations and resolving disputes and controversies. Contrary to the assumptions of some modern economists, "efficiency" is not the only moral value that the law can or should serve—even if efficiency is elevated to the level of large-scale social efficiency as a goal of so-called "welfare economics." Many utilitarian economists embrace this overall objective of social efficiency, but it is not universally shared.

Philosophers who emphasize deontological principles (such as duties to be honest, trustworthy, or loyal) provide a competing point of view.[11] Religious leaders and traditions also emphasize substantive ethical duties as a check on calculations of self-interest (or even aggregated collective interest). These duties serve as grounding principles to govern individual decision-making in everyday practical situations.

---

[9] See, e.g., Edward P. Lazear, "Economic Imperialism," 115 *Quarterly Journal of Economics* 99 (2000).

[10] Thomas Mayer, *Truth Versus Precision in Economics* (Edward Elgar 1993), p. 82. In fact, more complexity and differences of opinion characterize the world of economics than some economists and law-and-economists would like to admit. For an argument for "a more modest economics" that balances formal abstract modeling with a respect for empirical methods, see id., p. 7.

[11] An attempt has recently been made to advance a "unified theory" of ethics bringing together competing views of utilitarian, deontological, and social contract theories. Derek Parfit, *On What Matters*, vol. 1 (Oxford University Press 2011). However, most contemporary philosophers and legal scholars still fall into one of the three major camps. Most economists tend to follow a version of utilitarianism.

Democracy offers yet another potentially competing value. On at least one interpretation of democratic government, elected representatives should deliberate about competing policy prescriptions and values, and then make choices through political processes which are in turn expressed through the adoption of formal legislation. The democratic value of "following the law" then becomes another moral reason to decide to adhere to one course of action rather than another.[12]

With respect to business firms, this complexity of normative values means that business leaders will often find themselves having to choose among different recommended courses of action. Although they may prefer to rationalize decisions as "efficient," high-level managers will inevitably also find themselves in situations that call for the invocation or at least serious consideration of other moral values. Business ethics expresses one set of normative constraints and positive values for decision-making. Following the law expresses another set of normative constraints and positive exhortations. Negative constraints include: Don't lie, cheat, or steal. Positive norms include: Act with honesty, loyalty, fairness, justice, and integrity. According to many serious philosophical and religious views, one cannot reduce these values to economic calculations of self-interest or collective social welfare.

An authoritative expression of the plurality of values in business management appears in the American Law Institute's statement of the "purpose" or "objective" of business corporations. (As described more fully in the chapters of this book, corporations have become the preeminent legal form of modern business enterprise in terms of economic and organizational size.) In addition to pursuing a "primary" objective of profit and economic gain, on this view, a corporation as an organizational person is "obliged, to the same extent as a natural person, to act within the boundaries set by law" and may "take into account ethical considerations that are reasonably regarded as appropriate to the responsible conduct of business."[13] Scholars may quibble about whether law should be mandatory and ethics permissive, as this language seems to suggest. But the main point here is that this official summary supports the idea of competing values and purposes in business. Even though they are organized primarily for economic purposes, corporations and other business firms are not only profit-maximizing machines. Business firms are organizations composed of people, and they should therefore operate according to human values that are not expressed only by cold calculations of profit and loss.[14] The view that business enterprises should maximize wealth and profits without regard to law and ethics—along the lines of some version of the formula that "greed is good"—is an artifact of an overly abstracted economics rather than a

---

[12] For reflections on the normative features of legal rules and reasoning, see, e.g., Frederick Schauer, *Thinking Like a Lawyer: A New Introduction to Legal Reasoning* (Harvard University Press 2009).

[13] American Law Institute, *Principles of Corporate Governance: Analysis and Recommendations*, sect. 2.01 (1994). Business corporations may also "devote a reasonable amount of resources to public welfare, humanitarian, educational, and philanthropic purposes," which many laws authorize and many ethical traditions encourage. Id.

[14] For an elaboration on this theme, arguing that non-economic objectives should have been integrated more centrally into the ALI's statement of objective, see James Boyd White, "How Should We Talk About Corporations? The Languages of Economics and of Citizenship," 94 *Yale Law Journal* 1416 (1985).

product of traditional sources of legal and ethical reasoning. As the legal scholar James Boyd White argues, "the language of economics is inadequate" to describe what business corporations and other firms "do and ought to do."[15] Legal theory is needed too.

Even some of the strongest proponents of a focused economic objective in business recognize that law and ethics impose constraints. For example, in a famous essay urging business corporations to abjure temptations to "do good" as a "corporate social responsibility," the economist Milton Friedman argues that business executives should act in accordance with the desires of the company's owners, "which generally will be to make as much money as possible." Friedman also agrees, however, that the executive must also do so "while conforming to the basic rules of the society, both those embodied in law and those embodied in ethical custom."[16] Others argue that law and ethics impose positive duties for "good citizenship" as well as negative constraints.[17]

A *fourth reason* to develop a legal theory of the firm is that the competing values expressed by law open the possibility for significant variance, experimentation, and reform with respect to the future of business enterprise. Some traditional views of economics shackle the imagination with respect to the purposes of firms. There is no natural law of corporations, for example, that mandates "shareholder value maximization" as the only permissible goal of management. This mantra is merely a prescription recommended by some economic theories of the firm—particularly some rather narrow financial theories that purport to reduce the operational complexity of corporate firms to a mathematical function. Although it may prove useful in many situations to focus on shareholder value as an important objective for business corporations, an appreciation of the legal foundations of firms opens a wider vista of possibilities. Even the mandate to "maximize shareholder value" usually sets no specific time horizon, for example, thus providing managers with considerable flexibility for interpretation of long-term strategy. More generally, there is no legal reason that the governing rules of business firms cannot be altered to account for an array of modern social challenges. In fact, as this book will discuss, there are many privileges as well as obligations that society bestows upon the legal "persons" of corporations and other firms which can be justified only by reference to larger concerns of social responsibility, including a need to account for the costs of "externalities" that firms may impose when pursuing profit and wealth. ("Externalities" refer to the economic costs that are not included in the "internal" decision-making processes of firms, and they may also encompass non-economic harms such

---

[15] Id., p. 1425.

[16] Milton Friedman, "The Social Responsibility of Business Is to Increase its Profits," *New York Times*, September 13, 1970 (magazine), p. 33.

[17] I am one of those in this camp espousing positive ethical duties. See Eric W. Orts, "Ethics, Risk, Environmental Management, and Corporate Social Responsibility," in *Environmental Protection and the Social Responsibility of Firms: Perspectives from Law, Economics, and Business* (Bruce L. Hay, Robert N. Stavins, and Richard H.K. Vietor eds.) (Resources for the Future Press 2005), pp. 184–96; Eric W. Orts, "From Corporate Social Responsibility to Global Citizenship," in *The INSEAD-Wharton Alliance on Globalizing: Strategies for Building Successful Global Businesses* (Hubert Gatignon and John Kimberly eds.) (Cambridge University Press 2004), pp. 331–52.

as physical injuries or harm to reputation, privacy, or violations of basic human rights.[18])

The unfolding historical narrative of business enterprise tells the story of changing laws and norms that represent an evolving balance among various normative objectives and constraints that are built into the social and legal structure of firms. This evolving normative balance does not mean that various values themselves are always "balanced" when participants in firms make decisions. Law is often designed and written to provide right answers in particular defined situations. And moral reasoning often leads to right answers in specific situations as well. The point is rather that law is normatively complex in a manner that allows for different social values (e.g. economic efficiency, justice, honesty, and loyalty) to be considered in different situations when they are most salient or compelling. A legal theory of the firm allows institutional space for different values to apply in different circumstances.

A *fifth reason* for reviving a legal understanding of business firms is to inform contemporary political debates about the role of business corporations and other firms in society. Current political treatments of the nature of corporations and firms are often unsophisticated with respect to a basic understanding of how the law creates and regulates firms. For example, the U.S. Supreme Court in the landmark case of *Citizens United* reinforced a view that business corporations count as full-fledged "persons" with constitutional rights of free speech in political elections.[19] This case raises deep and important questions of legal theory regarding the nature and purposes of business firms, as well as questions of how constitutional and political theory should deal with the evolving place of business firms and other organizations within democratic societies. *Citizens United* is important because it significantly shifts the political structure of the United States toward allowing an unprecedented amount of individual and corporate money to be channeled into electoral politics through political action committees (PACs) and otherwise.[20] "SuperPACs" representing large donations by business firms as well as individuals now have a great impact on U.S. Presidential campaigns as well as other federal and state elections.[21]

Arguments on both sides of the *Citizens United* debate would benefit from a more solid understanding of the legal underpinnings of business firms. During the writing of this book, for example, U.S. Presidential candidate Mitt Romney

---

[18] On externalities and the firm, see also Chapter 1, page 22 and accompanying note 61.

[19] *Citizens United v. Federal Election Commission*, 130 S. Ct. 876 (2010).

[20] Id. See also *SpeechNow.org v. Federal Election Commission*, 599 F.3d 686 (D.C. Cir. 2010) (extending *Citizens United* to allow unlimited individual contributions to PACs if used for "independent" communications in electoral campaigns).

[21] U.S. elections in 2012 broke records in terms of the amount of money spent in federal political campaigns. See, e.g., Nicholas Confessore, "Spending: The $6 Billion Election," *New York Times*, November 1, 2012, p. A14 (noting that total spending broke the previous record by at least $700 million). See also Russ Feingold, "The Money Crisis: How *Citizens United* Undermines Our Elections and the Supreme Court," 64 *Stanford Law Review Online* 145 (2012) (observing that current U.S. elections "will be financially dominated by big money, including, whether directly or indirectly, big money from the treasuries of corporations of all kinds").

responded to a question on the campaign trail about corporate taxation with a simple retort that "corporations are people, my friend."[22] The comedian Stephen Colbert then highlighted the issue in a satirical campaign to convince the public of the proposition that indeed "corporations are people."[23] *Citizens United* engendered a counter-movement to amend the Constitution to declare that corporations specifically are not "people" or "persons" for First Amendment purposes.[24] Underlying this controversy, in which both sides tend to leap quickly to either "pro" or "con" positions, are important and difficult questions about the nature and purposes of organizing people in corporations and other business firms, as well as nonprofit, charitable, and political associations. Only after understanding the complexities of these organizations can one adequately address questions about whether and how these organizational entities and persons should be recognized and treated in constitutional law. To insist that either "corporations are people" or "corporations are not people" elides the complex reality that business firms, including corporations, are in fact recognized legally as "persons" for some purposes and "not persons" for others. As discussed further in Chapter 1, the category of legal "persons" is itself a central one in legal theory. It applies to both human beings (e.g. "citizens" compared with "slaves" or "aliens") and various organized entities (including nation-states, for example, as well as business firms). Because the current political debate in the United States does not take account of these legal complexities, it tends to become falsely dichotomous. This characterization extends even to the divided Justices on the Supreme Court. As I argue in Chapter 7, both majority and dissenting opinions in *Citizens United* leave the concept of the corporation itself radically undertheorized. A deeper and more broadly accessible understanding of the legal nature of business firms would allow for the development of more sophisticated answers to potentially divisive questions about the political role of business firms in democratic societies.

A *sixth reason* for this book is its timeliness. Perhaps the time is now ripe for a recovery of legal theories of the firm in light of recent events that have revealed the failure of purely economic theories in the world of business and financial organization. A siren song of neoclassical economics has encouraged a hands-off approach to the regulation of business. By most authoritative accounts, however, this call for deregulation contributed to the largest meltdown of global financial markets since the Great Depression.[25]

---

[22] Ashley Parker, "'Corporations Are People,' Romney Tells Iowa Hecklers Angry Over His Tax Policy," *New York Times*, August 12, 2011, p. A16.

[23] For Colbert's campaign, see Charles McGrath, "Colbert Pushes 'Corporations Are People' Referendum," *New York Times*, December 6, 2011, <http://thecaucus.blogs.nytimes.com> (accessed September 29, 2012).

[24] See, e.g., Andy Kroll, "Can Citizens United Be Rolled Back?" *Mother Jones*, December 15, 2011, <http://www.motherjones.com> (accessed September 29, 2012).

[25] For a contemporaneous review of causes and culprits, see, e.g., "'A Race to the Bottom:' Assigning Responsibility for the Financial Crisis," Knowledge@Wharton, December 9, 2009, <http://knowledge.wharton.upenn.edu> (accessed September 29, 2012). For lucid accounts arguing that economists bear significant responsibility, see also Richard A. Posner, *A Failure of Capitalism: The Crisis of '08 and the Descent into Depression* (Harvard University Press 2009); Richard

A relatively unconstrained "free market" with respect to business institutions has also likely produced or at least exacerbated significant social problems of global inequality of wealth and environmental destruction. At least, a survey of the most pressing problems of modern global society in the twenty-first century does not allow for a sanguine view of unregulated markets as the universal and unfailing solution to these kinds of large social problems. Government and law continue to have essential roles to play. Another of the primary lessons of this book is that business firms do not exist entirely "free" of legal rules and frameworks. The establishment of relatively free markets of self-organizing firms and independently operating exchanges of goods and services is instead a structural product of preexisting legal structures which change over time.

This book contributes to an understanding of how business firms are created and governed in modern society. I hope that this understanding will serve as a foundation for better informed regulatory interventions and reforms. I hope also that it will provide inspiration for new entrepreneurial experiments and innovations in business. Regulatory alternatives of different legal forms of business enterprise are available that allow for the selection of different purposes and objectives (or combinations of purposes and objectives) of the firm. Competing values within business vocations appear as well, ranging along a spectrum from an unrelenting focus on profit maximization to the recognition of important ethical and legal principles as guiding stars. As discussed in greater detail in Chapter 5, new "social hybrid" business forms challenge traditional assumptions that the "profit" motive must always be separated institutionally from "social" objectives that aim, for example, at alleviating poverty or enhancing environmental sustainability.

I do not presume to choose among these various competing values—or advocate for some against others—and probably this kind of ethical choice is impossible to do in general non-situational terms.[26] My intuition is that economic efficiency should often take precedence when determining particular "rules of the game" for business firms, but not always. But even if economic efficiency is a goal, it is important to ask "efficiency for whom?" The current rules of the game for business may well contribute to widening global patterns of inequality of wealth distribution both within countries and among countries, though these rules may also contribute to general increases in overall global well-being. In some cases, non-economic values such as honesty, loyalty, or fairness should also be considered, recognized, and preferred. In yet other cases, one should consider whether legal rules promote justice, safety, and environmental protection, even when they may have significant

---

A. Posner, *The Crisis of Capitalist Democracy* (Harvard University Press 2011). For the official post-mortem, see Financial Crisis Inquiry Commission, *The Financial Crisis Inquiry Report* (Public Affairs 2011).

[26] On the likelihood of the "incommensurability" of different moral values, see Nien-hê Hsieh, "Incommensurable Values," *Stanford Encyclopedia of Philosophy*, <http://plato.stanford.edu/entries/value-ibncommensurable/> (July 23, 2007) (accessed September 29, 2012). See also Isaiah Berlin, "The Pursuit of the Ideal," in *The Proper Study of Mankind: An Anthology of Essays* (Henry Hardy and Roger Hausheer eds.) (Farrar, Straus and Giroux, 1998), pp. 1–16 (offering a pluralist view of incommensurable ends).

economic costs. Following economic efficiency alone as the preeminent guiding value for business firms and their regulation will most likely lead to an increasingly unjust, unhealthy, and perhaps even uninhabitable planet.

* * *

A prefatory word should be said also about how the legal theory of the firm advanced here fits with other views that have been developed about the nature of corporations and other business enterprises. Legal theories of the corporation and other business entities have ancient roots, and the arguments here take account of this historical legacy.[27] A legal theory of the firm can also positively influence the selection of historical topics. For example, recognizing the important difference between privately organized firms and state-owned firms, as discussed in Chapter 5, may suggest an historical focus on how particular societies have evolved to support each of these general types of business organization.

Also, as discussed above, influential economic theories of the firm should be revised to incorporate features of the legal theory advanced here.[28] Although economic theories of the firm have great value, they tend to employ partial and impoverished understandings of law. Economic theories therefore require significant supplementation on this score.[29] At a minimum, economic theories should take account of the legal manner in which the "entities" and "persons" of firms are created, maintained, and changed over time.

In addition to history and economics, political science is centrally important—and other academic disciplines are relevant as well, including anthropology, sociol-

---

[27] An historical understanding of the evolution of business firms in global perspective is important and not as well studied or known generally as it should be. For exceptions, see, e.g., Alfred D. Chandler, Jr., *Scale and Scope: The Dynamics of Industrial Capitalism* (Harvard University Press 1990); John Micklethwait and Adrian Wooldridge, *The Company: A Short History of a Revolutionary Idea* (Modern Library 2003); *A History of Corporate Governance Around the World* (Randall K. Morck ed.) (University of Chicago 2005); *The Invention of Enterprise: Entrepreneurship from Ancient Mesopotamia to Modern Times* (David S. Landes, Joel Mokyr, and William J. Baumol eds.) (Princeton University Press 2010).

[28] The literature on economic theories of the firm is immense. For an introduction, see *The Economic Nature of the Firm*, op. cit.; *The Nature of the Firm*, op. cit.; Roberts, op. cit. For leading treatments from different perspectives, see R.H. Coase, *The Firm, the Market, and the Law* (University of Chicago Press 1988); Richard M. Cyert and James G. March, *A Behavioral Theory of the Firm* (Blackwell Business, 2nd ed., 1992); Harold Demsetz, *Ownership, Control, and the Firm: The Organization of Economic Activity* (Basil Blackwell 1988); Oliver Hart, *Firms, Contracts, and Financial Structure*, op. cit.; Michael C. Jensen, *A Theory of the Firm: Governance, Residual Claims, and Organizational Forms* (Harvard University Press 2003); Edith Penrose, *The Theory of the Growth of the Firm* (Oxford University Press, 3rd ed., 1995); Oliver E. Williamson, *The Economic Institutions of Capitalism*, op. cit.

[29] I have outlined this argument previously. Eric W. Orts, "Shirking and Sharking: A Legal Theory of the Firm," 16 *Yale Law and Policy Review* 265 (1998). Others have advanced related arguments about the need for economists to include more law in their view of firms. See Geoffrey M. Hodgson, "The Legal Nature of the Firm and the Myth of the Firm-Market Hybrid," 9 *International Journal of Economics and Business* 37 (2002); Katsuhito Iwai, "Persons, Things and Corporations: The Corporate Personality Controversy and Comparative Corporate Governance," 47 *American Journal of Comparative Law* 583 (1999); Scott E. Masten, "A Legal Basis for the Firm," 4 *Journal of Law, Economics, & Organization* 181 (1988); Jean-Phillipe Robé, "The Legal Structure of the Firm," 1 *Accounting, Economics, and Law: A Convivium* (2011) (article 5).

ogy, and social psychology. This book on legal theory is meant to provide clarification of only one important dimension of business firms in modern society. It intends to supplement other perspectives, not to trump or replace these other points of view. At the same time, the book maintains that a legal perspective on the firm is an essential one.

* * *

Although this book is theoretical in its method, its ultimate aim is practical. I hope that providing a better legal understanding of the nature and purposes of business firms will better inform both business people and policy makers about the full range of their options. As legally authorized and constructed institutions, firms are best understood as social organizations composed of *business people* in the broad sense of the word. Although the primary signals that they follow are calibrated in the language and symbolic mathematics of economics—namely, profit and loss, financial value, and (for corporations) stock prices—business firms are human enterprises with representatives who speak in the legal language of power and authority.[30] They are organized as *business persons*. A legal theory of the firm provides a starting point for understanding this basic social truth—and elaborating its implications for both business management and public policy.

The theory offered here is radical, though not in the sense of "new." It is radical in the etymological sense of returning to conceptual roots that have been overlooked and often forgotten. Oliver Sacks refers to what he calls "scotoma," that is, a tendency in the physical sciences toward a loss of knowledge over time, which then requires occasional "rediscoveries" of old truths.[31] A version of scotoma afflicts the study of the law of business organizations today. For example, basic principles of agency law (reviewed in Chapter 2) provide the foundations for the growth of "trust" in business relationships. But an overgrowth of economic theory has hidden some of these legal roots for too long. Rediscovering the legal roots of the firm and translating them into a modern vernacular will provide a solid standpoint from which to address many issues regarding the management and regulation of firms in the future.

---

[30] Cf. White, op. cit. (discussing different "languages" used for talking about business firms). Further examination of this main point is also given in Chapters 1 and 2.

[31] Oliver Sacks, "Forgetting and Neglect in Science," in *Hidden Histories of Science* (Robert B. Silvers ed.) (New York Review Books 1995), p. 141, cited in Laura G. Pedraza-Fariña, "Patent Law and the Sociology of Innovation," 2013 *Wisconsin Law Review* 813 (2013).

Acknowledgments

As a footnote-attentive reader may adduce, this book emerged from what began as a larger project called *Rethinking the Firm: Theories of the Business Enterprise*. This larger work had gone so far in the research and writing process as to be under contract also with Oxford University Press, and due to an error of optimism (to be charitable with myself) was even listed as forthcoming for purchase from Amazon. As indicated in various footnotes, I hope to continue to work on other relevant theories of the firm dealing in the disciplines of history, economics, philosophy, and political theory and to publish this work in the future. At this juncture, however, I am very happy to thank my editor at Oxford, David Musson, for both his patience and flexibility in the face of the growing size and unwieldiness of my initial project and his recommendation (which was simultaneously made by my step-daughter, Dana Hagar) to expand an overly large single chapter dealing with legal theories of the firm into the present book. Other people within the organizational person of Oxford University Press who deserve acknowledgement include Niko Pfund, who convinced me to choose Oxford as a publisher over a few excellent rivals, and Matthew Derbyshire. Thanks are also due to Emma Booth who masterfully guided me through various aspects of the final stages of the book publishing process.

The list of other natural and organized persons to thank is very long. Harvard University and the Wharton School of the University of Pennsylvania supplied the time and money that made the research and writing of this book possible. The original idea for the project was hatched during a sabbatical at Harvard's Center for Ethics and the Professions, and much of the hardest thinking and writing occurred during another sabbatical taken from Wharton and Penn at home in Philadelphia. I thank my Department chairpersons at Wharton during these times, Janice Bellace and the late Tom Dunfee, for their support.

I am grateful for comments received at multiple presentations of various parts of this project at Wharton and Penn, as well as at NYU School of Law. Teaching two seminars on "Social Theory and the Business Enterprise" at Wharton and NYU Law were helpful in the development of my ideas, as were earlier presentations to faculty at the University of Bergamo, Florida State School of Law, the Law and Society Association, Sydney Law School, Temple University Law School, and Widener University School of Law (Delaware campus). Students in many versions of my Law of Corporate Management and Finance in Global Perspective course at Wharton (and its rough equivalent when visiting at various law and business schools) have had a formative influence. Jae Seon Choi deserves thanks for his work on an initial draft of the bibliography. I also thank Michael Carnevale, Caroline D'Angelo, and Mima Mohammed for cite-checking the manuscript. Lynn Selhat provided helpful professional editorial suggestions for the Preface, Introduction, and Conclusion. Amy Sepinwall gave helpful comments on penultimate versions of the Introduction,

Chapter 1, and Chapter 7. Three anonymous reviewers provided very useful suggestions as well.

The people who are owed the largest debt for their support and tolerance are my wife, Julie Orts, and my son, Emmett Orts. Julie is the "traffic" to my "weather." And Emmett honed his video-gaming skills, did homework, and walked the dog during many long Dad-is-writing hours. I am grateful also to other members of my immediate family: my parents, Keith and Carol; my siblings, Daryl, Sylvia, and Corinne (and their families); my step-daughters, Dana and Emily; my father-in-law Peter Perine and late mother-in-law Carol Perine; and my ex-wife and continuing co-parent, Janet Burns, and her mother, Joan Burns. Janet and Joan were especially helpful during the beginning stages of this project. I also thank my neighbors on Saint Mark's Square, as well as several organizational persons and the people associated with them: the Bachelors Barge Club, the First Unitarian Church of Philadelphia, and the Green Line Café.

Other friends, colleagues, co-workers, and students deserve mention as well (and my apologies to those whom I will inevitably but unintentionally omit). I thank all of my colleagues and students (and former colleagues and students) at the University of Pennsylvania as a group, and a number of them are found in Arts and Sciences and the Law School as well as Wharton. (This list is also long, and they know who they are.) The same goes for the cohort of faculty fellows at Harvard during my sabbatical there. (I'll name our leader: Dennis Thompson.) In addition, the following individuals deserve special thanks for their sundry roles as friends, advisers, former teachers, student assistants, office assistants, and otherwise: Rob Atkinson, Ken Beldon, Jeannette Chang, Jack Coffee, Julie Cohen, Cory de Torres, Dakota Dobyns, Tamara English, Harvey Goldschmid, Kent Greenawalt, Jennifer Hill, Ira Katznelson, the late Susan Kelly-Andrews, Jen Kollar, Charlie Krueger, Dan Kryder, Sean Laane, Lowell Lysinger, David Macauley, Gregory Mark, Peter Mayer, Larry Mitchell, Michael O'Malley, Mia Powell, Ricky Revesz, William H. Roberts, Hal Rosen, Joel Seligman, Jeffrey Sheehan, Jenna Shweitzer, Keith B. Smith, Robert S. Smith, Joanne Spigonardo, Lynn Stout, Peter Strauss, Geoffrey Strong, Ed Swaine, Aidan Synnott, Gunther Teubner, Cherly Vaughn-Curry, Natacha Vidal, Joseph Vining, Conna Weiner, and Harlan Wilson. All errors of course are mine.

Note on Footnotes

A prefatory caution is in order, especially for the non-academic reader. This is a work of legal theory, and some may find the book tough going in following the reasoning and arguments. Nevertheless, I have tried to make this book as accessible as possible to the general educated reader. The legal nature of modern business firms is complex, but this book attempts to provide a basic explanation to a broad audience of how business enterprises are built, maintained, and changed over time. Intended readers include students and scholars, employees and managers, investors and policy makers, and citizens and consumers. I have therefore endeavored to make my arguments and prose as nontechnical as possible. Some academic debates that general readers may find arcane are relegated mostly to footnotes (which general readers may do well to skip).[1] Readers are also encouraged to skip portions of the text that may involve questions that are too theoretical, academic, or otherwise not directly relevant to their interests and understanding.

The footnotes and references are in an adapted legal "Bluebook" style. For articles and citations of cases, the volume number is given first, followed by the title of the article or case reporter, and then followed by the first page number and year of publication. I give the full name of law reviews and other journals for the benefit of general readers and interdisciplinary scholars. "Note" or "Comment" refers to work authored by law students. For internet-based sources, I use the highest level link that is searchable. The bibliography includes only selected references (i.e. not all of the sources cited in the footnotes).

---

[1] Following in the best traditions of legal scholarship, this book is heavily footnoted, and I make no apology for the practice. For an inspiring defense and history of the art of giving references for one's statements, see Anthony Grafton, *The Footnote: A Curious History* (Harvard University Press 1999).

Introduction—The Recognition
and Boundaries of the Firm

[T]he normative integration of societies takes place only by way of institutionalizing principles of recognition that regulate in a comprehensible way the
forms of mutual recognition through which its members become involved in
the societal context of life.[1]

— Axel Honneth

We cannot know what something is without knowing how it is marked off
from other things.[2]

— W.V. Quine

Law plays an essential role in the social recognition, conceptual definition, and
historical evolution of business enterprises, also known as firms. Business enterprises refer to social institutions that are distinguished from the individual people
who compose them primarily through legal methods and in a manner accepted
socially and politically over time.

Law supplies the social technology by which business enterprises are constructed
and maintained. One may usefully contrast "physical technologies" (such as improvements in energy production or the invention of new modes of communication and transportation) with "social technologies" such as law.[3] Without the
social technology and "forms" provided by law, business firms would be indistinguishable from informally organized social groups, clubs, or gatherings of people
pursuing similar interests.[4] Law also distinguishes business firms from other formally organized social entities, such as nation-states and nonprofit charities.[5]

---

[1] Axel Honneth, "Recognition and Justice: Outline of a Plural Theory of Justice," 47 *Acta Socio-
logica* 351, 354 (2004).

[2] W.V. Quine, *Ontological Relativity and Other Essays* (Columbia University Press 1969), p. 55.

[3] See Richard R. Nelson, *Technology, Institutions, and Economic Growth* (Harvard University Press
2005), pp. 153–65, 195–209.

[4] Another important "social technology" with respect to business firms not discussed in detail here
is accounting. I discuss the historical importance of accounting for the emergence of firms elsewhere.
Eric W. Orts, "A Short History of the Business Enterprise" (unpublished manuscript, available from
the author on request). See also Chapter 1, pages 33–4 and accompanying notes 111–14.

[5] On the importance of "formality" in the construction and recognition of institutions, including
business firms, see Arthur L. Stinchcombe, *When Formality Works: Authority and Abstraction in Law
and Organizations* (University of Chicago Press 2001). See also Robert S. Summers, *Form and Function
in a Legal System: A General Study* (Cambridge University Press 2005).

(Other important legally created and circumscribed entities include marriages and family relationships. As discussed in Chapters 2 and 5, the connections between families and business firms can be especially close, but nevertheless remain distinct. Distinctions that separate for-profit firms, nation-states, and nonprofit organizations are further discussed in Chapter 5.)

Law recognizes firms as organizational "entities" with rights and responsibilities that are enforceable in court—thus endowing them with "legal personality." In this book, I examine the legal principles and practices that allow for the social recognition of organized amalgamations of people in business firms. I argue that firms receive and deserve recognition as organizational persons because they consist of individual people.[6] At the same time, these organizational persons are and should be recognized to possess important legal responsibilities, as well as legal privileges.

The legal constitution of business enterprises imbues them with collective purposes, which are primarily, though not exclusively, to pursue profitable investments, to organize work, and to take advantage of other economic opportunities. The law recognizes the ability of business firms to govern themselves though *internal structures* of decision-making authority. At the same time, the law draws *external boundaries* that mark off firms as institutions distinct from other individual or organizational "persons" and "entities." In other words, the law both recognizes the existence of firms and patrols the boundaries of firms as institutions within a larger society composed of a number of different kinds of institutions.

In this book, I assume without elaboration that firms qualify as social "institutions," while recognizing that there is a lively debate in sociology and other disciplines about the exact meaning of an "institution." "There are almost as many uses of the word 'institution,'" one scholar observes, "as there are authors."[7] For my purposes here, a sufficient definition of an "institution" is "some sort of establishment of relative permanence of a distinctly social sort." This definition has the advantage of embracing the "only idea common to all usages of the term."[8] Another useful and compatible definition of "institution" refers to different types of "social pattern or order" that "owe their survival to relatively self-activating social processes."[9] The law, as this book will explain, provides the means by which the

---

[6] On the social importance of the "recognition" of individual people in general, see *Multiculturalism: Examining the Politics of Recognition* (Amy Gutmann ed.) (Princeton University Press 1994) (including essays by Charles Taylor, Jürgen Habermas, and K. Anthony Appiah); Axel Honneth, *The Struggle for Recognition: The Moral Grammar of Social Conflicts* (Joel Anderson trans.) (Polity Press 1995).

[7] Johann Peter Murmann, *Knowledge and Competitive Advantage: The Coevolution of Firms, Technology, and National Institutions* (Cambridge University Press 2003), p. 19, citing Richard R. Nelson and Bhaven N. Sampat, "Making Sense of Institutions as a Factor Shaping Economic Performance," 44 *Journal of Economic Behavior and Organization* 31 (2001).

[8] Everett C. Hughs, "The Ecological Aspect of Institutions," 1 *American Sociological Review* 180 (1936), quoted in Lynne G. Zucker, "The Role of Institutionalization in Cultural Persistence," in *The New Institutionalism in Organizational Analysis* (Walter W. Powell and Paul J. DiMaggio eds.) (University of Chicago Press 1991), p. 83.

[9] Ronald L. Jepperson, "Institutions, Institutional Effects, and Institutionalism," in *The New Institutionalism in Organizational Analysis*, op. cit., p. 145.

"self-activating social processes" known as firms are created, maintained, and changed over time.

In describing firms as institutions, the legal theory advanced here may be categorized correctly as part of an interdisciplinary wave of "new institutionalism" in other disciplines, including economics, ethics, history, political science, and sociology.[10] My legal account draws also on an "old institutionalism" associated with the work of social theorists such as John Commons, Emile Durkheim, Friedrich Hayek, Joseph Schumpeter, Adam Smith, Thorstein Veblen, and Max Weber.[11]

This book outlines the main institutional features of the business enterprise from a legal perspective. Chapter 1 begins with a review of long-standing conceptual difficulties with understanding the firm to be an organizational "entity" with "legal personality." This idea is foundational for a modern legal theory of the firm. The chapter argues for a resurrection of some old ideas regarding the nature of the business corporation (which, as explained here, is one specific kind of firm). Jurisprudential discussion about corporations and firms generally as legal *fictions*, *entities*, and *persons* are a key to understanding the nature of business firms and how they have evolved. Some contemporary economists (as well as some legal academics strongly influenced by economics) have tended in recent years to be impatient and dismissive of these legal ideas, but Chapter 1 argues that legal ideas conceiving of firms as fictions, entities, and persons operating in society are necessary and foundational. (And by "foundational" I mean only that these legal characteristics are essential for a pragmatic understanding of business firms. I do not mean that these foundational features express ultimate or self-evident truths, such as in "foundationalism" in ethics.[12])

Laws pertaining to the creation of *agency relationships*, *organizational contracts*, and *private property* count as an additional set of foundations needed for the construction, growth, and management of modern business firms. Chapter 2 considers these dimensions of the firm. As noted in the Preface and discussed in passing in this chapter, various economic theories of the firm have emphasized one or another of these elements (e.g. agency, contracts, or property rights). But

---

[10] See, e.g., *The New Institutionalism in Organizational Analysis*, op. cit.; Mary Douglas and Steven Ney, *Missing Persons: A Critique of Personhood in the Social Sciences* (University of California Press 1998); Chrysostomos Mantzavinos, *Individuals, Institutions, and Markets* (Cambridge University Press 2001); Charles Perrow, *Complex Organizations: A Critical Essay* (Random House, 3rd ed., 1986); Dennis F. Thompson, *Restoring Responsibility: Ethics in Government, Business, and Healthcare* (Cambridge University Press 2005); Peter A. Hall and Rosemary C.R. Taylor, "Political Science and the Three New Institutionalisms," 44 *Political Studies* 936 (1996); Paul Pierson and Theda Skocpol, "Historical Institutionalism in Contemporary Political Science," in *Political Science: The State of the Discipline* (Ira Katznelson and Helen Milner eds.) (W.W. Norton 2004).

[11] See Jack Knight, *Institutions and Social Conflict* (Cambridge University Press 1992), pp. 4–9; W. Richard Scott, *Institutions and Organizations* (Sage, 2nd ed., 2001), pp. 2–17; Arthur L. Stinchcombe, "On the Virtues of the Old Institutionalism," 23 *Annual Review of Sociology* 1 (1997); Lars Udehn, *Methodological Individualism: Background, History and Meaning* (Routledge 2001), pp. 256–7.

[12] Cf. Dale Jamieson, "Method and Moral Theory," in *A Companion to Ethics* (Blackwell Publishers 1993), pp. 476–87.

I maintain that one must have a clear conception of how these disparate elements fit together, and only legal theory can supply this understanding. The business entities and persons outlined in Chapter 1 provide a framework for understanding the different features of agency, contracts, and property described in Chapter 2—and how these elements fit together to compose the panoply of real-world business firms.

Legal distinctions between "public" and "private" spheres of social life, particularly with respect to property ownership and freedom of association, are also important. Chapter 3 takes up the important distinction between *public* and *private* business firms, a distinction which tracks different conceptions and allocations of property in modern societies. Following other commentators, I suggest that humanity is currently witnessing a competition between societies characterized primarily as engaged in "market capitalism" in which privately organized and owned enterprises predominate (e.g. the United States and Europe) and those which may be called "state capitalist" systems in which government-owned and -operated firms are prevalent (e.g. China and, increasingly, Russia).[13] Chapter 3 describes how the legal distinction between *public* and *private* helps to determine how these different social approaches to firms are put into practice and how, potentially, they may change over time. A main point is that the division of different kinds of business firms—private, public, and public–private hybrids—is accomplished through legal methods of recognition and differentiation. Market competition plays a major role in selecting the most efficient of these business forms in particular situations, but this economic competition depends on an underlying legal and political foundation allowing for the recognition and development of different kinds of firms.

Chapter 4 turns to consider another important legal dimension of firms, namely, questions of liability and responsibility. These general questions divide into two subsidiary topics: (1) the extent to which firms as organizations are or should be responsible and legally liable for the social harms they may cause (i.e. *enterprise liability*); and (2) the extent to which various business participants are or should be responsible and legally liable for these social harms (i.e. *business participant liability*).

In current legal practice, the recognition of the "entities" of firms (including corporations as well as other limited liability forms) often limits the legal responsibility of both the business entities of firms themselves and the business participants within them. Contemporary legal scholars have discussed both enterprise liability and limited liability for business participants from an economic perspective, but Chapter 4 provides a foundational legal background underlying this debate. It shows how the law frames the discussion with respect to the recognition of business enterprises as "persons" with potential organizational liability. Law draws the boundaries of a firm

---

[13] For the basic argument, see Ian Bremmer, *The End of the Free Market: Who Wins the War Between States and Corporations?* (Portfolio 2010), pp. 4–6, 23, 25–54 (distinguishing between "state capitalism" and "free-market capitalism"); David Brooks, "The Larger Struggle," *New York Times*, June 15, 2010, p. A29 (referring to "state capitalism" and "democratic capitalism"). For an account of the varieties of "state capitalism," see also "Special Report: State Capitalism," *Economist*, January 21, 2012, pp. 3–18.

for the purposes of finding liability (or not) of both the firm itself (such as in parent–subsidiary corporate structures) and participants within firms (including investors, managers, and employees). A larger theme in the chapter describes the resulting implicit social balance of liability and limited liability of business persons (both enterprise entities and individuals). The ability to arbitrage legal attributes regarding potential liability in the construction of firms (and other legal entities) has large practical implications, especially in a globalizing world in which jurisdictional boundaries may be easily gamed by financially sophisticated and wealthy players.

Organizational law—including the law of corporations, partnerships, limited liability companies, and other specific forms of business enterprise—sets out a menu of structural options for privately organized firms (as well as state-owned enterprises, which remain especially prominent in some countries such as China). Chapter 5 presents this menu and sets forth an organizational taxonomy and legal nomenclature of the various forms of business enterprise.

The specific laws of enterprise organization, particularly the law of corporations, add other important features to modern firms. These include the expansion of shareholder ownership through "splitting the atom" of private property held in corporate form—and in some cases the public trading of these atomized shares of ownership. (These changes allowed for the evolution of some of the organizational principles of limited liability described in Chapter 4. The revolution in corporate property including the fission of corporate ownership is also discussed in Chapter 2.[14]) Basic principles of organizational law also distinguish business firms from other kinds of social entities, such as political governments and nonprofit organizations. Chapter 5 outlines the importance of these distinctions, as well as providing an overview of the main choices of the legal forms of business available to business participants and entrepreneurs.

Chapter 6 examines the legally defined boundaries of the firm. These boundaries relate to the regulation of firms both *internally* (through the operation of rules enabling self-governance) and *externally* (including legal rules that discourage the negative behavior or encourage the positive behavior of firms and their participants). For example, an attribute of the legal recognition of firms is the ability to create a business entity (such as through a corporate charter) and then to construct *internal rules* for its governance (such as adopting a set of bylaws). In effect, the legal recognition of independent firms allows business participants to set their own internal rules with respect to boundary-setting issues such as the scope of authority and participation in profits of the firm. Examples of external legal rules that affect the boundaries of firms include (1) liability rules attributing *external responsibility* for the conduct of a firm's agents to the firm as a whole; and (2) requirements for some kinds of firms to have mandatory accounting or reporting about their organization and operations to an *external public*.

Chapter 6 draws on previous chapters to reinforce why and how legal recognition is centrally important in understanding the nature of business enterprise. It provides

---

[14] For the seminal diagnosis, see Adolf A. Berle and Gardiner C. Means, *The Modern Corporation and Private Property* (Transaction Publishers 1991) (rev. ed. 1968) (1932).

examples, following early insights by the legal theorist H.L.A. Hart, of how the boundaries of a firm can change depending on the question asked.[15] In other words, it argues that particularly difficult questions in law, economics, and social theory concerning the boundaries of the firm have legal answers: but the answers are not always simple. And they often shift according to the context. For example, an employee may act as an agent of the firm and bind it contractually when acting with designated legal authority in negotiations with a customer or supplier. But the same employee may be treated differently when the question is whether he or she has a voice in governance decisions or a share of the firm's profits. Similarly, a creditor can usually claim only an arm's-length contractual relationship with a firm to whom a loan is made. But the characteristics of this relationship may change if and when the firm goes bankrupt. The creditor may then step into a role of having primary influence (along with other creditors) over the governance of the firm, including options for forcing its liquidation or reorganization.

Chapter 7 provides two practical applications of the legal theory of the firm elucidated in this book. Executive compensation in corporations is one practical issue that an institutional legal theory can illuminate. The chapter shows how some influential economic theories have led to simplistic prescriptions which have contributed to significant imbalance and injustice in compensation practices. A more comprehensive legal theory offers a corrective in perspective. Controversies about political free-speech rights of corporations, such as addressed in the *Citizens United* case, provide another example.[16] Adopting an institutional legal theory, the chapter argues, deepens analysis on both sides of the debate and suggests possible compromises, such as mandatory disclosure requirements of the political activities of firms.

A conclusion restates some of the arguments made for a legal theory of the firm and its practical relevance for contemporary issues. In future work, I hope to elaborate on other leading theoretical perspectives informing modern views of the business firm. These include not only the perspective of economics, but also history, political theory, philosophy, and sociology. Here, however, I limit myself to arguing for the importance of an essentially *legal theory of the firm*.

***

With respect to the overall theoretical tilt of this book, it would be fair to characterize my project as both conservative (or "radical" in the original sense of going back to the "roots" of an issue) and progressive. The book is conservative in the sense that it argues for a return to older notions that describe the business enterprise as a legal fiction, an organizational entity, and a constitutional person. These older debates have lately been abandoned by some as too abstract or conceptually difficult, especially given a methodological commitment to examine only individual actors in social analysis. There is a long-standing divide in social

---

[15] H.L.A. Hart, "Definition and Theory in Jurisprudence," in *Essays in Jurisprudence and Philosophy* (Oxford University Press 1983), pp. 21–3, 31–3, 40–5.

[16] *Citizens United v. Federal Election Commission*, 130 S. Ct. 876 (2010).

theory between this approach, which has become known as "methodological individualism," and an approach known as "methodological holism," which takes a larger point of view from the perspective of society as a whole. The institutional approach advanced here squares the circle to include both of these methods. It sees individual actors as essential, but it also recognizes that social institutions of groups of individuals acting in concert are necessary too. In this book I argue that old ideas such as "legal personality" remain relevant and necessary. Reviving them underscores the importance of understanding firms as social institutions. Firms are greater than the sum of their individual parts, and attempting to reduce them to their individual components does violence—or at least radically understates—their social and institutional reality.

At the same time, if a recovery of older legal principles governing the nature of business firms is conservative in spirit, then the potential consequences of this recovery are also progressive. At least, an understanding of the legal flexibility and plasticity of modern firms allows for a broader range of potential business practices and policy prescriptions than are often imagined today. The legal theory of the firm offered here therefore has relevance for addressing a number of contemporary problems. The example of executive compensation given in Chapter 7 illustrates how a too-narrow economic theory of the firm can produce some large unintended consequences (such as creating high-powered incentives for major financial frauds) which a more traditional and holistic legal theory may better comprehend and counter.

More broadly, a legal theory of the firm allows us to contemplate the construction of business firms for various "hybrid" purposes. Some kinds of firms, for example, may be able to combine the profit motive with other social objectives, such as the reduction of poverty or the advancement of environmental sustainability. It may be true that economic competition will make survival difficult for firms that choose to complicate their guiding objective beyond a univocal focus on profits. In principle and practice, however, there is nothing to prevent firms from pursuing multiple objectives. They can both walk (pursue profits) and chew gum (act ethically).[17] In fact, current law already commands firms and their participants to meet minimal standards of ethical and legal behavior, in addition to pursuing profits. Although it is common today to think of ethics and law as normative constraints on the economic objective of profit-seeking, this is also not the only way to think about business objectives. Understanding the legal constitution of business as an integral part of the larger society allows for a conceptually richer appreciation of its role. A legal theory of the firm emphasizes the possibility of reform in the following sense: If the inherited forms and practices of business enterprise lead to deleterious or unhappy social consequences, then these forms and practices should change. One can therefore paint the future of business firms in society as bright, as long as thoughtful and optimistic people embrace the freedom to make change happen at various institutional levels.

---

[17] I owe my colleague Alan Strudler for the use of this metaphor in this context.

1

Foundations of the Firm I:
Business Entities and Legal Persons

Whether and how to recognize business enterprises as organizational "entities" and legal "persons" that bear enforceable rights, privileges, and responsibilities has been one of the most vexing issues in the history of legal thought. These issues, though often raised with respect specifically to corporations, are relevant to business firms in general.[1] Debates about whether business firms are simply "legal fictions" created by the state or "real entities" that exist independently as institutions trace at least to classical Roman times.[2] These debates mirror an historical tension between "top-down" and "bottom-up" perspectives on business enterprises. An appreciation of these two perspectives helps to explain and resolve the differences among the main competing legal theories of the firm.

An institutional theory of the firm

"Top-down" legal theories see business firms as creatures of the state. The Roman jurist Gaius expressed this view as follows:

Partnerships, *collegia*, and bodies of this sort may not be formed by everybody at will; for this right is restricted by statutes, *senatus consulta* [rules], and imperial *constitutiones* [edicts]. In a few cases only are bodies of this sort permitted. For example, partners in tax farming, gold mines, silver mines, and salt works are allowed to form corporations. Likewise, there are certain *collegia* at Rome whose corporate status has been established by [law], for example, those of the bakers and certain others and of the shipowners. . . . Those permitted to form a corporate body consisting of a *collegium* or partnership . . . have the right on the pattern of

---

[1] The literature on this topic is both broad and deep. For an overview, see Alfred F. Conard, *Corporations in Perspective* (Foundation Press 1976), pp. 417–45. Contemporary treatments derive from original discussions in Europe, especially in Germany and France. Id., pp. 417–19 (citing especially the work of Friedrich von Savigny and Otto von Gierke in Germany and René Clemens in France). See also Ron Harris, "The Transplantation of the Legal Discourse on Corporate Personality Theories: From German Codification to British Political Pluralism and American Big Business," 63 *Washington and Lee Law Review* 1421 (2006).

[2] See Reuven S. Avi-Yonah, "The Cyclical Transformations of the Corporate Form: A Historical Perspective on Corporate Social Responsibility," 30 *Delaware Journal of Corporate Law* 767 (2005). For an historical treatment of this jurisprudence in the United States, see Gregory A. Mark, Comment, "The Personification of the Business Corporation in American Law," 54 *University of Chicago Law Review* 1441 (1987).

the state to have common property, a common treasury, and an attorney...through whom...what should be transacted and done in common is transacted and done.[3]

On this ancient view, business firms exist only at the behest and at the pleasure of government.

More recently, the U.S. Supreme Court expressed this top-down conception of the firm in a famous, often repeated declaration by Chief Justice John Marshall in the *Dartmouth College* case: "A corporation is an artificial being, invisible, intangible, and existing only in contemplation of law. Being the mere creature of law, it possesses only those properties which the charter of its creation confers upon it, either expressly, or as incidental to its very existence."[4] The top-down view sees the business corporation—and, by extension, any business enterprise—as the subordinate subject of law and, derivatively, of the governments that charter or otherwise recognize them.[5]

The "bottom-up" point of view of the participants in business firms yields a different, almost opposite legal theory. Although the law may provide the basic social structure and "rules of the road" for the creation and operation of business firms, participants who invest their own wealth, time, labor, and knowledge in a business enterprise tend to favor the recognition of legal rights and obligations that inhere in the enterprise itself. Participants see firms as representing, derivatively, their own interests and expectations, rather than those of a sponsoring government. Although the Roman emperors were intolerant of this participants' point of view, the long-term history of the business enterprise suggests that the emergence of a bottom-up view has gained traction in various geographical locations over the *longue durée*.[6] Traces of the bottom-up view appear even in the ancient Roman debates, though they are less easy to make out than the top-down declarations of control by emperors.[7] At least some early Roman firms had the right to pass the equivalent of bylaws to govern their own affairs.[8]

A bottom-up view comports also with the long-term historical trajectory described by Friedrich Hayek of a "spontaneous order" of firms that grow in different shapes and sizes once a basic legal infrastructure has been put into place.[9] Hayek

---

[3] Dig. 3.4.1 pr.-1 (Gaius, Provincial Edict 3) (Alan Watson trans. 1985), quoted in Avi-Yonah, op. cit., p. 773. *Collegia* included private clubs, religious groups, and informal economic organizations.

[4] *Dartmouth College v. Woodward*, 17 U.S. 518, 636 (1819). Modern cases that cite this language favorably include *CTS Corp. v. Dynamics Corp. of America*, 481 U.S. 69, 89 (1987) and *Citizens United v. Federal Election Commission*, 130 S. Ct. 876, 950 (2010) (Stevens, J., dissenting).

[5] In fact, *Dartmouth College* held against the government, finding that a royal charter creating a private institution could not be constitutionally altered by New Hampshire under the Contracts Clause. 17 U.S. at 624–53. The case is discussed further below in Chapter 3 with respect to the public/private distinction.

[6] Fernand Braudel, *The Perspective of the World: Civilization and Capitalism, 15th-18th Century, vol. III* (trans. Siân Reynolds) (University of California Press 1992), pp. 619–23.

[7] See Avi-Yonah, op. cit., pp. 775–6 (citing passages from Ulpian). Different legal theories of business organization have been "cyclical" in terms of their adoption and influence. Id., pp. 767, 770–813.

[8] See Samuel Williston, "History of the Law of Business Corporations Before 1800," 2 *Harvard Law Review* 105, 121 (1888).

[9] See Friedrich A. Hayek, *Law, Legislation, and Liberty: Volume 1, Rules and Order* (University of Chicago Press 1973), pp. 35–54; Friedrich A. Hayek, *The Road to Serfdom: Text and Documents*

accounts for the top-down versus bottom-up dichotomy as the difference between an imposed or "made" social order (*taxis*) and a "grown" or spontaneous social order (*kosmos*).[10] For Hayek, economic markets constitute a "catallaxy," that is, "the special kind of spontaneous order produced by the market through people acting within the rules of the law."[11] Although business firms must comply with relevant law, on this view, they also create and define themselves—and then make a legitimate claim to an independent right to existence and legal recognition on the basis of this self-creation.

In the United States, the Supreme Court has at least implicitly endorsed this bottom-up point of view as well, such as in *Santa Clara County v. Southern Pacific Railroad*. This case extended the constitutional principle of "equal protection under the law" to business corporations as well as individual human beings as "legal persons."[12] (Some scholars, emphasizing that this case declared corporations to be "persons," have urged a nefarious conspiracy theory claiming that corporate lawyers hijacked the Fourteenth Amendment designed to protect former slaves to serve corporate masters instead. But this historical interpretation has been debunked.[13])

The *Santa Clara* case held that the aggregation of private property in a business corporation deserves constitutional respect (in the specific context of the assessment of an unequal corporate tax) because the property belonged, derivatively, to the individual investors in the enterprise.[14] In this manner, the Court adopted a bottom-up view of the individual interests represented by the corporation. The Supreme Court has more recently extended this legal notion of the constitutional protection of corporate "persons" in other contexts, such as in the controversial *Citizens United* case, which asserted First Amendment free-speech rights for business corporations in political elections.[15] Despite the top-down language of *Dartmouth*

(University of Chicago Press 2007) (1945), pp. 71–3. See also John Gray, *Hayek on Liberty* (Routledge, 3rd ed.,1998), pp. 25–55, 118–25.

[10] Hayek, *Law, Legislation, and Liberty: Volume 1, Rules and Order*, op. cit., pp. 35–54.

[11] Friedrich A. Hayek, *Law, Legislation, and Liberty: Volume 2, The Mirage of Social Justice* (University of Chicago Press 1976), pp. 108–9. See also Gray, *Hayek on Liberty*, op. cit., pp. 34–40. As Gray explains, Hayek's idea of "spontaneous order" includes three distinct elements: (1) *an invisible-hand thesis* that "social institutions arise as a result of human action but not by human design"; (2) *a tacit or practical knowledge thesis* that "our knowledge of the world, and especially of the social world, is embodied first of all in practices and skills, and only secondarily in theories"; and (3) *a thesis of the natural selection of competitive institutions* that cultural traditions as "whole complexes of practices and rules of action and perception" undergo "continuous evolutionary filtering." Id., pp. 33–4. I do not address all of these elements here. Suffice it to say that I agree with Hayek that the bottom-up view of a "spontaneous order" describes one side of the theoretical problem of the nature of firms. But I emphasize the other side too: the top-down *taxis* of law as well as the bottom-up *kosmos* of self-organizing markets.

[12] 118 U.S. 394 (1886). See also Avi-Yonah, op. cit., pp. 793–4.

[13] See Mark, op. cit., pp. 1463 and n. 62. See also James Willard Hurst, *The Legitimacy of the Business Corporation in the United States, 1780 to 1970* (University Press of Virginia 1970), pp. 66–8 (finding insufficient evidence for this "conspiracy theory" of constitutional law).

[14] See Mark, op. cit., pp. 1463–4. For a more recent case limiting the principle of equal protection as applied to business corporations, see *Western and Southern Life Insurance Co. v. State Board of Equalization of California*, 451 U.S. 648 (1981). But cf. *Granholm v. Heald*, 544 U.S. 460 (2005) (voiding under the Commerce Clause legislation discriminating against out-of-state firms selling wine).

[15] *Citizens United*, op. cit. See Chapter 7 below for further discussion of this case.

College, then, some constitutional cases involving business enterprises adopt a bottom-up view, rather than simply allowing the government to adopt and enforce any new rules or impositions at all with respect to its "creatures." The Supreme Court recognizes and protects constitutional rights for corporations and other business entities as "persons" in some cases but not others.[16]

The jurisprudence of recognizing business enterprises to have "personality" and treating them as "entities" is complex. Legal scholars who have ventured into this literature, however, have consistently identified three major legal theories of the business enterprise.[17] Two of these theories represent the top-down and bottom-up perspectives. I will label them the *concession theory* (top-down) and the *participant theory* (bottom-up). A third—which I will call the *institutional theory*—captures an intermediate perspective that views firms as existing at a social level between political states and individual people. The institutional theory helps to explain and clarify the meaning and usefulness of both top-down and bottom-up theories. These two legal theories remain important and often applicable, as long as either one or the other is not adopted as the only theoretical truth. In my view, the institutional theory allows for a coherent explanation of the main legal theories of the firm. For a schematic overview of some key features of these theories, see Table 1.1.[18]

The *concession theory* of business enterprise represents the top-down perspective of the political state. It holds that business enterprises, including corporations, are simply the creations of government. For example, the English East India Company existed because the King granted a charter to create it.[19] On this theory, it follows also that the act of creation authorizes the King to determine the nature and scope of the activities of his institutional "creature."[20] From this perspective, business

---

[16] For treatments of this topic from different perspectives, see, e.g., Phillip I. Blumberg, *The Multinational Challenge to Corporation Law: The Search for a New Corporate Personality* (Oxford University Press 1993), pp. 24–5, 30–45; Jess M. Krannich, "The Corporate 'Person': A New Analytical Approach to a Flawed Method of Constitutional Interpretation," 37 *Loyola University Chicago Law Journal* 61 (2005); Carl J. Mayer, "Personalizing the Impersonal: Corporations and the Bill of Rights," 41 *Hastings Law Journal* 577 (1990); Larry E. Ribstein, "The Constitutional Conception of the Corporation," 4 *Supreme Court Economic Review* 95 (1995); Note, "Constitutional Rights of the Corporate Person," 91 *Yale Law Journal* 1641 (1982).

[17] The extent to which scholars agree on a tripartite division of the leading theories is remarkable. See Avi-Yonah, op. cit., pp. 771 (noting that "the same three theories of the corporation" have recurred over the course of "two millenia"); H.L.A. Hart, "Definition and Theory in Jurisprudence," in *Essays in Jurisprudence and Philosophy* (Oxford University Press 1983), pp. 24–5 (describing "three great theories of corporate personality"). See also John C. Coates IV, Note, "State Takeover Statutes and Corporate Theory: The Revival of an Old Debate," 64 *New York University Law Review* 806, 808–24 (1989); Mark M. Hager, "Bodies Politic: The Progressive History of Organizational 'Real Entity' Theory," 50 *University of Pittsburgh Law Review* 575, 579–80 (1989); Ron Harris, op. cit., pp. 1423–4; Michael J. Phillips, "Reappraising the Real Entity Theory of the Corporation," 21 *Florida State University Law Review* 1061, 1063–73 (1994); Sanford A. Schane, "The Corporation Is a Person: The Language of a Legal Fiction," 61 *Tulane Law Review* 563, 564–9 (1987).

[18] This approach may represent an example of dialectical reasoning. On the usefulness as well as the dangers of triadic dialectical reasoning, see Karl R. Popper, "What Is Dialectic?" 49 *Mind* 403 (1940).

[19] This theory has also been called the "grant theory." See, e.g., Mark, op. cit., p. 1452.

[20] One theorist goes so far as to call this the "creature theory." See, e.g., Schane, op. cit., pp. 565–9. The metaphor has led some opponents of corporations to imagine them as artificial monsters. See, e.g., I. Maurice Wormser, *Frankenstein, Incorporated* (McGraw-Hill 1931).

Table 1.1 The main legal theories of the firm

	Social perspective	Primary focus
Concession theory	Top-down view that political states "grant" firms rights to exist	Government as law-giver
Participant theory	Bottom-up view that firms are created by the individual people who compose them	Individual participants
Institutional theory	Intermediate view that firms are understood as institutions both formed according to legal rules and organized and run by individual people	Firm itself as an "entity" (or group of entities)

firms exist only because governments say so. They exist, in other words, only "by concession" of government. This theory is compatible with strong versions of state capitalism. Firms are viewed as subordinate (and perhaps even subservient), and they are subject to strict government oversight and direction.[21]

The *participant theory* of business enterprise takes a bottom-up perspective of individual people who aggregate together within a firm. On this view, states may allow for the existence of firms, and governments may grant some of the original charters for companies and corporations. Once these authorizations are given, however, and once the individual participants invest their wealth, time, labor, and knowledge in advancing the purposes of the enterprise, there is a shift in legal emphasis over time. The individual participants begin to possess cognizable rights and interests within the firm that the state should not, according to this theory, extinguish by fiat.

The advent of legal templates for the creation of business organizations—such as the general incorporation statutes adopted in the United States and Great Britain in the nineteenth century and then spreading throughout the world—reinforced this bottom-up, participant theory of firms. General or "free" incorporation statutes were adopted first in the United States (at the level of different states, beginning with New York in 1811) followed closely by Great Britain (at the national level in 1844). They responded to political pressures against the "special privileges" of companies or corporations chartered by special acts of legislation or by monarchs.[22] Once governments removed themselves from the

---

[21] Friedrich von Savigny advanced an early version of this view in Germany. See, e.g., Katsuhito Iwai, "Persons, Things and Corporations: The Corporate Personality Controversy and Comparative Corporate Governance," 47 *American Journal of Comparative Law* 583, 601–2 (1999); Arthur W. Machen, Jr., "Corporate Personality," 24 *Harvard Law Review* 253, 255 (1911).

[22] See Hurst, op. cit., pp. 25–33, 135; Henry Hansmann, Reinier Kraakman, and Richard Squire, "Law and the Rise of the Firm," 119 *Harvard Law Review* 1333, 1386–7, 1394–6 (2006); Mark, op. cit., pp. 1450, 1453–4. The adoption of general incorporation statutes for businesses in the United States followed an earlier type of general incorporation statute for religious or charitable institutions which included for-profit businesses that could demonstrate a "public service," such as insurance companies and banks. Ronald E. Seavoy, "The Public Service Origins of the American Business Corporation," 52 *Business History Review* 30 (1978).

direct "chartering" of business firms (with continuing exceptions, such as government corporations or business licensing requirements), they tended to follow a version of the participant theory.

The approach of market capitalism followed by most countries today emphasizes free markets of self-organizing firms. This approach supports the participant theory of the firm, though competing varieties of market capitalism may have different views about who counts as a legitimate business "participant," particularly with respect to regular or rank-and-file employees.[23] Some legal systems (and some firms) tend to recognize employees as true participants, and others tend to categorize employees as mere "inputs" to a firm's production processes. These different views of firms, their relationship to government, and the role of employees (among other variables) reflect theoretical controversies in different disciplines, including law, economics, and political theory, as well as geographical and cultural differences.

In any event, the participant theory, broadly construed, maintains that the business enterprise is created as an aggregate entity by and for its participants. The firm "belongs" to its participants and not the government. This "belonging" of members to an organization depends on the recognition of this relationship by the legal order, as Hans Kelsen emphasized, which is much different than saying that the relationship depends directly on a top-down governmental authorization or "concession."[24] The legal recognition of a firm follows from recognition of the aggregated rights and interests of the people who constitute it.

A third view develops an intermediate position. The *institutional theory* sees firms as socially established entities that are *both* authorized and recognized by governments *and* organized and managed by individual participants. The institutional recognition of the business enterprise as a legal "entity" or "person" interposes a conceptual separation between the political state and the firm's individual participants. Once a regular legal process for the governmental recognition and individual creation of firms has become established, business firms become social institutions. In legal terms, they become "entities" and "persons" with specified legal rights and obligations. The most important of these rights and obligations (which are assumed without much reflection in legal practice today) include: (1) the holding of a legal name; (2) the designation of a place of residence or citizenship; (3) the ability to sue and be sued in court; (4) the power to own tangible and intangible property, including real estate and other capital; (5) the capacity to make contracts, incur debt, and enter into other financial arrangements in the name of the firm; and (6) the right to self-govern by adopting founding documents, bylaws, and other "private statutes."[25]

---

[23] On "market capitalism" versus "state capitalism," see Introduction, page 4 and accompanying note. Themes regarding this distinction are also further discussed in Chapters 3 and 5 below.

[24] Hans Kelsen, *General Theory of Law and State* (Anders Weberg trans.) (Harvard University Press 1945), pp. 98–9.

[25] See Williston, op. cit., pp. 116–17 (quoting Coke and Blackstone on these points with respect to corporations). Most of these general rights and obligations apply to other basic legal forms of business

Law plays a dual role here, integrating top-down and bottom-up theories. First, the government adopts statutes, supplemented by judicial decisions, which set forth the "rules of the game" for the establishment and governance of firms. These rules are then adjusted over time and within constitutional limits to address various policy issues that arise. Constitutional limits in the United States, for example, include a prohibition of the expropriation or "taking" of the property of a business enterprise without "just compensation," such as in the "nationalization" of a private business firm converting it to government ownership.

Second, individual participants rely on and use this established legal framework to create firms by entering into organizational contracts, as well as formally registering these firms with the government, when and if required. Individual participants arrange for the self-governance of their firms by doing the following: (1) adopting "constitutional" documents (such as the charter and by-laws of a corporation); (2) issuing governing resolutions via designated representatives (such as the board of directors in a corporation); and (3) following policies that authorize managers to run the firm through an ordering and structuring of the activities of subordinates.[26] (As discussed in Chapter 5 below, variations in the governance methods of firms depend in part on the legal type of firm selected, e.g. corporation, partnership, or limited liability company.)

The institutional theory of the firm is broad enough to encompass the main features of both the concession and participant theories. As such, it describes most of the world with respect to the legal structure of business enterprises today. This approach is also consistent with the philosophical and sociological approach to the firm that is advanced by "institutional" theorists in various disciplines. The institutional theory shows how the legal system squares the circle of social and individual perspectives on the firm, and it also allows for legal analysis and historical change over time from both "macro" and "micro" points of view.

Note that the institutional theory advanced here emphasizes the recognition of firms as "entities" and "persons," but it does not require subscribing to what has been called the "real entity" theory associated most prominently and notoriously with the German legal theorist Otto von Gierke. The strongest version of this "real entity" theory holds that intermediary institutions such as business enterprises should be considered to have a metaphysically "real" existence and an "organic" institutional permanence separate from their individual participants.[27] Gierke even

---

enterprise, such as partnerships, but corporations tend to have the broadest array of powers as "entities" or "persons." See Robert C. Clark, *Corporate Law* (Aspen 1986), pp. 15–21.

[26] Cf. Melvin Aron Eisenberg, *The Structure of the Corporation: A Legal Analysis* (Little Brown 1976), p. 1 ("Corporate law is constitutional law; that is, its dominant function is to regulate the manner in which the corporate institution is constituted, to define the relative rights and duties of those participating in the institution, and to delimit the powers of the institution vis-à-vis the external world").

[27] For an account of this theory and its influence in the English-speaking world through the translations of Frederic Maitland and Ernst Freund (among others), see Mark, op. cit., pp. 1464–78. See also William W. Bratton, Jr., "The New Economic Theory of the Firm: Critical Perspectives from History," 41 *Stanford Law Review* 1471, 1490–1 (1989).

went so far as to posit a "physico-spiritual unity" of a "real corporate personality."[28] No such metaphysical assertions are made here. Instead, my argument is that business enterprises are social institutions created by human beings—and thus both "artificial" and "fictional" (rather than metaphysically "real"). Nevertheless, firms have a social ontological existence because they are artificial fictions that are legally reinforced in the real world. They are therefore "fictions" that become "real" and "actual" in an everyday, pragmatic sense.

An institutional theory of the business enterprise that recognizes both the top-down authority of government and the bottom-up authority of participants in intermediate institutions is consistent with the jurisprudence of Robert Cover. In Cover's view, law is best conceived as having a bottom-up feature—a norm-generating "jurisgenesis"—as well as a top-down "imperial" aspect.[29] Various non-state institutions, including religions and other organizations, develop a plurality of normative systems or worlds (*nomos*). Governments then act through statutes and other legally enforceable rules to establish an "imperial" order in particular areas of social life and conduct. Courts and judges hold an intermediate position. They are "jurispathic" in that they suppress associational norms when they conflict with "imperial" law. On one hand, then, judges are "people of violence" because they impose a single law within their jurisdiction backed by the force of the state. On the other hand, judges are "people of peace" because they often play the role of finding compromises and resolving disputes between normative worlds without resorting to violence.[30]

Cover writes that "modern corporation law continues to bear the formal character of a grant of norm-generating authority" in the United States and, to extend his argument, elsewhere in the world. Cover refers to "company town[s]" and the original Massachusetts Bay colony in the United States as historical examples of strongly independent norm-generating associations.[31] The delegation of internal law-making authority to promoters, organizers, and managers of firms remains a strong feature of contemporary enterprise law. Business participants make their own rules—and create their own "nomos"—subject to the "imperial" constraints of governing law.

Although political states have often suppressed business enterprises (and other independent groups) or bent them to serve only political purposes in the manner of Roman emperors, the *longue durée* of history suggests that the idea of "associational autonomy" has become relatively strongly established in many places in the world.[32] To this extent, non-state institutions—including but not limited to business enterprises—become a source of bottom-up normative arguments for

---

[28] Iwai, op. cit., p. 616 (citing Maitland).

[29] Robert M. Cover, "The Supreme Court, 1982 Term—Foreword: Nomos and Narrative," 97 *Harvard Law Review* 4, 4–18 (1983).

[30] Id., pp. 40–6, 53.

[31] Id., pp. 30–1.

[32] Id., pp. 31–2. See also Eric W. Orts, "A Short History of the Business Enterprise" (unpublished manuscript, available from the author on request). For interdisciplinary treatments of "associational autonomy," see *Freedom of Association* (Amy Gutmann ed.) (Princeton University Press 1998).

the authority to make their own legal rules and interpretations. For Cover, the norm-generating features of freedom of association should translate into the legal recognition of the rights of certain groups. In his words: "Freedom of association implies a degree of norm-generating autonomy on the part of the association. It is not a liberty to *be* but a liberty and capacity to create and interpret law—minimally, to interpret the terms of the association's own being."[33] At the same time, the exercise of this associational freedom is subject to legal limits.

Influential theorists have argued forcefully against a need to select among the several different legal theories of the business enterprise described above. H.L.A. Hart, for example, argues that "though these theories spring from the effort to define notions actually involved in the practice of a legal system they rarely throw light on the precise work they do there."[34] He recommends a practical institutional approach. Hart brushes aside unhelpful debates, such as whether a firm is "a mere abstraction, a fiction, a metaphysical entity," and he calls for closer attention to "the legal rules of the game" about how terms such as the "corporation" are actually used and what legal consequences follow.[35]

Similarly, John Dewey surveys the debates surrounding the idea of corporate personality and recommends caution. The idea of a legal "person," he says, is empty: it "signifies what law makes it signify." If one agrees that the legal reference to a "person" is simply to designate "a right-and-duty-bearing unit," then the most important questions shift from "regarding the nature of things" to thinking "in terms of consequences."[36]

In my view, both Hart and Dewey support a pragmatic institutional approach to legal theories of the business enterprise.[37] Dewey warns against relying too heavily on either the "concession theory" or the "fiction theory" because they have been used historically to support conflicting ends that are politically or otherwise determined.[38] He concludes that attention should focus on "concrete facts and

---

[33] Cover, op. cit., p. 32 (original emphasis). For a controversial case in which the U.S. Supreme Court recognized a "right of expressive association" for groups, see *Boy Scouts of America v. Dale*, 530 U.S. 640 (2000) (striking down a state law prohibiting discrimination on the basis of sexual orientation as a violation of associational rights). But see *Roberts v. United States Jaycees*, 468 U.S. 609 (1984) (holding that a private business group did not have the right to exclude women); *Rumsfeld v. Forum for Academic and Institutional Rights, Inc.*, 547 U.S. 47 (2006) (upholding military recruiting access requirement to universities against a group-rights challenge).

[34] Hart, "Definition and Theory in Jurisprudence," op. cit., p. 25.

[35] Id., pp. 43–7.

[36] John Dewey, "The Historic Background of Corporate Legal Personality," 35 *Yale Law Journal* 655, 655–6, 660 (1926).

[37] Some may object that my interpretation of support by Hart and Dewey for an institutional theory is misplaced. Dewey in particular has been given credit (or blame) for contributing to "the decline of corporation theory" in the United States. Mark, op. cit., pp. 1478–83. See also Bratton, op. cit., pp. 1508–10 (discussing Dewey's influence on legal scholars). A close reading of Dewey, however, suggests that he did not take the extreme position that the idea of legal personality should be abandoned. Dewey argued only that the idea itself should not drive legal and policy-related conclusions about the rights and obligations of legal persons. Hard policy questions remain concerning the definition and boundaries of organizational legal persons, but this does not mean that the "persons" themselves somehow disappear from the analysis.

[38] Dewey, op. cit., pp. 655–7, 663–9.

relations" rather than theories of legal personality.[39] Attention to the "concrete facts
and relations" of the firm leads to a consideration of how the law creates these
institutions, what the rules of the game are for them, and what social consequences
obtain. The "concrete facts and relations" of the business enterprise refer, at least in
part, to the legal infrastructure that permits their construction, recognizes them,
and channels their activities. In addition, Dewey observes that legal results related
to corporate personality have been driven by many different "non-legal considerations," including "considerations popular, historical, political, moral, philosophical, metaphysical and, in connection with the latter, theological."[40] These policy
considerations should be made explicit.

Hart expresses a similar view when he argues that "the essential elements of the
legal corporation" become visible through how legal rules apply in particular
contexts and circumstances to express a "unity" or "identity" in the actions of
groups of people.[41] The complexity of law, however, requires analytical care: one
should not extrapolate a finding of legal "identity" under one set of circumstances
to apply without reflection to another set of circumstances. (This concern relates
also to the issue of the shifting boundaries of firms discussed further below,
especially in Chapters 4, 5, and 6.)

A legal theory that sees the business firm as institutionally created can embrace in
a pragmatic and therefore substantively open fashion the elements of the two other
main theories, which focus on the prerogatives of both government and participants, respectively. One may read Dewey to say that adopting an intermediate
institutional theory of this kind commits one to taking a substantive political and
economic position.[42] And this is true to a degree. At a minimum, the institutional
theory assumes that both government and business participants have legitimate,
substantive claims that deserve recognition. To this extent, the institutional theory
does not adopt an entirely "positive" legal theory. It recognizes substantive institutional limits that extend minimal necessary roles to both governments and business
participants, thus combining elements of both concession and participant theories.[43]

The institutional theory of the firm is minimalist with respect to substantive
political content because it leaves open for elaboration both (1) what substantive
legal rules and restrictions government may impose; and (2) how far the aims and
interests of business participants should be legally protected.[44] In other words, the

---

[39] Id., p. 673.

[40] Id., p. 655.

[41] Hart, "Definition and Theory in Jurisprudence," op. cit., p. 30.

[42] Dewey, op. cit., pp. 670–3. Specifically, Dewey makes this point against the early organic or "real
entity" theorists such as Gierke, as well as more recent interpreters such as Harold Laski. Id. See also
Harold J. Laski, "The Personality of Associations," 29 *Harvard Law Review* 404 (1916).

[43] Cf. H.L.A. Hart, *The Concept of Law* (Oxford University Press, 2nd ed., 1997), pp. 193–200
(describing a "minimum content of natural law" included in a theory of positive law). I will not elaborate
extensively on the jurisprudential implications, except to say that the institutional legal theory of the firm
advanced here is compatible with several different jurisprudential orientations, including most if not all
contemporary versions of legal positivism, legal realism, and natural law theory.

[44] One may take a stronger *political* position with respect to the usefulness or normative desirability
of societies that recognize, respect, and encourage the formation of intermediate non-state institutions,
including business enterprises. These justifications might include an argument in favor of a vibrant

scope and breadth of substantive claims made by government (for regulation) and business participants (for limits on regulation and protection of their rights and interests) remain open for determination—both theoretically (through scholarly study and policy debate) and institutionally (through legal and political processes). Following the advice of Hart and Dewey, it makes better sense to decide specific policy questions with respect to the law applicable to business firms in particular contexts and situations rather than in general.

In addition, an institutional approach allows for the possibility that multiple values and purposes may apply to decide particular regulatory questions. Relatively open procedural methods, such as democratic government and deliberative judicial decisions, enable choices among different values and purposes to apply in different situations, depending on the social context and the legal questions raised. Different values may also apply more strongly in some circumstances than others. For example, the economic consequences of a particular legal rule are not always easily known or estimated, and in these cases ethical arguments may have stronger persuasive force.

An institutional theory of the firm describes a broad middle ground between the extremes that result from strict adherence to either a concession theory or a participant theory. Again, this institutional theory provides a moderate perspective by (1) recognizing that governmental regulation of firms makes sense on a policy level, but leaving open the substantive content and scope of this regulation for elaboration through political and legal processes; and (2) recognizing that some of the prerogatives and rights of individual participants represented in business firms deserve legal protection against government intrusion.

On one hand, with respect to the prerogatives of government, multiple alternative policy objectives are available for selection. Some economists and law-and-economists advocate the objective of promoting economic efficiency and overall wealth creation. This value is sometimes promoted as the only permissible objective to pursue in business regulation.[45] Neo-mercantilist or "industrial policy" proponents aim to advance national economic development, which has been one justification used to support state capitalism and the promotion of nationalistic economic competition among different varieties of market capitalism.[46] In contrast with economics, philosophers often advocate justice and fairness as policy alternatives that focus, for example, on the inequality of wealth distribution.[47] They may appeal

"civil society" (as well as governmental protection of individual rights) and an argument that the existence of independent organizations of sufficient size and strength provide an institutional check on tendencies toward absolute government. But these questions of political theory lie outside the scope of this book.

[45] See, e.g., Louis Kaplow and Steven Shavell, "Fairness Versus Welfare," 114 *Harvard Law Review* 961 (2001) (arguing that values of social welfare should trump other considerations).

[46] For an example of a debate along these lines with respect to national U.S. and Japanese policies in the 1980s, compare Robert B. Reich, "Making Industrial Policy," 60 *Foreign Affairs* 852 (1982), with Charles L. Schultze, "Industrial Policy: A Dissent," 2 *Brookings Review* 3 (1983).

[47] See, e.g., Liam Murphy and Thomas Nagel, *The Myth of Ownership: Taxes and Justice* (Oxford University Press 2002) (arguing in favor of "negative" and "progressive" taxes from considerations of justice and fairness); Jared D. Harris, "What's Wrong with Executive Compensation?" 85 *Journal of*

also to other basic moral values such as honesty (e.g. the prohibition of fraud) or respect for property (e.g. the prohibition of theft). These moral values derive from either deontological (duty-based) or utilitarian (consequentialist) moral principles.[48] Laws against insider trading, for example, may express primarily moral rather than economic principles.[49] Governments may adopt any of these multiple values or objectives and promote them through the enactment and interpretation of laws applicable to business enterprise.

On the other hand, a concern for the legal protection of the rights and interests of business participants recommends limits on governmental regulation, including (1) a prohibition of "takings" of private property (including business capital and financial investments) without compensation; and (2) guarantees of basic freedoms of self-organization and association.[50] These kinds of constitutional and other legal limitations recognize that business firms are "self-created" rather than "state-created."[51] Takings jurisprudence, which draws difficult conceptual lines between private property and its permissible regulation, fits also within a more general idea in constitutional law of protecting settled expectations, especially with respect to property interests, while recognizing that the legal definition of property itself changes over time.[52] Future-oriented, forward-planning business people tend to value stability, certainty, and the preservation of "settled expectations" in the law, which may also support other social and economic objectives.[53] The growth of sustainable long-term economic development and cultural cohesion may depend in part on a relatively stable legal order.

Business Ethics 147 (2009) (examining executive compensation levels on ethical grounds). For a critique of U.S. corporate law for ignoring concerns about wealth distribution, see Ronald Chen and Jon Hanson, "The Illusion of Law: The Legitimating Schemas of Modern Policy and Corporate Law," 103 *Michigan Law Review* 1, 121–5 (2004).

[48] A line between deontological theories (positing fundamental moral duties) and utilitarian theories (deriving moral principles from expected or proven social consequences, most often in terms of measures of human welfare) divides modern ethical philosophy. See, e.g., Dale Jamieson, "Method and Moral Theory," in *A Companion to Ethics* (Blackwell Publishers 1993), p. 477. Other theoretical views are possible which prioritize a process of "moral theorizing" in practical circumstances rather than looking to apply a priori principles. See, e.g., id., pp. 478–86. For an attempt to unify competing ethical theories, see Derek Parfit, *On What Matters*, vol. 1 (Oxford University Press 2011).

[49] See, e.g., Alan Strudler and Eric W. Orts, "Moral Principle in the Law of Insider Trading," 78 *Texas Law Review* 375 (1999).

[50] On constitutional "takings," see, e.g., Richard A. Epstein, *Takings: Private Property and the Power of Eminent Domain* (Harvard University Press 1985); William A. Fischel, *Regulatory Takings: Law, Economics, and Politics* (Harvard University Press 1995). On freedom of association, see pages 16–17 and accompanying notes 32–3.

[51] Laski, op. cit., p. 413.

[52] See Laurence H. Tribe, *American Constitutional Law* (Foundation Press, 2nd ed., 1988), pp. 587–613.

[53] See Frederic R. Coudert, *Certainty and Justice: Studies of the Conflict Between Precedent and Progress in the Development of the Law* (D. Appleton 1914). For a theory emphasizing the preservation of expectations, see Niklas Luhmann, *Law as a Social System* (Klaus A. Ziegart trans.) (Fastima Kastner et al., eds.) (Oxford University Press 2004); Niklas Luhmann, *A Sociological Theory of Law* (Elizabeth King and Martin Albrow trans.) (Routledge and Kegan Paul 1985). See also Thomas D. Barton, "Expectations, Institutions, and Meanings," 74 *California Law Review* 1805 (1986) (book review).

Two extremes: concession theory and participant theory

By embracing the perspectives of both government and business participants, the institutional theory of the firm described here is consistent with most existing legal systems in the world today. The substantive virtues of this institutional theory are illustrated by considering the extreme outcomes that would follow from adhering *only* to the concession theory or *only* to the participant theory.

The concession theory, taken alone, is too authoritarian with respect to the business enterprise. It may have appealed to ancient Roman emperors and old English monarchs, but in part exactly for this reason it conflicts with a contemporary viewpoint that accords basic respect to individual human rights, including positive freedoms of association and negative freedoms against arbitrary dispossession.[54] To subject business enterprises entirely to the whims of government (even one that is democratically elected) would run roughshod over the most basic rights that most countries today recognize for individual citizens—who are also individual participants in business firms—such as human rights to property and freedom of association. The Universal Declaration of Human Rights, for example, enshrines the following provisions.

- "Everyone has the right to own property alone as well as in association with others."[55]

- "No one shall be arbitrarily deprived of his [or her] property."[56]

- "Everyone has the right to freedom of peaceful assembly and association."[57]

- "Everyone has the right to work, to free choice of employment, to just and favorable conditions of work and to protection against unemployment."[58]

Most nation-states provide for similar or analogous legal protections of these rights in their constitutions or basic laws.[59]

Some modern versions of state capitalism adopt a strong concession view, which influential policy makers seem to hold today in China, Russia, and elsewhere, which can often violate basic rights. This view, at least when taken to its extreme, is incompatible with the varieties of capitalism (and their accompanying legal regimes) that recognize and respect basic political and economic rights. And it

---

[54] For the distinction between positive and negative freedom, see Isaiah Berlin, "Two Concepts of Liberty," in Isaiah Berlin, *The Proper Study of Mankind: An Anthology of Essays* (Farrar, Straus and Giroux 1998) (Henry Hardy and Roger Hausheer eds.), pp. 191–242. The value of freedom to engage in economic activity, including participation in private business enterprise, is also central in Hayekian theory. See, e.g., Hayek, *Law, Legislation, and Liberty: Volume 1, Rules and Order*, op. cit.; Hayek, *Law, Legislation, and Liberty: Volume 2, The Mirage of Social Justice*, op. cit.

[55] Universal Declaration of Human Rights (1948), sect. 17(1).

[56] Id., sect. 17(2).

[57] Id., sect. 20(1).

[58] Id., sect. 23(1).

[59] See, e.g., Jeremy Waldron, *The Right to Private Property* (Oxford University Press 1988), p. 18 (noting protection of property rights "around the world").

almost goes without saying that these rights of associational freedom, property ownership, and labor must be respected in actual practice as well as simply written into formal constitutions or statutes.

Extreme versions of the participant theory of the firm also go too far. Standing alone, this theory amounts to nothing much more than a theory of anarchy (or at least a very strong libertarianism). On its own terms and taken to its logical conclusion, this theory of the firm asserts that *only* the interests of individual participants matter. Even though the legal framework that makes firms possible is provided by government—in addition to any specific organizational privileges that might be extended (such as limited liability, discussed further below and in Chapter 4)—the extreme version of this theory posits that government should refrain from setting *any* limits to what participants may do through the organization and use of firms. Some of the so-called *Lochner*-era cases of the U.S. Supreme Court in the 1930s, which struck down broad-based business regulations such as min-imum-wage laws as unconstitutional infringements of basic rights to "liberty," approached this extreme.[60] To forbid any government regulation of business enterprises that would abridge private contracts or private property would swing the institutional pendulum too far in the direction of protecting entrenched business participants and disregarding legitimate public interests expressed through government.

Admitting that business firms play a central role in modern social life and therefore share an institutional responsibility for negative as well as positive conse-quences for their actions should prove sufficient to demonstrate that adopting an extreme version of the participant theory goes too far. Given the foundational role of government in providing the legal infrastructure for firms, it seems relatively uncontroversial that some level of further regulation may be needed (with the extent and scope of the regulation left open for further elaboration). This regulation may include both the prohibition of harmful activities and the encouragement of positive actions by firms. In economic terms, regulation may counter "negative externalities" (such as environmental pollution) and encourage "positive external-ities" (such as reducing crime by encouraging the expansion of employment).[61] In fact, the very idea of an economic "externality" assumes a corresponding organiza-tional "internality." It is within firms that the *internal* economic calculations and decisions are made—which do not include the *external* social costs or benefits that these decisions may impose outside of the firm. Economic accounts of "external-ities" regarding business decision-making therefore recognize (at least implicitly) the institutional existence of firms as real legal "persons" or "entities" that follow internal self-governing processes.

---

[60] For a review of cases, see Laurence H. Tribe, *American Constitutional Law*, vol. 1 (Foundation Press, 3rd ed., 1999), pp. 1332–81. Even at the high-water mark of this era, however, more regulatory measures were constitutionally upheld than struck down. Id., p. 1344 and n. 4.

[61] See, e.g., Harold Demsetz, "Toward a Theory of Property Rights," 57 *American Economic Review* 347, 348–9 (1967).

Woodrow Wilson may have expressed the point too strongly when he said:

A corporation [or other business firm] exists, not of natural right, but only by license of law, and the law, if we look at the matter in good conscience, is responsible for what it creates. . . . If law is at liberty to adjust the general conditions of society itself, it is at liberty to *control* these great instrumentalities which nowadays, in so large part, determine the character of society.[62]

Wilson's use of the word "control" suggests that he may fall somewhat closely to the extreme of the concession theory rather than an institutional perspective.[63] A more moderate interpretation of Wilson's observation, however, seems difficult to deny: namely, that the government should play an important role in setting the ground rules and basic operational parameters for the creation, organization, and management of business enterprises. From the perspective of legal theory, the substantive provisions of the regulation of business firms (as well as constitutional or other structural limitations on such regulation) are best left open for elaboration through political and deliberative processes.

If contemporary China and Russia are places where concern about an overly rigorous application of the concession theory of business enterprise is justified, the United States may illustrate the perils of adopting an extreme version of the participant theory. At present, the business-related jurisprudence in the mainstream of academic law in the United States (and, to a lesser extent, in other English-speaking countries) borrows its substantive legal theories of the firm mostly from the discipline of economics, following the success (in terms of institutional influence in leading law and business schools) of the law-and-economics movement.[64] This approach tips the balance too far toward participants and against government interests.

Law-and-economics is well-described as "a leading example of a highly successful legal ideology" with particularly strong influence in business-related fields, including the law of enterprise organization.[65] (Note that to say that a philosophical or jurisprudential movement is "ideological" is not to say that other approaches are "non-ideological." The question is rather whether the theoretical assumptions and views expressed are right, true, or useful.) Law-and-economics as a jurisprudential

---

[62] Woodrow Wilson, Governor's Inaugural Address, Minutes of Assembly of New Jersey, January 17, 1911, pp. 65, 69, reprinted in *The Public Papers of Woodrow Wilson* (Ray Stannard Baker and William E. Dodd, eds.) (Harper 1925–7), vol. II, pp. 273–5, and quoted in *Louis K. Liggettt Co. v. Lee*, 288 U.S. 517, 559 n. 37 (1933) (Brandeis, J., dissenting in part)) (emphasis added).

[63] Prior to becoming President, Woodrow Wilson played a significant historical role in the development of corporate law in the United States as Governor of New Jersey. The state of New Jersey had become a haven for incorporations, and then Governor Wilson led a charge for reform. As a result, many leading corporations moved to incorporate themselves in Delaware (which had copied New Jersey's permissive statute)—following a famous "race to the bottom" (or, according to scholars favoring regulatory competition, a "race to the top") in U.S. corporate law. For an overview, including Wilson's role, see Christopher Grandy, "New Jersey Corporate Chartermongering, 1875–1929," 49 *Journal of Economic History* 677 (1989). See also Chen and Hanson, op. cit., p. 143.

[64] For the classic and most influential example of this approach, see Richard A. Posner, *Economic Analysis of Law* (Aspen, 7th ed., 2007).

[65] Spencer Weber Waller, "The Law and Economics Virus," 31 *Cardozo Law Review* 367, 367–8, 379–90 (2009).

movement has had deep influence, especially in U.S. law schools. One recent historical analysis concludes: "Simply measured in terms of the penetration of its adherents in the legal academy, law and economics is the most successful intellectual movement in the law in the last thirty years, having rapidly moved from insurgency to hegemony."[66]

The influence of economic theories with respect to the business enterprise has been especially acute.[67] The currently dominant economic theories of the firm focus almost exclusively on individual participants—a consequence of methodological individualism. Law-and-economics jurisprudence with respect to business firms tends therefore to favor the principles of freedom of contract, freedom of association, and the protection of private property of the *participants* in business rather than to adopt the perspective of *government*. In other words, a deregulatory and even anti-regulatory bias (except perhaps for regulatory or constitutional protection of individual participants' rights) is built into a legal theory that takes contemporary neoclassical economic models as its guide. There are exceptions, and law-and-economics scholarship has grown to become highly diverse normatively as well as methodologically. It is also quite possible for economic analysis to take a broader view. For example, one well-known founder of law-and-economics has focused his fire on both *the failure of government* to regulate in a manner that would have prevented or at least significantly reduced the risks of the financial meltdown of 2008, as well as on *the failure of economists* to predict the problems.[68] Nevertheless, the overall bias or critical "tilt" of law-and-economics scholarship is well-known and derives from the underlying theoretical positions taken by the leading neoclassical economists.[69] Recent historical accounts reveal also that at least some of the influence of law-and-economics derives from anti-regulatory political as well as intellectual sources, especially through the funding of private think tanks and law-and-economics centers in law schools.[70]

[66] Steven M. Teles, *The Rise of the Conservative Legal Movement: The Battle for Control of the Law* (Princeton University Press 2008), p. 216. For an assessment of the influence of law and economics from an insider to the movement, see William M. Landes, "The Empirical Side of Law & Economics," 70 *University of Chicago Law Review* 167 (2003). See also Robert C. Ellickson, "Trends in Legal Scholarship: A Statistical Study," 29 *Journal of Legal Studies* 517 (2000) (finding an increases in law-and-economics work published in law journals from 1982 to 1996); William M. Landes and Richard A. Posner, "The Influence of Economics on Law: A Quantitative Study," 36 *Journal of Law and Economics* 385 (1993) (finding significant increases in terms of citation counts of law-and-economics work).

[67] For a heavily influential example in U.S. corporate law, see Frank H. Easterbrook and Daniel R. Fischel, *The Economic Structure of Corporate Law* (Harvard University Press 1996). See also Brian R. Cheffins, *Company Law: Theory, Structure, and Operation* (Oxford University Press 2007) (applying economic analysis in British law); Reinier R. Kraakman et al., *The Anatomy of Corporate Law: A Comparative and Functional Approach* (Oxford University Press, 2nd ed., 2009) (applying economic analysis in comparative perspective). For another leading source that employs economics as its lodestar, see William A. Klein, John C. Coffee, Jr., and Frank Partnoy, *Business Organization and Finance: Legal and Economic Principles* (Foundation Press, 11th ed., 2010).

[68] Richard A. Posner, *A Failure of Capitalism: The Crisis of '08 and the Descent into Depression* (Harvard University Press 2009); Richard A. Posner, *The Crisis of Capitalist Democracy* (Harvard University Press 2010).

[69] For a critique along these lines, see Chen and Hanson, op. cit, pp. 7–66.

[70] See Kim Phillips-Fein, *Invisible Hands: The Businessmen's Crusade Against the New Deal* (W.W. Norton 2009), pp. 162–3, 167; Teles, op. cit., pp. 90–134, 181–219.

In any event, most law-and-economics views of the firm, including so-called "contractarian" theories of the firm discussed in Chapter 2, adopt a relatively extreme version of the participant theory of the firm. Dissenting legal academics warned that followers of law-and-economics who adopted an exclusively "aggregate" rather than an "entity" theory of the business firm would lead to unpleasant consequences, but their voices were not heeded.[71] The global financial meltdown beginning in 2008—which most observers believe to have been caused mainly by a combination of factors including general deregulation, an overly laissez-faire approach to investment banking, and the under-regulation of new financial products (such as credit default swaps, subprime mortgages, and various kinds of securitizations)—may have taken the shine off the deregulatory presumptions of traditional law-and-economics.[72] As of this writing, however, the larger global trends with respect to regulation and the influence of traditional law-and-economics in the United States and elsewhere are unclear.

In addition, the business participants considered most relevant for law-and-economics theories, which closely follow neoclassical economic models, are capital investors or "owners." One can roughly divide capital investors in business enterprises into the categories of "creditors" (who make various kinds of loans) and "equity owners" (including both shareholders in corporations and investing members of other firms such as partners who claim a share of residual profits of a business). Some legal theorists continue to insist on a distinction between debt and equity as essential, but actual practice has become more complex, including the use of hybrid debt–equity instruments.[73] Blurring the distinction between debt and equity is not new. As one commentator worried as early as 1928:

> Stockholders and creditors are . . . two distinct classes of people, whose interests in the corporation are of such different natures as to be often diametrically opposed. . . . Should resort to devices under which rights are conferred to be either the one or the other, as expediency may later dictate, continue to grow in popularity, the effect must be the ultimate breaking down of the barrier between stockholders and creditors, a result which will necessitate the re-writing of an important part of the law of corporations.[74]

In contemporary practice, a "financial revolution" in investment products and options has indeed expanded the focus of financial views of the firm beyond simple assumptions of "shareholders as owners" and challenged the mantra of "shareholder value maximization" as the univocal objective of corporate firms.[75]

---

[71] See Bratton, op. cit.; David Millon, "Theories of the Corporation," 1990 *Duke Law Journal* 201, 201–4, 220–31 (1990). For an early critique, see also Arthur Allen Leff, "Economic Analysis of Law: Some Realism about Nominalism," 60 *Virginia Law Review* 451 (1974).

[72] See Preface, page xix and accompanying note 25.

[73] For further explanation, see Eric W. Orts, "Shirking and Sharking: A Legal Theory of the Firm," 16 *Yale Law and Policy Review* 265, 306–9 (1998).

[74] E. Ennalls Berl, "The Vanishing Distinction Between Creditors and Stockholders," 76 *University of Pennsylvania Law Review* 814, 822–3 (1928).

[75] See Henry T.C. Hu, "New Financial Products, the Modern Process of Financial Innovation, and the Puzzle of Shareholder Welfare," 69 *Texas Law Review* 1273 (1991); Peter H. Huang and Michael S. Knoll, "Corporate Finance, Corporate Law, and Finance Theory," 74 *Southern California Law*

Much more narrowly but nevertheless predominantly, many economists and law-and-economists hold the view that the business participants who matter most are the equity investors: for example, shareholders in corporations rather than creditors or lenders. When taken into legal theory unadulterated, this economic view of the firm threatens to reduce the scope of policy analysis by focusing only on a select group of business participants (and arbitrarily excluding others) and at the same time ignoring the larger institutional and legal realities of firms. Even for theories that focus only on the financial ownership of firms, it is now recognized that a focus on the "entity" of the firm (and various entities often constructed within firms) is required in order to make sense of competing financial claims, at least when conflicts arise among equity owners, creditors, and the many "hybrid" financial interests in modern firms.[76]

In addition, other business participants are considered important in different societies—sometimes equally so—including non-owner managers and employees as well as other capital providers and financial owners. The varieties of capitalism in different parts of the world today are distinguished in part by the different levels of legal protection provided to various groups of participants within firms. (A complete specification of the "varieties of capitalism" in the world today is beyond the scope of this book.[77] For the purposes here, I simply assume that several varieties of capitalism exist and elaborate how law contributes to the creation and maintenance of some aspects of this variety.) Politics as well as economics determine the relative legal status accorded to different participant groups in different countries. Variations are also negotiated in the form of specific organizational contracts and property structures (such as different voting and profit-participation rights for different equity and debt interests). One useful global analysis of interests within firms and the relative legal protections accorded to them in different countries refers to a tripartite divide within large firms among the following main groups: (1) investors (notably shareholders as well as creditors); (2) managers; and (3) other

---

Review 175 (2000); Frank Partnoy, "Financial Innovation in Corporate Law," 31 *Journal of Corporate Law* 799 (2006); Raghuram G. Rajan and Luigi Zingales, "The Influence of the Financial Revolution on the Nature of Firms," 91 *American Economic Review* 206 (2001).

[76] See, e.g., Hu, op. cit., pp. 1306–9. On the misuse of business entities in several high-profile scandals, see also William W. Bratton and Adam J. Levitin, "A Transactional Genealogy of Scandal: From Michael Milken to Enron to Goldman Sachs," 86 *Southern California Law Review* 783 (2013).

[77] On different systems, see, e.g., *Big Business and the Wealth of Nations* (Alfred D. Chandler, Jr. et al. eds.) (Cambridge University Press 1997); *Creating Modern Capitalism: How Entrepreneurs, Companies, and Countries Triumphed in Three Industrial Revolutions* (Thomas K. McCraw ed.) (Harvard University Press 1997); *A History of Corporate Governance Around the World* (Randall K. Morck ed.) (University of Chicago Press 2005); *Varieties of Capitalism: The Institutional Foundations of Comparative Advantage* (Peter A. Hall and David Soskice eds.) (Oxford University Press 2001). See also William J. Baumol, Robert E. Litan, and Carl J. Schramm, *Good Capitalism, Bad Capitalism, and the Economics of Growth and Prosperity* (Yale University Press 2007); Charles Hampden-Turner and Alfons Trompenaars, *The Seven Cultures of Capitalism: Value Systems for Creating Wealth in the United States, Britain, Japan, Germany, France, Sweden, and the Netherlands* (Doubleday 1993); Ronald Dore, William Lazonick, and Mary O'Sullivan, "Varieties of Capitalism in the Twentieth Century," 15 *Oxford Review of Economic Policy* 102 (1999).

employees.[78] A purely economic analysis of the firm focused only on financial owners elides the competing and often conflicting interests of these different groups.

The existence of firms as persons

Following an exclusive focus on business participants rather than the firm as an institution, one standard economic view has been to consider firms as merely "fictions"—thus recapitulating the misuse of a single theory of legal personality warned against by the likes of Hart and Dewey.[79] Some economists, when pushed on the subject, conclude that there is really no topic for a theory of the firm to address at all. Eugene Fama, for example, is fairly explicit with respect to the implications of his financial theory of the firm. Rejecting "classical models" of the firm that emphasize ownership and management of assets, Fama sees the firm as "a set of contracts among factors of production, with each factor motivated by its self-interest."[80] On this view, the "ownership of the firm" is "an irrelevant concept."[81] The logical conclusion: There are no firms, but only an immense aggregate of individuals contracting and trading with each other. Firms, to the extent that they exist, are merely one form among many "sets of contracts" that may be chosen. This conclusion is not surprising, given that a method focusing only on individuals— namely, the set of human beings who enter into contracts and own property—is assumed at the beginning of the analysis. In other words, "firms" as entities or persons with an ontological reality separate from the human beings that constitute them are not believed to exist because of a priori methodological assumptions. Human beings exist, but firms don't.

The institutional reality of business enterprises belies this assertion of the non-existence of firms. Asserting the non-existence of firms from an economic perspective denies or at least misunderstands the role of law in the institutional creation, construction, and maintenance of firms. It also flies in the face of a blizzard of contrary perspectives from other disciplines, including law, which reveal and explain the social reality of firms.

Note that even the starting assumption of a natural human being as the relevant "person" or unit assumed for economic analysis is problematic and requires law for definition and recognition. As the legal scholar Joseph Vining observes: "There is no such thing as a natural person [in law]. . . . A human being shifts among any

---

[78] Peter A. Gourevitch and James Shinn, *Political Power and Corporate Control: The New Global Politics of Corporate Governance* (Princeton University Press 2005), pp. 10–13, 57–83, 95–278.

[79] See, e.g., Michael C. Jensen and William H. Meckling, "Theory of the Firm: Managerial Behavior, Agency Costs and Ownership Structure," 3 *Journal of Financial Economics* 305, 310–11 (1976).

[80] Eugene F. Fama, "Agency Problems and the Theory of the Firm," 88 *Journal of Political Economy* 288, 289 (1980).

[81] Id., p. 290.

number of identities during the day, during the year, and during his or her life: sports player, parent, drug taker, dancer, corporate director, juror, investor, automobile salesman, artist, and so forth."[82] Like firms, natural human beings are given fictional names at birth, and limits are placed on whether human beings have access to courts with respect to age and mental acuity (such as in the concept of "capacity" in contract law), as well as national citizenship and other qualifications (as reflected in various provisions of immigration laws).

In addition, human beings, as well as firms, seek "standing" before courts in different kinds of roles. Again as Vining explains, "when a 'real' person comes before a court he [or she] does not come as a whole—... but in one of his [or her] roles, as a tenant farmer, perhaps, or a drug user, or a religious believer, or an investor."[83] Similarly, a firm can seek legal "standing" or recognition in different roles: as an employer, as a party to a contract with a supplier of goods, or as a bearer of certain constitutional rights.

The legal recognition of firms as "entities" or "persons" in these respects cannot be avoided or short-circuited through appeals to economics, because economic analysis itself depends on the legal recognition and definition of the relevant "units," including human beings as well as firms. With respect to theories of the firm, law is therefore a necessary starting point for any coherent economic analysis. Major errors in economics and law-and-economics have occurred when scholars invoke vaguely defined legal concepts (such as "implicit contracts" or "agency costs") without a sufficient appreciation of the richness of the legal meaning and context of these concepts.

From a legal point of view, then, the idea that "there are no firms" (and only individual human beings) is a non-starter. Firms as well as markets are created by law.[84] Firms exist as legal "entities" and "persons" because statutes and courts have recognized them as such for centuries and continue to do so today in almost all modern societies. The legal infrastructure supporting the business enterprise as an institution relies on these concepts. For example, the very idea of a "shareholder" depends on the legal recognition of an organizational entity (namely, the corporation) in which one may hold or own a "share." The role of a "manager" or a "director" presumes the existence of an organizational "entity" to be managed or directed. At least one recent economic theory of the firm is generally consistent with the emphasis placed here on legal definition and recognition. A firm, on this view, is "a nexus of specific investments: a combination of mutually specialized assets and people . . . [within] a complex structure that cannot be instantaneously replicated."[85]

---

[82] Joseph Vining, *Legal Identity: The Coming of Age of Public Law* (Yale University Press 1978), p. 59.

[83] Id.

[84] In discussing the difference between markets and firms, two influential legal commentators suggest that degrees of "firmishness" might replace attempts to distinguish firms and markets. Klein, Coffee, and Partnoy, op. cit., pp. 19–20. However, this idea presupposes that one can have a solid conception of a "firm" in mind from which varying degrees of "firmishness" could then be deduced or approximated.

[85] Luigi Zingales, "Corporate Governance," reprinted in *The Economic Nature of the Firm: A Reader* (Randall S. Kroszner and Louis Putterman eds.) (Cambridge University Press, 3rd ed.,

Even if one concedes that firms are "artificial legal fictions," they are legal fictions with social consequences that are real, practical, and large. The nation-state is another example of an "artificial fiction." Like business firms, the nation-state has a legal and institutional reality (in the social rather than the metaphysical sense), and few would deny that the "imagined communities" of nation-states exist and matter greatly in practical affairs.[86] The legal scholar Arthur Machen made the point as follows: "The state, like other corporations, is actually an impersonal entity; by a legal fiction or metaphor, that impersonal entity is regarded as a person. Uncle Sam is a fictitious person; but the government of the United States is a reality."[87] Nation-states matter because constitutional and international law recognize these entities—and people who live within the geographical and conceptual boundaries of nation-states empirically believe in them. Alexis de Tocqueville said: "The government of the Union rests almost entirely on legal fictions. The Union is an ideal nation which exists, so to say, only in men's minds and whose extent and limits can only be discerned by the understanding."[88] The belief in a nation-state reinforced by the legal recognition of this belief makes it practically real.

Money is another example of an "artificial" and "fictional" institutional invention which is, objectively, merely some bits of more or less colorful paper or shiny pieces of metal (or symbolic representations on computer screens).[89] Few, if any, would deny that money exists or amounts to "merely a legal fiction." The institutions of law, politics, and markets make the representation of "money" socially real, meaningful, and consequential. The same is true of the business firm, which the law creates, recognizes, and defines as a type of institutional "person" and "entity."

Much ink has been spilled over concepts such as "legal fictions," "legal entities," and "legal persons." Unfortunately, as the likes of Hart and Dewey point out, these concepts have too often been used categorically to support one or another substantive legal theory of the firm—or sometimes rejected entirely as unhelpful. Taking an institutional perspective allows one to explain and demystify these ideas, finding them both useful and descriptive, without either becoming a slave to the ideas or feeling a need to jettison them.

2009), p. 71. The author qualifies this economic definition of the firm with the caveat that it "does not necessarily coincide with a legal definition." Id. But it is actually closer to a foundational legal understanding than most other economic definitions, allowing for legal variations in different circumstances with respect to participants included and legal structures adopted. See also Raghuram G. Rajan and Luigi Zingales, "Power in a Theory of the Firm," 113 *Quarterly Journal of Economics* 387 (1998); Raghuram G. Rajan and Luigi Zingales, "The Firm as a Dedicated Hierarchy: A Theory of the Origins and Growth of Firms," 116 *Quarterly Journal of Economics* 805 (2001).

[86] See Benedict Anderson, *Imagined Communities: Reflections on the Origins and Spread of Nationalism* (Verso, 2nd ed., 2006).

[87] Arthur W. Machen, Jr., "Corporate Personality," 24 *Harvard Law Review* 346, 347 (1911).

[88] Aviam Soifer, "Reviewing Legal Fictions," 20 *Georgia Law Review* 871, 872 (1986) (quoting Tocqueville).

[89] For a discussion of the "social construction" of money as an "institutional fact," see John Searle, *The Construction of Social Reality* (Free Press 1995), pp. 32–3, 41–3, 52–3, 63, 76, 79–81, 119.

Legal fictions

To an average citizen, the idea of "legal fictions" may seem daunting or, worse, evidence of pettifoggery: the use of arcane legal concepts to achieve hidden, politically determined results by lawyers and those who hire them. A general theme in the history of jurisprudence has been to perceive legal fictions as problematic and unhelpful, obscuring the application of clear, scientific principles. Jeremy Bentham, for example, compared the use of fictions in law to swindling in trade.[90] And legal fictions can sometimes be used in this fashion.

At the same time, the use of legal fictions provides a means by which legal change can occur—pouring new wine of changing content into old legal bottles of established concepts.[91] Lawyers use fictions all the time. In fact, it is often difficult to say when an idea transforms from a "legal fiction" into an established "legal truth." Even some of the most central legal ideas, such as a "contract," are fictional in the sense that the recognition of an enforceable promise (with consequences involving either judicial enforcement or the payment of money in damages) depends on the interpretation of legal sources of authority and the institutional invocation of this authority. One may say that natural "agreements" and "promises" occur through the use of language and human interaction.[92] But it is law that determines whether a particular promise or agreement amounts to an enforceable "contract." A contract is therefore a legally determined social fact and an "artificial fiction." Over time, as the practice of making promises and enforcing contracts based on them becomes institutionally imbedded and relied upon in a particular culture, the fictional origins of the idea are forgotten as the concept becomes socially "real" through experience and settled cultural expectations.

Another example of a legal fiction is the business corporation. One can describe corporations as "legal fictions" in the sense that they are invented (in general) and created (in specific instances) by human beings who use established legal methods and processes to do so. However, once a framework of corporate statutes has been established, and once specific business firms are up and running, the corporation as an institution is no longer a "mere fiction." It becomes socially real through its construction and maintenance in accordance with a specific set of internal and external legal rules, principles, and understandings. As one legal philosopher puts it, "very old fictions are no longer considered as such."[93] Particularly useful legal fictions become converted over time into "juristic truth."[94]

---

[90] Lon L. Fuller, *Legal Fictions* (Stanford University Press 1967), p. 2 (citing Bentham).

[91] See id., pp. 1–3 (discussing Bentham, Blackstone, Jhering, and others).

[92] See, e.g., T.M. Scanlon, "Promises and Contracts," in *The Theory of Contract Law: New Essays* (Peter Benson ed.) (Cambridge University Press 2001), pp. 86–117 (arguing that breaking promises and "lying promises" are morally wrong without regard to background legal institutions or likely enforcement).

[93] Pierre du Tourtoulon, *Philosophy in the Development of Law* (Macmillan 1922), quoted in Fuller, op. cit., p. 15 n. 36.

[94] Fuller, op. cit., p. 23.

Policy debates may then arise concerning the principled foundations that support particular legal fictions such as a "contract" or a "corporation." In contract law, for example, the assertion of moral principle (keeping promises as a moral duty owed to people living in society together) may diverge from the assertion of economic principle (designing legal rules to achieve the greatest efficiency) as justifications for enforcing promises.[95] "Mixed theories" of ethics and efficiency can resolve or at least describe these kinds of normative conflicts.[96]

At the same time, one should remember that legal fictions—even useful ones—remain legal fictions. Therefore they remain open to the possibility of change. "A fiction becomes wholly safe," warns the legal scholar Lon Fuller, "only when it is used with a complete consciousness of its falsity."[97] Because ideas such as the "corporation" and other business forms are fictions, they are also malleable. Again in Fuller's words: "Some fictions should be rejected; some should be redefined. Redefinition is proper where it results in the creation of a useful concept... "[98] Law defines business firms, and it can therefore re-define them.

Legal fictions differ from literary fictions. The key difference is that legislatures and courts back legal fictions with institutional authority and, as a last resort, organized force.[99] Yet there is nothing necessarily permanent about the adoption of a legal fiction. Legislatures and courts may dismantle, disregard, or reform legal fictions if and when they are no longer useful or no longer found to advance the social policies for which they were originally established. Again to follow Hart and Dewey, the legal fictions that designate the "entities" and "persons" of the business enterprise are not written in stone. Legal institutions invent and reinforce these fictions over time because they are found socially beneficial, and their continued use should then depend on whether they are working well or not. When a legal fiction is not working for the purposes intended, it should be either adapted or discarded.[100]

Law is not alone among the disciplines in using "fictions." Economics employs the fiction of the "rational actor." Political theorists and philosophers refer to imaginative "social contracts." And scientists employ theoretical constructs that are at least partly fictional or created imaginatively.[101] Lon Fuller, following the German philosopher Hans Vaihinger, asserts that conceptual fictions are even "an indispensable instrument of human thinking."[102]

---

[95] See Stephen A. Smith, *Contract Theory* (Oxford University Press 2004), pp. 41–2, 106–19, 140–58.

[96] Id., pp. 158–61.

[97] Fuller, op. cit., p. 10.

[98] Id., p. 22.

[99] See Soifer, op. cit., pp. 882–3 (noting the difference and observing that "the nexus between even the most powerful literary fiction and actual force is quite attenuated").

[100] For further discussion of the use and misuse of legal fictions, see Fuller, op. cit. See also Nancy J. Knauer, "Legal Fictions and Juristic Truth," 23 *St. Thomas Law Review* 1 (2010).

[101] See Fuller, op. cit., pp. 98–110, 107.

[102] Id., pp. 93–123. But cf. Louise Harmon, "Falling Off the Vine: Legal Fictions and the Doctrine of Substituted Judgment," 100 *Yale Law Journal* 1 (1990) (renewing concern about the misuse of legal fictions).

From this perspective, rhetorical references to business corporations as "Frankenstein's monsters" may capture the truth of their artificial creation, but business firms in various legal forms are no more dangerous or unusual than other legal fictions, such as "contract" or "property."[103] Legal fictions can become socially embedded as institutions, and the resulting historical inertia and "path dependence" can make change very difficult along many social dimensions.[104] The legal infrastructure of business enterprise engenders reliance and even economic dependence of many participants on the "rules of the game." Appreciating the fictional features of business firms, however, allows one also to gain the critical perspective needed to reform them over time as social circumstances and needs change. Because the legal forms of business are fictions, they can be *re*-formed.

On the topic of whether business firms of various kinds should be considered "fictional" or "real," one is tempted to follow the position taken by the legal theorist John Chipman Gray who noted an "old saying" that "everybody is born either a nominalist or a realist." He concluded that it is unhelpful to argue for either point of view.[105] My view offers a different compromise, arguing that the legal entities and persons known as business firms are best considered *both* "fictional" *and* "real." Institutional fictions become real over time through the social and legal practices that recognize them. This theoretical approach combines nominalism and realism. Understanding the firm as a "legal fiction" highlights the prerogatives of government (including legislatures and courts) to change the legal forms of business enterprise, as well as the rules applicable to them when social conditions or relevant knowledge changes. Understanding the firm as "socially real" recognizes that people participating in business build up interests and expectations over time and presume (with justifications that the law often recognizes, respects, and enforces) that the forms and rules relied upon will remain relatively stable, thus supplying solid institutional foundations for productive work and commerce.

Legal entities

From an institutional perspective, describing firms as "entities" is not problematic once one appreciates the flexibility of using legal fictions. "Entities" are artificial creations of the legal imagination. There is nothing strange or unusual in the use of

---

[103] For references to business corporations as Frankenstein's monsters, see Wormser, op. cit. See also *Liggett v. Lee*, op. cit., 288 U.S. at 567 (Brandeis, J., dissenting in part).

[104] See Lucian Arye Bebchuk and Mark J. Roe, "A Theory of Path Dependence in Corporate Ownership and Governance," 52 *Stanford Law Review* 127 (1999) (describing both "structure-driven" and "rule-driven" path dependence in institutional evolution). See also W. Brian Arthur, *Increasing Returns and Path Dependence in the Economy* (University of Michigan Press 1994); S.J. Liebowitz and Stephen E. Margolis, "Path Dependence, Lock-in, and History," 11 *Journal of Law, Economics, & Organization* 205 (1995); Paul Pierson, "Increasing Returns, Path Dependence, and the Study of Politics," 94 *American Political Science Review* 251 (2000); Stephen Redding, "Path Dependence, Endogenous Innovation, and Growth," 43 *International Economic Review* 1215 (2002).

[105] John Chipman Gray, *The Nature and Sources of the Law* (Macmillan, 2nd ed., 1927), pp. 52–3.

entities to understand firms and how they work legally. One entity is the institutional "unity" of an enterprise such as a "corporation" (or an instantiated "body"). Considering the enterprise as an entity looks to the organizational coherence of the management, decision processes, and operations of a business as a framework for legal thinking.[106] One might even go as far as Joseph Vining who argues:

> Entities, units of reference, building blocks may be essential to thought itself. . . . A large part of thinking *seems* to consist of the rearranging or modifying of already given units of reference. But the establishment of a unit of reference is often the critical point in reasoning or discussion, legal or nonlegal, and when one is unpersuaded by an argument but does not quite know why, analysis often shows that one has tacitly rejected the unit of reference being used.[107]

Lon Fuller makes a similar argument: "[T]he notion of 'unity' or 'identity' has no meaning out of a complete context of thought-operations. 'Unity' and 'identity' are matters of subjective convenience. Conceptually one may postulate entities whenever it is convenient to do so."[108] For example, the creation and recognition of firms as legal entities gives them "standing" to sue and be sued in courts in their own (fictional) names. "Standing" is simply a legal term recognizing the ability of a legal person "to be heard by a judge."[109]

The "naming" of entities is another example of a "real fiction" used for individual humans (and often their pets) with application to business firms as well. A name is invented (by parents or bestowed through custom), and it then becomes "real"—as the name used to refer to the particular individual—through social practice, repetition, and reinforcement (e.g. the use of one's "name" in the family, in school, and on legal documents). Similarly, the naming of organizations occurs through the "naming devices" of corporate charters or partnership agreements—with the organizational name then reinforced as "real" through social practice, repetition, and reinforcement: such as through contracts in the firm's "name" used with employees, suppliers, customers, and creditors, as well as in the marketing of products and services by advertising and word-of-mouth.[110]

The legal conception of the firm as an entity also permits a defined and identified collective unit to hold and manage private property, to make contracts with people and other recognized entities, and to enforce or become the target of other legal responsibilities (including specific statutory capacities and obligations). Legal recognition of the business firm as an entity operationalizes the accounting concept of

---

[106] See Adolf A. Berle, Jr., "The Theory of Enterprise Entity," 47 *Columbia Law Review* 343 (1947).

[107] Vining, *Legal Identity*, op. cit., p. xii (original emphasis).

[108] Fuller, op. cit., p. 120.

[109] Vining, *Legal Identity*, op. cit., pp. 55–6 (reviewing the origin of the term). See also page 28 and accompanying note 83.

[110] On the deeper philosophy of naming, see Saul A. Kripke, *Naming and Necessity* (Harvard University Press 1980).

a firm as having its own "fisc" and treasury.[111] Law creates an entity (*firma*) that corresponds to the accounting entity (*ragione*) as well as the credit entity (*ditta*).[112]

This does not mean that modern legal and accounting entities are co-extensive. As discussed further below, especially in Chapters 2 and 6, the legal boundaries of the entities called firms vary according to the questions asked. Accounting boundaries, especially in corporate groups with parent-and-subsidiary or other complex organizational structures, can vary widely. For example, a firm may use overall consolidated accounting statements for U.S. income tax reporting purposes and, at the same time, use separate subsidiary profit-and-loss statements or other accounting methods to manage subordinate business units within a larger firm structure. Legal determinations are often required to determine the appropriate "enterprise entity" in resolving particular questions and cases.[113] For example, a common thread in some turn-of-the-century financial scandals in the United States (including those involving Enron's implosion and Goldman Sachs' enabling of a hedge fund short in the housing market) involved the highly creative and legally questionable use of off-balance sheet accounting "entities" for various kinds of transactions.[114] The simpler point here is that a foundational concept of the firm as a legal entity is necessary for these kinds of questions even to arise (and then to be answered).

In addition, the designation of an entity is important for recognizing responsibility for harmful actions or, in legal terms, "liability." Business participants may use legal entities to limit their liability, perhaps most notably through legal policies favoring limited liability for the shareholders and creditors of corporations. Commentators sometimes focus too closely on the limits to personal liability extended to shareholders (and managers).[115] Creditors who finance business entities through arms-length contracts also enjoy limited liability for the potentially harmful actions of the firms to whom they lend—as long as they do not assume effective managerial control of the enterprises that they finance.[116]

---

[111] For a review of the importance of accounting in this connection, see Orts, "A Short History of the Business Enterprise," op. cit. For discussion of accounting concepts with respect to the delineation of the business firm, see also Kenneth S. Most, "Sombart's Propositions Revisited," 47 *Accounting Review* 722 (1972); Basil S. Yamey, "Accounting and the Rise of Capitalism: Further Notes on a Theme by Sombart," 2 *Journal of Accounting Research* 117 (1964); James O. Winjum, "Accounting and the Rise of Capitalism: An Accountant's View," 9 *Journal of Accounting Research* 333 (1971).

[112] Werner Sombart, "Medieval and Modern Commercial Enterprise," in *Enterprise and Secular Change: Readings in Economic History* (Frederic C. Lane ed.) (Richard D. Irwin, Inc., 1953), p. 31. See also Thorstein Veblen, *The Theory of Business Enterprise* (Mentor 1932) (1904), pp. 49–67 (discussing "loan credit" as an important feature of business enterprise).

[113] See, e.g., Berle, op. cit., pp. 348–50 (discussing the example of determining the appropriate "entity" in parent-subsidiary cases with reference to consolidating accounting statements as a guide for legal results).

[114] See Bratton and Levitin, op. cit.

[115] See, e.g., Berle, op. cit., p. 343 (1947) (noting that the "primary business advantage" of the corporation is the "insulation of individual stockholders composing the corporation from liability for the debts of the corporate enterprise," as well as "the distribution of responsibility" among corporate managers and officers).

[116] For a classic case illustrating a situation where a creditor becomes liable to third parties for exercising managerial control under agency law, see *A. Gay Jenson Farms Co. v. Cargill, Inc.,* 309

The concept of "asset partitioning" helps to explain the use of the legal entity in limiting the liability and risk of capital providers. Essentially, the recognition of the firm as an entity and the firm's ability to own assets in its own name allow for setting financial priorities between creditors and equity owners for claims on these designated assets. The legal entity of the firm may also "shield" creditors and equity owners from personal liability in some circumstances.[117] According to the legal scholars Henry Hansmann and Reinier Kraakman, there are two general types of asset partitioning. "Affirmative asset partitioning" refers to a priority that *creditors of the firm* are given to the assets dedicated to the firm and owned by the firm as an entity. In the event of financial trouble, the creditors of the firm get priority over both the equity owners of the firm and any personal creditors of the equity owners. For example, if a single firm with a single owner has assets of $1 million, and the owner goes personally bankrupt, then the creditors of the firm can make claims against the $1 million dedicated to the firm ahead of claims made against the owner personally. "Defensive asset partitioning" refers to an entity "shield" that is recognized to protect the *equity owners of the firm* from personal liability for claims made against them by creditors of the firm in excess of a firm's own dedicated assets.[118] Adapting the previous example, imagine that the single firm with designated assets of $1 million produces defective products that result in a liability of $5 million. A corporate entity will "shield" the owner's personal assets against claims exceeding the $1 million amount invested in the firm.

Taking advantage of legal "asset partitioning," the creditors and shareholders of a corporate enterprise put only the amount of funds invested in the corporation at risk: they do not usually have to worry about additional liability for harms or obligations that may exceed the amount of capital owned by the corporation in the event of financial failure or bankruptcy. And creditors enjoy some security of a first claim on a firm's dedicated assets. Different business forms, which are further described in Chapter 5, allow for more or less protection in terms of the legal strength of "partitioned" assets in an entity.[119]

There are exceptions to this rule of limited liability even with respect to corporations, which are usually thought to provide the strongest form of asset partitioning.[120] (Criteria that justify exceptions to permit "piercing the entity" to find

---

N.W.2d 285 (Minn. 1981). Agency law and limited liability are further discussed in Chapters 2 and 4.

[117] See Henry Hansmann and Reinier Kraakman, "The Essential Role of Organizational Law," 110 *Yale Law Journal* 387 (2000).

[118] Id., pp. 393–6; see also Paul G. Mahoney, "Contract or Concession? An Essay on the History of Corporate Law," 34 *Georgia Law Review* 873, 876–7 (2000) (referring to the same idea as "forward" and "reverse" partitioning). In work with another author, Hansmann and Kraakman substitute "entity shielding" for "affirmative asset partitioning." Hansmann, Kraakman, and Squire, op. cit., pp. 1362–3.

[119] Hansmann and Kraakman, "The Essential Role of Organizational Law," op. cit., pp. 394–7.

[120] See, e.g., Berle, op. cit., pp. 352–4 (reviewing cases disregarding corporate entities when used for illegal, fraudulent, or "objectionable" purposes); Clark, op. cit., pp. 35–92 (describing "limits to limited liability" for shareholders, such as in fraudulent conveyance law and "piercing the corporate veil" cases); Conard, op. cit., pp. 424–3 (reviewing various criteria for exceptions to limited liability); Franklin A. Gevurtz, *Corporation Law* (West Group 2000), pp. 69–111 (same).

liability are discussed in Chapter 4.) One can achieve the legal results of asset partitioning, however, only by recognizing and respecting the "entity" of a business enterprise. Other legal methods of asset partitioning are not feasible, mostly for reasons of transaction costs in terms of the extensive contracting that would be otherwise required.[121]

Joseph Vining is therefore on the mark when he writes: "Limitation of the liability that would otherwise flow from private law analysis—the limitation that is a characteristic feature of modern industrial and commercial organization—is largely the recognition and separation of entities."[122] Hansmann and Kraakman conclude also that the recognition of entities is "essential" for the organization of business enterprise.[123]

More broadly speaking, the designation of firms as entities raises questions of their governance, decision-making authority, and control. Many issues in the law of enterprise organization involve "the recognition of entity" with respect to these dimensions as well.[124] In contrast to some contemporary authors who treat the idea of firms as entities strictly from an economic perspective, Vining observes that attributes of "power" and "authority" are involved as well as "wealth" whenever dealing with "entities beyond the material or individually human."[125]

Some legal complexities and difficulties arise in terms of different kinds of entities that may possess more or less economic or social "reality." For example, corporate subsidiaries are recognized as legal entities and used in the structures of holding companies and large multinational enterprises.[126] (Historically, there was resistance to the idea that corporations or other business enterprises such as trusts should be allowed to hold stock in other corporations or entities, but these kinds of multi-entity corporate groups became solidly established over time and "grew to occupy a commanding role in American industry and eventually in the world economy as well."[127]) These legally complex enterprises are usually managed in a relatively centralized fashion.[128] Toyota, for example, exercises relatively unified management control of its business from its central headquarters in Japan, even though it has also created a number of legal entities as subsidiaries for manufacturing and sales operations in other locations, such as the United States.[129] Multinational

---

[121] Hansmann and Kraakman, "The Essential Role of Organizational Law," op. cit., pp. 406–23.

[122] Joseph Vining, *From Newton's Sleep* (Princeton University Press 1995), p. 320.

[123] Hansmann and Kraakman, "The Essential Role of Organizational Law," op. cit., pp. 387, 390, 440.

[124] Vining, *From Newton's Sleep*, op. cit., p. 320.

[125] Id., pp. 319–20.

[126] See, e.g., Conard, op. cit., pp. 165–9; Eric W. Orts, "The Legitimacy of Multinational Enterprise," in *Progressive Corporate Law* (Lawrence E. Mitchell ed.) (Westview Press 1995), pp. 248–9, 251–2.

[127] Blumberg, op. cit., p. 58.

[128] However, there are exceptions. Corporate conglomerates and other business firms, for example, are sometimes managed in a purposefully *decentralized* manner in order to devolve operational decision-making authority in the firm to lower managerial levels in the organization.

[129] See, e.g., Renè Belderbos and Leo Sleuwaegen, "Japanese Firms and the Decision to Invest Abroad: Business Groups and Regional Core Networks," 78 *Review of Economics and Statistics* 214, 216 (1996).

business enterprise structures thus raise interesting issues of "corporate geography."[130]

Corporate law in most jurisdictions recognizes subsidiaries as useful entities for various purposes, such as establishing domestic corporate residence or citizenship for doing business and limiting the extent of liability for the corporate parent.[131] Policy justifications for this extension of limited liability to parent–subsidiary and other complex entity structures may include the encouragement of international trade as well as flexibility for larger firms to enter into new corporate ventures with different combinations of investors. The "primary motives" for parent–subsidiary structures may also include: "increased facility in financing; the desire to escape the difficulty, if not the impossibility, of qualifying the parent company as a foreign corporation in a particular state; the avoidance of complications involved in the purchase of physical assets; the retention of the good will of an established business unit; the avoidance of taxation; the avoidance of cumbersome management structures; [and] the desire for limited liability."[132] Parent–subsidiary corporations often create entity-within-entity structures, however, which go beyond policy justifications of "asset partitioning" to protect individual participants. Strong arguments have been made that courts and legislators should subject parent–subsidiary and other entity-within-entity structures to greater scrutiny when they are invoked to limit the liability for harm caused by a larger enterprise and attributable to decisions made for the benefit of the participants in the larger business as a whole. This approach would follow an "enterprise entity" or "single enterprise" theory for finding liability.[133]

Jurisdictional issues are also important when considering whether and when to extend liability to corporate parents. These issues arise both at the national and global levels.[134] And questions of "piercing the entity" in parent–subsidiary

---

[130] For an introduction to the field, see Richard Walker, "A Requiem for Corporate Geography: New Directions in Industrial Organization, the Production of Place and the Uneven Development," 71 *Geografiska Annaler: Series B, Human Geography* 43 (1989).

[131] See, e.g., Blumberg, op. cit., pp. 58–60 (recognizing limited liability in parent–subsidiary structures but noting that it appears to have evolved as "a historical accident"); Orts, "The Legitimacy of Multinational Enterprise," op. cit., pp. 254–8 (reviewing the use of subsidiaries for purposes of establishing corporate citizenship in different jurisdictions).

[132] William O. Douglas and Carrol M. Shanks, "Insulation from Liability Through Subsidiary Corporations," 39 *Yale Law Journal* 193, 193 (1929).

[133] See, e.g., Berle, op. cit.; Conard, op. cit., pp. 428–9; Douglas and Shanks, op. cit., pp. 210, 217–18; Note, "Liability of a Corporation for Acts of a Subsidiary or Affiliate," 71 *Harvard Law Review* 1122 (1958). See also Robert J. Rhee, "Bonding Limited Liability," 51 *William and Mary Law Review* 1417, 1456–8 (2010) (favoring a "theory of enterprise liability" determined by a practical "control" test). But see, e.g., Stephen B. Presser, *Piercing the Corporate Veil* (Clark, Boardman, Callaghan 1992), pp. 1–53 to 1–57 (arguing that economic principles justify extending limited liability to corporate parents); Stephen B. Presser, "The Bogalusa Explosion, 'Single Business Enterprise,' 'Alter Ego,' and Other Errors: Academics, Economics, Democracy, and Shareholder Limited Liability," 100 *Northwestern University Law Review* 405, 420–7 (2006) (rejecting "single enterprise" and other theories of parent liability).

[134] See, e.g., Janet Cooper Alexander, "Unlimited Shareholder Liability Through a Procedural Lens," 106 *Harvard Law Review* 387 (1992); Henry Hansmann and Reinier Kraakman, "A Procedural Focus on Unlimited Shareholder Liability," 106 *Harvard Law Review* 446 (1992); Jennifer A. Schwartz, Comment, "Piercing the Corporate Veil of an Alien Parent for Jurisdictional Purposes:

situations arise also in bankruptcy law.[135] The point here is not to resolve all of these complex legal questions, but only to point out that the recognition of business "entities" is essential in all of them.

Another example shows how a legal entity can have virtually no "real" institutional existence at all. In triangular mergers in the United States—a legal procedure by which three corporate entities are used to merge or consolidate two companies—a new legal entity is often created as a subsidiary in order to accomplish the merger. The newly formed entity then simply disappears after the merger is concluded. For example, a target corporation X may be merged into a subsidiary Y of an acquiring corporation Z. Once merged into subsidiary Y, target X as a separate entity is dissolved, leaving only corporation Z and its subsidiary Y. (See Figure 1.1 for a schematic representation.) The reality of the third entity here appears only formally in the law's imagination—a fiction that is nevertheless useful to accomplish the practical ends of the two primary institutional players (namely, X and Z corporations).[136] The transient and ephemeral nature of the entity used to achieve a triangular merger suggests one reason to avoid adopting a *real entity* institutional theory as complete.[137] As long as this method of corporate combination accomplishes objectives that are otherwise deemed effective, fair, and sound as a matter of public policy, however, there appears to be no reason to fear the use of fictional legal entities in this fashion.[138]

A Proposal for a Standard That Comports with Due Process," 96 *California Law Review* 731 (2008); William A. Voxman, Comment, "Jurisdiction over a Parent Corporation in Its Subsidiary's State of Incorporation," 141 *University of Pennsylvania Law Review* 327 (1992).

[135] For a classic debate on this topic, see Jonathan M. Landers, "A Unified Approach to Parent, Subsidiary, and Affiliate Questions in Bankruptcy," 42 *University of Chicago Law Review* 589 (1975); Jonathan M. Landers, "Another Word on Parents, Subsidiaries and Affiliates in Bankruptcy," 43 *University of Chicago Law Review* 527 (1976); Richard A. Posner, "The Rights of Creditors of Affiliated Corporations," 43 *University of Chicago Law Review* 499 (1976). See also Richard Squire, "Strategic Liability in the Corporate Group," 78 *University of Chicago Law Review* 605 (2011) (revisiting this debate in light of current practices).

[136] For explanation of triangular mergers, see Clark, op. cit., pp. 430–3 (summarizing reasons for them, including avoiding liability, avoiding shareholder votes that may otherwise be required, and tax considerations). See also Klein, Coffee, and Partnoy, op. cit., pp. 120–2.

[137] This refers to the overly strong versions of an "institutional entity theory" such as adopted by Gierke. See pages 15–16 and accompanying notes 27–8. See also Otto von Gierke, *Community in Historical Perspective* (Mary Fischer trans., Antony Black ed.) (Cambridge University Press, 1990) (1868); Otto von Gierke, *Political Theories of the Middle Age* (Frederick Maitland trans.) (Cambridge University Press 1987) (1913).

[138] Klein, Coffee, and Partnoy use the triangular merger example in contradistinction to their argument against what they call the "reification" of the business enterprise. Influenced strongly by economic models of the firm, these scholars argue against the use of reification (or the recognition of a business as an entity) for analytical purposes "except when the complexity of the actual relationships becomes so unmanageable as to make it necessary to reify." Klein, Coffee, and Partnoy, op. cit., p. 117. I agree that this analytical perspective with its focus on individual business participants is useful, but I disagree with it to the extent that this view seems to reject recognition of legal persons and entities as descriptive concepts and sees them as unfortunate "exceptions" rather than as basic concepts needed for understanding of the business enterprise as an institution. See id., pp. 117–18. See also G. Mitu Gulati, William A. Klein, and Eric M. Zolt, "Connected Contracts," 47 *UCLA Law Review* 887, 890–3 (2000) (arguing against "reification" and the use of "entities" in legal analysis of firms and adopting a version of the economic "nexus of contracts" theory of the firm, which essentially

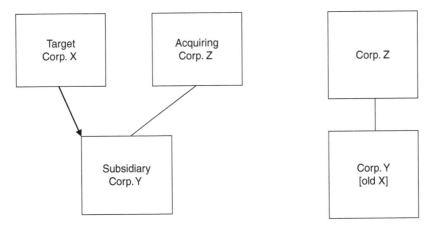

Fig. 1.1 Triangular corporate merger (schematic)

A third example of the use of legal entities refers to options for the "form-shifting" of business enterprises or, more colorfully, their propensity for "shape-shifting."[139] Given a menu of different legal options (which are reviewed further in Chapter 5 below), a firm can "shapeshift" from one form to another in terms of its governance structure (e.g. from a partnership to a corporation) and capital structure (e.g. from a closely held corporation with only a few shareholders to a publicly held corporation with many shareholders). Corporate shapeshifting, as the legal scholar Frank Partnoy describes the phenomenon, is "a transformation of corporate form involving the creation or use of a new legal entity and one or more changes in structure, including capital structure and the allocation of control rights."[140] Business forms other than corporations can also shapeshift—including, for example, sole proprietorships, partnerships, or limited liability companies trans-forming into corporations (or vice versa). The general "choice of business form" problem for a start-up enterprise is only an initial choice and can be later altered. One basic option includes an initial decision to "incorporate" as a small start-up business to gain various legal advantages. More complex transactions can include a decision to "go private," that is, when a large corporation with many public shareholders changes into a privately held corporation (often accomplished with the assistance of private equity firms which specialize in the performance of this sort of legal and financial alchemy). Or a firm may decide to use "special purpose entities" for capital accounting purposes.[141] Partnoy includes "public company regulatory arbitrage" by hedge funds and the use of various financial techniques to change a firm's capital structure as additional examples of corporate shapeshifting.

---

denies the usefulness of the concept of a firm as an entity). I contest the "connected contracts" thesis in Chapter 2.

[139] Frank Partnoy, "Shapeshifting Corporations," 76 *University of Chicago Law Review* 261 (2009).
[140] Id., p. 262.
[141] See id., pp. 264–6.

These techniques often use newly formed and legally recognized entities for these changes, such as "special purpose entities" and "structured finance."[142] These kinds of special entities have recently come under sustained legal fire as essentially fraudulent to the extent that they are used to misrepresent the true lines of economic control and responsibility in particular transactions.[143]

Whether different kinds of shapeshifting transactions should be legally allowed or encouraged requires an appeal to policy considerations, such as whether they are fairly done (with respect to the treatment of various business participants) and whether they contribute to overall social welfare. As Partnoy observes, it is not self-evident that the constant and often rapid shapeshifting of legal entities provides economic value to society as a whole or whether it often functions instead as a method to enrich some business participants at the expense of others. As Partnoy observes: "On one hand, shapeshifting can reflect the efficiency of markets as corporate structures move to their most highly valued shape.... On the other hand, shapeshifting can reflect the extraction of private value or the transaction costs associated with inefficient legal rules."[144] In particular, there is good reason to be skeptical of "cyclical shapeshifting"—such as a pattern of going public through an initial public offering, then going private, then going public again, et cetera.[145] Repeated or frequent shapeshifting may indicate wealth transfers among different groups within a firm rather than building long-term economic value for all participants and society as a whole. At least, the ability to make these kinds of changes in business structures illustrates another instance of the importance of "entities" (and accounting for them) in a legal theory of the firm.

Legal persons

If the conception of business firms as artificial and fictional entities may seem relatively passive or abstract—described in terms of accounting-like "partitions" of assets and legalistic manipulation of entities to achieve various business purposes—then thinking of firms as "legal persons" adds an active and more energetic quality to a legal theory of the firm. Legal personality brings the somewhat abstract ideas of firms as "fictions" and "entities" back to practical reality. As Joseph Vining explains, the "problem of legal persons" is a subset of the "larger problem" involving the "process of defining and designating entities."[146]

Again, there is nothing to fear in the ensuing legal discussions concerning what "persons" and "entities" to recognize. The legal work of "communicating and agreeing" about the recognition of legal persons is constantly "shifting and changing" and "is as common as it is fascinating."[147] Authoritative "restatements" and "summaries" of law in the United States support a broad view of the recognition of "persons." The American Law Institute in its *Principles of Corporate*

---

[142] Id., pp. 266–9, 283–7.   [143] See Bratton and Levitin, op. cit.
[144] Partnoy, op. cit., pp. 287–8   [145] Id., pp. 269–70, 278.
[146] Vining, *Legal Identity*, op. cit., p. xii.   [147] Id.

Governance adopts the following broad definition: "'Person' means (a) an individual, (b) any form of organization, including a corporation, a partnership or any other form of association, any form of trust or estate, a government or any political subdivision, or an agency or instrumentality of government, or (c) any other legal or commercial entity."[148] Similarly, the American Law Institute's *Restatement (Third) of Agency* defines "person" to include any "organization or association" or "other legal entity that has legal capacity to possess rights and incur obligations."[149]

Business firms are not mere disembodied entities but rather collective groups of "people in action."[150] Thinking of the firm as a legal person animates it with the ability to exercise power and authority through human representatives. The representatives of firms include those given the ordinary everyday power and authority to make decisions, namely, managers, officers, and directors. In the United States, the "business judgment rule" bestows significant discretion to corporate managers and directors to exercise independent decision-making authority on a wide range of decisions under ordinary circumstances.[151] Other countries also allow for a similar delegation of broad authority to managers and directors of firms.[152]

Basic founding documents, such as partnership agreements and corporate charters, combine with authorizing legislation, such as partnership laws and corporation codes, to provide the legal pillars for the institutional "persons" of firms.[153] Usually, managers and executives speak for the person of the firm. Depending on the circumstances, other groups can also speak for the interests of the firm: creditors in the case of bankruptcy or shareholders in the case of fundamental disputes regarding major changes in business structure or challenges to managers' or directors' decisions, or protection of their voting rights. With some exceptions, however, creditors do not represent firms, and the protection of their interests is limited to contracts made directly with the managers and designated leaders of the firm. (In bankruptcy, the situation changes because creditors are given priority in terms of governance and distribution of assets in case of liquidation or reorganization.) Also, shareholders do not represent firms, unless the percentage size of their financial stake gives them effective control (such as in some closely held corporations), in which case the majority shareholders are effectively also the managers. Shareholders of large public corporations usually have a role in corporate governance limited to selecting a board of directors and exercising oversight through access to corporate records and, in some cases, bringing derivative litigation in the name

---

[148] American Law Institute, *Principles of Corporate Governance: Analysis and Recommendations* (1994), sect. 1.28.

[149] American Law Institute, *Restatement (Third) of Agency* (2006), sect. 1.04(5).

[150] Conard, op. cit., pp. 442–5.

[151] See, e.g., Clark, op. cit., pp. 123–5; Klein, Coffee, and Partnoy, op. cit., pp. 156–61.

[152] Other countries have adopted the equivalent of the business judgment rule. See Klaus J. Hopt, "Comparative Corporate Governance: The State of the Art and International Regulation," 59 *American Journal of Comparative Law* 1, 39–40 (2011) (noting adoption of the rule by judicial decision or statute in Germany, Switzerland, Japan, and Australia).

[153] See *Restatement (Third) of Agency*, op. cit., sect. 1.03, cmt. c (observing that authority within business firms "originates both with the statute through which the organization achieves a legally recognized form and with the organization's constitutional documents").

of the corporation challenging actions of directors or officers as violations of their corporate duties.[154] In almost all everyday situations, then, executives and other managers represent the firm as a person. Firms as legal persons—composed (almost always) of collectively owned assets and teams of people who work together—gain social meaning and reality through the actions of their representatives.

Firms of any significant size and complexity depend, then, on their executive *leadership*. The leaders of firms express their organizational purposes, set their objectives, and represent the firm's collectively organized interests.[155] In complex firms with some degree of hierarchical organization, leadership is a quality that can be exercised in a bottom-up as well as a top-down manner.[156] (This assertion that leaders express a firm's purposes and objectives is subject to the caveat, however, that the firm's founding documents or "private legislation" can define and limit these purposes and objectives. Although firms depend on leaders to represent them, leaders would have nothing to represent without a foundational recognition of the firm as an organizational legal person. And internal "constitutional" limitations on leadership authority and power can be included in the founding documents of a firm.)

Understanding the firm as a legal person with human representatives that speak and act on its behalf reflects common sense as well as traditional legal interpretations. Presidents and prime ministers lead nation-states. Generals lead armies. Deans and principals lead schools. Although it is true that leaders of organizational persons represent the interests of other human beings who compose the collective entity, it is also true that these leaders speak, in their leadership roles, on behalf of the legal person itself—representing the organizational entity. The idea of business representation and leadership does not depart from this general pattern. Chief executive officers lead corporations. Managing partners lead law and accounting firms. Strictly speaking, it is difficult if not impossible to imagine a country, an army, a school, or a business firm without some embodiment of a leader or a leadership group. Leaders represent organizational legal persons. Each of them is delegated responsibility for advancing the purposes and speaking on behalf of the organizational "entity." Business firms are no different than any other organization in this respect, except that they specialize in commerce.

The selection of leadership for organizations also implicates governance structures. Here it is sufficient to observe that the governance structures of private organization are open for significant variation selected by the major business participants (such as the founding owners writing a corporate charter) in contrast

---

[154] See *Principles of Corporate Governance*, op. cit., sects. 3.01, 3.02, 5.10, 7.01 to 7.17 (describing roles of managers, directors, and controlling shareholders, as well as shareholder derivative lawsuits).

[155] For a classical treatment of institutional leadership in a manner consistent with the account of firms given here, see Philip Selznick, *Leadership in Administration: A Sociological Interpretation* (University of California Press 1958).

[156] See, e.g., Michael Useem, *Leading Up: How to Lead Your Boss So You Both Win* (Crown Business 2003) (discussing strategies for leadership from within an organization aimed a higher levels).

to the governance structures of nation-states (such as the U.S. Constitution). These variations of legal forms of firms are further examined in Chapter 5.

The social theory of Thomas Hobbes provides useful insights with respect to the idea of legal personality and its practical representation in the world. For Hobbes, corporations (or, in his day, "merchant companies") as well as commonwealths are "made by words."[157] They do not exist except through human speech, language, and action. In fact, legal persons of all kinds do not exist, according to Hobbes, in any a priori sense. For Hobbes, language precedes the naming of persons. Arguably, this view fits with a number of other legal categorizations of persons—such as the difference between "citizens" and "aliens" (based on nationality claims). This view fits also with strongly fictional versions of legal personality, that is, those that maintain that law can designate almost anything as a "legal person."[158] On this view, a legal person is entirely dependent on law for its existence. If one takes away the law that defines a legal person, "there is no more left than the smile of the Cheshire Cat after the cat had disappeared."[159]

Even natural individual human beings, the foundational "persons" recognized in the bottom-up participant theories of the firm, are created through speech, language, and social action. (In contrast, the persons assumed in economic versions of participant theories of the firm are usually radically undertheorized. The individuals assumed in methodological individualism are often mere ciphers.[160]) For Hobbes, "persons are essentially spokespersons who can give their word to others and thereby 'personate' themselves."[161] The ability to speak a language is one prerequisite. The ability to reason is another.[162] Human beings who speak and reason have the coincident ability to "personate" and represent themselves to other human beings.

This view corresponds to a contemporary philosophical view that would restrict reference to "legal persons" only to rational, communicative human beings.[163] Etymology supports this interpretation as well. In Latin, *persona* refers to "a theatrical mask." Its roots are from *per* meaning "through" and *sonare* meaning "sound."[164] A "person," then, represents himself or herself to others through sound, speech, and language.

---

[157] See Philip Pettit, *Made with Words: Hobbes on Language, Mind, and Politics* (Princeton University Press 2008), pp. 70–81, 115–16.

[158] For a review of current approaches in this vein, see Ngaire Naffine, "Who are Law's Persons? From Cheshire Cats to Responsible Subjects," 66 *Modern Law Review* 346, 350–4 (2003).

[159] Id., p. 353, quoting Bryant Smith, "Legal Personality," 37 *Yale Law Journal* 283, 294 (1928).

[160] See Note, "What We Talk About When We Talk About Persons: The Language of a Legal Fiction," 114 *Harvard Law Review* 1745, 1768 (2001) (observing that legal discussions about "persons" remain "grossly undertheorized"). But see Naffine, op. cit. (categorizing current legal and philosophical theories of "legal persons").

[161] Pettit, op. cit., p. 2 (describing Hobbes' "theory of personhood").

[162] Id., pp. 24–54, 141, 144–6.

[163] See Naffine, op. cit., pp. 362–5 (citing proponents of this view including Michael Moore and Elizabeth Wolgast).

[164] Pettit, op. cit., p. 59. But see Max Radin, "The Endless Problem of Corporate Personality," 32 *Columbia Law Review* 643, 645–7 (1932) (agreeing with this etymology but arguing that "person" is used more commonly in the modern sense of "a human being"). Following Dewey, Radin argues for a

So-called "dumb" animals are not ordinarily considered persons in this sense because they do not have capacity for language and reason (though they may speak and communicate in a more rudimentary fashion, e.g. dogs barking or cats meowing).[165] Babies, young children, and severely mentally ill or incapacitated human beings arguably fall into the same category. In Hobbes' words, "children, fools, and madmen" are excluded from the ability to act as "natural" persons.[166] However, if animals, incapacitated or immature people, and other "entities" (such as fetuses or even frozen embryos) are deemed to have basic legal rights (such as the right not to be treated cruelly or the right to inherit property), then these rights can be "represented" by full-capacity human beings who can use language as well as rational thought. Like firms or other organizational legal persons, animals and incapacitated or immature human beings can gain status as "legal persons" through the representation of capable human beings who can exercise language, reasoning, and legal argument on their behalf.[167]

The next step is the representation of a collective person—not of oneself (or an animal or incapacitated human being), but rather the representation of a collective group of people. For Hobbes, this representation is accomplished in a participant-based process.[168] The creation of a collective person is enabled by "rallying behind the words of a collective representative or spokesperson."[169] This is the origin, for Hobbes, of "the ability of people to incorporate—to come together and act as a single corporate [or other organizational] person."[170] The philosopher Philip Pettit nicely describes these two steps as "using words to personate" (that is, for people to represent themselves through language, thought, and communication in society) and "using words to incorporate" (that is, the ability for people to create and represent collective organizations).[171] The use of "corporation" here is used in a general rather than a technical legal sense referring to a specific modern business form. The *corportio* (corporation) as distinguished from a *congregatio* (congregation) refers to an organizational entity that "exists, in a sense, over and beyond its members," but nevertheless "needs members to speak and act for it." When representatives of a *corportio* do so—"when people act in that role"—"they put aside their own identities." They become *universi* (representatives) in this role and "cease to perform as *singuli* or individuals."[172] On this view, the construction of organized "legal persons" beyond the singly speaking, reasoning human being

pragmatic use of "corporate personality" as "a matter of necessity and convenience," while recognizing its "nominalist," flexible character. Id., pp. 652, 665–7, citing Dewey, op. cit.

[165] Pettit, op. cit., p. 60.

[166] Id., p. 56 (quoting Hobbes).

[167] See also Naffine, op. cit., pp. 357–61, 365–7.

[168] For a contrary philosophical view that collective organizations precede the individual human being in terms of the ontological creation of "persons," see Roger Scruton and John Finnis, "Corporate Persons," 63 *Proceedings of the Aristotelian Society, Supplementary Volumes* 239 (1989). In my view, this philosophical disagreement recapitulates, though at a deeper level, the theoretical debate about whether the recognition of firms begins as a "bottom-up" or "top-down" process. Perhaps the best answer is the institutional one given here of "both."

[169] Pettit, op. cit., p. 2 (describing Hobbes' "theory of group agency").

[170] Id., p. 70.   [171] Id., pp. 55–81.   [172] Id., p. 70.

becomes possible through a secondary institutional process of representation and the legal recognition of groups.

One does not have to accept the deeper philosophical claims that Hobbes makes about the nature of language and meaning to agree with his points about legal personality and organization. Just as human beings can through language and reason "personate" themselves, they can by the same means "personate" or represent collective groups. These groups can be public (such as the Hobbesian Leviathan of the sovereign political state). Or they can be private, including business firms, as well as nonprofit organizations with educational, religious, political, philanthropic, or other social objectives. Fundamentally, these "group persons" cannot exist without some form of legal representation or "personification."[173]

Rather than a misty obfuscation that prevents clear analysis of the component parts of firms, then, legal personality is an essential component of any realistic legal theory of the firm. An attribution of legal personality is needed for business firms to have social meaning: not only with respect to procedural abilities to exert "standing" in courts, but also practical abilities to conduct ordinary, everyday transactions through representatives—or, in legal terms, "agents"—by means of contracts, through the instrumentalities of private property, and within the constraints imposed by the organization's own internal rules and society's external laws.

The concept of legal persons acting through designated representatives raises important issues of governance and formulation of "collective purpose." Governance of firms refers to the operation of both (1) voluntary, internally imposed rules created by founding documents and other agreements made by business participants (such as corporate charters and bylaws); and (2) externally imposed legal rules (such as the requirement that a large public corporation must have a board of directors). These governance rules allow for the firm to act as an "organizational principal" and to delegate authority to managers and its other "agents." (Recognition of organizational principals and the role of agents are also foundational for a legal theory of the firm as discussed in detail in Chapter 2.)

The idea of a "collective purpose" or "collective intention" of an organizational person does not refer to metaphysical versions of a "general will." In a practical sense, these ideas refer only to the rules set in place by voluntary organizational agreements (such as charters or bylaws) and external law (including statutes and court decisions), as well as the expressions made by representatives exercising their authority according to these rules and practices. Leaders, managers, and other agents who are delegated governance authority through these procedures possess a recognized ability to speak, act, and otherwise communicate on behalf of the firm.

Notions of collective purpose or collective intention of business firms—and the methods used to ascertain them—deserve further attention from legal scholars. A resurgence of general interest in these topics has occurred in philosophy,

---

[173] For an examination of "group persons" in this "juristic" sense, see Andrew Vincent, "Can Groups Be Persons?" 42 *Review of Metaphysics* 687, 704–12 (1989).

sociology, and linguistics.[174] Firms surely differ with respect to the kinds of collective purposes or intentions in different situations. Most firms are probably more cohesive in this respect than the collective intentions of modern legislatures such as the U.S. Congress.[175] For purposes here, however, it is sufficient to observe that interpretations of the organizational intentions and purposes of firms—as expressed in bylaws, shareholder resolutions, employment hand-books, managerial orders, etc.—have important legal, moral, and operational consequences.

Recognizing legal personality as an important dimension of theories of firm worries some contemporary commentators. According to one leading text, for example, recognizing a business firm as a legal "entity" leads down a slippery slope in which it also "becomes a putative person." In this fashion, they say, "reification sometimes leads to anthropomorphism—that is, treating the corpor-ation [or other firm] as if it were a human being."[176] Economists tend to worry even more than jurists about legal personality, probably because the idea poses a threat to their view that methodological individualism is the only true path to social knowledge.[177] If firms are legal persons acting in markets along with individuals as argued here, however, then neoclassical economic models of the firm require revision.

It is true that thinking of firms as "entities" encourages thinking about them in terms of "persons" because the ideas are related. It is also true that an uncritical extrapolation of the idea of a "person" or "personality" to business enterprises can lead in troublesome directions. For example, the legal scholar Joel Bakan's examin-ation of the corporation as a person derives its approach to "corporate personality" from clinical psychology. He concludes from this analysis that modern business corporations qualify as "pathological" according to standard tests used to evaluate individual human personalities.[178]

---

[174] See, e.g., Michael A. Bratman, *Faces of Intention: Selected Essays on Intention and Agency* (Cambridge University Press 1999); Margaret Gilbert, *Sociality and Responsibility: New Essays in Plural Subject Theory* (Rowman and Littlefield 2000); Raimo Tuomela, *The Importance of Us: A Philosophical Study of Basic Social Notions* (Stanford University Press 1995). Cf. Abby Wright, Comment, "For All Intents and Purposes: What Collective Intention Tells Us about Congress and Statutory Interpret-ation," 154 *University of Pennsylvania Law Review* 983 (2006) (examining how the U.S. Congress as a "collective entity" can express a "collective purpose" in its statutes).

[175] See Wright, op. cit., pp. 997, 1015–24 (observing how "it is perfectly natural to speak of a club planning an event or a company designing a new product," but Congress "can be said to have shared intentions" only in a more limited sense).

[176] Klein, Coffee, and Partnoy, op. cit., p. 118. For an argument that one should not worry so much about making various distinctions when dealing with legal concepts and principles that occur along a spectrum of possibilities, see Frederick Schauer, "Slippery Slopes," 99 *Harvard Law Review* 361 (1985).

[177] See, e.g, Jensen and Meckling, op. cit., p. 311 ("the personalization of the firm implied by asking questions such as 'what should be the objective function of the firm,' or 'does the firm have a social responsibility,' is seriously misleading," and "thinking about organizations as if they were persons with motivations and intentions [is erroneous]").

[178] Joel Bakan, *The Corporation: The Pathological Pursuit of Profit and Power* (Free Press 2004). See also the documentary with the same title and based on the same material by Mark Achbar, Jennifer Abbott, and Joel Bakan (Zeitgeist Films 2004). Consonant with my general thesis here, Bakan views the corporation as "an institution" (though he does not discuss other forms of business enterprise). Bakan, op. cit., p. 1.

This approach may have a rhetorical value in calling attention to the importance of the role of business corporations in connection with responsibility for some serious social problems. It may also highlight some "inhumane" consequences of corporate laws and call into question laws and norms that may encourage or mandate "profit only" or "wealth maximization" orientations to business management. However, it is not analytically useful in terms of theories of the firm to transfer concepts from individual clinical psychology into the realm of organizational personality. The social problems that the legal recognition of organizational persons may help to generate—and, more precisely, the rules and social practices applicable to the management and governance of these persons—are better addressed from the perspectives of law, economics, politics, philosophy, and other social disciplines, rather than diagnosed through an extension of individual psychology. *Social* psychology is probably relevant, especially with respect to the public perceptions of business firms, social behavior in securities trading, and perhaps other business-related behavior, but an in-depth discussion of this disciplinary perspective is left outside the scope of this book. In addition, it is appropriate to inquire how organizational structures and incentives of business enterprise affect the individual psychology of human beings who make decisions within the firm and on behalf of the firm's objectives. In this respect, critics are correct to point out that a relentless and uncompromising pursuit of profit in some business firms will lead to damaging consequences—or, in economic jargon, "negative externalities."[179] Legal reform and other social action seeking guidance from other disciplines, however, are the more likely effective remedies. After all, one cannot prescribe medication or confinement to a hospital for a so-called "pathological" corporation.

At the same time, once one realizes and guards against the possibility of misinterpreting the meaning of "legal person" (that is, by remembering that it is a flexible legal idea adopted to achieve certain social ends and purposes), it becomes apparent that thinking about business enterprises as legal persons is very useful. The idea of the legal person has been extended for convenience to recognize, animate, and "personify" other entities without generating confusion. For example, inanimate ships are recognized as "persons" in admiralty law. No less an authority than Oliver Wendell Holmes concludes: "It is only by supposing the ship to have been treated

---

Bakan's view that the "corporation's legally defined mandate is to pursue, relentlessly and without exception, its own self-interest, regardless of the often harmful consequences it might cause to others," however, is not supported by most legal sources. Id., pp. 1–2. Some economic theories of the firm come close to advocating this extreme view, but legal accounts are usually more moderate, such as the American Law Institute's qualification of the "objective" of "corporate profit and shareholder gain" by the mandate to act "within the boundaries set by law" and to "take into account ethical considerations." See Preface, pages xvi and accompanying note 13. At least, this authoritative statement of the corporate objective suggests that Bakan's claim that the corporation is "a psychopathic creature" that "can neither recognize nor act upon moral reasons to refrain from harming others" is overstated. Bakan, op. cit., p. 60. For a critique along similar lines, see also Ian B. Lee, "Is There a Cure for Corporate 'Psychopathy'?" 42 *American Business Law Journal* 65, 65–73 (2005).

[179] See Bakan, op. cit., pp. 60–1, 70–3.

as if endowed with personality, that the arbitrary seeming peculiarities of the maritime law can be made intelligible, and on that supposition they at once become consistent and logical."[180] One can say the same about much of the law of business enterprise. Of course, judges and legislators do not pretend that ships or business firms are truly animate objects; they are instruments of people acting collectively. But "[w]hatever the hidden ground of policy may be," as Holmes continues, "their thought still clothes itself in personifying language."[181] The moral of the story follows: The recognition of legal persons is perfectly fine and often useful, as long as one keeps in mind the policy reasons for thinking in this manner and the social consequences that are likely to obtain. One need not agree with proposals to extend the recognition of legal persons further afield—such as to include wild animals, other features of the natural environment (such as wilderness preserves), or other "unconventional entities"—to appreciate and accept the usefulness of ascriptions of legal personality to business firms.[182]

Non-Western legal systems also recognize the legal personality of business firms. In Islamic law, for example, commercial enterprises are recognized to possess a legal personality through the development of concepts of *dhimma* ("juristic container within a person") and *waaf* ("properties left in perpetuity"), both of which allow for a segregation of assets in firms.[183] Chinese law also recognizes business firms—including state-owned enterprises—as endowed with separate legal personalities.[184] As one legal scholar has noted, "in the Confucian view, the collective was morally prior to the individual. Hence, for traditional Chinese law, collective legal personality was a given."[185]

These developments indicate another important feature of recognition of the legal personality of firms: a demarcation between firms and the political state (which, under most theoretical accounts is seen as a legal person too, again as in Hobbes' Leviathan).[186] A world of legally recognized organizational persons pro-

---

[180] O. W. Holmes, Jr., *The Common Law* (Little Brown 1881) (Legal Classics Library reprint ed. 1982), pp. 26–7. See also Blumberg, op. cit., pp. 212–14.

[181] Holmes, op. cit., p. 30.

[182] For an argument for the recognition of entities in the natural environment, see Christopher D. Stone, "Should Trees Have Standing?—Toward Legal Rights for Natural Objects," 45 *Southern California Law Review* 450 (1972). See also Christopher D. Stone, "Should Trees Have Standing? Revisited: How Far Will Law and Morals Reach? A Pluralist Perspective," 59 *Southern California Law Review* 1, 8 (1985) (arguing for "a more expansive inquiry into the legal and moral status of... unconventional entities generally—not merely lakes and mountains, but robots and embryos, tribes and species, future generations and artifacts"); *Sierra Club v. Morton*, 405 U.S. 727, 741–3 (1972) (Douglas, J., dissenting) (maintaining that standing should be recognized for the representation of "ecological unit[s]").

[183] See Mahdi Zahraa, "Legal Personality in Islamic Law," 10 *Arab Law Quarterly* 193, 202–6 (1995). See also Nabil Saleh, "Arab International Corporations: The Impact of the Shari'a," 8 *Arab Law Quarterly* 179, 180–2 (1993) (recognizing legal personality deriving from *dhimma* and *waaf*, but noting that these entities do not confer limited liability under Islamic law).

[184] Tingmei Fu, "Legal Person in China: Essence and Limits," 41 *American Journal of Comparative Law* 261 (1993).

[185] Teemu Ruskola, "Conceptualizing Corporations and Kinship: Comparative Law and Development Theory in a Chinese Perspective," 52 *Stanford Law Review* 1599, 1606–7 (2000).

[186] On theories regarding the political state as a legal person, see Vincent, op. cit., pp. 705–6, 708–9.

vides an institutional layer that separates large political nation-states from individual people.[187] In this respect, business firms as well as other human associations arguably compose an intermediate organizational level between nation-states and individuals known as "civil society." (Whether and how business firms should be considered as belonging to the institutions of "civil society" in political and social theory is an important topic, but one lying outside the scope of this book.)

As Dewey, Hart, Fuller, and other theorists have pointed out, legal persons extend only as far as the law allows. This is true of individual people as well as organizations. For example, an individual "citizen" is accorded the full protection of laws within the jurisdiction of a nation-state. A non-citizen or "alien" is often denied certain rights and legal recognition.[188] An extreme historical example of the denial of recognition of legal personality of human beings appears in the institution of slavery or, even worse, instances of genocide.[189] The point of raising these comparisons here is simply to show that the idea of a legal person is not somehow a "natural" category extended to cover only individual human beings. It is inevitable that the granting of specific rights and responsibilities—such as the powers to sue and be sued, enter into contracts, and own property—bestow recognition of business firms as "persons" in a rudimentary legal understanding of the term. To avert one's eyes from this social reality is to adopt an extreme and untenable position that firms do not exist in legal imagination and legal practice. This basic point was made by the Oxford jurist William Martin Geldart a century ago:

> The object of arrangement and classification is to bring together what is like, to separate what is distinct. But to tell us at one moment that only persons are the subjects of legal rights and duties ... that they are "deemed" to be persons by the law, is merely to play fast and loose with the language. If corporate bodies are *really* like individuals the bearers of legal rights and duties, they must have something in common which qualifies them to be such; and if that is not personality, we may fairly ask to be told what it is. Or if the rights and duties attributed to them are not really theirs, we may again fairly ask to be told whose they are.[190]

Once firms are recognized legally as persons, real consequences follow in practice.

From an institutional perspective, many questions involving the legal personality of firms remain open. Some issues—such as whether a firm can appear in court and

---

[187] The nature of institutional legal persons deserves much greater academic discussion than it currently receives. For exceptions, see Meir Dan-Cohen, *Rights, Persons, and Organizations: A Legal Theory for Bureaucratic Society* (University of California Press 1986); Meir Dan-Cohen, "Between Selves and Collectivities: Toward a Jurisprudence of Identity," 61 *University of Chicago Law Review* 1213 (1994).

[188] For an examination of the topic in U.S. law, see Gerald L. Neuman, *Strangers to the Constitution: Immigrants, Borders, and Fundamental Law* (Princeton University Press 1996). See also Frederic R. Coudert, "The Rights and Remedies of Aliens in National Courts," 5 *American Society of International Law Proceedings* 192 (1911) (discussing the historical trend toward recognizing rights of aliens).

[189] See, e.g., Milton Meltzer, *Slavery: A World History* (Da Capo Press, rev. ed., 1993); Samantha Power, *A Problem from Hell: America and the Age of Genocide* (Basic Books 2002).

[190] W.M. Geldart, *Legal Personality* (Oxford University Press 1924), p. 10 (reprint of inaugural lecture delivered at Oxford in 1910) (original emphasis).

be represented by a lawyer—are now relatively well settled, though hard questions remain with respect to some details of this representation. For example, jurisdictional questions about whether or not a firm should count as a full-fledged "citizen" arise in a manner analogous to individuals.[191] Also, lawyers who represent firms have ethical responsibilities to represent the business enterprise as a whole, which is often a difficult task given the complicated structures of modern firms.[192] Questions of the attribution of some human characteristics to firms as persons, such as whether firms may be describing as having a "race" for certain legal purposes, provide yet another example.[193]

Other substantive issues, such as whether and to what extent constitutional rights applicable to individuals should apply as well to business firms—and whether and to what extent criminal laws should apply to firms—continue to be contested as well. Objections have been made to expanding both constitutional law and criminal law to business firms, at least with respect to business corporations.

In U.S. constitutional law, the argument has been made that constitutional rights are meant to protect individual people only—not organizational persons.[194] This argument has not been persuasive over time, however, and constitutional rights for corporations (and other business firms) have been recognized in various areas, though not universally.[195] (Chapter 7 revisits this question with respect to the corporate constitutional rights to political free speech.)

With respect to whether criminal law should apply to business firms, there are two schools of thought.[196] On one view, organizational persons do not possess the requisite intention (*mens rea*) needed for criminal culpability, and criminal law should therefore apply only to individual human beings who have this capacity.[197] A few civil law countries reject the idea of corporate or enterprise-level criminality, though the general trend is to recognize such liability.[198] A second view approves

---

[191] See, e.g., Blumberg, op. cit., pp. 168–201; Robert R. Drury, "The Regulation and Recognition of Foreign Corporations: Responses to the 'Delaware Syndrome,'" 57 *Cambridge Law Journal* 165 (1998).

[192] See Geoffrey C. Hazard, Jr., "Ethical Dilemmas of Corporate Counsel," 46 *Emory Law Journal* 1011 (1997); William H. Simon, "Whom (Or What) Does the Organization's Lawyer Represent? An Anatomy of Intraclient Conflict," 91 *California Law Review* 57 (2003); E. Norman Veasey and Christine T. DiGuglielmo, "The Tensions, Stresses, and Professional Responsibilities of the Lawyer for the Corporation," 62 *Business Lawyer* 1 (2006).

[193] See Richard R. W. Brooks, "Incorporating Race," 106 *Columbia Law Review* 2023 (2006) (discussing recent cases holding that "race" can be legally attributed to business firms).

[194] See, e.g., *Wheeling Steel Corp. v. Glander*, 337 U.S. 562, 576–81 (1949) (Douglas, J., dissenting).

[195] See Blumberg, op. cit., pp. 30–5; Mayer, op. cit.; Ribstein, op. cit.; Note, "Constitutional Rights of the Corporate Person," op. cit.

[196] See John C. Coffee, Jr., "'No Soul to Damn: No Body to Kick': An Unscandalized Inquiry into the Problem of Corporate Punishment," 79 *Michigan Law Review* 386, 407 (1981).

[197] See, e.g., William S. Laufer, "Corporate Culpability and the Limits of Law," 6 *Business Ethics Quarterly* 311, 313 (1996) ("Many philosophers, ethicists, and criminologists question whether corporate entities should be criminally . . . responsible for the actions of employees.")

[198] See, e.g., Coffee, op. cit., p. 444; see also V.S. Khanna, "Corporate Criminal Liability: What Purpose Does It Serve?" 109 *Harvard Law Review* 1477, 1490–1 (1996) (noting strict European legal standards for imposing corporate criminal liability and observing that Germany is a holdout to the trend toward adopting a regime of corporate criminal liability).

criminal liability for business firms and other organizations on policy grounds of deterrence as well as retribution.[199]

Despite some of the strong objections to constitutional and criminal law extensions to include firms as legal persons, it is probably fair to say that in many jurisdictions, such as in the United States, new subfields have arisen to include what might be called *corporate constitutional law* and *corporate criminal law*. Or, more precisely, in terminology that encompasses the contemporary variety of available legal forms of firms, we might speak of the constitutional law and criminal law of business persons.

The questions in these subfields can also interrelate. For example, assuming that criminal law applies to business corporations, different U.S. constitutional rights protecting them as criminal defendants may apply—or not. The Supreme Court has held that the Fifth Amendment's protection against "double jeopardy" (trying a person for the same crime twice) applies to firms such as corporations.[200] But the Court held that a business firm may not invoke the Fifth Amendment's right against "self-incrimination."[201]

Adopting an institutional legal perspective does not resolve all of the questions about whether and how the legal fictions, entities, and persons of business firms should be recognized for various purposes. It also does not resolve many complex and important questions about how these firms, once recognized, should be legally treated. At least, though, an institutional legal theory of the firm provides a foundation for beginning to evaluate and answer these questions—again from the perspectives of different potential policy goals and principles. An institutional theory of the firm asserts that concepts of "fictions," "entities," and "persons" are foundational to understanding business enterprises. And this is not a new claim.[202]

---

[199] See, e.g., Note, "Developments in the Law—Corporate Crime: Regulating Corporate Behavior through Criminal Sanctions," 92 *Harvard Law Review* 1227, 1231–41, 1365–8 (1979). But see Khanna, op. cit. (arguing against corporate criminal liability as unsatisfactory on deterrence grounds and favoring alternatives of civil enforcement).

[200] See, e.g., *United States v. Martin Linen Supply Co.*, 430 U.S. 564 (1977).

[201] See, e.g., *Doe v. United States*, 487 U.S. 201 (1988).) See also Blumberg, op. cit., pp. 38–40; *Eastern Enterprises v. Apfel*, 524 U.S. 498, 557 (1998) (Breyer, J., dissenting); *Hale v. Henkel*, 201 U.S. 43 (1906) (discussing theories of corporation in application of constitutional principles in criminal context).

[202] For historical perspective, see *Corporate Personality in the 20th Century* (Ross Grantham and Charles Rickett eds.) (Hart Publishing 1998) (collecting essays discussing one of the earliest English cases recognizing firms as separate "entities" and "persons," *Salomon v. Salomon & Co.*, [1847] A.C. 22, HL, which held that a sole proprietor may invoke the corporate form against claims for personal liability from creditors). *Salomon* has been described as "a celebrated case" which "haunts every discussion of corporate entity and limited liability." Bernard F. Cataldo, "Limited Liability with One-Man Companies and Subsidiary Corporations," 18 *Law and Contemporary Problems* 473, 478 (1953). See also Paul Vinogradoff, "Juridical Persons," 24 *Columbia Law Review* 594, 595–7 (1924).

2

Foundations of the Firm II:
Agency, Contracts, and Property

Firms are, in various respects, legal fictions, entities, and persons. These ideas carry theoretical weight and translate into institutional reality through social practice and recognition. Dismissing these ideas as indefinite or antiquated fails to appreciate their continuing influence. The concepts are essential when carving out the scope of limited liability, executing mergers and acquisitions, or applying criminal or constitutional law in the context of business enterprises. Joseph Vining is therefore correct to observe that "corporate law" (which may be extended to include the law of enterprise organization more generally) "is not a branch of the law of property, or contract, or tort. It is not a combination of them, nor reducible to them."[1] Instead, "the entity is in question" whenever business enterprises are involved.[2] One cannot avoid legal fictions and attributions of legal personality when dealing with business firms either.

At the same time, several other substantive legal fields are also foundational for understanding the composition of modern firms. A description of these additional foundations is needed to paint a complete picture of the business enterprise in legal theory.

Because modern business enterprises are ubiquitous and many-faceted, almost all areas of law involve them—from specific laws that focus particularly on business firms (such as antitrust, consumer protection, or securities regulation) to general laws focused on the protection of the public interest from business externalities (such as environmental law). Here, I focus on only three additional types of law which are foundational for understanding business enterprises in terms of their basic *composition*: the law of agency, the law of contracts, and the law of property. Although each of these legal building blocks of the firm may begin with individualist conceptions, each of them also adapts and expands its principles and rules to mesh with the institutional reality of business enterprises.

---

[1] Joseph Vining, *From Newton's Sleep* (Princeton University Press 1995), p. 321. For an opposing argument favoring this kind of reduction in legal principles, see, e.g., Richard A. Epstein, *Simple Rules for a Complex World* (Harvard University Press 1995). For critique of Epstein's views, see Heidi Li Feldman, "Libertarianism with a Twist," 94 *Michigan Law Review* 1883 (1996) (book review); Eric W. Orts, "Simple Rules and the Perils of Reductionist Legal Thought," 75 *Boston University Law Review* 1441 (1995) (book review). See also R. George Wright, "The Illusion of Simplicity: An Explanation of Why the Law Can't Just Be Less Complex," 27 *Florida State University Law Review* 715 (2000) (canvassing different causes of legal complexity).

[2] Vining, op. cit., pp. 322–3. As Vining observes, "the focus of argument" for the legal analysis of business firms is "ontological work, work with entities." Id.

Agency law

Firms of any complexity beyond a single individual cannot exist without the law of agency. Although somewhat overshadowed in recent years by academic debates that focus on other elements of business enterprise—such as organizational contracts discussed below—agency law provides an essential foundation for the legal structure of modern firms.[3]

The basic idea of legal agency is a simple one. Individuals in modern societies who are deemed to be sufficiently rational (that is, adults who are not insane) have the capacity to act as "principals" and "agents" with respect to each other in conducting their everyday affairs. Essentially, an agency relationship allows for one person (the principal) to confer authority and power to another (the agent) to "represent" him or her in actions taken on behalf of the principal.[4] Legal agency is recognized in civil law as well as common law countries, though with some differences.[5] Inherent in the transfer of authority and power in the creation of an agency relationship is a minimal level of trust and an expectation that the agent will, in fact, *represent* the principal's interest to third parties with some degree of loyalty. In legal terms, agency is therefore defined as a "fiduciary relationship." The scope of the fiduciary relationship in agency is quite broad, at least in the United States, though its requirements may often be changed by mutual agreement of principal and agent.[6] Agency in this sense is not simply a social practice or informal norm because it is *the law*—which means that courts will enforce the expectations of responsibility inherent in this "fiduciary relationship" when necessary and appropriate.

The expectation of enforcement distinguishes the legal idea of agency from the idea of agency as used in other disciplines such as economics or philosophy.[7] Economic concepts of agency often presume the phenomenon of legal agency without fully comprehending the legal basis and social consequences of the concept, especially with respect to its essential grounding in the idea of a fiduciary relationship involving minimal expectations of trust or loyalty.[8] The scope of the fiduciary responsibilities owed by agents and principals is often open to further elaboration in particular contexts or situations. As Justice Felix Frankfurter observed:

---

[3] I have argued previously for a legal theory of the firm that emphasizes the importance of agency law and draw on some of those arguments here. Eric W. Orts, "Shirking and Sharking: A Legal Theory of the Firm," 16 *Yale Law and Policy Review* 265 (1998). See also Donald C. Langevoort, "Agency Law Inside the Corporation: Problems of Candor and Knowledge," 71 *University of Cincinnati Law Review* 1187, 1191 (2003) ("That corporation law builds on the foundation of agency law is beyond doubt").

[4] See American Law Institute, *Restatement (Third) of Agency*, sect. 1.01 (2006) ("Agency is the fiduciary relationship that arises when one person (a 'principal') manifests assent to another person (an 'agent') that the agent shall act on the principal's behalf and subject to the principal's control, and the agent manifests assent or otherwise consents so to act").

[5] For an historical overview, see Wolfram Müller-Freienfels, "Law of Agency," 6 *American Journal of Comparative Law* 165 (1957).

[6] *Restatement (Third) of Agency*, op. cit., sect. 1.01 and cmt. e.

[7] See id., sect. 1.01, reporter's notes, cmt. b.

[8] For legal elaboration, see Tamar Frankel, "Fiduciary Law," 71 *California Law Review* 795 (1983).

[T]o say that a man [or a woman] is a fiduciary only begins analysis; it gives direction to further inquiry. To whom is he [or she] a fiduciary? What obligations does he [or she] owe as a fiduciary? In what respect has he [or she] failed to discharge these obligations? And what are the consequences of his [or her] deviation from duty?"[9]

The idea that one might assume a standard or uniform "agency relationship" measurable in comparative "costs," as some economists do, doesn't jibe with a robust legal understanding of agency.

In addition, the legal enforcement of a norm may have the long-term consequence of establishing the norm socially as a matter of custom and everyday expectations. A general empirical assumption is nevertheless that the formal force of law stands behind the social norms and everyday expectations of agency relationships. Metaphorically, business practices and transactions are accurately described often to occur in "the shadow of the law."[10] One might even argue that the historical consequences of recognizing the ability of individuals to enter freely into various agency relationships influenced or set the historical stage for the emergence of philosophical ideas of agency understood as the human capacity for "autonomy" and independent action. But an analysis of this possibility is beyond the scope of this book.

The long-term consequences of the establishment of the idea of legal agency have been cumulatively explosive. Although somewhat slow to develop historically, agency relationships are now ubiquitous and far-reaching. Ancient Roman law did not develop a full-fledged conception of agency, but it had master–servant relationships based on the patriarchal family and slavery.[11] Precursors of modern agency can also be found in ancient Greek, Egyptian, and Jewish law. Modern principles of agency—which empower individuals acting in their own capacity as well as on behalf of social organizations—began to flourish in the seventeenth century around the time of the Enlightenment and the rise of capitalist business enterprises. Legal principles underpinning modern agency developed along parallel tracks in both common law and civil law systems.[12]

Today, agency is "recognized in all modern legal systems" and regarded "as an indispensable part of the existing social order."[13] Oliver Wendell Holmes described it as one of "the great departments of the law."[14] Two contemporary legal scholars exclaim: "Agents are everywhere around us. They invest our money, help us work, and plan our lives. No matter where we turn, they are working. Even our agents

---

[9] *S.E.C. v. Chenery Corp.*, 318 U.S. 80, 85–6 (1943).

[10] Cf. Robert H. Mnookin and Lewis Kornhauser, "Bargaining in the Shadow of the Law: The Case of Divorce," 88 *Yale Law Journal* 950 (1979).

[11] See, e.g., Wolfram Müller-Freienfels, "Legal Relations in the Law of Agency: Power of Agency and Commercial Certainty," 13 *American Journal of Comparative Law* 193, 193–4 (1964). See also Henry Hansmann, Reinier Kraakman, and Richard Squire, "Law and the Rise of the Firm," 119 *Harvard Law Review* 1333, 1362 (2006) (observing that "Roman law famously had no general concept of agency").

[12] Müller-Freienfels, "Legal Relations in the Law of Agency," op. cit., pp. 193, 196–7.

[13] Müller-Freienfels, "Law of Agency," op. cit., pp. 165–6 (noting that basic agency law is "admitted in nearly all jurisdictions" and "everywhere prevalent").

[14] O. W. Holmes, Jr., "Agency," 4 *Harvard Law Review* 345, 348 (1891).

have agents and we ourselves probably act as agents for others. The web of agency enmeshes us all."[15] These scholars provide a good summary of reasons for the popularity of modern agency relationships as well:

Agency allows us to live better in three different ways. First, we may not have time to pursue our own interests as vigorously as we would like. Many possibilities go unexplored and many of those we do explore go unexploited. Hiring an agent simply allows us to do more. . . . Two or more people—the right people, anyway—can simply do more than one.

Second, even if we have the time, we may not have the knowledge and skills we need to pursue our own interests effectively. We may know what we want to do but not how to do it. Many of us, for example, engage others to invest our money not because we are pressed for time, but because we fear that we would make poor investment decisions. The right professional, we hope, will improve and steady our returns. In this way, a well-chosen agent may carry out our aims more effectively than we ourselves could. . . .

Third, agents can allow us to pursue our activities more cheaply. If we compartmentalize our projects, we can engage others to work on them who do not need the broad range of skills necessary to complete the overall projects. Such division of labor permits specialization, which brings its own returns and frees actors from having to master a wider range of knowledge than is necessary. Actors can thus focus more directly on serving us than on acquiring skills. Additionally, if our agents save us money, we ourselves will have more resources to devote to more of our own pursuits.[16]

The web of agency relationships extends particularly to the business enterprise. From the simple idea of individual agency—requiring only three parties of A (the principal), B (the agent), and C (a third party affected by the agency relationship)—the complex organized structures of modern business firms are built.

Unlike contracts which require only two parties (plus the government or a third-party to enforce the agreement), agency relationships need at least three parties to be meaningful.[17] This tripartite relationship immediately implies a structure of authority and power between principal and agent with a social dimension regarding the meaning of this relationship for a third party. In other words, agency relationships create a principal–agent team with consequences for a third party (or, more usually, a number of potential third parties) in society. The three categories of principal, agent, and third party create six permutations for legal analysis: principal to agent, principal to third parties, agent to principal, agent to third parties, third parties to principals, and third parties to agents. These permutations are followed in scholarly treatments of the topic of agency law as a whole.[18] In this chapter, I focus specifically on how agency law supplies the essential basis for the construction of power and authority within the business enterprise.

Agency relationships within firms can be both vertical (hierarchical) and horizontal (mutual). The simplest and most common example of a vertical agency relationship in a business firm is employment. When A hires B as an employee

---

[15] Samuel Issacharoff and Daniel R. Ortiz, "Governing Through Intermediaries," 85 *Virginia Law Review* 1627, 1635 (1999).
[16] Id., pp. 1635–6.
[17] See, e.g., Orts, "Shirking and Sharking," op. cit., pp. 273–4.
[18] See, e.g., *Restatement (Third) of Agency*, op. cit.

agent, then *A* ordinarily has the authority to direct *B*'s actions within the scope of *B*'s employment. The terms of employment are established by contract, but agency law supplies some basic assumptions. These include the following.

(1) *A* exercises authority, power, and control over the scope, description, and details of *B*'s work. As described in the *Restatement (Third) of Agency*:

An essential element of agency is the principal's right to control the agent's actions. Control is a concept that embraces a wide spectrum of meanings, but within any relationship of agency the principal initially states what the agent shall and shall not do. . . . Additionally, a principal has the right to give interim instructions or directions to the agent once their relationship is established. Within an organization the right to control its agents is essential to the organization's ability to function, regardless of its size, structure, or degree of hierarchy or complexity.[19]

(2) *B* owes a fiduciary duty to work on behalf of *A* and, at a minimum, not to work against *A*'s interests. Again in the words of the *Restatement*:

As agents, all employees owe duties of loyalty to their employers. The specific implications vary with the position the employee occupies, the nature of the employer's assets to which the employee has access, and the degree of discretion that the employee's work requires. However ministerial or routinized a work assignment may be, no agent, whether or not an employee, is simply a pair of hands, legs, or eyes. All are sentient and, capable of disloyal action, all have the duty to act loyally.[20]

(3) *B* possesses authority to act on behalf of *A* with respect to third parties in connection with the business, which includes both contracts entered into and torts committed by *B*.[21]

These features of agency describe a hierarchical relationship, at least in the simplest cases of employment, with employer *A* having the authority and power to direct the work of employee *B*. There are variations in terms of the scope of authority and independence that an employee agent may exercise. Even in flat, relatively non-hierarchical organizations, however, agency relationships exist that determine, in the final analysis, who is hired and fired, as well as less momentous decisions with respect to the allocation of work, promotions, compensation, and other work-related activities. Organizational principals such as corporations and other firms introduce further complexities in agency relationships of ownership, employment, and management, as discussed further below.

In the simplest case of a horizontal or mutual agency relationship, *X* and *Y* may decide to enter into a business together as partners rather than in an employment relationship. Although *X* and *Y* may decide on various details of the business—such as how to share contributions of initial capital, responsibility for profit and loss, and responsibility for everyday management or operations of their business—the

---

[19] *Restatement (Third) of Agency*, op. cit., sect. 1.01, cmt. f.

[20] Id., sect. 1.01, cmt. g.

[21] Id., sects. 6.01, 6.02, 6.03 (ability of agents to bind principals in contracts with third parties); id., sects. 7.03(2)(b), 7.07, 7.08 (tort liability of principals for acts of agents within the scope of their employment accrue through the principle of vicarious liability).

agency relationship in a simple partnership is mutual and horizontal with respect to legal authority. In other words, a basic principle of partnership holds that X and Y are mutual agents of each other.[22] More precisely, they are both "co-agents" with respect to the partnership business entity and its management. Co-agents "have agency relationships with the same principal," and co-agent relationships are "a common phenomenon within organizations."[23]

Even the simplest firms can quickly become more complex with respect to their internal agency relationships. Most partnerships, for example, hire employees as well. Adding partners expands horizontal agency relationships; adding employees adds vertical agency relationships. See Table 2.1 for a graphical illustration of the vertical and horizontal dimensions of agency.

In addition, the laws of agency and enterprise organization allow for the creation of what may be called "agency chains"—including "superior and subordinate co-agents" and "subagents" within the firm structure.[24] As Deborah DeMott, the academic reporter for the most recent *Restatement of Agency*, explains: "Multiple agencies, focused on the same agent, create multiple chains of imputation, attribution, and duties. Multiple agency chains may run parallel or may intersect and create conflicting duties to one degree or another."[25] Subagents, including agents who are subordinate to superior agents, often owe allegiance to the same principal.[26] To account for these more complex agency relationships, the law of agency recognizes that firms act as "organizational principals."[27]

Firms, acting as "juridical persons," appoint representatives.[28] The organization's governing body designates agents or, when speaking directly on behalf of the enterprise itself, "quasi-principals." For example, the chief executive officer (CEO) in many large modern corporations often acts as a "quasi-principal" because the

Table 2.1 Basic legal agency relationships within firms

	Legal authority	Leading examples
Vertical agency	Hierarchical; top-down	Employment; corporate board and officer structures; parent–subsidiary corporations
Horizontal agency	Mutual; relatively equal power sharing	General partnership; corporate joint ventures

[22] See, e.g., Uniform Partnership Act, sect. 301(1) (1997) ("Each partner is an agent of the partnership for the purposes of its business"). See also Saul Levmore, "Love It or Leave It: Property Rules, Liability Rules, and Exclusivity of Remedies in Partnership and Marriage," 58 *Law and Contemporary Problems* 221, 227 (1995) ("partnerships are easily and most often described as mutual agency relationships").

[23] *Restatement (Third) of Agency*, op. cit. sect. 1.04(1) and cmt. a.

[24] Orts, "Shirking and Sharking," op. cit., pp. 280–2 (describing "agency chains").

[25] Deborah A. DeMott, "The Lawyer as Agent," 67 *Fordham Law Review* 301, 308–9 (1998).

[26] *Restatement (Third) of Agency*, op. cit. sect. 1.04(8)–(9) and cmts. h and i.

[27] Id., sects. 1.03 and cmt. c, 3.04 and cmt. d.

[28] Id., sect. 1.03, cmt. c (describing organizations as "juridical persons").

CEO usually holds the authority in a corporation to conduct, approve, or delegate the most ordinary and everyday business decisions on behalf of the firm itself. As the *Restatement (Third) of Agency* explains,

Private-sector organizations formed as corporations have a governing body ordinarily known as a board of directors . . . that, by statute, must take specified types of actions and that also, by statute, is assigned ultimate supervisory responsibility for the corporation's business and affairs. Directors commonly appoint officers for the corporation. Officers hold defined executive positions carrying titles [such as CEO]; the nature and scope of each officer's authority may be defined by statute, by the corporation's constitutional documents, by specific resolutions adopted by the directors, and by custom associating specific functions with a particular position.[29]

In the corporate context, the board of directors acts effectively as the top-level representative of the firm as a "principal" for purposes of hiring and delegating authority to agents. Given that CEOs are commonly delegated a very broad range of authority, they act as "quasi-principals" for many business purposes and actions.[30]

More precisely, top executives in business corporations often play a dual role in their positions. They act as top-level "superior agents" who have been delegated (by the firm's shareholders and boards of directors) significant power and authority to act on behalf of the organization as a whole.[31] And they also act as the embodiment of the corporation itself as a "quasi-principal" for most business purposes regarding other internal agents as well as external third parties. In this sense, many CEOs of large corporate enterprises are the equivalent of "modern princes" in terms of the scope of their authority and power.[32]

Agency law, recognizing firms as legal persons with the capacity to act as organizational principals, allows for the construction of business enterprises of a great variety—from the very small to the very large. From a legal point of view, agency law is therefore foundational for the existence of any business enterprise beyond a "pure sole proprietorship," which consists of only one individual person without any internal agency relationships (including no employees and no equity partners or contributors).[33] Even in most sole proprietorships, one or more

---

[29] See id., sect. 1.03

[30] See Orts, "Shirking and Sharking," op. cit., p. 282. See also Deborah A. DeMott, "Organizational Incentives to Care About the Law," 60 *Law and Contemporary Problems* 39, 49 n. 43 (1998) (suggesting that the term "quasi-principals" may "introduce a better fit between terminology and reality" with respect to the "de facto authority and power" exercised by corporate executives); Peter C. Kostant, "Breeding Better Watchdogs: Multidisciplinary Partnerships in Corporate Legal Practice," 84 *Minnesota Law Review* 1213, 1231 (2000) ("Corporations are hierarchical institutions in which powerful agents in superior positions really function as quasi-principals").

[31] *Restatement (Third) of Agency*, op. cit. sect. 1.03, cmt. c ("A juridical person that is an organization manifests its assent to be bound by the acts of individuals through the observable connections between the individual and the organization. An organization manifests assent to an individual by appointing that person to a position defined by the organization. Such appointment often occurs through the acts of superior agents").

[32] Orts, "Shirking and Sharking," op. cit., p. 282. Cf. also Vining, op. cit., p. 321 ("In a world thought to be more egalitarian, the agents now governed by corporate law are those who might individually have been principals in premodern eras").

[33] Orts, "Shirking and Sharking," op. cit., pp. 300–1. Pure sole proprietorships are described along with other types of firms in Chapter 5 below.

employees are hired, immediately creating an internal agency relationship structure. In very large firms, agency relationships add complexity along both vertical and horizontal dimensions of organizational authority.

All firms (except the pure sole proprietorship and some one-person corporations) are therefore composed in legal terms of "a nexus of agency relationships."[34] This "nexus" is created by the recognition of the firm as a legal entity or person, which serves as a fulcrum for the construction of various internal agency relationships, including managerial lines of authority, employment, and structures of ownership and governance.

The agency relationships of firms account for the exercise of considerable power and authority in society by business representatives. In addition, the *internal agency relationships* in firms describe important features of their *legal boundaries*.

The internal agency relationships of a firm allocate legal authority to a firm's agents (and quasi-principals) to bind the firm contractually. They also expose the assets of the firms to potential liability for harms caused to third parties outside the firm, as discussed further below in this chapter and in Chapter 4.

The internal agency relationships of the firm create ownership structures as well, as illustrated by the simple case of a partnership. The ownership structures of firms can expand more broadly—beyond the scope of agency law alone and with the aid of statutory frameworks—to include complex capital structures of equity shareholder ownership and credit financing, such as those that appear in large-scale public corporations. These variations are accomplished through novel divisions of property within firms, also as discussed later in this chapter, especially with respect to the structure of business corporations.

Contrary to some popular economic theories of the firm, shareholders are *not* considered to be the principals of corporate firms. The *Restatement (Third) of Agency* states explicitly that a "true agency" is "not present" in "the relationship between a corporation's shareholders and its directors."[35] Instead, the role of shareholders in legal theory is limited to the authority to select the members of the board of directors, along with some other legally designated rights, such as the inspection of corporate books and records or, in extreme cases, participating in a hostile tender offer or proxy contest. (For the uninitiated: A tender offer is a structured legal mechanism by which a controlling interest of publicly held shares of a corporation may be purchased by an acquirer. A proxy contest, which is a straightforward competition for shareholders' votes, describes the other method by which control of a public corporation may be taken. In the United States, tender offers and proxy contests may also sometimes be combined, and both are regulated in detail by federal statutes.[36])

In the case of a single-shareholder-owned corporation—or a corporation with a "controlling interest" of ownership—the power to select management will align

---

[34] Orts, "Shirking and Sharking," op. cit., pp. 271–2, 296–306, 311.

[35] *Restatement (Third) of Agency*, op. cit., introduction, p. 5.

[36] For an overview, see William A. Klein, John C. Coffee, Jr., and Frank Partnoy, *Business Organization and Finance: Legal and Economic Principles* (Foundation Press, 11th ed., 2010), pp. 185–207.

exactly with shareholder ownership. In other words, controlling shareholders "self-select" themselves as managers too. In corporations with a more broadly distributed or complex shareholder structure, however, the board of directors is considered legally to represent the interests of the corporation as a whole. The board delegates to its managers and officers as "principal agents" the authority and power to conduct the business of the corporate enterprise.[37]

It is important also to point out that although agency law is essential for a legal theory of the firm and understanding its internal legal structure, agency relationships are not co-extensive with the organization of firms. Firms as organizational persons can also enter into agency relationships that are *external* to the firm. Examples include hiring "outside counsel" to represent a firm in a legal dispute or entering into a long-term "outsourcing" contract for services to the firm. The legal terms for these relationships themselves refer to the legal fact that the transactions occur "outside" the boundaries of the firm. Hiring *outside* counsel in an arm's-length relationship to the firm contrasts with the inside role of the general counsel of a firm who both represents the firm and is employed full-time by the firm. Similarly, *outsourcing* services (such as for business software development or customer call answering services) contrasts with the traditional internal hiring of employees who are subject to the firm's direct oversight and control.[38] As discussed further in Chapter 4, outsourcing can provide economic benefits by managing the legal lines of potential liability of the firm (and its managers and owners) for the actions of employees. Outsourcing may also be used to reduce statutory benefits required to be paid by the firm for employees. See Table 2.2.

Although many kinds of agency relationships exist outside of the boundaries of firms as well as inside, agency law is an essential legal component that allows for building firms and their internal structures of authority and ownership. Agency law does not describe completely how the law defines the boundaries of the firm for various purposes. Much of the law regarding business enterprise nevertheless involves ascertaining the appropriate boundaries of actions that both (1) allow for

Table 2.2 Internal and external agency relationships within and with firms

	Legal description	Leading examples
Internal agency relationships	Recognition of organizational principals as well as various kinds of agents (and quasi-principals) acting within the legal structure of a firm	Firm as an organizational principal; governing body of firms (e.g. boards of directors); chief executive officers; all managers and employees
External agency relationships	Arm's-length contracts with services providers outside the boundaries of the firm who nevertheless act as designated agents of the firm	Outside counsel (e.g. for litigation); outsourcing of specific services (without features of employment)

---

[37] See American Law Institute, *Principles of Corporate Governance: Analysis and Recommendations* (1994), sects. 1.29 and 1.30 (describing "Principal Manager" and "Principal Senior Executive").
[38] See Orts, "Shirking and Sharking," op. cit., pp. 274–5, 304–5.

the authorization of a firm's actions (such as contracts made with third parties); and (2) expose the firm to liability for consequences of its actions (such as for personal injuries caused to third parties by a firm's employees). These boundaries of the firm are drawn in part by agency law. Table 2.2 illustrates schematically some of the differences between internal and external agency relationships in firms.

Contracts

Organizational contracts are used to create agency relationships as well as to make agreements that create firms and their management structures. These kinds of contracts are also essential to include as another building block in a legal theory of the firm. Most agency relationships, for example, result from contractual agreements. And a simple partnership is established by a contract that creates a mutual agency between the partners with respect to the partnership business entity.[39]

Although the vast majority of agency relationships are created by contracts, legal agency (namely, the ability to act as a representative for another) cannot be reduced to contract law. To express the difference succinctly (though perhaps too generally to capture all cases): agency law primarily involves issues of *representation* and *authority*, and contract law mainly involves issues of *exchange* and *bargaining*.

Both agency law and contract law comprise what H.L.A. Hart refers to as "power-conferring rules." These kinds of legal rules recognize and reinforce the capacities of individuals to enter into the construction of their own organizations and agreements.[40]

In practice, agency and contracts interact a great deal. Most features of basic agency relationships may be changed or altered by contractual agreement to the contrary, but not all of them. For example, an agreement to create an agency relationship that would involve *no* fiduciary duty at all—or a similar expectation that the agent would act only in the agent's own self-interest and *against* the principal's interest—would destroy the most basic reasons for entering into a relationship of agency in the first place.

Contracts as well as agency law are a foundational element of firms. A myriad of legal contracts compose many specific details of both the internal relationships within firms (including organizational relationships of authority and ownership) and the external dealings of the firm with third parties in commercial markets (such as with suppliers, creditors, distributors, advertisers, and consumers). In modern capitalist economies characterized by the relative freedom of organization, production, and consumption, contracts become ubiquitous. Contracts govern zillions of economic sales, purchases, agreements, deals, and other privately negotiated arrangements among a multitude of individual and organizational persons. As the

---

[39] See, e.g., Uniform Partnership Act, sect. 103(a) (1997) (noting that "relations among the partners and between the partners and the partnership are governed by the partnership agreement").
[40] H.L.A. Hart, *The Concept of Law* (Oxford University Press, 2nd ed., 1994), p. 41.

legal scholar Karl Lleweyllan explains, contracts enable "group self-government."[41] He goes on to say that "the major importance of legal contract is to provide a framework for well-nigh every type of group organization and for well-nigh every type of passing or permanent relation between individuals and groups."[42]

Enterprise-organizers choose the initial legal structure of firms—ranging from sole proprietorships to complex corporations—and they may also alter various features of a firm's structure over time.[43] This initial choice of business form and governance set-up involves contracts made among the founding organizers who create a firm. (The role of enterprise-organizers in the creation of different legal forms of enterprise is further discussed in Chapter 5.)

It is important to distinguish between the initial organizational choice (with a relatively greater freedom and range of options) at the beginning or "start-up" of a business enterprise and later "midstream" organizational changes contemplated once a business has been operating for a period of time. As the legal scholar Lucian Bebchuk emphasizes: "The questions of contractual freedom in the initial charter and in midstream (that is, after the corporation has been formed and its initial charter set) are different and require separate examination."[44] The primary reason for differential treatment is that business participants make decisions and commitments over time, which establishes economic and legal expectations, as well as expectations for fairness among participants. These expectations are relevant to consider when making organizational changes.

Legal rules impose constraints on organizationally related contracts at the various stages of development of firms. Commentators refer to these legal requirements as "mandatory rules" (such as the prohibition against insider trading) as opposed to "enabling rules" which allow for a relatively free choice of legal form and structure (such as choosing to organize a firm as either a partnership or a corporation).[45] Although some contractual provisions in firms must follow "mandatory"

---

[41] Karl N. Llewellyn, "What Price Contract?—An Essay in Perspective," 40 *Yale Law Journal* 704, 728–31 (1931).

[42] Id., pp. 736–7.

[43] On "enterprise-organizers," see Orts, "Shirking and Sharking," op. cit., pp. 300–9. Cf. also Armen A. Alchian and Harold Demsetz, "Production, Information Costs, and Economic Organization," 62 *American Economic Review* 777, 789 n. 14 (1972) ("entrepreneur-organizer"); R.H. Coase, "The Nature of the Firm," 4 *Economica* (n.s.) 386, 388–9 (1937) ("entrepreneur-coordinator"). The idea of enterprise-organizers is also related to a broader conception of "entrepreneurs." See, e.g., Frank H. Knight, "Profit and Entrepreneurial Functions," 2 *Journal of Economic History* 126 (Supp. 1942); Joseph A. Schumpeter, "The Creative Response in Economic History," 7 *Journal of Economic History* 149 (1947).

[44] Lucian A. Bebchuk, "Foreword: The Debate on Contractual Freedom in Corporate Law," 89 *Columbia Law Review* 1395, 1399 (1989).

[45] On "mandatory" and "enabling" rules in business organization, see Anita Indira Anand, "An Analysis of Enabling vs. Mandatory Corporate Governance: Structures Post-Sarbanes-Oxley," 31 *Delaware Journal of Corporate Law* 229 (2006); John C. Coffee, Jr., "The Mandatory/Enabling Balance in Corporate Law: An Essay on the Judicial Role," 89 *Columbia Law Review* 1618 (1989); Melvin Aron Eisenberg, "The Structure of Corporation Law," 89 *Columbia Law Review* 1461 (1989); Jeffrey N. Gordon, "The Mandatory Structure of Corporate Law," 89 *Columbia Law Review* 1549 (1989); Jonathan R. Macey, "A Pox on Both Your Houses: Enron, Sarbanes-Oxley and the Debate Concerning the Relative Efficiency of Mandatory Versus Enabling Rules," 81 *Washington University Law Quarterly* 329 (2003).

requirements, voluntary "enabling" contracts of many varieties play an undeniably major role in the framework of modern firms.

Beginning in the 1970s (in economics and finance) and the 1980s (in the law), however, many scholars the United States (and to some extent elsewhere) went further and adopted the view that firms were *essentially* composed of contracts. In a favorite formulation, the firm was described as simply "a nexus of contracts."[46] Extreme versions of this view conceived the business firm as *only* a mass of different contracts that somehow cohered into a "nexus." Questions about the nature of the firm and its boundaries were deemed irrelevant. For example, one influential pair of economists argued that "it makes little or no sense to try to distinguish those things which are 'inside' the firm (or any other organization) from those things that are 'outside' of it. There is in a very real sense only a multitude of complex relationships (i.e. contracts) between the legal fiction (the firm) and the owners of labor, material and capital inputs and the consumers of output."[47]

From a traditional legal perspective, this view is conceptually confused. Firms are either "real" or they are not. They cannot be entirely fictional (and therefore ignored as unimportant) *and* serve as a real-world "nexus" for a myriad of contracts. Economists writing in this vein fail to appreciate the legal nature of the firm as a "fictional" but nonetheless socially and legally "real" institutional entity and person, as described in Chapter 1.

Nevertheless, many economists have continued to follow a radically decentralized conception of the firm—decomposing it into component contracts rather than maintaining a view of the firm as a separate organizational and legally recognized entity and person.[48] (There are prominent exceptions. Harold Demsetz, for example, recognized problems with the economic definition of the firm as a "nexus of contracts," particularly with respect to its vagueness.[49] He then suggested: "It might be useful to adopt legal notions of what a firm is and what it is not, for there do arise cases in which this determination is called forth because of the important impact it has on which body of law determines the liabilities of the parties involved."[50])

What have become known as "contractarian" theories of the firm follow a very strong commitment to methodological individualism, refusing to recognize that institutions or groups even exist (as an ontological category) separate from their individual members.[51] From this point of view, thinking of firms "as if they were

---

[46] Michael C. Jensen and William H. Meckling, "Theory of the Firm: Managerial Behavior, Agency Costs and Ownership Structure," 3 *Journal of Financial Economics* 305, 311 (1976) (describing the firm as "simply one form of legal fiction which serves as a nexus for contracting relationships" and "emphasizing the essential contractual nature of firms") (emphasis deleted).

[47] Id.

[48] See, e.g., Eugene F. Fama, "Agency Problems and the Theory of the Firm," 88 *Journal of Political Economy* 288 (1980); Benjamin Klein, "Contracting Costs and Residual Claims: The Separation of Ownership and Control," 26 *Journal of Law and Economics* 367 (1983).

[49] Harold Demsetz, "The Theory of the Firm Revisited," 4 *Journal of Law, Economics, & Organization* 141, 154–5 (1988).

[50] Id., p. 155. See also Preface, pages xiv and accompanying notes 5–7 (noting that economists such as Coase and Williamson recognize the need for a more expansive role for law in theories of the firm).

[51] See Chapter 1, pages 24–5 and accompanying notes 67–71.

persons with motivations and intentions" is an "error." Instead, firms are conceived to be the same as other "markets," such as "the wheat or stock market."[52]

Again, this view seriously misconceives the legal nature of firms and fails to comprehend the social reality of legal persons and entities as they are explained in Chapter 1. One main objective of this book is to counter this point of view—or at least to supplement it with an appreciation of organizational fictions, entities, and persons that are created and made socially real through the force of law.[53]

Insights gained from an economic approach emphasizing the role of contracts in firms has continuing value in thinking about various features of firms—especially with respect to the evolution of their shapes and sizes in competitive market environments. But this approach is inadequate from a legal perspective because a focus only on contracts misses the essential importance of the legal designations of entity, personality, and agency authority discussed above. An approach focusing exclusively on contracts also overlooks complex questions regarding the legal recognition of collective as well as individual ownership of property within firms.[54] The recognition of the firm as a legal entity or person resolves the analytical problem of conceiving of firms as involving both contractual relationships and property ownership structures. Understanding firms as persons provides a center from which (and about which) contracts are made. Understanding firms as persons also grounds the property relationships that compose them. (Property in the firm is further discussed in this chapter below.)

Perhaps surprisingly, many academic lawyers (mostly in the United States) have followed these economic accounts of firms that reduce them only to their component contracts. A school of self-described legal "contractarians" arose and became heavily influential in many U.S. law schools.[55] By 1989, the legal scholar (and Harvard Law School Dean) Robert Clark observed that the "modern contractual theory" of the firm "dominates the thinking of most economists and most economically oriented corporate law scholars who focus at all on the theory of the

---

[52] Jensen and Meckling, op. cit., p. 311.

[53] Elsewhere, I contest the radical philosophical and sociological claim that firms do not exist at all, regardless of the disciplinary lens, in greater theoretical depth. I also discuss nuances regarding the relationship between firms and groups as ontological categories that are omitted here as well. See Eric W. Orts, "The Business Enterprise as a Social Institution" (unpublished manuscript, available on request from the author). For major philosophical sources supporting the ontological argument for the existence of firms and other collective groups, see Christian List and Philip Pettit, *Group Agency: The Possibility, Design, and Status of Corporate Agents* (Oxford University Press 2011); John R. Searle, *The Construction of Social Reality* (Free Press 1995); Margaret Gilbert, *On Social Facts* (Princeton University Press 1989); Philip Pettit, "Responsibility Incorporated," 117 *Ethics* 171(2007).

[54] See also Orts, "Shirking and Sharking," op. cit., pp. 289–98.

[55] See Michael Klausner, "Corporations, Corporate Law, and Networks of Contracts," 81 *Virginia Law Review* 757–72 (1995) (describing the "contractarian paradigm"). See also Coffee, "The Mandatory/Enabling Balance in Corporate Law," op. cit., p. 1618 (describing "contractarians"); David Millon, "Communitarians, Contractarians, and the Crisis in Corporate Law," 50 *Washington and Lee Law Review* 1373, 1377–9, 1382 (1993) (describing "contractarians" as adopting an "anti-regulatory, individualistic stance" opposing mandatory rules).

corporation."[56] Some proponents of this approach have been appointed to sit as judges on powerful federal courts of appeals in the United States. The leading current example is Judge Frank Easterbrook, who co-authored one of the most influential contractarian treatments of corporate law.[57]

Riding the jurisprudential tsunami of law-and-economics (with its epicenter at the University of Chicago), these legal theorists adopted the economic "nexus of contracts" idea both descriptively and prescriptively. They agreed with the economists' claims that firms are essentially a "nexus of contracts"—or, in another influential formulation, "a series of bargains made under constraints."[58] Again, this approach has the virtue of recognizing the large number of relevant business participants in firms (from employees to investors), as well as the wide range of options available for the structuring of business enterprises.[59] However, the legal contractarians rejected the traditional understandings of the construction of business entities and the legal rules that developed to recognize and govern them. The legal scholar William Klein, for example, dismisses the important conceptions of agency law in organizations as "formalistic and simplistic" because they "stem from anachronistic notions of autocratic masters and their faithful or unfaithful servants."[60] Headlines describing unending examples of dictatorial, over-paid chief executives and massive securities frauds committed by supposed agents for others, however, would suggest that Klein's vision of the business world without considerable hierarchy and potential for violation of fiduciary duties is utopian. Against this view, Robert Clark criticizes "the strong form of the contractual theory" for implicitly rejecting the legal authority of "traditional rules" developed over time.[61] Theoretical support of ancient vintage for the wisdom of traditional rules appears in the writings of Cicero, Edmund Burke, and Friedrich Hayek.[62] These traditional rules of business organization include those of agency law and conceptions of firms as organized entities and persons.

Because contractarian theorists omit or deny the importance of legal recognition of the business enterprise itself as an entity and unit of analysis, they cannot provide an adequate account of the organizational fulcrum needed for contracts made both

---

[56] Robert C. Clark, "Contracts, Elites, and Traditions in the Making of Corporate Law," 89 *Columbia Law Review* 1703, 1705 (1989). See also Klausner, "Corporations, Corporate Law, and Networks of Contracts," op. cit., p. 759 n. 1 (noting "the contractarian approach so dominates corporate law scholarship" that "any attempt to list examples would be arbitrary").

[57] Frank H. Easterbrook and Daniel R. Fischel, *The Economic Structure of Corporate Law* (Harvard University Press 1996); see also Frank H. Easterbrook and Daniel R. Fischel, "The Corporate Contract," 89 *Columbia Law Review* 1416 (1989).

[58] Easterbook and Fischel, *The Economic Structure of Corporate Law*, op. cit., pp. 4–22, 34–5, 90–3 (adopting "nexus of contracts" approach); William A. Klein, "The Modern Business Organization: Bargaining Under Constraints," 91 *Yale Law Journal* 1521, 1563 (1982) (advancing "bargaining" model).

[59] See Easterbrook and Fischel, *The Economic Structure of Corporate Law*, op. cit., pp. 2–8, 14–15; G. Mitu Gulati, William A. Klein, and Eric M. Zolt, "Connected Contracts," 47 *UCLA Law Review* 887, 919–29 (2000).

[60] William A. Klein, op. cit., p. 1524.

[61] Clark, "Contracts, Elites, and Traditions in the Making of Corporate Law," op. cit., pp. 1705–6, 1712–13, 1726–30.

[62] Id., p. 1729 n. 58 (providing sources).

within and outside of the firm.[63] In other words, contractarians assume a "nexus" without an adequate account of it.

In response to this criticism, some contractarian theorists in law as well as economics bite the bullet and dispense with the "nexus" altogether. They argue that firms do not exist: there are only "connected contracts" of many varieties.[64] On this view, "there is no primacy, no core, no hierarchy, no prominent participant, *no firm*, [and] no fiduciary duty." Instead, there is only "*a set of interrelated agreements or relationships* among all participants in *an economic activity*—equity holders, debt holders, managers, workers, suppliers, and customers."[65] However, questions of definition and boundaries return to plague this reformulation of the contractarian thesis. What defines the "set" of interrelated agreements or relationships? What is the relevant scope of "the economic activity" involved for purposes of legal analysis as well as everyday business practice? Answers require appeals to notions of an "entity" or some other unit of analysis at the organizational level. The traditional view of firms constructed as legal entities and persons, as well as an understanding of legal structures of agency relationships and property, supply these answers.

Descriptively, then, the contractarian view (at least in its strongest manifestations) is wrong, as a number of academic commentators have pointed out. According to Robert Clark, the contractarian view is "extreme," "almost perverse," and "likely to blind us" to the features of firms that are most "distinctive, puzzling, and worth exploring."[66] Another prominent legal scholar, Melvin Eisenberg, agrees: "The characterization of the corporation as a nexus of contracts is...inaccurate. A corporation is a profit-seeking enterprise of persons and assets organized by rules. Some of these rules are determined by contract or other forms of agreement, but some are determined by law, and most are determined by the unilateral action of corporate organs or officials."[67] Although it is true that many contracts are involved in the structure and operation of firms, extreme claims that business firms are entirely or only composed of contracts overstate the legal reality, even in jurisdictions that highly value freedom of organization and association, such as the United States.[68] Even some law-and-economics scholars have come around to recognizing intractable problems in contractarian theory. Michael Klausner, for example, concludes that "while the contractarian theory was a useful starting point

---

[63] See, e.g., Easterbrook and Fischel, *The Economic Structure of Corporate Law*, op. cit., p. 12 (arguing for a focus on transactional contracts rather than the "entity" of a corporate firm).

[64] Gulati, Klein, and Zolt, op. cit. (advancing the "connected contracts" view).

[65] Id., p. 947 (emphasis added).

[66] Robert C. Clark, "Agency Costs Versus Fiduciary Duties," in *Principals and Agents: The Structure of Business* (John W. Pratt and Richard J. Zeckhauser eds.) (Harvard Business School Press, rev. ed., 1990), pp. 60–1.

[67] Eisenberg, "The Structure of Corporation Law," op. cit., p. 1487.

[68] For other earlier criticisms of contractarian theories, see William W. Bratton, "The Economic Structure of the Post-Contractual Corporation," 87 *Northwestern University Law Review* 180 (1992); William W. Bratton, "The 'Nexus of Contracts' Corporation: A Critical Appraisal," 74 *Cornell Law Review* 407 (1989); Victor Brudney, "Corporate Governance, Agency Costs, and the Rhetoric of Contract," 85 *Columbia Law Review* 1403 (1985); John C. Coffee, Jr., "No Exit? Opting Out, the Contractual Theory of the Corporation, and the Special Case of Remedies," 53 *Brooklyn Law Review* 919 (1988).

for economic analysis of corporate law, more recent research demonstrates that as a description of reality, or a basis for policy prescription, the theory falls short."[69]

Instead, as Eisenberg describes the structure of corporate law (in a manner which can be extended to cover other types of business firms), there are "three basic categories" of legal rules that "concern the internal organization" of business enterprises and "the conduct" of business participants within them.[70] These categories are enabling rules, default rules, and mandatory rules.

First, "enabling rules" recognize that business participants have considerable latitude to construct many of their own organizational structures and internal rules—by contracts, as well as by the various commitments of property and labor that constitute the contents of these contracts.[71] To this extent, firms are indeed composed of contracts made under the legal authority of these enabling rules. Even here, however, note that these enabling rules allow for the contractual creation of a business entity to hold property, make contracts, and have legal standing to pursue or defend claims. Contractarians tend to underemphasize the importance of these traditional kinds of legal empowerments of the business entity and person.

Second, default rules supply common terms for specific forms of business organizations by statute, but allow for "opting out" or "opting in" of various provisions. Contractarians tend to assume that these "default rules" approximate the bargains that average rational contracting parties would make if they had complete information about the issue. They consider them "off-the-rack" contract provisions that business participants may elect to change, if and when it makes sense to do so.[72] These default rules govern firms unless the enterprise-organizers and other business participants agree to "contract around" them.[73] Note that even though default rules may be changed, they may nevertheless favor some business participants, such as investors, against others, such as managers or employees.[74]

Third, "mandatory rules" exist which business participants cannot waive or alter by contract.[75] Examples include prohibitions against insider trading and bans on material misrepresentations of business accounts (i.e. fraud or "cooking the

---

[69] Michael Klausner, "The Contractarian Theory of Corporate Law: A Generation Later," 31 *Journal of Corporation Law* 779, 779 (2006).

[70] Eisenberg, "The Structure of Corporation Law," op. cit., p. 1461.

[71] Id. See also Coffee, "The Mandatory/Enabling Balance in Corporate Law," op. cit., p. 1618 (describing corporate law as "partly enabling, partly mandatory in character").

[72] See, e.g., Easterbrook and Fischel, *The Economic Structure of Corporate Law*, op. cit., pp. 34–5.

[73] For theories of default rules from an economic perspective, see Ian Ayres and Robert Gertner, "Filling Gaps in Incomplete Contracts: An Economic Theory of Default Rules," 99 *Yale Law Journal* 87 (1989); Jason Scott Johnston, "Strategic Bargaining and the Economic Theory of Contract Default Rules," 100 *Yale Law Journal* 615 (1990); Omri Ben-Shahar, "A Bargaining Power Theory of Default Rules," 109 *Columbia Law Review* 396 (2009). For discussion of the use and abuse of default rules in corporate law, see Tamar Frankel, "What Default Rules Teach Us About Corporations; What Understanding Corporations Teaches Us About Default Rules," 33 *Florida State University Law Review* 697 (2006).

[74] See David Millon, "Default Rules, Wealth Distribution, and Corporate Law Reform: Employment at Will Versus Job Security," 146 *University of Pennsylvania Law Review* 975 (1998).

[75] Eisenberg, "The Structure of Corporation Law," op. cit., p. 1461. See also Coffee, "The Mandatory/Enabling Balance in Corporate Law," op. cit., p. 1618.

books").[76] To the extent that mandatory rules exist for the construction and management of business firms which participants cannot "contract around," a description of firms simply in terms of the contracts that compose them is both incorrect and inadequate.

Eisenberg's description of enabling, default, and mandatory rules—or, more generally, a mix of what H.L.A. Hart calls "power-conferring" and "duty-imposing" rules—applies to business enterprises of all forms and sizes.[77] In Hart's words:

Rules conferring private powers must, if they are to be understood, be looked at from the point of view of those who exercise them. They appear then as an additional element introduced by the law into social life over and above that of coercive control. This is so because possession of these legal powers makes of the private citizen, who, if there were no such rules, would be a mere duty-bearer, a private legislator. He is made competent to determine the course of the law within the sphere of his contracts, trusts, wills, and other structures of rights and duties which he is enabled to build.[78]

This perspective provides another jurisprudential explanation of the bottom-up as well as top-down nature of the legal structures of business firms. Contracts play an essential role in the bottom-up construction and ongoing maintenance of these structures.

In general, firms with a fewer number of participants, and thus simpler legal structures, are probably defined to a greater extent by the contractual agreements that compose them than larger and more complex firms. Firms with larger numbers of business participants and more complex structures are more likely to involve greater numbers of mandatory or duty-imposing rules (as well as unadulterated default rules), if only because the practices of negotiating truly reciprocal contractual agreements to cover the interests and perspectives of increasing numbers of business participants become increasingly unlikely, expensive, and often impossible as an exponential function of increasing size and complexity.

Dimensions of the organizational complexity generated by large numbers of people organized in firms include both the "technical complexity" of many legal rules and the "normative complexity" of different values embraced by both business participants and the larger social world.[79] As the legal scholar (and former Delaware Chancellor) William Allen has therefore advised, lawyers who counsel enterprise-organizers and other businesspeople should "develop an artist's sensitivity to complexity in corporate

[76] See, e.g., Eisenberg, "The Structure of Corporation Law," op. cit., p. 1486 (describing insider trading and other examples of mandatory rules in corporate and securities law).

[77] See Eric W. Orts, "The Complexity and Legitimacy of Corporate Law," 50 *Washington and Lee Law Review* 1565, 1580–2 (1993). Cf. Hart, op. cit., pp. 26–49, 283–6.

[78] Hart, op. cit., pp. 40–1.

[79] See Orts, "The Complexity and Legitimacy of Corporate Law," op. cit., pp. 1574–612. In recognition of problems of organizational complexity and the limits of contracts as an instrument of planning, some theorists have adopted conceptions of "relational contracts." See, e.g., Charles J. Goetz and Robert E. Scott, "Principles of Relational Contracts," 67 *Virginia Law Review* 1089 (1981); Ian R. MacNeil, "Relational Contract: What We Do and Do Not Know," 1985 *Wisconsin Law Review* 483 (1985). However, the metaphor of "relational contracts" is not very precise or helpful in legal terms. The vagueness of this concept further indicates the weakness of strictly contractarian theories of the firm.

law."[80] The increasing organizational size, power, and complexity of firms is also likely to translate over time into political pressures to regulate them with respect to larger public policy objectives, such as the protection of public investors, consumers, employees, and the natural environment. These kinds of public regulation of business behavior often take the form of mandatory rules.

Normatively and as a matter of policy, contractarian theorists tend to argue for dismantling mandatory rules and to favor a regime of only enabling and default rules. (This tendency has led some critics to suggest that contractarian theories are in fact motivated by de-regulatory or anti-regulatory ideologies.[81]) The general argument for this approach is easy to see, though much less easy to prove. If the only objective of business firms were economic efficiency, then maximizing the degree of business participants' organizational choice might seem to follow.[82] Focusing on the specific content of mandatory rules, however, shows that this general thesis runs into problems.[83] For example, mandatory rules that prescribe basic levels of trust and loyalty in business relations, such as those expressed in agency-derived standards of fiduciary duties, may well conduce to increase overall levels of economic efficiency and social wealth.[84]

Moreover, values of trust and loyalty are widely seen to be commercially important, independently of contracts.[85] "Trust is an important lubricant of a social system," argues the economist Kenneth Arrow. "It is extremely efficient; it saves a lot of trouble to have a fair degree of reliance on other people's word."[86] The social theorist Francis Fukuyama concurs: "We often take a minimal level of trust and honesty for granted and forget that they pervade everyday economic life and are crucial to its smooth functioning."[87] The legal scholar Lawrence Mitchell writes: "Trust is one of the most important institutions binding our society.... Trust enables us to give others the power to manage our money and to run our businesses."[88] Jonathan Macey, another legal scholar, observes that the expectations

---

[80] William T. Allen, "The Pride and the Hope of Delaware Corporate Law," 25 *Delaware Journal of Corporate Law* 70, 73 (2000).

[81] See, e.g., Brudney, "Corporate Governance, Agency Costs, and the Rhetoric of Contract," op. cit., p. 1404, 1409–10, 1444; David Millon, "Theories of the Corporation," 1990 *Duke Law Journal* 201, 202–4, 229–31 (1990). See also Chapter 1, pages 23–5 and accompanying notes 65–72.

[82] See, e.g., Roberta Romano, "Answering the Wrong Question: The Tenuous Case for Mandatory Corporate Laws," 89 *Columbia Law Review* 1599 (1989) (arguing that mandatory rules are appropriate only if they effectively address identified economic "externalities").

[83] For the argument that a number of mandatory rules in corporate law have economic justifications, see Gordon, op. cit.

[84] See Robert Flannigan, "The Economics of Fiduciary Accountability," 32 *Delaware Journal of Corporate Law* 393 (2007).

[85] There is a large interdisciplinary literature on the importance of trust in society. For an introduction, see, e.g., *Trust in Organizations: Frontiers of Theory and Research* (Roderick M. Kramer and Tom R. Tyler eds.) (Sage 1996). See also Margaret M. Blair and Lynn A. Stout, "Trust, Trustworthiness, and the Behavioral Foundations of Corporate Law," 149 *University of Pennsylvania Law Review* 1735 (2001).

[86] Kenneth J. Arrow, *The Limits of Organization* (W.W. Norton 1974), p. 23.

[87] Francis Fukuyama, *Trust: The Social Virtues and the Creation of Prosperity* (Free Press 1995), p. 152.

[88] Lawrence E. Mitchell, "Trust. Contract. Process," in *Progressive Corporate Law* (Lawrence E. Mitchell ed.) (Westview Press 1995), p. 185.

of many business participants are often based on trust rather than on assurances of enforceable legal contracts.[89] Although Macey follows an adapted version of contractarian theory in his treatment of corporate governance, he recognizes that "a contractarian paradigm" alone is insufficient to account for the legal treatment of equity investors and other "incomplete contracts" within firms.[90] He distinguishes between *contracts* and *promises*, and he argues that the more general category of "promises" allows for a range of expectations, including non-contractual, norm-based expectations of trust and fiduciary duties owing to shareholders and other investors. At least, Macey recognizes the importance of social norms and trust as well as contracts.[91] Other scholars would go further and argue that legal rules and principles that express moral values such as fairness, trust, loyalty, and honesty should be honored and enforced regardless of economic considerations—even, and perhaps especially, in business contexts.[92]

Property

One explanation for the "nexus" that contractarians struggle to find in their theory of the firm is a simple one, though it becomes more complex on closer examination: private property and ownership. Business firms of any significant size and scope involve the allocation of capital to the enterprise. The fulcrum of the firm lies in the assets that are dedicated to business purposes.

An exception may appear in the pure sole proprietor who uses personal property (such as a computer) to begin a business (such as the online resale of books or other items). Even here, a business firm exists and depends on the institutions of property, contracts, and agency. The allocation of assets to the firm is informal, however, and not as clearly demarcated in very small enterprises as compared with larger, more formally organized ones. As noted above in Chapter 1, the development of accounting as a social technology complementary to the laws of enterprise organization has been essential for the delineation of property assets belonging to the firm separately from an individual owner or family (i.e. as an "entity" and "person").[93]

Organizational contracts and agency relationships emanate from the "nexus" of the capital allocated to the firm which, as also described in Chapter 1, is then

---

[89] Jonathan R. Macey, *Corporate Governance: Promises Kept, Promises Broken* (Princeton University Press 2008), p. vii.

[90] Id., pp. 5–8, 16–27.

[91] Id., pp. vii, 40–2, 274.

[92] On the non-contractual foundations of fiduciary duties, see, e.g., Victor Brudney, "Contract and Fiduciary Duty in Corporate Law," 38 *Boston College Law Review* 595 (1997); Deborah A. DeMott, "Breach of Fiduciary Duty: On Justifiable Expectations of Loyalty and Their Consequences," 48 *Arizona Law Review* 925 (2006). On loyalty as a value, see George P. Fletcher, *Basic Concepts of Legal Thought* (Oxford University Press 1996), pp. 172–86; Simon Keller, *The Limits of Loyalty* (Cambridge University Press 2007); Josiah Royce, *The Philosophy of Loyalty* (Vanderbilt University Press 1995) (1908). See also Chapter 1, pages 19–20 and accompanying notes 47–9.

[93] See Chapter 1, pages 33–4 and accompanying notes 111–14. See also Jane Gleeson-White, *Double Entry: How the Merchants of Venice Created Modern Finance* (W.W. Norton & Co. 2012).

formally owned by the firm as a legal entity and institutional person. This feature of a "property nexus" explains why legal and ethical principles such as trust, loyalty, and fiduciary duty remain so important. Because business enterprises almost always involve the management of assets belonging to others who are not directly involved in everyday operations, the use and control of "other people's money" frame the heart of the legal responsibilities of business management.[94] As Louis Brandeis expressed the basic idea: "The goose that lays golden eggs has been considered a most valuable possession. But even more profitable is the privilege of taking the golden eggs laid by somebody else's goose."[95]

Property in the form of organized capital is therefore another foundation of the legal composition of the business enterprise. Historically, modern business firms organized on an independent basis arose in tandem with the establishment of private property regimes in land and other freely owned personal property and capital. Capital became represented in the form of money and managed through the emerging financial institutions of loans, other credit instruments, and banks, as well as invested directly as ownership interests in firms.[96] Banks were originally mostly private firms, but then evolved to include public institutions—including government-directed central banks.[97] Bonds issued by governments as well as banks and companies are another important part of the financial story.[98]

Free labor adds another essential ingredient to the mix. Employment relationships consist in the exchange of labor, knowledge, skills, and other commitments of intangible "human capital" for payments in wages and otherwise.[99] Employees arguably "own" their labor as a form of private property, but it is also accurate to say that employees "own" their wages and other compensation paid in return for their services.[100] In other words, labor is "commodified."

Commodification refers to the social and legal recognition that certain things, items, products, and services may be traded (i.e. bought and sold). An historical prerequisite for modern firms described here includes the widespread commodification of both land and labor. (Legally enforced boundaries forbid some other sorts of commodification, such as slavery, bribery, corruption, and vote buying in politics, as well as some forms of gambling, sexual services, and the purchase and sale of babies or human organs.)[101]

---

[94] See Louis D. Brandeis, *Other People's Money and How the Bankers Use It* (Frederick A. Stokes 1914), pp. 17–19.

[95] Id., pp. 17–18.

[96] For a history of the rise of financial institutions that supported independent business enterprises, see Niall Ferguson, *The Ascent of Money: A Financial History of the World* (Penguin Press 2008).

[97] Id., pp. 41–58.

[98] Id., pp. 65–118.

[99] See Gary S. Becker, *Human Capital: A Theoretical and Empirical Analysis, with Special Reference to Education* (University of Chicago Press, 3rd ed., 1993).

[100] On the idea of "self-ownership," see Jeremy Waldron, *The Right to Private Property* (Oxford University Press 1988), pp. 398–408. Other compensation in addition to wages and salary paid in cash include profit-sharing arrangements such as stock options.

[101] See, e.g., Orts, "Simple Rules and the Perils of Reductionist Legal Thought," op. cit., pp. 1453–5 (collecting sources). See also Michael J. Sandel, *What Money Can't Buy: The Moral Limits of Markets* (Farrar, Straus, and Giroux 2012); Debra Satz, *Why Some Things Should Not Be for Sale*

Thus, from the basic ingredients of private capital, free labor, organizational contracts, agency relationships, and the legal recognition of business entities, modern firms are created.[102] The institutional combination of property, contracts, agency, and organizational recognition describes a "legal matrix" from which business enterprises are organized and compete over time in markets for the provision of goods, services, resources, and information. Unlike its Hollywood parallel, this matrix is not fictional, except in the sense in which established legal fictions have real consequences.[103] The legal matrix of business enterprises nevertheless remains invisible to many people—a hidden social structure which reading this book will unveil!

At first blush, private property as a basic foundation of modern firms may appear self-evident without need for elaboration. But the organization of modern property in business firms quickly becomes more complex on a closer analysis.

Tangible property

One may begin a closer analysis of the role of property in the firm by imagining the physical and tangible property of the firm—in traditional accounting terms, "the plant and equipment"—to include the land, buildings, machinery, and other physical "things" in a business. Owners of this physical property have the authority to manage the firm by virtue of the fact that they have rights of control over this property.

"Anyone who frees himself from the crudest materialism," however, "readily recognizes that as a legal term property denotes not material things but certain

---

(Oxford University Press 2010); Michael J. Trebilcock, *The Limits of Freedom of Contract* (Harvard University Press 1993). For a survey of the current jurisprudential debate, see also Note, "The Price of Everything, the Value of Nothing: Reframing the Commodification Debate," 117 *Harvard Law Review* 689 (2003).

[102] I elaborate on the historical dimensions of the rise of independent firms elsewhere. Eric W. Orts, "A Short History of the Business Enterprise" (unpublished manuscript, available from the author on request). For sources describing various aspects of this historical evolution, see *A History of Corporate Governance Around the World: Family Business Groups to Professional Managers* (Randall K. Morck ed.) (University of Chicago Press 2005); *A History of Private Life* (Philippe Ariès and Georges Duby general eds.) (Harvard University Press 1987–91) (five volumes); Fernand Braudel, *Civilization and Capitalism, 15th–18th Century* (trans. Siân Reynolds) (University of California Press 1992) (three volumes); Alfred F. Conard, *Corporations in Perspective* (Foundation Press 1976); Norman Davies, *Europe: A History* (Oxford University Press 1996); Friedrich A. Hayek, *Law, Legislation and Liberty* (University of Chicago Press 1973–9) (three volumes), Eric Hobsbawm, *The Age of Revolution: 1749–1848* (Vintage Books ed. 1996) (1962); David S. Landes, *The Unbound Prometheus: Technological Change and Industrial Development in Western Europe from 1750 to the Present* (Cambridge University Press 1969); John Micklethwait and Adrian Wooldridge, *The Company: A Short History of a Revolutionary Idea* (Modern Library 2003); Michael Novak, *The Fire of Invention: Civil Society and the Future of the Corporation* (Rowman & Littlefield 1997); Karl Polanyi, *The Great Transformation: The Political and Economic Origins of Our Time* (Beacon Press 1944); Max Weber, *Economy and Society* (Guenther Roth and Claus Wittich eds.) (University of California Press 1978) (two volumes); Henry Hansmann, Reinier Kraakman, and Richard Squire, "Law and the Rise of the Firm," 119 *Harvard Law Review* 1333 (2006).

[103] Cf. *The Matrix* (Warner Bros. 1999).

rights."[104] In other words, people enter into various relationships of agency and contracts, and they decide on legal forms of business organization, from differing positions of power based on their respective ownership and claims to ownership of the physical property of the business.

This account tracks in part the "property rights" economic theory of the firm noted above.[105] More recently, there has been a turn in legal scholarship as well toward recognizing the importance of private property dimensions in the law of business enterprise (particularly corporate law) as opposed to the long-running fashion of contractarian theories.[106] Although this approach provides a necessary correction to the contractarians, however, there is a nascent danger that the new "proprietary theories" may crowd out an appreciation of other dimensions of business law outlined here—including contracts! For example, one version of this theory asserts that "proprietary foundations" are central with a "contractarian superstructure" dependent on these foundations.[107] Prioritizing "property" over "contracts" is not necessarily helpful, however, because both are intrinsically important in firms.

In the legal theory of the firm advanced here, the basic elements of both property and contracts are combined with other important features, including relationships of agency authority and the recognition of business entities and persons. To suggest that agency and trust law are essentially extensions meant to protect private property rights is an example of possible misinterpretation if the element of property is emphasized too strongly.[108] As argued in this book, agency relationships within firms involve allocations of authority and power that have larger social implications, especially when recognizing the size and scope of organizational entities as principals and the corresponding degrees of power delegated to their individual agents (or quasi-principals). This power is conferred through organizational contracts structuring agency relationships, not only through a simple extension of property rights within firms.

Nevertheless, the nexus of property ownership serves as the legal grounding for contracts for labor internal to the firm (including employment agreements with managers and various levels of employees)—as well as external contracts through which the firm conducts its business (including, for example, contracts with suppliers of raw materials or other production "inputs," contracts with outside service providers for advertising or legal advice, and contracts with the firm's customers). An appreciation of the physical, tangible property owned by the firm provides clarification of how firms are born and grow—and yet retain an essential "core" or "center" in the collective ownership of their constitutive property.[109] Like

---

[104] See Morris R. Cohen, "Property and Sovereignty," 13 *Cornell Law Quarterly* 8, 11–12 (1927).

[105] See Preface, page xiv and accompanying note 8. See also Orts, "Shirking and Sharking," op. cit., pp. 295–6 (arguing that "the property theory of the firm represents an advance from contractarian theories" for purposes of a legal theory of the firm).

[106] See, e.g., John Armour and Michael J. Whincop, "The Proprietary Foundations of Corporate Law," 27 *Oxford Journal of Legal Studies* 429 (2007).

[107] Id., pp. 449, 464.

[108] Id., pp. 449, 463.

[109] For a theory of private property beginning with the recognition of rights to material things, but recognizing the limits of this approach in complex modern circumstances, see Waldron, op. cit., pp. 31–40. I do not enter here on the deeper questions of fundamental philosophical justifications of

Table 2.3 Internal and external contracts within and with firms

	Legal description	Leading examples
Internal contracts	Governance contracts that compose the firm as an organizational entity with respect to property and agency relationships	Founding documents of "legal form" (e.g. partnership agreements, corporation charters, and bylaws); executive compensation; other employment contracts
External contracts	Commercial contracts with outside providers of "inputs" to the firm and contracts with purchasers of the firm's goods, services, or information	Suppliers; distributors; marketing/legal services; customers

agency, contracts occur both internally and externally to the firm as an entity with a "nexus" defined by property rights and ownership. See Table 2.3 for an illustration.

Intangible property

Although physical, tangible property and its private ownership remain important in modern society, the idea of private property has become much more complicated—especially with respect to the notion of "intangible assets" that derive from the operations of business firms as organized entities. Intangible, non-material assets include property rights that are created by legal fiat (in recognition of human creativity and inventiveness) as "intellectual property." This category includes patents, copyrights, and trademarks. These kinds of assets are particularly important with respect to technological change and economic competition—and the legal boundaries of the firm are affected in part by the scope given to intellectual property rights.[110]

To recognize that intellectual and other intangible property rights are created legally is not to denigrate their importance. Arguments favoring the recognition of these rights parallel similar policy justifications seen in the recognition of other "legal fictions" such as money and corporations. Because the legal recognition and enforcement of intellectual property rights differ among countries (in China as compared with the United States, for example), the scope of firms internationally is potentially limited to the same extent.[111]

private property. For an outline of "rights-based" justifications, see id., pp. 62–445. For an introduction to other justifications, see Stephen R. Munzer, *A Theory of Property* (Cambridge University Press 1990).

[110] For examinations of intellectual property and theories of the firm, see Oren Bar-Gill and Gideon Parchomovsky, "Law and the Boundaries of Technology-Intensive Firms," 157 *University of Pennsylvania Law Review* 1649 (2009); Dan L. Burk, "Intellectual Property and the Firm," 71 *University of Chicago Law Review* 3 (2004). See also Mira Wilkins, "The Neglected Intangible Asset: The Influence of the Trade Mark on the Rise of the Modern Corporation," 34 *Business History* 66 (1992).

[111] On cultural attitudes toward intellectual property in China, see William P. Alford: *To Steal a Book Is an Elegant Offense: Intellectual Property Law in Chinese Civilization* (Stanford University Press 1995).

Intellectual property law also recognizes, though only partially, the larger role played by the creation, management, ownership, and use of business-relevant "knowledge" and "cognition" as an important economic attribute determining the competitive success of firms, which is the focus of some other economic theories of the firm.[112] Specific, practical, and applied knowledge in the everyday work processes and operations of particular firms—or what the ancient Greeks described as *mētis*—describes intangible features of economic value.[113] The experience of workers in a particular occupation and profession that allows them to make judgment calls or apply "rules of thumb" in some situations but not others illustrates this kind of practical knowledge. Another kind of practical knowledge—what the ancient Greeks called *techne*—translates more directly into modern legal terms, such as in the rights to use a new technical or scientific invention through the exercise of a patent.[114]

Additional value in firms can also derive from building commercial "goodwill" over time, such as in a firm's reputation for high-quality products or customer-friendliness in responding to inquiries or complaints. The old accounting idea of goodwill captures the economic reality that a firm as a "going concern" is commonly worth much more than the total economic value of its tangible assets.[115] Today, other methods of valuation that do not rely on goodwill estimations, such as discounted cash flow analysis, are more commonly used. Nevertheless, the economic value of a firm's reputation, though not easily measured, is widely recognized.[116]

A related source of intangible value lies in the formation of a firm's commercial "identity," as established through the marketing and branding of both itself and its products and services. This identity formation and projection is accomplished through the use of copyrights and trademarks, as well as through internal governance

---

[112] See, e.g., Masahiko Aoki, *Corporations in Evolving Diversity: Cognition, Governance, and Institutions* (Oxford University Press 2010); John Peter Murmann, *Knowledge and Competitive Advantage: The Coevolution of Firms, Technology, and National Institutions* (Cambridge University Press 2003); Mario Morroni, *Knowledge, Scale and Transactions in the Theory of the Firm* (Cambridge University Press 2006); Ikujiro Nonaka, Ryoko Toyama, and Toru Hirata, *Managing Flow: A Process Theory of the Knowledge-Based Firm* (Palgrave Macmillan 2008); Robert M. Grant, "Toward a Knowledge-Based Theory of the Firm," 17 *Strategic Management Journal* 109 (1996); Bruce Kogut and Udo Zander, "Knowledge of the Firm, Combinative Capabilities, and the Replication of Technology," 3 *Organization Science* 383 (1992); Bruce Kogut and Udo Zander, "A Memoir and Reflection: Knowledge and an Evolutionary Theory of the Multinational Firm 10 Years Later," 34 *Journal of International Business Studies* 505 (2003).

[113] Cf. James C. Scott, *Seeing Like a State: How Certain Schemes to Improve the Human Condition Have Failed* (Yale University Press 1998), pp. 6–7, 331–9.

[114] Id., pp. 319–23 (distinguishing between *mētis* and *techne*).

[115] See, e.g., John R. Commons, *Legal Foundations of Capitalism* (Augustus M. Kelly, reprint ed., 1974) (1924), pp. 160–2; Note, "An Inquiry into the Nature of Goodwill," 53 *Columbia Law Review* 660, 694 (1953).

[116] On the value of the reputation of firms, see, e.g., Grahame Dowling, *Creating Corporate Reputations* (Oxford University Press 2001); Charles J. Fombrun, *Reputation: Realizing the Value from the Corporate Image* (Harvard Business School Press 1996); Charles J. Fombrun and Cees B.M. Van Riel, *Fame and Fortune: How Successful Companies Build Winning Reputations* (Financial Times Prentice Hall 2008).

and management processes.[117] A firm's identity and its value may change over time in response to market pressures and social developments.[118] Building and maintaining a firm's identity in a global environment pose special challenges.[119] Even with these complexities, the construction of an "identity" of business persons describes another property-related component of its economic value, its legal definition, and its internal cultural understanding.

Taken together, the intangible assets represented by the reputation, knowledge, organization, identity, processes, and "expected profits" (or, in modern financial terms, "cash flows") of the firm describe an important category of private property in the firm. Early institutional economists such as John Commons and Thorstein Veblen recognized the importance of these kinds of intangible assets represented by business firms. One might refer to *institutional assets* to describe these kinds of property. These assets refer to the economic value, beyond the physical "plant and equipment" and intellectual property owned by a firm, deriving from the organizational benefits of a business firm's management, structure, and operational processes.

As Commons explained, business capital is not only "the present value of expected net income" following from "the primitive notion of property as physical things held for one's own use by an owner." It also includes intangible predictions of "expected transactions on commodity markets and money markets," as well as "expected additions to income to be derived, not from physical things, but from expected profitable transactions with persons."[120] The legal theorist Stephen Munzer has restated this view: "It is perfectly sound to think of property both as things . . . and as relations among persons or other entities with respect to things. . . ."[121]

Similarly, Veblen described business capital as representing the "earning-capacity" of a firm based on the "recurring valuation of the company's properties, tangible and intangible." The "nucleus of the capitalization" of a firm encompasses intangible assets such as its "established customary business relations, reputation for up-right dealing, . . . [and] exclusive control of particular sources of materials." Veblen included intellectual property in trademarks, patents, and copyrights—as well as protected trade secrets—on this list.[122] (Commons acknowledged an intellectual debt to Veblen regarding his ideas of intangible property.[123]) Financial techniques that analyze a firm's overall "free cash flow" and other quantitative measures supply modern, more sophisticated methods for estimating the economic

[117] See, e.g., David A. Aaker and Erich Joachimsthaler, *Brand Leadership: Building Assets in an Information Economy* (Free Press 2000); Vithala R. Rao, Manoj K. Agarwal, and Denise Dahlhoff, "How Is Manifest Branding Strategy Related to the Intangible Value of a Corporation?" 68 *Journal of Marketing* 126 (2004).

[118] See, e.g., Dennis A. Gioia, Majken Schultz, and Kevin G. Corley, "Organizational Identity, Image, and Adaptive Instability," 25 *Academy of Management Review* 63 (2000).

[119] See George S. Day and David J. Reibstein, "Managing Brands in Global Markets," in *The INSEAD-Wharton Alliance on Globalizing: Strategies for Building Successful Global Businesses* (Hubert Gatignon and John R. Kimberly eds.) (Cambridge University Press 2004), pp. 184–206.

[120] Commons, op. cit., p. 168.

[121] Munzer, op. cit., p. 17.

[122] Thorstein Veblen, *The Theory of the Business Enterprise* (Mentor 1932) (1904), pp. 70–1.

[123] Rick Tillman, *Thorstein Veblen and His Critics, 1891–1963: Conservative, Liberal, and Radical Perspectives* (Princeton University Press 1992), pp. 130–3.

value of these intangible institutional assets included in the total property of the firm. Free cash flow is a financial measure of a firm's incoming revenue "in excess of that required to fund all projects that have positive net present values when discounted at the relevant cost of capital."[124] It therefore includes a valuation of a firm's intangible as well as tangible property.

The fragmentation of ownership and control

The increasing intangibility of property represented in firms represents a dynamic and radical change in the institution of private property itself. Although Commons and Veblen first recognized this change, the best expression of the "revolution" in private property rendered by the business firm—particularly in the form of the corporation—appears in the seminal book by Adolf Berle and Gardiner Means, *The Modern Corporation and Private Property*.[125]

Berle and Means followed Commons and Veblen in their recognition of the importance of the growth of intangible property in large business enterprises.[126] They then went further and diagnosed a "revolution" accomplished by the owner-ship structures of the corporate enterprise which have "destroyed the unity that we commonly call property." The "dissolution of the atom of property," they argued, "destroys the very foundation on which the economic order of the past three centuries has rested." They attributed the cause of this dissolution to the rise of the business corporation and its fragmented ownership structure.[127] Berle and Means also identified a famous "separation of ownership and control" in corporations in the United States.[128]

The observation of this separation had been made earlier, though not with the same quantitative rigor, by both Veblen and John Maynard Keynes.[129] Veblen observed as early as 1904 that "the management is separated from the ownership or property, more and more widely as the size of corporation finance widens." This phenomenon occurred in connection with what he called "absentee ownership," his pejorative term for the increasingly prevalent practice of financing firms from a distance without participating in their operational management.[130] Keynes made

---

[124] Michael C. Jensen, "Agency Costs of Free Cash Flow, Corporate Finance, and Takeovers," 76 *American Economic Review* 323, 323 (1986). For an early description, distinguishing cash-flow from earnings analysis, see Diran Bodenhorn, "A Cash-Flow Concept of Profit," 19 *Journal of Finance* 16 (1964). For historical background, see Scott P. Dulman, "The Development of Discounted Cash Flow Techniques in U.S. Industry," 63 *Business History Review* 555 (1989).

[125] Adolf A. Berle and Gardiner C. Means, *The Modern Corporation and Private Property* (Transaction Publishers 1991) (rev. ed. 1968) (1932), pp. xli, 7.

[126] Id., pp. xxiii–xxv (Berle's 1967 preface), 64–5.

[127] Id., pp. 7–9.

[128] Id., pp. 110–16, 297–8.

[129] The initial footnote in *The Modern Corporation and Private Property* refers to Veblen's last work. Id., p. 4, citing Thorstein Veblen, *Absentee Ownership: Business Enterprise in Recent Times: The Case of America* (Transaction Publishers 1997) (1923).

[130] See Edward S. Herman, *Corporate Control, Corporate Power* (Cambridge University Press 1981), pp. 7–8 (quoting Veblen).

similar observations in the 1920s, noting the tendency of corporate shareholders to become "almost totally disassociated from the management."[131]

Berle and Means' restatement and empirical documentation of the separation of ownership and control in corporations fueled a large amount of legal research in the United States and, to lesser extent, elsewhere in the world.[132] As scholars have recognized, the separation between a diffused ownership of many shareholders and centralized management in corporations has not spread widely beyond the United States and several other English-speaking countries.[133] In the United States, though, according to one leading legal scholar, the separation of ownership and control became "the master problem for research."[134]

Although the separation-of-ownership-and-control thesis is now widely known and discussed, Berle and Means' original argument has too often been narrowly interpreted. This narrow interpretation focuses only on the separation in large, publicly traded corporations between shareholders and top managers. The shareholders, on this view, are posited (incorrectly) as the only true "owners" of corporations. And the top managers are described (mostly correctly) as have having grown over time to exert significant "control" of corporations.

This narrow interpretation also tends to follow a heavily prescriptive version of the separation-of-ownership-and-control thesis in arguing (against the conclusions and recommendations of Berle and Means themselves) that the separation of ownership and control between shareholders and managers should, normatively, be closed. The legal scholar Roberta Romano has observed this tendency in contemporary research and noted its "irony." In fact, rather than arguing for closing the separation of ownership and control, Berle and Means "celebrated" it as allowing for the potential emergence of "public-regarding" and "independent corporate managers" who did not answer too reactively or directly to shareholders.[135]

The narrow but well-populated stream of legal research that argues for closing the institutional separation between shareholder ownership and managerial control on economic grounds does not seem to have strong empirical foundations with respect to the diagnosis of a real problem. One reason for doubt appears in the historical persistence of an "equity premium" for long-term investments in publicly traded corporate shares in the United States and elsewhere (as compared with investments in debt, loans, or other financial instruments).[136] Empirical work confirms that investments in stock markets have outperformed investments in

---

[131] Id., pp. 8–9 (quoting Keynes).

[132] See Brian R. Cheffins, "The Trajectory of (Corporate Law) Scholarship," 63 *Cambridge Law Journal* 456, 479–81 (2004). See also Brian R. Cheffins, "Does Law Matter? The Separation of Ownership and Control in the United Kingdom," 30 *Journal of Legal Studies* 459 (2001).

[133] See, e.g., Mark J. Roe, "Political Preconditions to Separating Ownership from Corporate Control," 53 *Stanford Law Review* 539 (2000) (arguing that differences with respect to social democracy and organized labor provide one good explanation for this phenomenon).

[134] Roberta Romano, "Metapolitics and Corporate Law Reform," 36 *Stanford Law Review* 923, 923 (1984).

[135] Id., pp. 923–4, 1014; see also Berle and Means, op. cit., pp. 310–13.

[136] See, e.g., Jeremy J. Siegel and Richard H. Thaler, "Anomalies: The Equity Premium Puzzle," 11 *Journal of Economic Perspectives* 191 (1997).

corporate bonds and treasury bills in most developed countries over long periods of time.[137] If the separation of ownership and control in large corporations had dire economic implications for shareholders, then the source of this equity premium is puzzling. Even if there are organizational costs (often called "agency costs") inherent in the separation of financial ownership and managerial control, other economic benefits from the institutional separation—such as the occupational specializations enabled in finance and management, respectively—appear to outweigh them, at least for many business firms in many situations. Arguably, the returns on equity compared with debt or other investments could be even higher with legal reforms or structural changes, but from a macroeconomic perspective it is not at all obvious that there is a major problem that needs to be fixed.[138] At least, long-term positive equity returns suggest that the current global system of corporate investment is not radically broken or in need of massive regulatory intervention. This is not to say that there are no specific problems with respect to financial, corporate, and securities regulation that deserve attention, especially in light of ongoing financial scandals and instabilities following the Great Credit Crash of 2008. The point is rather that the presumed macro-problem of the corporate separation of ownership and control appears to have been overstated. It has garnered too much scholarly attention compared with other pressing issues.

The problematization of the separation of ownership and control in corporations has spawned two major proposed approaches to law reform. One approach, which may be called the *shareholder empowerment solution*, argues for legal changes to close the separation by empowering shareholders as "owners" to exercise more effective control of corporations, such as through enhanced shareholder voting rights or stronger enforcement of corporate fiduciary duties owed to shareholders. Examples of shareholder empowerment reforms include allowing for shareholder nominations to corporate boards, making hostile takeover bids easier, and removing hurdles for shareholder lawsuits accusing corporate managers and directors of misfeasance.[139] The legal scholar Lucian Bebchuk is one of the strongest contemporary advocates for this approach.[140]

---

[137] See Jeremy J. Siegel, *Stocks for the Long Run* (McGraw-Hill, 4th ed., 2007) (reviewing U.S. stock performance compared with alternative investments). See also Elroy Dimson, Paul Marsh, and Mike Staunton, *Triumph of the Optimists: 101 Years of Global Investment Returns* (Princeton University Press 2002) (reviewing data from sixteen different countries and finding positive long-term returns favoring investments in corporate stocks compared with investments in bonds and government treasuries).

[138] For a contrary view, relying on comparative studies of share prices in the United States over a relatively limited time span, see Lucian Bebchuk, Alma Cohen, and Allen Ferrell, "What Matters in Corporate Governance?" 22 *Review of Financial Studies* 783 (2009) (noting significant share price differentials with respect to several categories of relevant legal variables). See also Paul Gompers, Joy Ishii, and Andrew Metrick, "Corporate Governance and Equity Prices," 118 *Quarterly Journal of Economics* 107 (2003) (finding stronger protections of shareholders to correlate with higher economic performance of large U.S. firms in the 1990s as measured in terms of share price).

[139] See, e.g., Cheffins, "The Trajectory of (Corporate Law) Scholarship," op. cit., p. 480.

[140] See Lucian A. Bebchuk, "The Myth of the Shareholder Franchise," 93 *Virginia Law Review* 675 (2007); Lucian A. Bebchuk, "Letting Shareholders Set the Rules," 119 *Harvard Law Review* 1784 (2006); Lucian A. Bebchuk, "The Case for Increasing Shareholder Power," 118 *Harvard Law Review* 833 (2005).

Note that arguments for empowering shareholders vis-à-vis managers, creditors, or other participants in a corporation do not necessarily depend on the larger thesis that the separation-of-ownership-and-control must be entirely "closed." One may argue instead that it simply makes sense from an economic or social point of view to adjust the legal balance of corporate governance toward shareholders—and against managers, creditors, or employees—while recognizing that the institutional reality of the separation-of-ownership-and-control is likely to continue. In fact, the reform measures most commonly advocated are intended to exert structural pressure on managers to focus on increasing shareholder value, rather than to eliminate the institutional separation. In other words, the separation is taken as given: reforms are intended simply to increase the legal powers of shareholders to act across this institutional gap.

A second approach, which may be called the *management ownership solution*, recommends financial restructuring transactions that unify ownership and control in corporate managers by transforming them into owners, such as in management-led buyouts designed to eliminate public shareholders and replace them with manager-owners. These "going private" transactions are usually accomplished though the use of leverage, that is, issuing new corporate debt in order to pay current shareholders for a controlling equity stake of the firm. (These transactions are accomplished legally through the alchemy of corporate "shapeshifting."[141]) The financial scholar Michael Jensen has been a prominent advocate for these kinds of management ownership solutions. He has gone so far as to argue that "going private" deals will solve the separation problem and eventually result in an "eclipse" of the public corporation as a common legal form of enterprise.[142] However, there are also risks with this approach. Increasing leverage in these transactions may also increase systemic risks of business failures by focusing on short-term incentives (i.e. debt payment schedules) rather than long-term investments (i.e. equity returns).[143]

See Table 2.4 for a graphical depiction of the two proposed reform strategies of the shareholder empowerment and managerial ownership solutions.

Oversimplifications can occur with respect to both of these proposed solutions to the extent that shareholders are miscast conceptually as "principals" and managers as their "agents" in complex corporate firms. As discussed earlier in the first section of this chapter, the law of agency and business organization combine to create complex structures of authority, power, and ownership that defy this reductionist logic.

Much of the literature advocating a closing of the separation of ownership-and-control in public corporations follows an adaptation of economic theories of "agency costs."[144] In summary, this vast literature (again, mostly in the United States) assumes that shareholders are roughly analogous to principals,

---

[141] See Chapter 1, pages 39–40 and accompanying notes 139–45.

[142] See, e.g., Michael C. Jensen, "Eclipse of the Public Corporation," *Harvard Business Review*, Sept.–Oct. 1989, pp. 69–74.

[143] See, e.g., Michael Useem, "Business Restructuring, Management Control, and Corporate Organization," 19 *Theory and Society* 681, 694–5 (1990).

[144] For a description of economic "agency costs" theories of the firms, see Orts, "Shirking and Sharking," op. cit., pp. 275–8.

Table 2.4 Recommended solutions to the separation of ownership and control

	Perceived problem	Examples/recommendations
Shareholder empowerment solution	Shareholders do not exercise sufficient "control" or "oversight" of managers who have consolidated decision-making power in large corporate firms over time. Prominent proponent: Lucian Bebchuk	Enhanced corporate governance provisions and laws to increase shareholder "voice" and voting; prohibition of antitakeover devices; expansion of rights of shareholders to sue managers and directors for violations of fiduciary duties
Management ownership solution	Managers do not have enough "skin in the game" to make decisions to maximize economic gains for the firm. Prominent proponent: Michael Jensen	Management-led buyouts; leveraged private equity structures; long-term "eclipse" of the public corporation

and managers are expected to serve them as agents.[145] From a structural legal point of view, however, this entire literature is based on a mistaken assumption. Shareholders are not legally principals, and managers are not merely agents of shareholders. Managers are agents of the organizational principal itself, namely, the firm as an entity.[146] Managers are legally bound to serve shareholders only derivatively and secondarily. The institutional "separation" has its legal source in the very structure of the property revolution in modern corporations diagnosed by Berle and Means. To "close" it would undo this organizational revolution.

Legal arguments that managers *should* act as direct agents of shareholders assume a prescriptive answer to the observed phenomenon of the separation of ownership and control. The traditional legal structure of business enterprise does not require this prescriptive approach. Instead, competing economic and policy arguments may support the continued evolution of business structures, including publicly owned corporations, based on fragmented ownership, rather than attempting to reverse this historical development by forcibly "closing" the separation of ownership and control by one means or another.

Moreover, the implications for these recommended changes are significant because they affect not only how organizational power and authority in large firms are exercised (control), but also how business capital is held and invested (ownership). In a world characterized by concentrated capital in large firms, following either the shareholder empowerment or managerial ownership solution would have the predictable consequence of shifting the overall social distribution of wealth to either shareholders or managers, respectively.

Alleged gains to overall economic efficiency of structurally eliminating the separation of ownership and control have also not yet been proven; and they are doubtful given that economic incentives for various business participants have

---

[145] See, e.g., Cheffins, "The Trajectory of (Corporate Law) Scholarship," op. cit., p. 482–3.
[146] See pages 58–61 and accompanying notes 24–37.

probably encouraged the development of fragmented ownership over time. (The assumption that economic incentives have favored the development of current corporate structures is admittedly Hayekian in the sense that current structures are presumed to have evolved for beneficial reasons, unless proven otherwise.[147]) Alleged macroeconomic improvements that would be gained by closing the corporate separation of ownership and control are usually based on microeconomic theoretical models of "agency costs." The legal complexity of contemporary business enterprises, however, reveals these models to be too simplistic.

An exclusive focus on the bilateral institutional separation of shareholders and managers oversimplifies the revolution that has occurred with respect to the property organized in most large modern firms. Berle and Means traced the revolutionary change in enterprise ownership in large part to the increasing capital requirements of new technologies and the ever-expanding global reach of business firms. The corporation as a preferred mode of legal organization for business enterprise became dominant at least in part because it enabled the accumulation of large amounts of capital from a broad range of sources through "the dissolution of the atom of private property" and "the quality of multiple ownership."[148]

Given the concentration of very large business firms in the modern world, if "multiple ownership" did not become the rule, then a massive amount of wealth would likely be held either by a very few people individually or national governments. In fact, this highly concentrated ownership structure has become a social problem in many parts of the world in which a very few number of families connected closely to the national government exercise ownership rights over large corporate pyramids or state-owned enterprises, as discussed further in this chapter below. There is also an argument (not further developed here) that societies with more fragmented corporate ownership structures will become (or remain) both more egalitarian and more democratic than societies with highly concentrated and hierarchical ownership structures.

Rather than seeing the separation of ownership and control as an institutional illness that should be cured, then, one can view the business corporation with fragmented ownership as a positive institutional innovation that has allowed for exponential increases in the scale and scope of business production and distribution—with attendant economic efficiencies and growth, as well as corresponding risks and potential harms.[149] (Chapter 4 discusses the risks and harms of large enterprises and the legal liability rules regarding them.) Economies of scale "result when the increased size of a single operating unit producing or distributing a single product reduces the unit cost of production or distribution." Economies of scope are "economies of joint production or distribution" that result "from the use of

---

[147] See Chapter 1, pages 10–11 and accompanying notes 9–11.

[148] Berle and Means, op. cit., pp. 8–9, 17.

[149] For a comparative account of the rise of large corporate enterprises in Western societies, see Alfred D. Chandler, Jr., *Scale and Scope: The Dynamics of Industrial Capitalism* (Harvard University Press 1990), pp. 1–46. For other historical accounts of the rise of the business corporation, see Micklethwait and Wooldridge, op. cit; Novak, op. cit.

processes within a single operating unit to produce or distribute more than one product."[150] The historical trajectory of the development of private business firms suggests that in a modern world of globalized markets and mass production, many firms are likely to remain large, driven by big appetites for broadly sourced capital investment to serve wide-ranging demand.[151]

Seeking, like all the king's men in Humpty Dumpty, to put the smashed egg of private property back together again is retrogressive from an historical point of view, because returning to a world dominated by many small, lightly capitalized firms (or a concentrated minority of capitalist owners of only a few immense firms) is quite unlikely and perhaps impossible.[152] To a great extent, then, the specifications of shareholder empowerment and managerial ownership solutions to the oversimplified problem of a bilateral separation of shareholder ownership and managerial control are unlikely to prove especially helpful on a large scale.

The "multiple" and "fragmented" ownership structures of corporate enterprise beyond the simple bilateral divide between shareholders and managers is also more descriptive when a global perspective is adopted. The separation in large corporations between widely dispersed shareholders and centralized managers remains for the most part exceptional to the United States, Great Britain, and a few other English-speaking countries (such as Australia and Canada).[153] Even in the United States large firms today exhibit many *multilateral* dimensions of ownership. In addition to shareholders, for example, ownership interests in modern corporations appear in the forms of debt financing (which can itself become fragmented among many individual creditors), interlocking and interrelated corporate structures (such as corporate holding companies and pyramids), and the ownership of private property that firms create as entities and allocate in the form of retained earnings. Modern firms are thus usually better characterized not by a simple separation of ownership and control, but by a *fragmentation of ownership and control* along several dimensions. See Table 2.5.

Debt financing

One may begin a deeper analysis of modern enterprise ownership, as does Veblen, with debt. Bankers and other financiers loan capital to business firms, thereby

---

[150] Chandler, op. cit., p. 17.

[151] See Orts, "A Short History of the Business Enterprise," op. cit.

[152] But see E.F. Schumacher, *Small Is Beautiful: Economics As If People Mattered* (Harley and Marks 2000) (1975) (offering an alternative vision of the future that relies on a reconfiguration of human expectations and desires, as well as a radical reduction in average firm size). Note that even if one accepts that larger firms are inevitable in many fields (such as aerospace, automobiles, and energy), it is possible to imagine that many smaller enterprises may succeed in other areas (such as "artisan services" and local cooperative production). See, e.g., David Segal, "Economic Fix-Its," *New York Times*, November 28, 2010, p. WK1 (describing various small business solutions).

[153] See, e.g., John C. Coffee, Jr., "The Rise of Dispersed Ownership: The Roles of Law and the State in the Separation of Ownership and Control, 111 *Yale Law Journal* 1 (2001); Roe, "Political Preconditions to Separating Ownership from Corporate Control," op. cit.

Table 2.5 The fragmentation of ownership in modern firms

	Small firms	Large firms
Equity ownership	Ownership of firm's equity usually held by one owner-operator or a small group of owners (e.g. general partnership or closely held corporation)	Broad ownership of the "shares" of a corporate firm—often held in small or large amounts by public shareholders[a]
Debt ownership	Ordinary bank loans or supply/distribution credit agreements	Corporate debt issues that can be widely distributed and owned

[a] Broad public shareholding of firms is common mostly in Anglo-American countries.

creating contractually denominated claims on future earnings, profits, and cash flows. As Veblen observed, the importance of financial debt and credit in a theory of the business enterprise requires a reformulation of the understanding of the "capital" of a firm as constantly changing in terms of its financial valuation in debt and securities markets.[154] The legal rights to future payments on debt (including bonds, debentures, loans, and other variations) represent potential ownership interests in the firm.

Creditor–debtor relationships are best considered both contracts and property interests.[155] They are contracts, but also have property-like features. In extreme cases, namely, if and when a firm cannot pay the debts owed, creditors have rights in bankruptcy to seize the assets of the firm in at least partial satisfaction of their claims. The simplest example of a creditor's right to exert an ownership interest in a firm is a "secured" loan which is hedged by a legal claim to attach a particular asset owned by the debtor in the event of default on payments. Bankruptcy laws also give creditors primacy in making claims on general assets remaining in the event of the failure of a firm.[156]

Debt takes very different forms and is extended to firms by very different categories of creditors. Debt can be held privately or traded on public markets, and it can be provided by large institutional investors, wealthy individuals, or trade creditors.[157] In the United States and some other countries, "[b]ank lenders provide the bulk of financing for small- and medium-sized firms."[158] In Germany, Japan, and elsewhere, bank financing is also central to large firms.[159] Large corporations increasingly finance themselves through issuing their own corporate debt in private placements or public offerings.[160] In the aggregate, then, creditors of

---

[154] Veblen, *The Theory of the Business Enterprise*, op. cit., pp. 49–86.

[155] See Thomas W. Merrill and Henry E. Smith, "The Property/Contract Interface," 101 *Columbia Law Review* 773, 833–4 (2001).

[156] See Edward M. Iacobucci and George G. Triantis, "Economic and Legal Boundaries of Firms," 93 *Virginia Law Review* 515, 518–19, 524–34 (2007). See also Merrill and Smith, op. cit., pp. 833–43.

[157] See, e.g., Iacobucci and Triantis, op. cit., pp. 549–51.

[158] George G. Triantis and Ronald J. Daniels, "The Role of Debt in Interactive Corporate Governance," 83 *California Law Review* 1073, 1082 (1995).

[159] See, e.g., Mark J. Roe, "Some Differences in Corporate Structure in Germany, Japan, and the United States," 102 *Yale Law Journal* 1927 (1993).

[160] See, e.g., Triantis and Daniels, op. cit., p. 1083.

modern firms exert considerable influence, which may sometimes become the equivalent of financial "control."[161]

In this context, it makes sense to draw a distinction between *financial structural control* and *managerial operational control*. Control of the firm in an everyday operational sense refers to the internal relationships of agency authority and power discussed in Chapter 1. This kind of control is conferred mostly to executive managers. However, debt financing can also create highly powered incentives (via severe consequences imposed for default) on top managers to meet strict schedules for interest payments. In financial terms, increasing the amount of debt (and therefore increasing pressure on managers to service this debt) is often intended to reduce the "managerial slack" that arises from the separation of ownership and control diagnosed by Berle and Means.[162]

Post-dating Berle and Means, another "financial revolution" has changed the complexion of enterprise ownership with respect to the mix of debt and equity financing in many large firms.[163] Determining the optimal mix or "ratio" of debt and equity financing in a firm's capital structure has become a major topic in the finance literature as well as a preoccupation in practice.[164] This ratio expresses the amount of leverage in a firm. Increased leverage increases pressures within firms to generate higher cash flows and profits, especially over the short-term. At the same time, increased leverage may increase the probabilities of future bankruptcy and reduce the resilience of firms to exogenous risks and economic shocks. Following the famous Modigliani–Miller hypothesis in finance, which argued (though with various assumptions and caveats) that debt and equity financing were essentially equivalent in terms of economic valuations of the firm, the debt financing and corresponding leverage of firms has expanded. And the number of debt-driven deals involving mergers, acquisitions, and other kinds of restructuring transactions has increased, especially in the United States.[165] (Many leveraged deals in the

---

[161] The role of creditors, though emphasized in Veblen, was downplayed by Berle and Means. For a discussion of financial control exercised by creditors as well as by shareholders, see, e.g., Herman, op. cit., pp. 114–61. See also Triantis and Daniels, op. cit.

[162] See, e.g., Triantis and Daniels, op. cit., pp. 1074–6. Not incidentally, a prominent proponent of using increased debt to motivate managers refers to "the control hypothesis." Jensen, "Agency Costs of Free Cash Flow, Corporate Finance, and Takeovers," op. cit., p. 324. Cf. also Eugene F. Fama and Michael C. Jensen, "Separation of Ownership and Control," 26 *Journal of Law and Economics* 301, 304 (1983) (distinguishing between "decision management" and "decision control" in complex firms).

[163] See, e.g., Raghuram G. Rajan and Luigi Zingales, "The Influence of the Financial Revolution on the Nature of Firms," 91 *American Economic Review* 206 (2001) (discussing effects on firm organization of increasing availability of debt financing). See also Merton H. Miller, "Financial Innovation: The Last Twenty Years and the Next," 21 *Journal of Financial and Quantitative Analysis* 459, 459 (1986) (noting that "the word revolution is entirely appropriate for describing the changes in financial institutions and instruments that have occurred in the past twenty years").

[164] See, e.g., Iacobucci and Triantis, op. cit., pp. 543–59.

[165] For the original article, see Franco Modigliani and Merton H. Miller, "The Cost of Capital, Corporation Finance and the Theory of Investment," 48 *American Economic Review* 261 (1958). See also Merton H. Miller, "The Modigliani-Miller Propositions After Thirty Years," 2 *Journal of Economic Perspectives* 99 (1988). On the increase in U.S. corporate debt prior to the Great Credit Crash of 2008, see Nouriel Roubini and Stephen Mihm, *Crisis Economics: A Crash Course in the Future of Finance* (Penguin Press 2010), pp. 82–3. European banks were heavily overleveraged as well. Id., pp. 116, 127.

United States also take advantage of tax and accounting preferences for corporate debt rather than equity, which is separate policy question.[166])

A general acceptance of this open approach to debt and leverage explains the invention and use of high-yield debt (or, pejoratively, "junk bonds") to finance corporate control transactions as well as general corporate investment projects.[167] According to one scholar, junk bonds are "just another risky security."[168] Some real-world implications of following this debt-friendly financial theory, however, may yet hold surprises. Debt financing, by requiring periodic payments, is more rigorously enforced and less forgiving than equity financing (or the use of retained earnings) for long-term investments. One critique of some practical applications of the Modigliani–Miller hypothesis of the financial equivalence of debt and equity is that it may underestimate the systemic economic risks and costs of bankruptcies.[169] In general, there has been a backlash against the broad use of financial leverage in the economy following the Great Credit Crash of 2008, which may carry over to the use of corporate debt and the heavy leveraging of business enterprises.[170] But it is also possible that "business as usual" attitudes toward debt and leverage will return once the crisis has passed and been forgotten.[171]

A related critique of heavy reliance on debt financing returns to focus on the puzzle of the "equity premium" which has been observed for corporate shares as opposed to corporate debt over relatively long time horizons.[172] One explanation of the puzzle may be that equity-financed firms undertake long-term business risks in the face of uncertainties about future returns as well as the timing of these returns. Equity financing may therefore allow for greater risk-taking by firms in some situations of greater uncertainty than debt financing.[173]

Higher ratios of equity to debt may also enhance the resilience of firms in weathering systemic economic downturns.[174] For example, some finance scholars who advocated for greater leveraging ratios had criticized Ford Motor Company for

---

[166] See Martin Lipton, "Corporate Governance in the Age of Finance Corporatism," 136 *University of Pennsylvania Law Review* 1, 9–11 (1987); Merton H. Miller, "Leverage," 46 *Journal of Finance* 479, 479–80 (1991). See also Herwig J. Schlunk, "The Zen of Corporate Capital Structure Neutrality," 99 *Michigan Law Review* 410 (2000) (arguing for the elimination of favorable tax treatment of corporate debt as opposed to equity).

[167] See Klein, Coffee, and Partnoy, op. cit., pp. 254–5; Lipton, op. cit., pp. 11–13, 63.

[168] Miller, "Leverage," op. cit., pp. 481–2.

[169] See, e.g., Murray Glickman "A Post Keynesian Refutation of Modigliani–Miller on Capital Structure," 20 *Journal of Post Keynesian Economics* 251, 253–63 (1997–98). But cf. Miller, "Leverage," op. cit., p. 484 (1991) (arguing that from "a bloodless finance perspective" bankruptcy means simply that shareholders have "lost their entire stake in the firm" and creditors become the new equity owners).

[170] Cf. Roubini and Mihm, op. cit., pp. 80–5.

[171] See, e.g., Roger Lowenstein, *The End of Wall Street* (Penguin Press 2010), pp. 273–98.

[172] On the "equity premium," see pages 79–80 and accompanying notes 136–7.

[173] See, e.g., Ravi Bansal and Amir Yaron, "Risks for the Long Run: A Potential Resolution of Asset Pricing Puzzles," 59 *Journal of Finance* 1481 (2004) (modeling future growth prospects, consumption volatility, and "fluctuating economic uncertainty" as providing an explanation for the equity premium phenomenon). For other solutions that have been proposed, see Siegel and Thaler, op. cit.

[174] See Hyman P. Minsky, "The Evolution of Financial Institutions and the Performance of the Economy," 20 *Journal of Economic Issues* 345, 348–52 (1986).

holding "too much cash" in the late 1980s and early 1990s.[175] More recently, though, Ford has been hailed as far-sighted for its conservative earnings retention policy, which enabled it to avoid the fate of the bankruptcy and government bailout suffered by General Motors and other companies in the Great Credit Crash of 2008. Ford's corporate losses during the ensuing recession were only slightly less than the amount of earnings that the company had earlier been criticized for retaining.[176] Other finance scholars, such as Hyman Minsky, had warned that an aggregate expansion of debt and leverage may cause a general structural instability in modern capitalist economies.[177]

Regardless of the wisdom of increasing debt financing and leverage as a matter of policy, there is no doubt that enterprise-level debt has grown to play a significant role in the ownership structure of modern business enterprises. Enterprise debt cannot be dismissed as "merely a contract" in a legal theory of the firm.[178] Even though the legal forms of debt arrangements are mostly governed by contractual provisions, enterprise-level debt has legal features of *springing rights of ownership and control* in circumstances of financial failure or severe stress.[179] Enterprise-level debt carries a contingent ownership interest in the firm. The Modigliani–Miller hypothesis in finance carries over to legal theory to the extent that the financial interchangeability of debt and equity (and the real-world practices that have followed from this insight) confirms the view that the modern capital of firms is composed of both equity and debt. Although *managerial operational control* remains usually with the managers who owe their positions to the equity ownership authority structures of an enterprise, the effective *financial structural control* of large firms is now very often shared between equity owners and creditors.

The fact that debt securities have features of ownership has implications for the extensive debate in the literature regarding "shareholder primacy" in corporations.[180] Managers in heavily leveraged firms are probably better described as focusing on "creditor primacy," given their need to meet periodic debt payments with little managerial slack. But this does not mean that they may then abdicate fiduciary duties to shareholders as well as the corporate enterprise as a whole.

---

[175] See, e.g., Jensen, "Eclipse of the Public Corporation," op. cit., p. 76.

[176] See, e.g., Bill Vlasic, "Ford Posts 6th Quarter of Profit in a Row," *New York Times*, October 27, 2010, p. B1.

[177] Hyman P. Minsky, "Capitalist Financial Processes and the Instability of Capitalism," 14 *Journal of Economic Issues* 505 (1980).

[178] Julian Velasco, "Shareholder Ownership and Primacy," 2010 *University of Illinois Law Review* 897, 929 (2010) (describing debt securities as "merely contracts").

[179] Orts, "Shirking and Sharking," op. cit., p. 307; see also Merrill and Smith, op. cit., pp. 833–4.

[180] For a sample of this literature, see Stephen M. Bainbridge, "Director Primacy: The Means and Ends of Corporate Governance," 97 *Northwestern University Law Review* 547 (2003); Richard A. Booth, "Who Owns a Corporation and Who Cares?" 77 *Chicago-Kent Law Review* 147 (2001); D. Gordon Smith, "The Shareholder Primacy Norm," 23 *Journal of Corporation Law* 277 (1998); Thomas A. Smith, "The Efficient Norm for Corporate Law: A Neotraditional Interpretation of Fiduciary Duty," 98 *Michigan Law Review* 214 (1999); Mark J. Roe, "The Shareholder Wealth Maximization Norm and Industrial Organization," 149 *University of Pennsylvania Law Review* 2063 (2001); Lynn A. Stout, "Bad and Not-So-Bad Arguments for Shareholder Primacy," 75 *Southern California Law Review* 1189 (2002).

A more integrated and flexible conception of fiduciary duty may be helpful in this context. For example, managers and controlling shareholders should arguably have duties of "fair dealing" with creditors in addition to their obligations spelled out in contractual debt provisions.[181]

Modern practices of debt financing further fragment the ownership of the business enterprise. This extensive use of corporate debt builds on previous developments along the same lines that predate the separation of equity ownership and managerial control emphasized by Berle and Means. As Veblen observed, the extension of debt creates an interest of "absentee ownership" in a firm, and debt financing played an important role in the rise of the business corporation as the dominant modern organizational form.[182] Decades before Berle and Means, Veblen referred to "the time-worn principles of ownership and control" that included debt as well as equity financing.[183] The different and often conflicting economic preferences of creditors and equity owners have also been addressed in a long-standing set of technical legal rules governing the structure of different kinds of "legal capital."[184] Again, the conceptual line between equity and debt is blurred in practice with respect to such instruments as convertible debt and preferred stock.[185] Creditors can also exert elements of financial control on their debtors by inserting various governance-related covenants in debt contracts.[186]

The distinction between "debt" and "equity" remains salient for a legal theory of the firm.[187] The increasing creativity in the invention of financial instruments, however, suggests strongly that a sharp conceptual separation between methods of business financing does not make much sense. Rather than a bilateral "separation of ownership and control," a multilateral and fragmented "balance of ownership and control" has evolved with respect to the shifting capital structures of most large modern firms. See Table 2.6.

---

[181] See Victor Brudney, "Corporate Bondholders and Debtor Opportunism: In Bad Times and Good," 105 *Harvard Law Review* 1821 (1992) (arguing for the judicial protection of creditors, especially public creditors). For arguments favoring a fiduciary duties to creditors, see, e.g., Richard A. Booth, "The Duty to Creditors Reconsidered—Filling a Much Needed Gap in Corporation Law," 1 *Journal of Business & Technology Law* 415 (2007); Simone M. Sepe, "Directors' Duty to Creditors and the Debt Contract," 1 *Journal of Business & Technology Law* 553 (2007). But see Frederick Tung, "The New Death of Contract: Creeping Corporate Fiduciary Duties for Creditors," 57 *Emory Law Journal* 809 (2008) (recognizing this trend but judging it "worrisome" from a contractarian perspective).

[182] Veblen, *The Theory of the Business Enterprise*, op. cit. pp. 49–67. See also Tuna Baskoy, "Thorstein Veblen's Theory of Business Competition," 37 *Journal of Economic Issues* 1121, 1127, 1132 (2003).

[183] Veblen, *Absentee Ownership*, op. cit., p. 5. See also Herman, op. cit., pp. 63–5 (noting the importance of "financial control" of firms by bankers, financiers, and other creditors, as well as "the curiosity" that Berle and Means did not include this category in their empirical study).

[184] See Bayless Manning and James J. Hanks, Jr., *Legal Capital* (Foundation Press, 3rd ed., 1990).

[185] See Chapter 1, pages 25–6 and accompanying notes 73–6. For a recent examination of the particularly difficult case of preferred stock, which is treated sometimes as equity and sometimes as debt, depending on the circumstances, see William W. Bratton and Michael L. Wachter, "A Theory of Preferred Stock," 161 *University of Pennsylvania Law Review* 1815 (2013).

[186] Klein, Coffee, and Partnoy, op. cit., pp. 255–9.

[187] See Robert Flannigan, "The Debt-Equity Distinction," 26 *Banking & Finance Law Review* 451 (2011).

Table 2.6 The balance of ownership and control in modern firms

	Description	Examples
Managerial operational control	Top managers exert effective operational control over the business enterprise	CEO delegated broad authority by corporate board of directors; firms with relatively low debt leverage
Financial structural control	Financial lenders exercise effective structural control over the business enterprise	Highly leveraged firms; firms in financial distress or near bankruptcy

Complex firm structures

Complex corporate structures, in which firms can themselves have ownership interests in other firms, present further legal features to include in a theory of the business enterprise. Examples include the holding companies and parent–subsidiary corporations mentioned in Chapter 1, as well as corporate pyramids organized in longer chains of ownership and control (such as the *chaebol* in Korea) and interlocking ownership by corporations of each others' shares (such as the *keiretsu* in Japan). These structures separate and fragment ownership and control along another dimension. They use combinations of legal entities, usually corporations, to create complex firm structures. See Table 2.7 for a summary. Note that the account given here focuses only on several of the most popular methods of integrating ownership and control in complex firms. Historically, firms have also used methods to control multinational operations. These other methods include agency branches and separated family-owned business entities.[188]

Table 2.7 Separation of ownership and control in complex firm structures

	Ownership	Control
Holding companies	Parent companies own stock (wholly or in part) of subsidiary companies	Parent companies usually exercise structural control, though operational control is sometimes delegated
Corporate pyramids	Hierarchical ownership of several levels of firms (e.g. Korean *chaebol*)	Apex firm in pyramid exercises structural and operational control
Interlocking corporate ownership structures	Related firms hold stock in each other as a "family" (e.g. Japanese *keiretsu*)	Structural control is held by a group of firms (potentially as an antitakeover defense); operational control exercised by each individual firm

---

[188] See Gordon M. Winder, "Webs of Enterprise 1850–1914: Applying a Broad Definition of FDI," 96 *Annals of the Association of American Geographers* 788 (2006). Agency branches follow organizational agency principles discussed previously, and family-organized business often depends on family ties to coordinate control.

Holding companies and parent–subsidiary structures multiply corporate entities within a single firm. An integrated structure of multiple entities allows the holding company or parent corporation as the "owner" to exercise control over its subsidiaries. The purposes for creating these structures include limiting liability (discussed further in Chapter 4) and doing multinational business in different geographic regions (mentioned in Chapter 1).[189]

One common structure utilizes "wholly owned subsidiaries" with 100 percent ownership and control retained by the parent corporation. It is also possible to divide ownership interests by offering equity stakes to minority interests at the subsidiary level. Governments in some parts of the world, such as China and India, require foreign corporations to grant specified percentages of minority shareholder ownership rights to domestic interests or otherwise restrict foreign direct investment in a manner that requires the use of parent–subsidiary or other complex enterprise structures.[190]

For a number of reasons, then, holding company structures and parent–subsidiary corporate groups have become common and recognized worldwide. The extent to which corporations and their subsidiaries are fully recognized legally on a global stage, however, is a question that raises some major controversies concerning how business "nationals" of one nation-state should be recognized and held legally responsible for their actions in other nation-states.[191] For the most part, I leave treatment of these questions outside the scope of this book, though some issues relating to global corporate responsibility are addressed in Chapters 4 and 5.

Corporate pyramids employ legal technologies to create chains of firms in a hierarchical relationship in which the top firm exerts effective ownership control over lower-level firms. Berle and Means included corporate pyramids in their empirical analysis of U.S. corporations.[192] As they observed with reference to early examples in the United States.

In the effort to maintain control of a corporation without ownership of a majority of its stock, various legal devices have been developed. Of these, the most important among the very large companies is the device of "pyramiding." This involves the owning of a majority of the stock of one corporation which in turn holds a majority of the stock of another—a process which can be repeated a number of times. An interest equal to slightly more than a

---

[189] As detailed in Chapter 4, complex firm structures can be used to shield corporate parent entities as well as individual investors from liability. On multinational motivations for holding company or parent–subsidiary structures, see Chapter 1, pages 36–7 and accompanying notes 126–33.

[190] See, e.g., Matthew Sweeney, Note, "Foreign Direct Investment in India and China: The Creation of a Balanced Regime in a Globalized Economy," 43 *Cornell International Law Journal* 207 (2010). See also Detlev F. Vagts, "The Multinational Enterprise: A New Challenge for Transnational Law," 83 *Harvard Law Review* 739, 783–5 (1970).

[191] For discussion of some of the salient issues, see, e.g., Eric W. Orts, "The Legitimacy of Multinational Corporations," in *Progressive Corporate Law*, op. cit., pp. 247–9; Joseph E. Stiglitz, "Multinational Corporations: Balancing Rights and Responsibilities," 101 *Proceedings of the Annual Meeting (American Society of International Law)* 3 (2007); Vagts, op. cit. For the basic legal structure, see Yitzhak Hadari, "The Structure of the Private Multinational Enterprise," 71 *Michigan Law Review* 729 (1973).

[192] Berle and Means, op. cit., pp. 69–74, 183–5. See also Herman, op. cit., p. 65 (noting that this "legal device" often translated to financial control).

quarter or an eighth or a sixteenth or an even smaller proportion of the ultimate property to be controlled is by this method legally entrenched. By issuing bonds and non-voting preferred stock of the intermediate companies the process can be accelerated. By the introduction of two or three intermediate companies each of which is legally controlled through ownership of a majority of its stock by a company higher in the series, complete legal control of a large operating company can be maintained by an ownership interest equal to a fraction of one per cent of the property controlled.[193]

An often overlooked finding of Berle and Means' study was that 22 percent of the 200 largest firms in the United States in 1930 were controlled through a "legal device," such as a pyramid structure, as compared with the 44 percent of firms characterized by the more famous "management control."[194]

Other legal control devices developed in the United States include dual class common stock and voting trusts. In dual class stock, one class of stock receives greater voting rights than another. Voting trusts are agreements that transfer voting power from shareholders in return for a "trust certificate."[195] These legal technologies further fragment ownership and control interests in firms through different divisions of authority, power, and property.[196]

If pyramids merely involved chains of wholly owned subsidiaries, then they would not add anything conceptually beyond the separation of ownership and control between the apex firm and its subsidiaries. As Berle and Means explained, however, an individual or family who owns the apex firm in a corporate pyramid can magnify its controlling interest exponentially with respect to lower-level firms and the minority non-controlling interests in them. In other words, control is consolidated in one set of equity ownership interests and separated from other minority ownership interests. This feature of financial structural control through pyramids is the focus of increasing attention in economic research.[197]

Additional layers of entities within pyramids have implications for operational control as well as financial control. In turn, effective operational control affects issues of potential liability, that is, whether the entity of a corporate subsidiary can shield a corporate parent from legal liability for harmful actions. To the extent that a subsidiary is effectively an "agent" of the parent, vicarious liability for the parent should arguably follow at least in some situations.[198]

Corporate pyramids have become widespread throughout the world today. One study, using a 20 percent equity ownership measure of control and surveying the

---

[193] Berle and Means, op. cit., pp. 72–3. See also Randall Morck, Daniel Wolfenzon, and Bernard Yeung, "Corporate Governance, Economic Entrenchment, and Growth," 43 *Journal of Economic Literature* 655, 661–4 and fig. 1 (2005) (explaining "control pyramids").

[194] Berle and Means, op. cit., p. 109.

[195] Id., pp. 71–4.

[196] See Lucian Arye Bebchuk, Reinier Kraakman, and George Triantis, "Stock Pyramids, Cross-Ownership, and Dual Class Equity: The Mechanisms and Agency Costs of Separating Control from Cash Flow Rights," in *Concentrated Corporate Ownership* (Randall K. Morck ed.) (National Bureau of Economic Research 2000), pp. 295–318.

[197] For an introduction, see Morck, Wolfenzon, and Yeung, op. cit.

[198] See Chapter 1, page 37 and accompanying note 133. Potential liability of corporate groups is further discussed in Chapter 4.

top largest firms measured by stock market capitalization, estimates that more than one-quarter of the largest companies in the world are structured as pyramids.[199] This estimate probably understates the full extent of the practice, given that some corporate pyramids can exert financial control with much less than 20 percent ownership. The study also does not count privately owned pyramids that do not trade in public securities markets.[200]

Ironically, corporate pyramids have become relatively less common in their apparent country of origin, the United States. Although a complete historical explanation has not yet been given, it appears that various kinds of regulation have significantly reduced the popularity of pyramids in the United States.[201] In many other countries, however, pyramids are important and have grown to become dominant.

The *chaebol* groups of South Korea illustrate the structure and reach of contemporary corporate pyramids.[202] The largest *chaebol* are governed by a founding family (with some exceptions) and control an average of forty subsidiaries.[203] Hyundai and Samsung, for example, each embrace as many as eighty companies.[204] *Chaebol* concentrate ownership and control in the hands of relatively few families and individuals.[205] The top thirty *chaebol* account for more than 60 percent of total assets and more than 70 percent of gross sales of all listed firms in South Korea.[206] Even though the total percentage of family ownership of *chaebol* is often small (averaging around 4 or 5 percent), *chaebol* pyramids translate even small percentages of equity ownership into financial structural control. Cross-shareholdings within *chaebol* also increase the influence of founding-family blocks with corporate groups of related companies.[207]

Over the last several decades, Hyundai, Samsung, and other *chaebol* have been under government pressure to break-up and reform.[208] From 1982 to 1993, family ownership of the thirty largest *chaebol* decreased from 17 to 9 percent.[209] By 2001, the percentage had slipped to only 4 percent.[210] Even though the percentages of family ownership in the *chaebol* are decreasing, however, the magnifying power of

---

[199] Rafael La Porta, Florencio Lopez-de-Silanes, and Andrei Shleifer, "Corporate Ownership around the World," 54 *Journal of Finance* 471, 499–500 and tbl. IV (1999).

[200] Id., p. 475.

[201] See Steven A. Bank and Brian R. Cheffins, "The Corporate Pyramid Fable," 84 *Business History Review* 435 (2010).

[202] See, e.g., Christopher Hale, "Addressing the Incentive for Expropriation within Business Groups: The Case of the Korean Chaebol," 30 *Fordham International Law Journal* 1 (2006).

[203] Curtis J. Milhaupt, "Property Rights in Firms," 84 *Virginia Law Review* 1145, 1162–4 (1998).

[204] Sea Jin Chang and Jaebum Hong, "Economic Performance of Group-Affiliated Companies in Korea: Intragroup Resource Sharing and Internal Business Transactions," 43 *Academy of Management Journal* 429, 429 (2000).

[205] Milhaupt, "Property Rights in Firms," op. cit., pp. 1162–3.

[206] See Morck, Wolfenzon, and Yeung, op. cit., p. 668, citing Kee-Hong Bae, Jun-Koo Kang, and Jin-Mo Kim, "Tunneling or Value Added? Evidence from Mergers of Korean Business Groups," 57 *Journal of Finance* 2695, 2699 (2002).

[207] See Curtis J. Milhaupt, "Privatization and Corporate Governance in a Unified Korea," 26 *Journal of Corporation Law* 199, 205 (2001).

[208] See, e.g., Craig Erlich and Dae Seob Kang, "Independence within Hyundai?" 22 *University of Pennsylvania Journal of International Economic Law* 709 (2001).

[209] Milhaupt, "Property Rights in Firms," op. cit., p. 1163, tbl. 1.

[210] "Unfinished Business," *Economist*, April 17, 2003 (online version) (citing study by Jang Ha-sung).

corporate pyramid structures still allow these relatively small percentages to exercise substantial financial control in South Korea.

Corporate pyramids appear in other countries as well. In Sweden, for example, the Wallenberg empire exerts control through a complex pyramid involving a number of firms, including the giant ABB. Wallenberg-controlled firms account for approximately half of the total capitalization of the Swedish Stock Exchange.[211] Elsewhere in Europe, pyramids are also common. Figures for the financial control of the total value of assets of firms in European countries by the top ten families in each country range from 10 to 20 percent (with Great Britain as an outlier with only 4 percent).[212]

Pyramids appear to be especially prominent in emerging economies.[213] In Israel, pyramids link a number of diverse businesses under the authority and control of a relatively small number of individuals and families. According to one estimate, a small number of tycoons control the top ten business groups, which account for approximately 30 percent of the Israeli economy.[214] Other well-known and notorious historical examples of pyramids that have also exercised political power include those of Marcos in the Phillippines and Suharto in Indonesia.[215]

One economic explanation for the popularity of pyramids may involve their relative attractiveness and stability for financing new or expanded business ventures, especially in places with unreliable or sparse legal and financial institutions.[216] This argument suggests that the apex parent firm in a pyramid plays a financing role for new or start-up businesses that join. This "internal market for capital" offered by the apex firm in a pyramid may compare favorably with external financing options, such as from banks, independent venture capitalists, or public capital markets. Reliable external financing may lag most acutely in countries with the weakest legal and financial institutions.

A related argument advanced by Yoshisuke Aikawa, the founder of the pre-war Nissan *zaibatsu* in Japan, holds that pyramids solve "the capitalist's quandary":

If a capitalist uses only his own money or his family's money, his scale of operations is too small. If he taps public equity markets, he risks losing control. But . . . a pyramidal group provides the best of both worlds—secure control and unlimited access to capital.[217]

Another explanation for pyramids in emerging economies focuses on strategies of cooperation among domestic enterprises to compete with foreign firms, especially large multinational corporations.[218]

---

[211] Morck, Wolfenzon, and Yeung, op. cit., pp. 664–5, 667.

[212] Id., p. 667 (measured as a percentage of market capitalization).

[213] Chang and Hong, op. cit., p. 429. See also Mauro Guillén, "Business Groups in Emerging Economies: A Resource-Based View," 43 *Academy of Management Journal* 362 (2000).

[214] Ethan Bronner, "Protests Force Israel to Confront Wealth Gap," *New York Times*, August 12, 2011, p. A1.

[215] Morck, Wolfenzon, and Yeung, op. cit., pp. 696–7.

[216] See Heitor V. Almeida and Daniel Wolfenzon, "A Theory of Pyramidal Ownership and Family Business Groups," 61 *Journal of Finance* 2637 (2006) (providing a formal model of this explanation).

[217] Morck, Wolfenzon, and Yeung, op. cit., pp. 674 (paraphrasing Aikawa). The idea that access to capital for pyramids is "unlimited," of course, is an overstatement. As discussed further in this section below, the pre-war *zaibatsu* in Japan were organized as family-based business groups as well.

[218] See, e.g., Guillén, op. cit. On cross-subsidization of the Korean *chaebol*, see also Hale, op. cit.

Other reviews of pyramids are less favorable, arguing that they allow a few wealthy individuals and families to control vast amounts of a particular country's productive assets—with adverse economic as well as political effects. As one group of scholars who have looked closely at the phenomenon of pyramids argues, "entrusting the governance of huge slices of a country's corporate sector to a tiny elite can bias capital allocation, retard capital market development, obstruct entry by outsider entrepreneurs, and retard growth."[219] The influence of corporate pyramids on politics through the influence of the concentrated wealth of a particular family or an individual also triggers major concern. A recent study of the close connections between corporate pyramids and government in Thailand, for example, highlights this issue.[220]

An additional complication arises in some countries, such as China, Canada, and France, when state-owned enterprises serve as the apex firms in pyramids.[221] (The distinction between state-owned public ownership and private ownership of firms is addressed in Chapter 3.) These structures can further fracture what Berle and Means described as the "atoms of property" in firms and raise knotty policy problems, such as whether to allow state-owned firms to compete with private firms in markets for corporate control.

For analytical purposes here, however, corporate pyramids have significant implications for a legal theory of ownership and control of firms. Whatever their motivations (from the point of view of their participants) or merits (on public policy grounds), pyramids present "another form of separating ownership of capital from control."[222] They multiply legal entities in order to enhance financial structural control by an apex firm over a number of lower-level subsidiaries, which are then allowed to exercise more or less managerial operational control.

Interlocking corporate ownership structures, notably cross-shareholding arrangements, describe a related use of business forms to insulate and integrate groups of firms. The leading example is the *keiretsu* cross-shareholding ownership structures in Japan.[223]

---

[219] See Morck, Wolfenzon, and Yeung, op. cit., p. 657.

[220] Pramuan Bunkanwanicha and Yupana Wiwattanakantang, "Big Business Owners in Politics," 22 *Review of Financial Studies* 2133 (2009).

[221] See, e.g., Joseph P.H. Fan, T.J. Wong, and Tianyu Zhang, "Organizational Structure as a Decentralization Device: Evidence from Corporate Pyramids" (working paper, February 2007), <http://papers.ssrn.com> (accessed September 28, 2012) (China); Morck, Wolfenzon, and Yeung, op. cit., p. 666 (France and Canada).

[222] La Porta, Lopez-de-Silanes and Shleifer, op. cit., p. 473.

[223] See Curtis J. Milhaupt, "A Relational Theory of Japanese Corporate Governance: Contract, Culture, and the Rule of Law," 37 *Harvard International Law Journal* 3, 25 (1996). Two prominent authors have argued that *keiretsu*, though widely discussed and examined by other scholars, "do not exist" and "never did." Yoshiro Miwa and J. Mark Ramseyer, *The Fable of the Keiretsu: Urban Legends of the Japanese Economy* (University of Chicago Press 2006), pp. 2–3, 37. They argue that *keiretsu* relationships are an "urban legend" concocted by Marxist scholars and socialist journalists in Japan, as well as left-leaning (or at least uncritical) fellow academic travelers in the United States. Id., pp. 2–3, 53–60. This argument is considerably overstated. See Randall Morck, Book Review, 45 *Journal of Economic Literature* 763 (2007). Whatever one may wish to call the phenomenon, a great deal of corporate cross-shareholding occurs in Japan (though, as discussed in the text, it is declining). And this cross-shareholding helps to explain why hostile takeovers in Japan have been relatively rare—and why

Keiretsu ownership structures developed from the ruins of the family-based *zaibatsu* business groups that existed in Japan prior to World War II. *Zaibatsu* trace their origins to medieval merchant firms, which grew into large conglomerate enterprises. Some of the family names of *zaibatsu* remain familiar today (though now organized in modern corporate form), such as Mitsui and Sumitomo.[224] After World War II, the United States occupation forces banned holding companies in Japan (ironically, given the widespread use of this form in the United States itself). The objective was to prevent the reestablishment of the *zaibatsu* which were alleged to have had close associations with imperial Japan and military production.[225]

Keiretsu horizontal co-ownership is created through a network of cross-shareholding among closely related companies, with each company owning small percentages of other companies in the same group.[226] Neither holding companies nor pyramids, the *keiretsu* at first followed patterns of conglomerate organization inherited from the *zaibatsu*. A few of the famous *zaibatsu* families continued to do business under these newer, more decentralized corporate structures, such as in the Fuji, Mitsubishi, Mitsui, and Sumitomo *keiretsu*. Other corporate cross-shareholding arrangements followed the rise of new firms, such as Toyota, and organized along functional lines to include suppliers and distributors, as well as banks. These are the so-called "vertical" *keiretsu* (emphasizing the role of suppliers), though they retain the key *keiretsu* feature of horizontal corporate cross-shareholding.[227]

Unlike the Korean *chaebol*, the Japanese *keiretsu* are not designed to consolidate financial or legal control in one company, though some *keiretsu* groups include "main banks" which exercise significant influence over related companies.[228]

---

many managers of Japanese companies are arguably more independent with respect to their shareholders than in the United States and some other countries.

[224] Marius B. Jansen, *The Making of Modern Japan* (Harvard University Press 2000), pp. 119–20.

[225] See, e.g., Michael L. Gerlach, "The Japanese Corporate Network: A Blockmodel Analysis," 37 *Administrative Science Quarterly* 105, 108–11 (1992); Milhaupt, "Property Rights in Firms," op. cit., pp. 1179–80. In fact, the *zaibatsu* banks had at first resisted the Japanese government's attempts to force them to make loans to military companies on a preferred basis, but the government overcame this resistance by centralizing financial control. See, e.g., Franklin Allen and Douglas Gale, *Comparing Financial Systems* (MIT Press 2000), pp. 39–40.

[226] See Ronald J. Gilson and Mark J. Roe, "Understanding the Japanese Keiretsu: Overlaps Between Corporate Governance and Industrial Organization," 102 *Yale Law Journal* 871 (1993); see also Randall Morck and Masao Nakamura, "Banks and Corporate Control in Japan," 54 *Journal of Finance* 319, 320 (1999) (defining *keiretsu* as a "group of companies linked by stable intercorporate shareholdings").

[227] See James R. Lincoln, Michael L. Gerlach, and Christina L. Ahmadjian, "Keiretsu Networks and Corporate Performance in Japan," 61 *American Sociological Review* 67, 68 and n. 2 (1996). See also Gilson and Roe, op. cit., p. 894.

[228] Some scholars refer to Japan as having a "main bank system." See, e.g., Gilson and Roe, op. cit., pp. 874–5. For a challenge to the idea of the "main bank system" as another "myth," see Miwa and Ramseyer, op. cit., pp. 61–88. Like the *keiretsu*, Miwa and Ramseyer argue that "the main bank system" "does not exist—and never did." Id., p. 88. As a source of financing, however, it appears that Japanese companies rely relatively heavily on loans rather than other means (such as equity offerings or retained earnings) to finance new projects and development. See, e.g., Allen and Gale, op. cit., pp. 49, 51 and tbl. 3.5. This dependence on debt financing gives banks a central role in Japanese corporate governance.

Instead, the word *keiretsu*, translated literally, means a "headless combine." It is best defined as "a form of corporate structure in which a number of organizations link together, usually by taking small stakes in each other and usually as a result of having a close business relationship, often as suppliers to each other."[229] The *kieretsu*-related firms, one scholar writes, "tend to share with other firms in their industries the existence of stable, identity-based shareholding, lending, and trading relationships."[230]

Aggregate levels of corporate cross-shareholding in Japan are relatively high— especially as compared with countries such as the United States, where corporate cross-shareholding is banned for public corporations. The total percentage of corporate cross-shareholding in Japan has fluctuated historically: from around 20 percent in 1950, to a peak of around 60 percent in the 1970s, and then down to around 20 percent again by 2000. Most recently, cross-shareholdings by banks and insurance companies in other corporations have decreased significantly, and foreign institutional investment has been increasing.[231] The current situation has been summarized as follows:

Corporate ownership in Japan is characterized by "stable shareholders" with reciprocally held cross-shareholdings among corporations and banks. The largest single shareholder, which is often the main bank, does not typically exceed a 5% stake [a limit set by law] but the web of small reciprocal cross-shareholdings often account for 20% of shares and stable shareholders over 40%. These horizontal groupings form a dense and stable network of long-term relationships.[232]

Scholars debate whether or not *keiretsu*-style organization makes sense for the long-term economic performance of Japanese firms. On one hand, there is evidence that independent companies have proven more profitable than some *keiretsu*-related companies.[233] On the other hand, some observers argue that networks of cross-shareholding companies support and monitor each other.[234] At least some Japanese firms participating in cross-shareholding ownership structures have shown significant resilience and economic success over time. Examples include Matsushita, Sony, and Toyota, which have been leaders in their respective industries.[235]

---

[229] "Keiretsu," *Economist*, October 16, 2009, <http://www.economist.com> (accessed September 28, 2012).

[230] Michael L. Gerlach, "Twilight of the Keiretsu? A Critical Assessment," 18 *Journal of Japanese Studies* 79, 115 (1992).

[231] See Hideaki Miyajima and Fumiaki Kuroki "The Unwinding of Cross-shareholding in Japan: Causes, Effects, and Implications," in *Corporate Governance in Japan: Institutional Change and Organizational Diversity* (Masahiko Aoki et al. eds.) (Oxford University Press 2007), pp. 79–124 and fig. 3.1.

[232] Gregory Jackson and Hideaki Miyajima, "Introduction: The Diversity and Change of Corporate Governance in Japan," in *Corporate Governance in Japan*, op. cit., pp. 3–4.

[233] See, e.g., Lincoln, Gerlach, and Ahmadjian, op. cit.; Stephen D. Prowse, "The Structure of Corporate Ownership in Japan," 47 *Journal of Finance* 1121, 1123 tbl. 1 (1992).

[234] See, e.g., Enrico Perotti, "Cross-Ownership as a Hostage Exchange to Support Collaboration," 13 *Managerial and Decision Economics* 45 (1992).

[235] See Allen and Gale, op. cit., p. 16. One interesting empirical study finds that cross-shareholding by non-financial corporations increases value, but cross-shareholding by banks does not. Miyajima and Kuroki, op. cit. The latter finding fits the traditional view that the economic interests of creditors and

Whichever argument is correct as a matter of empirical economics and public policy, the point here is a descriptive one. Corporate cross-shareholding structures associated with the *keiretsu* provide a significant degree of independence to the managers of many Japanese companies.[236] *Keiretsu*-style cross-shareholding provides one explanation for the relatively rare occurrence of hostile takeovers in Japan.[237] In fact, a primary historical motivation for the development of *keiretsu* may well have been to defend against takeovers.[238] The U.S. takeover entrepreneur T. Boone Pickens learned this lesson the hard way in 1988 when he acquired a 26 percent stake in Koito, a supplier of Toyota, and then found out that Toyota and five additional "stable shareholders" controlled 63 percent of the company—and were not interested in selling.[239]

Debt financing by banks who are also equity holders may further enhance *keiretsu*-related defenses to hostile takeovers. Percentages of debt cross-ownership approximate those of equity cross-ownership among the six largest *keiretsu*. For example, Sumitomo-related companies held both 27 percent of debt and 27 percent of equity ownership in each other in 1992.[240] Because the financing of hostile takeovers often requires debt leveraging, banks holding debt that would become riskier after a takeover may be motivated to use their equity positions to oppose the takeover.[241]

With respect to the legal structures of property ownership and financial control in firms, the lessons of Japanese corporate cross-shareholding practices add another level of organizational complexity. Like the *chaebol* pyramids, *keiretsu* cross-shareholding structures tend to reinforce the institutional independence of the management of firms. *Keiretsu* interpose an institutional layer between the ownership interests traceable directly to individuals and collectively organized ownership. In an effective *keiretsu*, each firm is essentially controlled by all the other managers of firms in the group (which means considerable deference is shown

---

shareholders may often conflict. The authors predict that at least some degree of corporate cross-shareholding in Japan will continue. Id., pp. 118–19.

[236] In their critique denying the existence of *keiretsu*, Miwa and Ramseyer seem to adopt a narrow definition of "cross-shareholding" to mean only direct cross-shareholding between two companies or a narrow set of affiliated companies. Miwa and Ramseyer, op. cit., pp. 20–2, 35–7. They establish that other scholars have made overly grand claims for the influence and scope of *keiretsu*. But they do not appear to disagree with the main argument made here, namely, that a large amount of corporate cross- or block-shareholding exists in Japan, and this structure (along with related debt-financing connections with equity-holding banks) translates into greater overall managerial independence in Japanese firms.

[237] See, e.g., Allen and Gale, op. cit., p. 16.

[238] See, e.g., Morck and Nakamura, op. cit., pp. 320–1 (finding that "intercorporate ownership in Japan developed expressly as a takeover barrier," first with respect to independent Japanese firms challenging the *zaibatsu* and more recently as a defense for foreign-based takeover attempts) (emphasis deleted).

[239] See Lincoln, Gerlach, and Ahmadjian, op. cit., p. 70–1; Morck, op. cit., p. 764.

[240] See Erik Berglöf and Enrico Perotti, "The Governance Structure of the Japanese Financial Keiretsu," 36 *Journal of Financial Economics* 259, 265 tbl. 2 (1994).

[241] Hostile takeover attempts in Japan, however, began to occur in the 2000s—and some scholars predict that they will continue. See, e.g., Miyajima and Kuroki, op. cit., p. 119. See also Curtis J. Milhaupt, "In the Shadow of Delaware? The Rise of Hostile Takeovers in Japan," 105 *Columbia Law Review* 2171 (2005). But see Dan W. Puchniak, "The Efficiency of Friendliness: Japanese Corporate Governance Succeeds Again Without Hostile Takeovers," 5 *Berkeley Business Law Journal* 195 (2008).

to each others' leaders in practice). Given the prominence of *keiretsu* networks in the country, Japan presents "perhaps the most extreme" form of corporate "separation of ownership and control" in the world.[242] Yet Japan has been one of the most successful national economies in the world, despite a severe recession in the 1990s. Japan was the second largest economy in the world (following the United States) until China overtook it in 2010.[243]

Retained earnings

A final source of ownership of private property in firms reinforces a primary lesson from a review of various kinds of separation of ownership and control—whether in Japan, Korea, the United States, or elsewhere. This source of firm ownership goes by the accounting name of "retained earnings." The role of retained earnings explains how and why many firms can grow so large and relatively autonomous in their management and operations.

Retained earnings refer to the monetary surplus that a firm earns in profits after all of its obligations and periodic debt payments have been paid, minus any dividends paid to shareholders (or other equity owners). From the perspective of financial investments in new projects within firms, there are three basic sources of potential funding: (1) retained earnings (or "ploughback"); (2) issuance of new debt; and (3) issuance of new equity.[244]

Distributions of earnings as profits to shareholders (or other equity owners) are periodically made in the form of dividend payments or otherwise. Methods of distributing profits include not only cash, stock, or other "special" dividends, but also share repurchases, which usually increase share value.[245] (Note that tax consequences often determine the method of a profit distribution, or even whether a distribution is made, but tax considerations are not covered in detail here.[246])

By making these dividend payments and other distributions, firms deliver on their promises to make profits for their investors over time and also signal their overall financial health and future prospects. By withholding or reducing dividends or other distributions, firms risk losing the confidence of their investors (who are often trading in securities markets) and decreasing the economic value of the firm.

Managers may choose whether to retain and reinvest the earnings of the firm, rather than to distribute them, with great latitude. In the United States and many other countries, the discretion for managers to make these decisions is protected by

---

[242] Allen and Gale, op. cit., p. 16.

[243] David Barboza, "China Passes Japan as Second-Largest Economy," *New York Times*, August 16, 2010, p. B1.

[244] See, e.g., William J. Baumol, Peggy Heim, Burton G. Malkiel, and Richard E. Quandt, "Earnings Retention, New Capital and the Growth of the Firm," 52 *Review of Economics and Statistics* 345 (1970).

[245] See Robert C. Clark, *Corporate Law* (Aspen 1986), pp. 593–698.

[246] See, e.g., Franklin Allen, Antonio E. Bernardo, and Ivo Welch, "A Theory of Dividends Based on Tax Clienteles," 55 *Journal of Finance* 2499 (2000).

the very broad and forgiving "business judgment rule," which expresses a general principle that the courts will not second-guess managers' decisions regarding everyday transactions and investments. This principle extends to decisions concerning the retention or distribution of earnings.[247]

Because managers of firms typically possess broad legal authority to decide to retain and reinvest some portion of earnings back into the firm itself, the category of retained earnings furnishes an independent source of financing.[248] Managers may capitalize retained earnings as cash (sometimes as an "equity cushion" against expected future volatility in commodity or product markets). Or they may reinvest retained earnings in new projects, new employees (or raising compensation for current employees), and the pursuit of other legitimate business purposes. New projects may include the development of new products or marketing campaigns. Other legitimate business purposes may include political lobbying or even philanthropy. As discussed further in Chapter 5, the scope of business purposes and objectives is not restricted to economic projections of future profitability. For example, a "reasonable" portion of a firm's earnings may be devoted to charitable or philanthropic purposes, at least under the governing law of the United States and many other countries. Flexibility of business purposes is also afforded by "social hybrid" forms of business, which are also discussed in Chapter 5.

To take the perspective of the firm's shareholders (or other equity owners)—and perhaps the firm's employees and managers as well—one may argue that the retention of earnings is justified when (1) a reinvestment of these funds in the firm are reasonably committed to projects aimed to increase future returns for the firm as a whole (and therefore the wealth of its investors and other participants); and (2) the costs of accessing other external methods of financing the firm's projects (i.e. "the costs of capital") are more than the costs of using retained earnings for the same purpose. Whether or not a particular project is more efficiently financed by retained earnings ("internal financing") or the issuance of new equity or debt ("external financing") will depend on the specific firm and its specific circumstances.

An unresolved debate in the finance literature discusses whether, as a more general rule, internal financing underperforms external financing.[249] Despite

---

[247] See Chapter 1, page 41 and accompanying notes 150–2. See also Victor Brudney, "Dividends, Discretion, and Disclosure," 66 *Virginia Law Review* 85, 104 (1980) ("prevailing legal doctrine holds dividend policy to be a matter of managerial discretion or business judgment"); Daniel J. H. Greenwood, "The Dividend Puzzle: Are Shares Entitled to the Residual?" 32 *Journal of Corporation Law* 103, 127–32 (2006) (describing the legal foundation of the "autonomous corporation" in the business judgment rule and broad interpretations of fiduciary duties).

[248] See, e.g., Clark, *Corporate Law*, op. cit., pp. 594–602 (discussing dividend decisions by managers).

[249] See Baumol, Heim, Malkiel, and Quandt, "Earnings Retention, New Capital and the Growth of the Firm," op. cit.; William J. Baumol, Peggy Heim, Burton G. Malkiel, and Richard E. Quandt, "Efficiency of Corporate Investment: Reply," 55 *Review of Economics and Statistics* 128 (1973); Richard A. Brealey, Stewart D. Hodges, and D. Capron, "The Return on Alternative Sources of Finance," 58 *Review of Economics and Statistics* 469 (1976); Irwin Friend and Frank Husic, "Efficiency of Corporate Investment," 55 *Review of Economics and Statistics* 122 (1973); George A. Racette, "Earnings Retention, New Capital and the Growth of the Firm: A Comment," 55 *Review of Economics and Statistics* 127 (1973); Geoffrey Whittington, "The Profitability of Retained Earnings," 54 *Review of Economics*

some evidence that internal financing with retained earnings often underperforms external financing with new equity or debt, this debate remains "inconclusive."[250] Given the vast variability of firms in terms of their organization, size, business sector, macroeconomic conditions, and many other variables, it is probably unlikely that a single empirical answer can be given to the question. "Excessive earnings retention" has also been cited as at least one economic motivation for hostile takeovers of some firms.[251] But an objective measure of what amount of retained earnings is "excessive" remains elusive and controversial. In any event, it remains true that under current law in the United States and most other countries, decisions about whether or not to retain earnings—and how to allocate any retained earnings internally within the firm—are generally reserved to the discretion of the firm's top managers.[252]

The traditional justification for this intrinsic separation of ownership and control in the firm with respect to retained earnings and dividend payments (and other distributions) has been one of professional specialization. Managers specialize in the businesses that they run and are therefore in the best position to determine whether and how new investments in the firm's business should be made. Investors specialize in determining whether particular business enterprises are good bets to finance.[253] As the legal scholar Daniel Fischel has argued, the business judgment rule is "particularly appropriate in the dividend context" because managers are

---

and Statistics 152 (1972); Geoffrey Whittington, "The Profitability of Alternative Sources of Finance—Some Further Evidence," 60 *Review of Economics and Statistics* 632 (1978).

[250] See, e.g., Dennis C. Mueller and Elizabeth A. Reardon, "Rates of Return on Corporate Investment," 60 *Southern Economic Journal* 430, 430 (1993).

[251] See, e.g., John C. Coffee, Jr., "Shareholders versus Managers: The Strain in the Corporate Web," 85 *Michigan Law Review* 1, 22–3 (1986). See also Richard A. Booth, "Junk Bonds, the Relevance of Dividends and the Limits of Managerial Discretion," 1987 *Columbia Business Law Review* 553 (1987).

[252] An argument has been proposed for a law reform to shift decisions about retained earnings and dividends from managers to investors. See Zohar Goshen, "Shareholder Dividend Options," 104 *Yale Law Journal* 881 (1995). Goshen argues for a mandatory rule granting shareholders an option to declare payments of dividends to themselves from retained earnings, which he believes will increase pressure on managers to use external financing by issuing new equity or debt. For support, he relies on the finance literature cited above, which suggests that external financing is more efficient than internal financing (though he does not seem to agree with suggestions that this research is inconclusive). Id., pp. 884–5, 887–93. For a contrary argument that market forces encourage managers to set dividend policies optimally without legal intervention, see Daniel R. Fischel, "The Law and Economics of Dividend Policy," 67 *Virginia Law Review* 699, 715 (1981) ("[M]anagers have no significant incentive to act contrary to the best interests of shareholders in setting dividend policy. Any systematic suboptimal dividend policy will have negative consequences in the managerial services market, the capital market, the product market, and, if prolonged, may trigger a proxy fight or a takeover"). See also Frank H. Easterbrook, "Two Agency-Cost Explanations of Dividends," 74 *American Economic Review* 650 (1984) (discussing empirical difficulties of testing efficiency of requiring dividend payments versus other methods of distributions of profits to equity owners). Goshen recognizes the radical nature of his proposal. No court in the United States has directed managers of a public corporate firm to pay dividends (rather than to retain earnings) in more than a century. Goshen, op. cit., p. 883, citing Merritt B. Fox, *Finance and Industrial Performance in a Dynamic Economy: Theory, Practice, and Policy* (Columbia University Press 1987), p. 375. For further criticism of the shareholder dividend option, see William W. Bratton, "Dividends, Noncontractibility, and Corporate Law," 19 *Cardozo Law Review* 409, 450–7 (1997) (noting informational and enforcement difficulties of the reform proposal).

[253] For this general perspective, see Frank H. Knight, *Risk, Uncertainty, and Profit* (Signalman reprint ed. 2009) (1921).

usually "better equipped" to make decisions than "uninformed and inexperienced judges or shareholders."[254] Because managers need investors, and vice versa, ongoing mutual assessments will occur with respect to managers' and investors' decisions about retaining earnings, making new investments, and seeking new sources of financing at various costs of capital. One possible reform that may enhance the quality of this interaction would encourage and perhaps mandate disclosure by managers to explain the basis for their dividend and retention policies to their investors and other business participants. But this policy debate lies outside of the scope of the description presented here.[255]

There are a few exceptions to the rule that judges do not interfere with dividend decisions. In the United States, for example, courts may intervene when controlling shareholders of a closely held corporation withhold (or reduce) dividends and distribute profits only to themselves by other means (such as by increasing their own compensation as managers), rather than sharing these profits with the firm's minority shareholders.[256] Also, serious problems may arise when managers declare dividends for shareholders against the wishes—and legal rights—of creditors. Debt covenants and fraudulent conveyance laws furnish some means of creditor protection against these practices.[257] The general rule in most circumstances is nevertheless that dividend and distribution decisions for most firms remain within the discretion of top managers.

From an historical perspective, the legal framework privileging retained earnings has enabled the growth of large and significantly autonomous firms. Many modern firms, as well as the financial institutions supporting them, have become large and complex over time—as well as significantly independent—because of the organizational flexibility created by the combination of retained earnings and the managerial discretion to declare and allocate them. The long-term increase in the size and complexity of firms correlates with other historical changes, including new technologies requiring large amounts of coordinated capital, globalization of product and service markets, and organizational efficiencies of scale and scope. Evolving legal technologies, such as the invention and widespread adoption of the business corporation, have also played an important historical role.[258]

Reflecting on the historical development of large, self-organizing, and significantly "autonomous" firms, much of the *Sturm und Drang* expressed about a need

---

[254] Fischel, "The Law and Economics of Dividend Policy," op. cit., pp. 716–17.

[255] See Bratton, "Dividends, Noncontractibility, and Corporate Law," op. cit., pp. 464–8; Brudney, "Dividends, Discretion, and Disclosure," op. cit. Cf. Aaron S. Edlin and Joseph E. Stiglitz, "Discouraging Rivals: Managerial Rent-Seeking and Economic Inefficiencies," 85 *American Economic Review* 1301 (1995) (arguing that managers are in a position to entrench themselves using informational advantages). But see Fischel, "The Law and Economics of Dividend Policy," op. cit. (arguing that additional disclosure is unnecessary given market pressures for optimal decisions about dividends and retained earnings).

[256] See, e.g., Benjamin Means, "A Voice-Based Framework for Evaluating Claims of Minority Shareholder Oppression in the Close Corporation," 97 *Georgetown Law Journal* 1207 (2009).

[257] See, e.g., Clark, *Corporate Law*, op. cit., pp. 596–698; Franklin A. Gevurtz, *Corporation Law* (West Group 2000), pp. 152–78.

[258] See pages 73, 78–9, 83–4 and accompanying notes 102, 125–34, 148–51. See also Chapter 1, page 13 and accompanying note 22.

to close the separation of ownership and control misses a central point. As the financial scholars Franklin Allen and Douglas Gale observe, managers in "self-organizing" firms have historically developed methods of "cooperative autonomy" focused on a "farsighted concern with the success of the firm" as a whole.[259] Allen and Gale call for the development of a corresponding theory of "autonomous, self-financing firms."[260] The legal theory of the firm presented here is consistent with this view and provides an account of how these "autonomous, self-financing firms" exist over time and operate in practice.

The largest source of the growth of private property within these firms is self-generated by the firm itself in the form of retained earnings. Almost everywhere in the world, despite the different varieties of capitalism that are followed in various places, business firms have financed a significant portion of their activities and new projects through retained earnings.[261] Allen and Gale note that "retained earnings is the primary method of finance" in most developed countries, including France, Germany, Japan, the United Kingdom, and the United States.[262] Similarly, the business scholar Colin Mayer finds that earnings retention leads all other sources of new financing for companies in these same five countries. (Other sources of finance include credit and other short-term debt, trade credit, corporate bonds, and issuance of new shares.[263]) Mayer's quantitative analysis of these five leading commercial nation-states reveals "a spectrum of financing patterns in which retentions are universally the dominant source of funding."[264] In another study, Mayer confirms his previous findings. "Retained earnings," in his words, "are the dominant source of finance in all OECD countries."[265] In the United States, approximately 75 percent of new capital within firms is raised through retained earnings.[266] Bank loans are the next most important basic source of finance for large firms globally, followed by the issuance of new corporate bonds and stocks which play a comparatively small role.[267]

Mayer finds that different secondary sources of finance play larger roles in some countries than in others. For example, France and Japan rely relatively more on bank financing, and the United States relies more heavily on bond issuances than other countries.[268] But in all of these countries, retained earnings are the leading source of financing in firms. This is probably also true today for state-owned and -operated firms (which are further discussed in Chapter 3). Even though they often do not act

---

[259] See Allen and Gale, op. cit., p. 17.

[260] Id., pp. 341–73.

[261] On the contemporary "varieties of capitalism," see Chapter 1, pages 26–7 and accompanying notes 77–8.

[262] Allen and Gale, op. cit., 363.

[263] Colin Mayer, "New Issues in Corporate Finance," 32 *European Economic Review* 1167 (1988).

[264] Id., p. 1173, 1174 fig. 2.

[265] Colin Mayer, "Corporate Governance, Competition, and Performance," 24 *Journal of Law and Society* 152, 164–5 (1997).

[266] See Goshen, op. cit., p. 882.

[267] Mayer, "Corporate Governance, Competition, and Performance," op. cit., pp. 164–5. See also Colin Mayer, "Financial Systems and Corporate Governance: A Review of the International Evidence," 154 *Journal of Institutional and Theoretical Economics* 144, 156 (1998).

[268] Mayer, "Financial Systems and Corporate Governance," op. cit., p. 156.

independently from their political masters, many state-owned firms may have developed significant operational independence in terms of allocating retained earnings.[269]

An appreciation of the prominent place of retained earnings in the property structure of modern firms supports the need for a legal theory to explain "autonomous, self-financing firms."[270] Again, giving managers significant autonomy to make these kinds of self-financing investment decisions may result in positive long-term returns for shareholders (and other equity owners) as compared with creditors, thus providing a potential explanation for the "equity premium" that has been empirically observed.[271] Successful firms that generate significant profits or "positive cash flows" over time are able to grow from internally financed new projects—which may include expansions of new equipment, addition of new employees, and a host of other alternative investments in the firm's business. These allocations occur internally—usually in management's discretion—though with an eye toward reactions from investors (both equity and debt holders) as well as other business participants (such as employees).

This description of the management and capital structure of modern firms brings the analysis of legal foundations back full circle to an appreciation of the firm as a legal "entity" and "person." Reinvestments of retained earnings—as well as financing decisions of other kinds—are ideally made by managers who are cognizant of their roles to act on behalf of the larger enterprise entity and its long-term economic success as an institutional business person.

The complexity of firm ownership

In general terms, as the analysis in this chapter has demonstrated, the ownership of property in firms is not a straight-forward proposition. Simplistic assertions of a need to respect and protect "private property rights" are therefore not likely to provide helpful answers to contemporary problems of firm ownership configurations and the legal rules governing them. Beginning from an idea of the simple allocation of an individual's property or capital to a business entity, the ownership of property within most firms today has grown much more complex. The legal recognition of firms as "entities" and "persons" has allowed for a creative expansion and division of property rights and obligations within them. Participants in firms enter into organizational contracts to allocate these rights and obligations, but the laws of business enterprise condition and limit the allowable scope of these contracts and the potential expansions and divisions of property rights.

---

[269] See Lisa A. Keister, "Capital Structure in Transition: The Transformation of Financial Strategies in China's Emerging Economy," 15 *Organization Science* 145, 147–8 (2004). In China in the 1980s, however, the retained earnings of state-owned enterprises were treated as income to the state and were not available to the managers of a state-owned firm for reinvestment, though higher profits led to greater loan financing from state-owned banks.
[270] See Allen and Gale, op. cit., pp. 341–7.
[271] See pages 79–80, 87 and accompanying notes 136–7, 172–3.

In this connection, the analysis of modern features of "ownership" provided by the legal scholar Tony Honoré is helpful. He catalogs eleven "incidents" of modern ownership of a particular property denominated X to include the following: (1) the right to possession of X; (2) the right to use X; (3) the right to manage X; (4) the right to income derived from X; (5) the right to the capital value of X; (6) the right to have security against the government's expropriation of X; (7) the power to transfer or give X to another person; (8) the right to exert whatever rights one has in X over either a specific term or an unlimited time; (9) the obligation to refrain from either using X or allowing X to be used in a manner that impermissibly harms others, (10) liability for legal judgments that may be executed against X; and (11) an expectation for the reversion of various rights to X after others have been allowed to exercise rights to use or benefit from X over a period of time.[272] Considering these incidents of ownership in connection with the business enterprise (without tracing the implications in detail for each one of them) reveals the complexity of the phenomenon of property organized and held within modern firms. An appreciation of the range of these features of modern ownership is sufficient to show, for example, that the simple bilateral interpretation of "the separation of ownership and control" between shareholders and managers cannot do justice to the complexity of property relationships in most firms. In a typical, relatively large business corporation, the firm itself exercises rights of "possession" and may invoke rights against government expropriation. The firm's managers have rights to direct the use of the firm's resources. The firm's employees may negotiate for profit-sharing or equity ownership rights, as well as wages. And the firm's various investors have different rights to participate in profits through receiving dividends or interest payments over time—or selling their shares or bonds to others. Financial instruments can fracture and recombine rights of both ownership and control into many variations. In other words, the property relationships within large firms have become intricate and complex along many of the various dimensions identified by Honoré.

Berle and Means were therefore correct to call attention to a much more radical fragmentation of ownership in modern firms than the formulation captured by a bilateral notion of separation of ownership and control between shareholders and managers. The practical management and public policy implications of this revolutionary change are similarly much more complicated than attempting somehow to "re-unify" ownership and control. The modern world of firms is radically fragmented with respect to the ownership of property, and the law has enabled and even encouraged this fragmentation to take place. Again, modern firms have broken the egg of pure and simple models of private property, and nostalgic remedies proposed to reassemble it are very unlikely to materialize. A complex modern world of collective ownership of property and allocations of control within firms is here to stay.

---

[272] This account draws on Jeremy Waldron's description of Honoré's work. Waldron, op. cit., p. 49, citing A.M. Honoré, "Ownership," in *Oxford Essays in Jurisprudence: A Collaborative Work* (Anthony Gordon Guest ed.) (Oxford University Press 1961), p. 108.

Reprise on Foundations:
The Legal Complexity of Modern Business Firms

As a review of their legal foundations indicates, modern business firms are not simple. They are the product of social developments over time along a number of legal dimensions, including their recognition as institutional "entities" and "persons" which endow them with specific legal capacities and powers. In addition, individual participants in firms use and combine other legal capacities and powers when constructing and managing these institutional entities and persons, including especially the laws of agency, contracts, and property.

The law relevant to firms includes both power-conferring and enabling rules, as well as duty-imposing and mandatory rules. The law of business enterprise also includes more flexible principles, which leave room for the application of general policies of economic efficiency, political justice, and ethical fairness to inform the various legal rules and regulations, as well as judicial decisions.[1]

Through a complex process of legal recognition and definition, business firms emerge, take shape, and evolve institutionally. Through the use of law, individual participants in firms formulate their own private deals, private legislation, and private governments. At the same time, the public authorities of government (including courts) set the external rules of the game governing the private construction, management, and financing of firms.

An additional complexity arises with respect to state-owned enterprises and other ways in which the government itself can act as a direct "participant" in firms (such as in owning shares after a bailout of a private company). Although this book focuses mostly on the creation, management, and financing of privately owned firms, the legal theory of the firm advanced here is intended to reach state-owned and -operated variations of firms as well. In particular, Chapters 3 and 5 address issues related to state-owned and -operated firms.

In the legal process of various countries, both business participants and governmental regulators appeal to various social, political, and economic values. My

---

[1] For an explication of the relationship of legal rules, principles, and policies, see, e.g., Ronald M. Dworkin, "The Model of Rules," 35 *University of Chicago Law Review* 14 (1967). This relationship between rules, principles, and policies in law engenders significant controversy in legal theory—with "positivists" such as H.L.A. Hart, for example, favoring a closer focus on the limitations and precision of rules, and "interpretivists" such as Dworkin arguing for a greater role (admittedly often political) for principles and policies. I will not dive further into this jurisprudential thicket, however, except to say that the legal theory of the firm developed here should appeal to various jurisprudential orientations.

argument here is not to recommend a particular prescriptive legal theory of the firm following one or more sets of pre-selected values (such as economic efficiency, political justice, or moral fairness). Instead, my goal has been to describe the technical complexity and various normative dimensions that appear to be important for any modern legal theory of the firm to include. An appreciation of this technical and normative complexity can itself help to provide perspective for the tasks of both everyday managers and policy makers in deciding the future course of business firms.[2]

An account of the legal foundations of firms provides a starting point as well for further analysis of the nature and purposes of firms in light of contemporary social needs and challenges. For example, one might hypothecate that issues of environmental sustainability have become increasingly pressing for the world in the last several decades. If so, then the legal rules governing business firms (as well as private considerations by business participants within firms) should therefore be altered with these changing circumstances in mind.[3]

With the legal foundations of the business enterprise set in place in the first two chapters, there are several other topics remaining to cover with respect to law and the firm. Chapter 3 next examines the legal lines drawn between the "public" and the "private" with respect to firms. Chapter 4 treats the interaction between the recognition of business firms and another important area of law, namely, legal liability for contracts and torts (i.e. legally wrongful acts or omissions). The chapter reviews the application of principles of enterprise liability and limited liability by which responsibility for wrongful harms or injuries are legally applied (and sometimes restricted) to firms and their participants. Legislation is also often designed to require firms and their participants to take responsibility for wrongful harm caused by their actions (or their legally cognizable inactions) to others—or what economists call negative externalities.[4] Chapter 5 consolidates the legal analysis done in the preceding chapters to offer a nomenclature and taxonomy of different kinds of modern firms. Chapter 6 returns to consider the legal complexity of the firm with respect to the shifting boundaries of the firm, especially given the potential for selection of different legal forms. Chapter 7 offers two practical applications to contemporary issues that the legal theory of the firm developed here may help to address: corporate executive compensation and political free-speech rights of business firms.

As indicated previously, the answers to questions about the nature of the firm and the firm's boundaries given in this book will not please those who yearn for

---

[2] Technical complexity refers to the different kinds of legal rules that apply, and normative complexity refers to competing values informing the adoption and application of these legal rules, as well as other non-legal kinds of everyday business decisions. See Eric W. Orts, "The Complexity and Legitimacy of Corporate Law," 50 *Washington and Lee Law Review* 1565, 1574–612 (1993).

[3] For an overview of contemporary challenges of sustainability and their relationship to business, see James Gustave Speth, *The Bridge at the End of the World: Capitalism, the Environment, and Crossing from Crisis to Sustainability* (Yale University Press 2008). For an earlier contribution, see Paul Hawken, *The Ecology of Commerce: A Declaration of Sustainability* (HarperBusiness, rev. ed., 2010) (1993).

[4] On externalities, see Chapter 1, pages 22, 47 and accompanying notes 61, 179.

bright lines and simple definitions. Instead, H.L.A. Hart's admonition remains correct: the nature and boundaries of the firm depend on the nature of the question being asked.[5] And there are many questions!

Hart makes this analytical point not only with respect to business firms such as "corporations," but also other legal ideas such as "rights." In other words, descriptions of these legal concepts in practice are required, rather than beginning from abstract attempts at philosophical definitions. Hart follows the legal theorist James Bryce in arguing that some "fundamental legal notions could perhaps not be defined, only described."[6] This approach fits with some tracks laid out in contemporary analytical philosophy, following in the footsteps of Ludwig Wittgenstein. My argument in Chapter 1, for example, that firms are constructed as legal "persons" does not argue that firms exist ontologically as "real" in a metaphysical sense. Although a full philosophical defense lies outside the scope of this book, I suggest that the existence of firms does not rise to the level of scientifically or philosophically verified "natural kinds."[7] Instead the firm is probably better described as a concept embracing different variations of what Wittgenstein calls "family resemblances": "a complicated network of similarities overlapping and criss-crossing."[8] The remaining chapters of this book attempt to further map this conceptual "network" of meanings known as the business firm.

[5] H.L.A. Hart, "Definition and Theory in Jurisprudence," in *Essays in Jurisprudence and Philosophy* (Oxford University Press 1983), pp. 19–23, 31–3, 40–5.

[6] Id., p. 47 (citing Bryce).

[7] See W.V. Quine, "Natural Kinds," in *Ontological Relativity and Other Essays* (Columbia University Press 1969), pp. 114–38.

[8] Ludwig Wittgenstein, *Philosophical Investigations* (G.E.M. Anscombe trans.) (Blackwell Publishing, 3rd ed., 2001), p. 27 (remarks 66–7).

3

The Public/Private Distinction:
Two Faces of the Business Enterprise

Although some legal commentators and social theorists have argued that an analytical distinction between "public" and "private" categories is incoherent and should be avoided, the modern business firm and its variations cannot be understood without it. Some legal theorists associated with the Critical Legal Studies movement in the United States, for example, have advanced the view that the public/private distinction is unhelpful.[1] Karl Marx also argued against the public/private distinction in social theory.[2] In contrast, my view is that the distinction is theoretically necessary, even though drawing legal lines between "public" and "private" in practice is often complicated and controversial, both descriptively and normatively.

The public/private distinction and its importance for business firms

The long-term history of the business enterprise reveals that the rise of a "private" realm of life separated from direct regulation by the "public" political state (and its rulers) was a prerequisite for the rise of privately organized business enterprises. And the law played an essential role in establishing this distinction. At least, the rise of a private realm of social life co-evolved with the development of private business organizations.[3] In addition to its relevance for commercial life, the public/private distinction is important with respect to the legal recognition of individual rights of privacy, individual freedom, and other basic human rights.

The line between "the public" and "the private" first arose formally in ancient Roman law. In Max Weber's words, it counts as "one of the most important distinctions in modern legal theory and practice."[4] The distinction between "public

---

[1] See, e.g. Morton J. Horwitz, "The History of the Public/Private Distinction," 130 *University of Pennsylvania Law Review* 1423 (1982); Duncan Kennedy, "The Stages of the Decline of the Public/Private Distinction," 130 *University of Pennsylvania Law Review* 1349 (1982); Karl E. Klare, "The Public/Private Distinction in Labor Law," 130 *University of Pennsylvania Law Review* 1358 (1982).

[2] For Marx's critique and its relation to Critical Legal Studies, see Gerald Turkel, "The Public/Private Distinction: Approaches to a Critique of Legal Ideology," 22 *Law & Society Review* 801 (1988).

[3] See Eric W. Orts, "A Short History of the Business Enterprise" (unpublished manuscript, available on request from the author). See also Chapter 2, pages 72–3 and accompanying notes 96–102.

[4] Max Weber, *Economy and Society* (Guenther Roth and Claus Wittich eds.) (University of California Press 1978), vol. 2, p. 641.

property" and "private property," for example, mostly likely first appeared in Rome among those recognized as political "citizens" (which excluded women and slaves). Some ancient Asian societies such as China recognized only public ownership of land, and some very early Germanic societies recognized only private land holdings.[5] Most modern societies today, however, recognize both public and private ownership of land, though in different proportions in different countries (e.g. publicly owned national parks versus privately owned real estate markets). Extreme variants of Marxism that had advocated the elimination of all private property by substituting public ownership by the state have almost entirely vanished. At the same time, most nation-states recognize some land and other property as government-owned. If everything is not "public," then something is "private," and vice versa. The world is now composed of a complex mix of both public and private property.

With respect to legal theories of the firm, the line between public and private property distinguishes the large categories of "state-owned enterprises" and "private business enterprises." In turn, the predominant balance between state-owned and privately owned enterprises in a particular society determines its more general character, namely in terms of what I have called "state capitalism" and "market capitalism."[6]

The institutional reality in different modern societies presents a shifting mix of state-owned and privately owned enterprises, as well as hybrid forms that combine public and private ownership structures and purposes, thus complicating both descriptive and normative analysis. State-owned and government-sponsored corporations appear even in societies that are predominantly oriented toward market capitalism, such as the United States. These enterprises represent a blending of private and public interests.[7]

For example, Fannie Mae and Freddie Mac are large government-sponsored corporations run as public/private hybrids to promote housing loans in the United States, and they have been found to be responsible at least in part for the Great Credit Crash of 2008.[8] The government-funded bailouts of large U.S. investment banks and automobile companies during the ensuing recession provide another example of how the line between "public" and "private" companies is not tightly sealed even in countries that follow a strongly held ideal of market capitalism.[9] In the teeth of the financial crisis in 2008 and 2009, taxpayer-funded bailouts of large firms were endorsed by both sides of the political spectrum, first by President George W. Bush and then President Obama. In terms employed here, taxpayer

---

[5] Nancy L. Schwartz, "Distinction Between Public and Private Life: Marx on the *Zoōn Politicon*," 7 *Political Theory* 245, 251 (1979).

[6] See Introduction, page 4 and accompanying note 13; Chapter 1, pages 12–13, 19, 21, and accompanying notes 19–21, 46.

[7] See A. Michael Froomkin, "Reinventing the Government Corporation," 1995 *University of Illinois Law Review* 543 (1995).

[8] See, e.g., Gretchen Morgenson and Joshua Rosner, *Reckless Endangerment: How Outsized Ambition, Greed, and Corruption Led to Economic Armageddon* (Times Books 2011).

[9] For an account of the transactions, see, e.g., David Zaring and Steven M. Davidoff, "Regulation by Deal: The Government's Response to the Financial Crisis," 61 *Administrative Law Review* 463 (2009).

bailouts may be framed as an infusion of temporary ownership investments by the government in privately owned enterprises. These bailouts differ from nationalizations of assets with respect to the time period of government ownership (i.e. temporary rather than permanent). Nevertheless, at the peak of the financial crisis one estimate found that the United States government had become one of the largest shareholders in private enterprises in the world, holding more than $959 billion in assets.[10]

Other government-owned and -operated business enterprises in the United States include the passenger railroad service (Amtrak), the general mail service (U.S. Postal Service), and public radio and television broadcasting (the Corporation for Public Broadcasting).[11] In addition, national ownership and leasing of extensive public lands (for mining, timber, and grazing livestock) illustrate the large role of government in providing resources to business enterprises in one of the most private market-oriented economies in the world.[12]

On the flip side, even in countries with a strong orientation toward state capitalism, such as China, many private enterprises exist and prosper. Many of the largest Chinese firms in banking, energy, mining, and steel continue to be state-owned.[13] But China's rapid growth in the last several decades owes largely to policy changes and legal reforms that have allowed for the start-up and expansion of many privately owned business enterprises, especially in rural towns and villages.[14] Township and village enterprises (TVEs) and other small businesses have served as "the dynamos of Chinese development" over the last few decades.[15] Some scholars describe TVEs as "collectively owned" enterprises with local government officials running the show.[16] Closer analysis, however, reveals that most TVEs are

---

[10] Benjamin A. Templin, "The Government Shareholder: Regulating Public Ownership of Private Enterprise," 62 *Administrative Law Review* 1127, 1128 (2010) (citing U.S. Treasury Department statistics). For reflections on the government's legal duties to private shareholders in these situations, see, e.g., Marcel Kahan and Edward B. Rock, "When The Government Is the Controlling Shareholder," 89 *Texas Law Review* 1293 (2011); J.W. Verret, "Treasury Inc.: How the Bailout Reshapes Corporate Theory and Practice," 27 *Yale Journal on Regulation* 283 (2010); Matthew R. Shahabian, Note, "The Government as Shareholder and Political Risk: Procedural Protections in the Bailout," 86 *New York University Law Review* 351 (2011). For an argument that the financial bailouts in the United States are part of a long-term and problematic pattern, see Jeff Madrick, *Age of Greed: The Triumph of Finance and the Decline of America, 1970 to the Present* (Knopf 2011).

[11] See Ian Bremmer, *The End of the Free Market: Who Wins the War Between States and Corporations?* (Portfolio 2010), p. 65; Louis Galambos, "State-Owned Enterprises in a Hostile Environment: The U.S. Experience," in *The Rise and Fall of the State-Owned Enterprise in the Western World* (Pier Angelo Toninelli ed.) (Cambridge University Press 2000), p. 273.

[12] Galambos, op. cit., pp. 279–80, 295.

[13] Bremmer, op. cit., pp. 134–7; Leng Jing, *Corporate Governance and Financial Reform in China's Transition Economy* (Hong Kong University Press 2009), pp. 23–4, 51–2, 57–8.

[14] See Leng Jing, op. cit., p. 67, 69; Jean C. Oi, *Rural China Takes Off: Institutional Foundations of Economic Reform* (University of California Press 1999), pp. 1–2.

[15] Edward S. Steinfeld, *Forging Reform in China: The Fate of State-Owned Industry* (Cambridge University Press 1998), pp. 1–2.

[16] See, e.g., Barry Naughton, *The Chinese Economy: Transitions and Growth* (MIT Press 2007), p. 271; Dani Rodrik, *One Economics, Many Recipes: Globalization, Institutions, and Economic Growth* (Princeton University Press 2007), p. 87.

privately owned sole proprietorships, household businesses, or "alliance enterprises" (*lianying*).[17]

A partial reversal toward increasing state ownership in China has occurred relatively recently. The government has announced and followed a policy known as "the state advances as the private sector retreats" (*guo jin min tui*).[18] However, the expansion of the private sector in China over the last several decades has been "stunning," given a starting place at which private firms were entirely illegal in the 1970s.[19] Private enterprises are currently estimated to account for at least half of China's total economic activity and 70 percent of its aggregate employment.[20] In 2005, more than 25 million private enterprises employed approximately 200 million people in China.[21] By another measure, the share of industrial output of state-owned enterprises fell from 80 percent at the end of the 1970s to only around 25 percent by the end of the 1990s.[22] China is therefore probably best described as a "hybrid" state capitalist system that includes many private firms as well as a number of large state-owned public enterprises. In the words of one observer, contemporary China is a "hybrid innovation" in which some business sectors are "very much private" and other "strategic sectors" are "owned by the government."[23]

The fact that real-life societies and organizations mix "public" and "private" features does not mean that the public/private distinction is therefore dispensable. Again, distinguishing the public and private aspects of firms may often prove difficult, complicated, and controversial, but it is nonetheless necessary.[24] As the legal scholar Christopher Stone has maintained: "A good society needs a commitment that public/private *matters*, even allowing that the terms are destined, over time, to matter in different ways in different areas."[25]

The law demarcates "public" and "private" in many particular fields in a descriptive and prescriptive manner. With respect to private property, for example, lawmakers consider various justifications for its recognition and then fit current legal rules to meet what they see as the most convincing justifications in particular

---

[17] See Yasheng Huang, "Debating China's Economic Growth: The Beijing Consensus or the Washington Consensus," 24 *Academy of Management Perspectives* 31, 34–5 (2010); Leng Jing, op. cit., p. 69.

[18] Bremmer, op. cit., p. 144; Huang, "Debating China's Economic Growth," op. cit., pp. 38–41; Yasheng Huang, *Capitalism with Chinese Characteristics: Entrepreneurship and the State During the Reform Era* (Cambridge University Press 2008), pp. 109–74, 233–40 (describing "a great reversal" in Chinese policy).

[19] Kellee S. Tsai, *Capitalism without Democracy: The Private Sector in Contemporary China* (Cornell University Press 2007), p. 3.

[20] Leng Jing, op. cit., p. 69; Steinfeld, op. cit., pp. 13.

[21] Tsai, op. cit., p. 3.

[22] Yongnian Zheng, *Globalization and State Transformation in China* (Cambridge University Press 2004), p. 4.

[23] See Stefan Helper, *The Beijing Consensus: How China's Authoritarian Model Will Dominate the Twenty-First Century* (Basic Books 2010), pp. 123–4.

[24] See Weber, op. cit., vol. 2, p. 643.

[25] Christopher D. Stone, "Corporate Vices and Corporate Virtues: Do Public/Private Distinctions Matter?" 130 *University of Pennsylvania Law Review* 1441, 1443 (1982) (original emphasis).

situations.[26] The same is true for justifications of private contract law and its applications to business enterprises.[27]

The designations of "public" and "private" refer also to other features of business firms beyond property and contracts, including the rights to self-organize and various freedoms that are recognized in the workplace.[28] Another important dimension of the public/private distinction refers to the source of social control of an organization. This dimension refers to whether the primary source of discipline and oversight for an organization is government or economic markets.[29]

Last but not least, the recognition of private business enterprises as "entities" or "persons" with legal capacities and powers to act in the social world is also essential, as discussed in Chapter 1. Contrary historical examples, such as the Roman emperors who suppressed the private associations known as *collegia* or Mao's repression of private business firms in China, support this claim of the need for legal recognition.[30] Without these conceptual and legal features which invoke the private/public distinction, the business firm cannot exist or persist as a separate institution.

The public/private distinction spawns difficulties and controversies with respect to the business enterprise at least in part because it recapitulates the top-down and bottom-up views of the firm described in Chapter 1.[31] The public viewpoint emphasizes the social recognition and regulation of business enterprises as entities and persons. The private viewpoint emphasizes the perspective and prerogatives of business participants. These public and private perspectives will sometimes conflict and even clash, but the institutional theory of the firm described in this book allows

---

[26] See, e.g., Morris R. Cohen, "Property and Sovereignty," 13 *Cornell Law Quarterly* 8 (1927–8). See also Stephen R. Munzer, *A Theory of Property* (Cambridge University Press 1990), pp. 25, 88–119; Jeremy Waldron, *The Right to Private Property* (Oxford University Press 1988), pp. 26–59.

[27] See, e.g., Morris R. Cohen, "The Basis of Contract," 46 *Harvard Law Review* 553 (1933). See also Stephen A. Smith, *Contract Theory* (Oxford University Press 2004), pp. 3–53; Melvin A. Eisenberg, "The Theory of Contracts," in *The Theory of Contract Law: New Essays* (Peter Benson ed.) (Cambridge University Press 2001), pp. 206–64.

[28] See Chapter 1, page 21 and accompanying notes 54–9. See also James L. Perry and Hal G. Rainey, "The Public–Private Distinction in Organization Theory: A Critique and Research Strategy," 13 *Academy of Management Review* 182 (1988).

[29] Perry and Rainey, op. cit., pp. 192–4. See also Charles E. Lindblom, *Politics and Markets: The World's Political-Economic Systems* (Basic Books 1977); Charles E. Lindblom, *The Market System: What It Is, How It Works, and What To Make of It* (Yale University Press 2001). For research comparing private and public organizations from a managerial perspective, see Hal G. Rainey and Barry Bozeman, "Comparing Public and Private Organizations: Empirical Research and the Power of the A Priori," 10 *Journal of Public Administration Research and Theory* 447 (2000).

[30] On the repression of *collegia*, see, e.g., Wendy Cotter, "The Collegia and Roman Law: State Restrictions on Voluntary Associations, 64 BCE–200 CE" in *Voluntary Associations in the Graeco-Roman World* (John S. Kloppenborg and Stephen G. Wilson eds.) (Routledge 1996), pp. 74–85.

[31] See Chapter 1, pages 9–14 and Table 1.1. Cf. Paul N. Cox, "The Public, the Private, and the Corporation," 80 *Marquette Law Review* 391, 394–6 (1997) (recognizing "a long history of the tension between the public and private character of the corporation"). At least some of Cox's analysis maps well to the views expressed here. For example, I embrace a version of what Cox calls "the separation argument" that maintains that law creates and protects a "private sphere" that is segregated from the political state. Id., pp. 408–10. I also agree with Cox that a number of competing values influence the law of business enterprise. Economic efficiency considerations vie in theory and practice with other ethical values such as respect for individual autonomy and dignity, trust, and loyalty.

for a balance between these perspectives to be worked out through both legal and political processes (in practice) and policy analysis governed by different values and modes of thought (in theory). At least some zone of recognition for private interests and rights is necessary, however, for a conception of private enterprise to emerge as an institution that has become relatively independent of the political state.

As discussed above with respect to China, even societies that continue to follow a strong version of state capitalism tend to recognize many private enterprises today. Contemporary Russia provides another example. Of course, whether and to what extent private business firms are actually "independent" or "free" in societies that advocate strong state capitalist policies is an empirical question. At least, these societies should keep in mind the historical lessons of Maoist China and the Soviet Union, which imposed extreme versions of Marxism to eliminate or radically suppress private enterprises. These historical experiments of the twentieth century proved economically ineffective, politically tragic, and environmentally disastrous. Other authoritarian states that have fettered the free development of business enterprise have also generally lagged historically in terms of economic development, though the extent to which particular political systems conduce to development remains empirically uncertain.[32] One legal requirement for economic development that appears to have gained general academic acceptance, however, is the effective protection of private property rights.[33]

A deeper philosophical argument for the public/private distinction is that the modern institution of the "state" or "government" itself cannot be conceived ontologically without it. Again as Christopher Stone argues: "[T]he public/private distinction is not only embedded in basic doctrines, it seems inherent in every major issue of law. The objection to rooting it out is not, alone, that it would make government worse (which, beyond some point, it would), but that it would make government unrecognizable."[34] Without a designation of what is "public" and what is "private," everything counts potentially as "public" (i.e. totalitarian government) or nothing does (i.e. a radical anarchy).

The etymology of "public" and "private" reinforces the point. Public (originating from the Latin *publicus*) refers to the people or "pertaining to the people of a community, nation, or state." The original word for private (*privatus*) means "deprived or set apart, as in being deprived of public office or set apart from government."[35] A general distinction between public and private spheres of life has now become deeply seated in most modern societies.[36] Although different

---

[32] See, e.g., Adam Przeworski and Fernando Limongi, "Political Regimes and Economic Growth," 7 *Journal of Economic Perspectives* 51 (1993) (summarizing various studies and finding no convincing statistical evidence of a correlation between democratic regimes and economic growth).

[33] Id., p. 51 ("While everyone seems to agree that secure property rights foster growth, it is controversial whether democracies or dictatorships better secure these rights"). See also Rodrik, op. cit.; Amartya Sen, *Development as Freedom* (Knopf 1999).

[34] Stone, "Corporate Vices and Corporate Virtues," op. cit., p. 1507.

[35] Perry and Rainey, op. cit., p. 183; Online Etymology Dictionary, <http://www.etymonline.com/> (accessed December 11, 2012).

[36] See Stone, "Corporate Vices and Corporate Virtues," op. cit., pp. 1442-3 (arguing that the public/private distinction has become a "metalegal" notion cutting across many areas of law).

societies and systems draw legal lines in different places with respect to different questions in this area, broadly recognized zones of human activity have been marked out legally as either "public" or "private."

(Note that the right of privacy is a related legal concept with large consequences in various areas, though most of them are not directly related to the law of business enterprise. There are some connections, however, such as regarding the privacy rights of employees against employers' surveillance of their personal lives either inside or outside the workplace.[37])

The most important question is therefore not whether to preserve the public/private distinction, but rather where and how to draw the legal lines between public and private in the context of specific concrete issues. In terms of the foundations of the business enterprise outlined in Chapters 1 and 2 above, the legal recognition and protection of some level of autonomy for self-organization through agency arrangements, organizational contracts, and the assembly of different constellations of property are needed for private business enterprises to arise and flourish. At the same time as the law "enables" and recognizes these activities, however, it also subjects them to "mandatory" limitations and requirements. In this sense, all modern law is "public," even when it regulates private activities in a protective or enabling manner in constituting the rules of the game for private organizations and market competition. And yet all law is also "private" in the sense that it applies to govern the actions of individual people. As the sociologist Emile Durkheim describes this apparent paradox,

[Public law] is for the regulation of the relations of the individual to the State.... [Private law is for the regulation] of individuals among themselves. But when we try to get closer to these terms, the line of demarcation which appeared so neat in the beginning fades away. All law is private in the sense that it is always about individuals who are present and acting; but so, too, all law is public, in the sense that it is a social function and that all individuals are, whatever their varying titles, functionaries of society.[38]

One example of line-drawing between public and private appears in debates about "privatization," namely, a public policy determination concerning whether particular categories of goods and services (such as military services, postal services, or prisons) should be produced and provided by the "public sector" (government) or the "private

---

[37] For an early and influential treatment of privacy as a legal principle, see Samuel D. Warren and Louis D. Brandeis, "The Right to Privacy," 4 *Harvard Law Review* 193 (1890). For more recent explanations, see, e.g., Ruth Gavison, "Privacy and the Limits of Law," 89 *Yale Law Journal* 421 (1980); Daniel J. Solove, "Conceptualizing Privacy," 90 *California Law Review* 1087 (2002). See also Jerry Kang and Benedikt Buchner, "Privacy in Atlantis," 18 *Harvard Journal of Law & Technology* 229 (2004) (comparing contemporary U.S and European perspectives). See also Preface to the Paperback Edition, page x.

[38] Emile Durkheim, *The Division of Labor in Society* (George Simpson trans.) (Free Press 1933), p. 68. One theoretical alternative might be to argue that "private rights" with respect to contracts or property rely on "natural law" principles (either God-given or rationally objective). But I will not enter into this jurisprudential debate here, except to indicate that recognizing a distinction between "private" and "public" can be consistent with either natural law or positive law theories. Differences would follow in practice with respect to answering specific line-drawing questions from the perspective of different theories. For example, a natural law theory may privilege claims based on objectively grounded property rights more strongly than positive law theories which may emphasize the democratic law-making features of legislation that impinge on property rights.

sector" (independent business firms).[39] One may also argue, as does the legal scholar Jody Freeman, that there is a two-way street. Policy makers may consider enlisting the private sector to promote public objectives and values through various legal means. The end can be accomplished through the adoption of legal rules that either provide incentives for public-regarding behavior (such as government-bestowed awards, labels, or disclosure requirements) or mandate specific behavior while recognizing the fundamentally private nature of the organization regulated.[40] In any case—whether one is considering privatization of previously government-organized work or considering incentives to promote public values in the work of private firms—the public/private distinction remains central to the debate. To say, as does Durkheim, that all law is public as well as private does not mean that the public/private distinction itself is lost. Instead, the law becomes the institutional vehicle by which the distinction is effectively composed in theory and enforced in practice.[41]

Consider, for example, the current controversy about whether and how private military companies should be employed by governments for deployments abroad. The use of mercenaries is certainly not new, but the organization of military services in modern private firms has arisen relatively recently.[42] Private military and security companies are now among the fastest growing business enterprises. ("Company" itself is a word of military origin—deriving from the Italian *con pane* which refers to the bread that members received as a benefit of group membership.)[43] A watershed event occurred with the U.S. invasion of Iraq in 2003. By one estimate, one-tenth of the people deployed in the Iraq War worked for private military and security companies. By 2004, approximately 20,000 people worked for about sixty different private companies in Iraq providing military or security services under the auspices of the U.S. military and its allies.[44]

---

[39] See, e.g., Talia Fisher, "A Nuanced Approach to the Privatization Debate," 5 *Law and Ethics of Human Rights* 73 (2011); Jon D. Michaels, "Privatization's Pretensions," 77 *University of Chicago Law Review* 717 (2010); Paul Starr, "The Meaning of Privatization," 6 *Yale Law and Policy Review* 6 (1988).

[40] See Jody Freeman, "Extending Public Law Norms Through Privatization," 116 *Harvard Law Review* 1285 (2003).

[41] Whether or not one should recognize separate categories of "public law" and "private law" is a related but different question. To some extent, the recognition of private rights in commercial life will lead to categories of regulation applicable to these activities that are separable from the public regulation of government. However, as Durkheim observed in the passage quoted in the text, most if not all law has both public and private aspects. It is therefore not likely that a jurisprudential separation between "public law" and "private law" can be strictly maintained. But see Randy E. Barnett, "Foreword: Four Senses of the Public Law–Private Law Distinction," 9 *Harvard Journal of Law and Public Policy* 267 (1986) (suggesting categories of this distinction with respect to litigants, standards, subjects, and enforcement).

[42] See, e.g., Deborah Avant, "Mercenaries," 143 *Foreign Policy* 20, 20–1 (2004); David Shearer, "Outsourcing War," 112 *Foreign Policy* 68, 69–70 (1998); Juan Carlos Zarate, "The Emergence of a New Dog of War: Private International Security Companies, International Law, and the New World Disorder," 34 *Stanford Journal of International Law* 75, 81–116 (1998). For an overview, see also Janice E. Thomson, *Mercenaries, Pirates, and Sovereigns: State-Building and Extraterritorial Violence in Early Modern Europe* (Princeton University Press 1994).

[43] P.W. Singer, *Corporate Warriors: The Rise of the Privatized Military Industry* (Cornell University Press 2003), p. 24. See also James R. Davis, *Fortune's Warriors: Private Armies and the New World Order* (Douglas and McIntyre 2002).

[44] Deborah D. Avant, *The Market for Force: The Consequences of Privatizing Security* (Cambridge University Press 2005), pp. 1–2.

Controversy surrounds the use and even the existence of these kinds of companies with respect to the line that should be observed between "public" and "private." On one hand, private military companies have been defended on the grounds that private organization of military power is likely to provide economic efficiencies that will make fighting wars cheaper for the governments that engage in them. Whether or not private military companies are justifiable or not would then depend on whether the war or other military action using these companies was sponsored by a government with "just cause."[45] On the other hand, the privatization of military force raises political concerns related to questions of democratic control of governmental commitments to warfare and moral concerns about corporate profitability tied to a need for violent engagements to continue (or begin). "War is far too important," as one scholar argues, "to be left to private industry."[46] Other scholars concur in this assessment that private military companies pose dangers with respect to principles and values of democracy and transparency.[47] A related concern appears in the potential use of private military or security companies not by governments, but by other private companies—such as mining, oil, or other natural resources companies seeking to maintain control of particular geographical areas and populations.

The main point here, however, is not to attempt to resolve these difficult issues involving private military companies on the merits. Instead, the example of the creation and use of private military companies highlights the salience of the public/private distinction. If some scope of recognition for private military companies is allowed, then the question of the appropriate legal lines to draw with respect to their public regulation and oversight comes directly into play.[48]

Two challenges: indeterminacy and structural critiques

Critics of the public/private distinction offer two general objections. First, some scholars argue that the public/private distinction is insufficient to support modern legal analysis because private and government institutions have become so integrated

---

[45] For this view, though recognizing the need for some public regulation, see Shearer, op. cit. See also Scott M. Sullivan, "Private Force/Public Goods," 42 *Connecticut Law Review* 853 (2010); Zarate, op. cit., pp. 148–53. On "just war" theory, see Michael Walzer, *Just and Unjust Wars: A Moral Argument with Historical Illustrations* (Basic Books, 4th ed., 2006).

[46] Singer, *Corporate Warriors*, op. cit., p. 242.

[47] See Avant, "Mercenaries," op. cit.; Martha Minow, "Outsourcing Power: How Privatizing Military Efforts Challenges Accountability, Professionalism, and Democracy," 46 *Boston College Law Review* 989 (2005). See also Eric W. Orts, "War and the Business Corporation," 35 *Vanderbilt Journal of Transnational Law* 549 (2002).

[48] See Laura A. Dickinson, "Public Law Values in a Privatized World," 31 *Yale Journal of International Law* 383 (2006); Oliver R. Jones, "Implausible Deniability: State Responsibility for the Actions of Private Military Firms," 24 *Connecticut Journal of International Law* 239 (2009); Jackson Nyamuya Maogoto and Benedict Sheehy, "Private Military Companies and International Law: Building New Ladders of Legal Accountability and Responsibility," 11 *Cardozo Journal of Conflict Resolution* 99 (2009); Minow, op. cit.; P.W. Singer, "War, Profits, and the Vacuum of Law: Privatized Military Firms and International Law," 42 *Columbia Journal of Transnational Law* 521 (2004); Zarate, op. cit.

and interrelated that attempting to derive and apply different rules to "public" or "private" institutions or persons is impracticable.[49] This argument against the public/private distinction is based at least in part on a more general claim of legal "indeterminacy."[50]

Yet it is not at all clear that a distinction must resolve all controversies and provide fully "determined" legal results to be useful. Even if one agrees that the law itself is radically indeterminate, this simply means that the social construction of law (i.e. what is "legal" or "illegal") must refer to other values and purposes that are found outside of various legal systems. In other words, law is often substantively open to the influence of other social norms and values as well as systemically closed with respect to its own legal processes and procedures.[51] The interaction among legal systems and other values from the worlds of economics, ethics, and politics (as well as the interaction of different legal systems with each other) is complex sociologically and as matter of jurisprudence. But it is sufficient for the purposes of this book to point out that indeterminacy is not a fatal charge to a legal distinction or principle, including the public/private distinction. "Indeterminacy" is rather a simple recognition of the inevitable reality of social change and evolution in the law.[52]

Ruth Gavison, an advocate for preserving the public/private distinction in feminist legal theory, makes this general point.[53] Arguing in favor of "privacy" or "private rights" in some circumstances—for example, to ban sexual harassment in the workplace or to forbid certain kinds of personal questions when interviewing for a new hire—is often analogous to arguing in favor of general principles such as "democracy."[54] The fact that a generalized value is difficult to apply in practice does not mean that the value should be discarded. Instead, the value or principle may be considered along with various legal materials as well as other values and principles when deciding a particular case or enacting a statute.

To give another example: consider whether employees should possess "public" rights of free speech in "private" workplaces and, if so, to what extent.[55] The

---

[49] See, e.g., Carol Harlow, "'Public' and 'Private' Law: Definition without Distinction," 43 *Modern Law Review* 241 (1980); Kennedy, op. cit.; Klare, op. cit. See also A. Claire Cutler, "Artifice, Ideology and Paradox: The Public/Private Distinction in International Law," 4 *Review of International Political Economy* 261, 273–5 (1997).

[50] See Gunther Teubner, "'And God Laughed...' Indeterminacy, Self-Reference and Paradox in Law," 12 *German Law Journal* 376, 381–2 (2011). For a defense that law is "determinate" in many respects, see Kent Greenawalt, *Law and Objectivity* (Oxford University Press 1992).

[51] For a statement of this position, see Teubner, op. cit., pp. 388–94.

[52] For an argument recognizing the indeterminacy of law but arguing for legal methods of interacting with other social institutions to increase legal determinacy, see Michael C. Dorf, "Legal Indeterminacy and Institutional Design," 78 *New York University Law Review* 875 (2003). Increasing legal determinacy and stability of expectations about legal rules is valuable, however, only if it serves some social values (such as commercial predictability) that are more important than other competing values (such as a need for change to address new social challenges).

[53] Ruth Gavison, "Feminism and the Public/Private Distinction," 45 *Stanford Law Review* 1 (1992).

[54] Id., pp. 12–13. Other feminist legal theorists argue against recognizing this distinction at least in some legal contexts. See, e.g., Frances Olsen, "Constitutional Law: Feminist Critiques of the Public/Private Distinction," 10 *Constitutional Commentary* 319 (1993).

[55] See, e.g., Robert F. Ladenson, "Free Speech in the Workplace and the Public–Private Distinction," 7 *Law and Philosophy* 247 (1988–89). Cf. also Tara J. Radin and Patricia H. Werhane, "The

concepts of "public" and "private" themselves do not resolve these kinds of controversies (and often must be compared with or balanced against other values or institutional goals), but they nonetheless refer to important social values that deserve to be taken seriously when deciding particular cases and when deriving legal rules and principles to apply to various situations.

The general indeterminacy argument against the public/private distinction in a legal theory of the firm therefore fails. Balancing "public" and "private" considerations in different situations is often conceptually and practically difficult as well as uncertain, but this fact does not supply a convincing argument to dismiss the distinction as useless. Instead, public-related values (such as the right to participate in democratic government) will sometimes trump private-related ones (such as the right to use and manage one's own property)—and vice versa.

A second criticism of the public/private distinction claims, following Marx, that recognizing private rights, especially in a business context, privileges one particular class of people (i.e. those who have property or "employers") against another class of people (i.e. those without property or "workers").[56] As the legal scholar Louis Seidman describes this argument,

Some critical scholars argued that reliance on legal rights was harmful. Liberal rights both grew out of, and reinforced, the public–private distinction. . . . Liberal rights were almost always conceptualized as claims by private persons against the state, rather than as claims to state resources to combat private oppression. Claims to . . . rights therefore both ignored and obfuscated the extent to which the private sphere was, itself, constructed by public decisions. This failure to detect state responsibility had the effect of taking off the table constitutional claims to radical redistribution of "private" resources and power.[57]

As Seidman explains, this is a "structural" argument of a Marxian variety that emphasizes the political determinism of economic class and political hierarchy. This argument is distinct from the previously considered "indeterminacy" argument that emphasizes the flexibility of political and legal interpretation.[58]

The "structural" objection to the public/private distinction presumes to follow a highly dubious bilateral class analysis. Marx's theory of history posited an enduring "class struggle" between the "haves" and "have nots," and it postulated "two great hostile camps . . . directly facing each other: Bourgeoisie and Proletariat."[59] But this bilateral Marxian view of social class and class conflict has been shown to be much too simplistic. The main objection is that social classes in modern societies are

Public/Private Distinction and the Political Status of Employment," 34 *American Business Law Journal* 245 (1996) (discussing other "public" issues such as the "employment at will" doctrine allowing for the discharge of employees without cause in private firms).

[56] See, e.g., Cutler, op. cit., pp. 262–4, 276–7; Klare, op. cit., pp. 1358–61, 1415–18; Betty Mensch and Alan Freeman, "Liberalism's Public–Private Split," 3 *Tikkun* 24, 25–6 (1988).

[57] Louis Michael Seidman, "Critical Constitutionalism Now," 75 *Fordham Law Review* 575, 578 (2006).

[58] Id., pp. 578–9.

[59] Karl Marx and Friedrich Engels, "Manifesto of the Communist Party," in *The Marx–Engels Reader* (Robert C. Tucker ed.) (W.W. Norton, 2nd ed., 1978), pp. 474. See also Robert C. Tucker, *The Marxian Revolutionary Idea* (W.W. Norton 1969), pp. 6–17.

much less cohesive and much more variable than a traditional Marxian analysis allows.[60] Instead of a bilateral class structure, it is more accurate to say that modern global society consists of "one great hierarchy of employment" (and also, it should be added, unemployment—given that Marx's category of a *lumpenproletariat* persists).[61] Friedrich Hayak warned against analytical oversimplification regarding "classes":

> We are in general far too likely to think of incomes within a given trade or profession as more or less uniform. But the differences between the incomes, not only of the most and the least successful doctor or architect, writer or movie actor, boxer or jockey, but also of the more and the less successful plumber or market gardener, grocer or tailor, are as great as those between the propertied and the propertyless classes.[62]

The analytical weakness of Marxian class analysis does not mean that major social issues such as radical inequality in the distribution of wealth or large-scale unemployment and poverty do not remain relevant and important. However, this weakness undermines the claim that the public/private distinction depends on an ideological preference for "private" interests of the wealthy against the "public" interests of the poor.

Nevertheless, a primary motivation for the structural challenge to the public/private distinction seems to be a legitimate concern that the invocation of a private right (especially in terms of private property and contracts) is a show-stopper with respect to further policy analysis or reform. As mentioned in Chapter 1, there have been times in U.S. constitutional history when the Supreme Court privileged rights to property and freedom of contract over other forms of modern legislation designed to protect employees and others.[63] The structural critics of the public/private distinction worry that the recognition of private rights of property or contract will lead to similar extreme results. They are concerned that a preoccupation with private rights will prevent the development of public regulation that will alter the rules of the game in business with respect to such issues as protecting the environment, protecting investors, and protecting employees, as well as issues regarding the regulation of the influence of business interests in politics.

A classical Marxist version of this argument maintains that the capitalist class inevitably dominates the political and legal process through its ownership of "the means of production."[64] The extent of political influence exerted by the interests of business is important to consider and, speaking normatively, to limit legally and

---

[60] For accounts supporting this view, see Ralf Dahrendorf, *Class and Class Conflict in Industrial Society* (Stanford University Press 1959); Terry Nichols Clark and Seymour Martin Lipset, "Are Social Classes Dying?," in *The Breakdown of Class Politics: A Debate on Post-Industrial Stratification* (Terry Nichols Clark and Seymour Martin Lipset eds.) (Johns Hopkins University Press 2001), pp. 39–54.

[61] Friedrich A. Hayek, *The Constitution of Liberty* (University of Chicago Press 1960), p. 119.

[62] Friedrich A. Hayek, *The Road to Serfdom: Text and Documents* (Bruce Caldwell ed.) (University of Chicago Press 2007) (1944), p. 141. For an overview of some the relevant academic literature, see Andrew Abbott, "The Sociology of Work and Occupations," 19 *Annual Review of Sociology* 187 (1993).

[63] See Chapter 1, page 22 and accompanying note 60.

[64] See, e.g., Karl Marx, "The German Ideology" and "Wage Labour and Capital," in *The Marx-Engels Reader*, op. cit., pp. 149–63, 207–17.

perhaps even constitutionally. (This is one reason that the *Citizens United* case, discussed further in Chapter 7, is so important.) But the Marxist assumption of the inevitability of capitalist domination of government (as well as its prescription of revolution and the nationalization of all productive property) is rejected here as too simplistic, too extreme, and lacking in empirical foundation. One might also observe that the revolutionary fragmentation of business property enabled by the invention of modern corporations and the development of securities markets as well as institutional investors (including mutual funds and pension funds) has significantly complicated Marx's account of the "ownership" of the means of production.[65] In at least in some modern economies, corporate ownership has been broadened considerably to include a much greater percentage of people in society than in the nineteenth century.[66]

Against the structural critique of the private/private distinction, one may also argue in favor of "worker's rights," for example, as opposed to traditional "property rights" or "contract rights" of owners. This argument stays within and in fact depends on the framework of the public/private distinction. Arguments invoking private rights may favor different groups that have historically had less influence (such as employees or dispersed shareholders) as well as groups that have usually held greater social power (such as top managers or wealthy owners). To recognize and use the public/private distinction does not foreordain the results of policy analysis or political argument on particular questions. Unless one is willing to go as far as Marx and deny any zone of legal coverage to private rights, the more moderate position adopted here seems preferable and more persuasive, namely: to recognize the legal distinction between public and private as salient—and then to allow and encourage policy debates with respect to where the lines should be drawn. Perhaps some legal lines should also be drawn more deeply in the social fabric than others, such as through the adoption of more permanent constitutional legal commitments to protect justifiable "private" and "public" rights or interests. But the issue of the depth of legal and political commitments to particular rights or principles is also open to debate.

In the same manner that private rights can vindicate the interests of workers in firms as well as business owners or managers, public constraints may also apply to workers (e.g. legal prohibitions against the destruction of property when conducting union organizing activities) as well as employers (e.g. a requirement to recognize and bargain with a legitimately organized union). In this sense, the alleged "indeterminacy" of the public/private distinction is actually a virtue in terms of allowing for significant flexibility for legal development (including the recognition of supplemental institutional entities such as labor unions) with respect to the "structural" issues. If the distinction itself does not determine legal results, then the indeterminacy claim undermines the structural claim that the public/private distinction locks in results favorable to the status quo. In other words, the first critique of

---

[65] See Chapter 2, pages 78–85 and Table 2.5 (describing the fragmentation of ownership and control in modern business enterprises).

[66] For a diagnosis of this phenomenon, see, e.g., Robert C. Clark, "The Four Stages of Capitalism: Reflections on Investment Management Treatises," 94 *Harvard Law Review* 561 (1981).

the public/private distinction based on indeterminacy undermines the second critique of the distinction based on ideological preferences. Other legal fields, such as those that aim to eliminate racial, gender, or other forms of discrimination, show also that recognizing private individual rights of different kinds appears to have had a progressive and morally positive influence. "Rights talk" in the commercial social context may lead to similar positive developments.[67]

Another political dimension regarding the public/private distinction appears when one reflects on the ability of private business firms to influence the political processes that determine their own regulation. There is no doubt that political controversy arises about the extent to which private business interests can and should participate directly in politics and the regulatory process. (See the discussion of *Citizens United* in Chapter 7.) Marx's view that the political state will inevitably privilege private interests over public regulation, however, makes a significant number of assumptions about how democratic government will work. Some individuals with authority and power over resources in different societies will inevitably influence political processes and decision-making to a greater extent than others, but this fact alone does not necessarily mean that a political oligarchy will result in which the rich will dominate the political process. In principle at least, it is not clear why the possession of wealth or other resources should disqualify citizens from influencing the political process of regulation, as long as these resources are not used coercively to silence or buy off other less well-endowed citizens and thereby control political results. These concerns support legal prohibitions against politically motivated coercion, such as bribery and vote-buying in elections, for example—and may support limitations on campaign contributions as well. (Again see Chapter 7.) A general political concern is warranted that an oligarchy of business-connected wealth could arise and exert a controlling influence on political processes and legal regulation. This is an ancient and continuing concern in political theory, and it is an important theme, though one that lies mostly outside the scope of this book.[68]

---

[67] But cf. Mary Ann Glendon, *Rights Talk: The Impoverishment of Political Discourse* (Free Press 1991) (arguing that invocations of individual rights in various fields should also include an emphasis on social responsibilities).

[68] See Aristotle, *Politics* (Ernest Barker ed. and trans.) (Oxford University Press 1958), p. 115 (describing "oligarchy" as a perverse form of government "directed to the interest of the well-to-do" as opposed to healthy forms of government "directed to the advantage of the whole body of citizens"). Aristotle's description owed much to an earlier one by Plato. See, e.g., H. Sidgwick, "Aristotle's Classification of Forms of Government," 6 *Classical Review* 141, 141–2 (1892). See also Andrew Lintott, "Aristotle and Democracy," 42 *Classical Quarterly* 114, 115–18 (1992). Etymologically, "oligarchy" means simply "rule by the few," and recent analysis has tended toward this more general usage rather than one based on the political influence of wealth. See, e.g., Darcy K. Leach, "The Iron Law of What Again? Conceptualizing Oligarchy Across Organizational Forms," 23 *Sociological Theory* 312, 315–18 (2005). Leach argues that oligarchy is best understood as "a particular distribution of illegitimate power that has become entrenched over time" and best contrasted with democratic procedures to assure accountability of organizational leadership. Id., pp. 316, 321–30. This approach comports with some of the concerns raised with respect to political influence of business enterprises, though one should note that the organizational structures of business enterprises are often "oligarchies by consent." Cf. id., p. 326 n. 15 (describing "business firms" in which "oligarchy is built into the structure of the organization"). I hope to address these kinds of issues regarding politics and business

Implications of the public/private distinction for a legal theory of the firm

To accept the importance of the public/private distinction does not mean to say that business enterprises are to be understood as only "private" rather than "public" entities. If the institutional theory of the firm advanced here is accepted, then business enterprises are neither entirely "private" nor entirely "public." Instead, firms have two faces: public *and* private. They are created, recognized, and regulated by public authorities, namely, governments. They are also composed of private interests and private participants who deserve some level of legal recognition by and protection from government. The relative balance between the public and the private elements of firms are continually contested in both theory and practice. But the contested nature of the balance between the public and private aspects of firms does not make this a distinction without a difference. The hard choices of regulation focus on the scope of recognition to be given to private organizations and the extent to which they should be required to shoulder public obligations of one kind or another.

Choices also arise as to whether some social activities are better managed by public groups and institutions (e.g. governments of various kinds and configurations) or private groups and institutions (e.g. privately owned and operated firms). Again, making these kinds of choices does not mean that the distinction withers away: quite to the contrary. The legal lines between the public and private features of business enterprise remain central and implicate many areas of modern social life. As Christopher Stone concludes, "the most complicated and perhaps most important questions do not involve whether to retain these two regions [of public and private] with their generally prevailing distinctions, but how we allocate between them."[69]

As a further illustration, consider the modern development of corporate securities markets and their regulation.[70] For purposes here, a "security" may be considered any transferable investment in a business firm, most often a corporation. With respect to the fragmented ownership structures reviewed in Chapter 2, these investments are often purchased and sold in relatively small denominations that amount collectively to very large amounts of aggregated capital. With respect to the public/private distinction, one may identify two general arguments with respect to

---

enterprises in future work. A key concept to elaborate may include a descriptive and normative argument for a "separation of business and state" in institutional terms in a manner analogous to the "separation of church and state" followed under current interpretations of the First Amendment of the U.S. Constitution. On the idea of the "separation of church and state" or, more accurately, "separation of religion and state," see, e.g., Philip Hamburger, *Separation of Church and State* (Harvard University Press 2004); Kent Greenawalt, "History as Ideology: Philip Hamburger's *Separation of Church and State*," 93 *California Law Review* 367 (2005) (book review).

[69] See, e.g., Stone, "Corporate Vices and Corporate Virtues," op. cit., p. 1508.

[70] For an introduction to U.S. law in this field, see Louis Loss, Joel Seligman, and Troy Paredes, *Fundamentals of Securities Regulation* (Aspen, 6th ed., 2011).

securities regulation. On one hand, a consensus has developed that the property interests represented by individual shareholders (as well as other investors) constitute "private property" that should be protected legally. On the other hand, the potential for large-scale fraud and manipulation of securities markets has led to the widespread and detailed regulation of those who act as intermediaries (such as "broker-dealers" or "investment advisers" in the United States) and who otherwise participate institutionally in the securities markets.[71]

To say that the securities markets and their regulation include both "public" and "private" features does not mean that the public/private distinction is either confused or unimportant. Instead, the modern law governing the trading of corporate securities both protects individual private property interests and regulates the public operations of the securities markets themselves (and the business firms and individuals who participate in and sometimes "make" these markets). Legal regulation contemplates public and private interests as well as public and private purposes.[72]

The public interests and purposes of regulation may include, for example, provisions to encourage systemic financial stability as well as general commercial accountability and transparency. According to one assessment of the recent government bailouts in the United States, a list of possible "principles" to follow when regulating include: "market driven" principles (non-regulation), "prudential investor standards" (meant to protect unsophisticated investors), "political insulation" (designed to protect portfolio managers from inappropriate political pressures), and "accountability and transparency" (traditionally invoked as protections against manipulation and fraud).[73] Systemic financial stability has been an overriding purpose of the large-scale revision of financial regulation in the Dodd–Frank Act in the United States.[74]

Other regulation of specific kinds of business firms carries a Janus-faced aspect as well. On one hand, the private right to go into business by self-organizing, entering into contracts, holding property, and otherwise acting freely in markets is protected by law. On the other hand, some kinds of business are singled out for special regulation in the public interest. Doctors, lawyers, accountants, real estate brokers, and other designated "professionals," for example, must often satisfy certain basic regulatory requirements and demonstrate minimum qualifications and competence in order to practice their professions. Licenses are often required.[75] Or some

---

[71] For an overview, see Clifford E. Kirsch, *Investment Adviser Regulation: A Step-by-Step Guide to Compliance and the Law* (Practicing Law Institute, 3rd ed., 2011); Norman S. Poser and James A. Fanto, *Broker-Dealer Law and Regulation* (Aspen, 4th ed., 2007).

[72] On "collective purposes," see Chapter 1, pages 44–6 and accompanying notes 168–75.

[73] Templin, op. cit., pp. 1203–14.

[74] For a critical overview, see David A. Skeel, *The New Financial Deal: Understanding the Dodd–Frank Act and Its (Unintended) Consequences* (Wiley 2011). See also *Regulating Wall Street: The Dodd–Frank Act and the New Architecture of Global Finance* (Viral V. Acharya et al. eds.) (Wiley 2010); Randall S. Kroszner and Robert J. Shiller, *Reforming U.S. Financial Markets: Reflections Before and Beyond Dodd–Frank* (Benjamin M. Freidman ed.) (MIT Press 2011).

[75] See J.F. Barron, "Business and Professional Licensing: California, A Representative Example," 18 *Stanford Law Review* 640 (1966).

business firms may have to follow particular laws aimed to regulate them in the public interest with respect to specific categories of risk—such as restaurants following municipal health/inspection codes or construction firms following building/housing codes.[76]

The combination of private rights and public regulation does not eliminate the public/private distinction. Instead, these real-life examples of regulated business firms show how the law works to establish business firms as an institution with two faces: one protecting the private interests of business participants and the other regulating business operations with an eye toward the public good.

The sociologist Paul Starr provides a sophisticated conceptualization of the various meanings of "public" and "private" in regulation.[77] "To speak intelligently about modern societies and politics without using the words public and private," Starr observes, "would be as great an achievement as writing a novel without the word 'the.' However, neither is necessarily the sort of achievement that other theorists or novelists would care to imitate."[78] One important use of the distinction marks off categories of social life that belong mostly to the political state or to the personal lives of individual people. Other meanings refer to conceptions of the "public or common good" as opposed to "private interests." Again in Starr's words:

[W]hen we speak of public opinion, public health, or the public interest, we mean the opinion, health, or interest of the whole of the people as opposed to that of a part, whether a class or an individual. Public in this sense often means "common," not necessarily governmental. The public-spirited or public-minded citizen is one concerned about the community as a whole.[79]

Some policy makers, especially those influenced by some recent trends in neoclassical economics and so-called "positive political theory," argue that the "public good" is itself a concept without a foundation. This theoretical perspective follows the so-called "public choice" method, which again as Starr notes, is "ill-named because the only choices it recognizes are essentially private."[80] In my view, everyday examples such as professional licensing, housing codes, and health requirements for restaurants should be sufficient to counter this argument. I agree that the "public good" is an essentially contested concept with respect to what is actually "good" as a policy matter with respect to particular social problems. Even one who opposes regulation in general (or most of the time), however, must admit that an argument that entirely free markets are better than regulation includes an implicit view of the "public good."

---

[76] On public health requirements, including inspections, see Emily A. Mok et al., "Implementing Public Health Regulations in Developing Countries: Lessons from the OECD Countries," 38 *Journal of Law, Medicine & Ethics* 508 (2010). On building and housing codes, see Neal Kumar Katyal, "Architecture as Crime Control," 111 *Yale Law Journal* 1039, 1102–8 (2002); Christopher D. Stone, "The Place of Enterprise Liability in the Control of Corporate Conduct," 90 *Yale Law Journal* 1, 18, 36 (1980).

[77] Starr, "The Meaning of Privatization," op. cit., pp. 7–13. See also Paul Starr, *Freedom's Power: The True Force of Liberalism* (Basic Books 2007), pp. 53–8.

[78] Starr, "The Meaning of Privatization," op. cit., p. 7.   [79] Id., pp. 7–8.   [80] Id., p. 23.

The lessons of *Dartmouth College*

The substantive consequences of the landmark *Dartmouth College* case, which was mentioned in Chapter 1 for its description of the corporation as a "mere creature of law," provides a concluding example of the social importance of the public/private distinction.[81] The case also provides an historical sense of how the distinction has developed legally with respect to business firms.

Although Chief Justice Marshall in his majority opinion intoned that the government of the state of New Hampshire had the ultimate authority to determine the rules of the game with respect to the formation of private organizations (such as Dartmouth College, as well as business corporations), the substantive thrust of the case set constitutional limits on how far governments can and should go in revising these legal rules once they are given. In other words, in terms introduced in Chapter 1, Marshall's often-quoted and rhetorical language that a corporation is "the mere creature of law" supported a public "top-down" concession theory of the firm.[82] At the same time, the substance of the Court's decision held in favor of the private "bottom-up" participants. In my interpretation, *Dartmouth College* illustrates the importance of the public/private distinction and supports the institutional theory of the firm advanced here.

First, to review the facts of the case: The state of New Hampshire attempted to take over the control and ownership of Dartmouth College, which had been founded through private charitable donations and managed under the authority of private trustees. In other words (though to use an anachronistic term), New Hampshire wanted to "nationalize" the college for purposes of enhancing state-run education. Although Dartmouth later evolved into a prestigious private secular university, its private founders established the school to teach Christianity to Native Americans.[83] (In the modern era, a question of the First Amendment's protection of freedom of religion against government interference might also have been raised. *Dartmouth College* has also been cited more recently in support of claims of academic freedom by private universities.[84])

The King of Great Britain had issued the original corporate charter for Dartmouth College prior to the American Revolution.[85] The New Hampshire Supreme Court

---

[81] *Dartmouth College v. Woodward*, 17 U.S. 518, 636 (1819).

[82] See Chapter 1, pages 10–15 and Table 1.1.

[83] *Dartmouth College*, op. cit., pp. 630–1.

[84] See, e.g., Matthew W. Finken, "On 'Institutional' Academic Freedom," 61 *Texas Law Review* 817, 820–1 (1983) (discussing arguments for Princeton University in a dispute with the state of New Jersey).

[85] *Dartmouth College*, op. cit., p. 626 (noting that the charter was granted "in the year 1769, incorporating twelve persons therein mentioned, by the name of 'The Trustees of Dartmouth College,' granting to them and their successors the usual corporate privileges and powers, and authorizing the trustees, who are to govern the college, to fill up all vacancies which may be created in their own body").

upheld the proposed state takeover, and the decision was appealed to the U.S. Supreme Court.[86]

The method of the proposed state takeover has a modern ring of familiarity for those who know the contemporary corporate law of mergers and acquisitions. By statute, the charter was to be amended to increase the number of Dartmouth's board of trustees, and the state would appoint new members as well as assert the authority to fill vacancies. A new "board of overseers" on which state officials would sit *ex officio* would also be created. A majority of the incumbent trustees refused to go along with the charter amendment, leading to the lawsuit and the appeal.[87]

Reversing the New Hampshire court, the U.S. Supreme Court found that the state had no constitutional authority to execute a takeover of a private organization in this fashion. Although the case is often cited as involving other important constitutional issues, the Supreme Court recognized the salience of the fact that a private institution was involved.[88] In holding in favor of Dartmouth College and its privately appointed trustees, the Court emphasized that "private donations" had been raised to create a "private corporation."[89] A minister had originally established the college "at his own expense," and "the funds of the college consisted entirely of private donations" (the largest donation coming, not surprisingly, from the Earl of Dartmouth).[90]

Dartmouth College drew attention to a long-term distinction between "private" and "public" corporations that traces historically to medieval times. An historical digression is needed to provide the conceptual context.

The word "corporation" has a long and convoluted history which often conflated public and private meanings. In ancient Roman law, the general term used to refer to associations of private individuals was *universitas*.[91] In more recent times, "corporation"—derived from the Latin *corpus* or "body"—became the linguistic successor to *universitas*. (If later generations followed Roman categories strictly, we would now call business firms "universities" rather than "corporations."[92]) The concept of the corporation evolved further in medieval times when religious legal debates focused on whether "corporate bodies within the church" had "perpetual

---

[86] Id., p. 625.   [87] Id., p. 626.

[88] On constitutional grounds, *Dartmouth College* was decided under the Contracts Clause which prohibited states from interfering with preexisting contracts. Id., pp. 643–54; U.S. Constitution, art. I, sect. 10. This jurisprudence has evolved substantially since then. The Contracts Clause, in particular, has declined as a basis for judicial intervention. In fact, it took only about a decade for the Supreme Court to cut back on its review of corporate charters under the Contract Clause, refusing to intervene on this ground in a dispute between two chartered bridge companies in Boston. See *Charles River Bridge v. Warren Bridge*, 36 U.S. 420, 536–53 (1837). For an account of constitutional law in this area, see, e.g., Laurence H. Tribe, *American Constitutional Law* (Foundation Press, 2nd ed., 1988), pp. 613–38. See also James W. Ely, Jr., "The Protection of Contractual Rights: A Tale of Two Constitutional Provisions," 1 *New York University Journal of Law and Liberty* 370 (2005); Ann Woolhandler, "Public Rights, Private Rights, and Statutory Retroactivity," 94 *Georgetown Law Journal* 1015 (2006).

[89] *Dartmouth College*, op. cit., pp. 632–5.

[90] Id., pp. 631–4.

[91] Alfred F. Conard, *Corporations in Perspective* (Foundation Press 1976), p. 127.

[92] Id., p. 132.

succession and a continuing body of property despite changing membership" in order to contest the expanding claims on church property made by governments.[93] Churches often wanted to claim continuing legal personality in order to maintain ownership of real estate contested by competing private interests or rising monarchies. Medieval social theorists then gradually began to use "corporation" to describe any self-governing body of citizens. Blending classical and theological sources, they referred to many different social entities as "corporations" (or *universitas*), including those described as a "household, neighborhood, city, kingdom, and [even] universe."[94] Eventually, "corporations" came to refer to different local and often self-governing geographical groups, including cities, boroughs, townships, and counties—as well as religious associations, commercial guilds (the harbingers of modern firms), and even the political state.[95]

Continuing in this general historical tradition, a "corporation" in the United States today can refer not only to a specific legal form of profit-making business enterprise (in various shapes, sizes, and configurations), but also to a non-profit association (oriented primarily toward a non-financial primary objective, at least in principle) or a municipal corporation (i.e. a city or township). In other words, "corporation" has replaced *universitas* as the common general term for associations of people organized for different purposes: profit, nonprofit/charitable, and governmental. Adding further linguistic fog from an international perspective, the British and some other English-speaking countries refer to a "company" rather than a "corporation" as their preferred term for a "chartered" or "incorporated" business enterprise.[96] This usage has the advantage of distinguishing "private companies" from various other kinds of government-dominated divisions. (Chapter 5 clarifies some of the modern nomenclature and categorization of various types of business firms today.)

Reflecting this conceptual history, Justice Joseph Story's concurring opinion in *Dartmouth College* describes the evolution of "private" and "public" corporations in the United States as follows.

Another division of corporations [in addition to a distinction based on founding purposes] is into public and private. Public corporations ... generally ... exist for public political purposes only, such as towns, cities, parishes and counties; and in many respects, they are so, although they involve some private interests; but strictly speaking, public corporations are such only as are founded by the government, for public purposes, where the

---

[93] Adolf A. Berle, Jr., and Gardiner Means, "Corporation," in *Encyclopedia of the Social Sciences* (Macmillan, 1931), p. 414. See also Ernst H. Kantorowicz, *The King's Two Bodies: A Study in Medieval Political Theology* (Princeton University Press 1957), pp. 206–8.

[94] Kantorowicz, op. cit., pp. 209–10. Referring to the "universe" as a corporation alludes to a theological idea known as the *corporate mysticum*, which lies far outside of the scope of discussion here!

[95] See Antony Black, *Political Thought in Europe, 1250–1450* (Cambridge University Press 1992), pp. 15, 18–19, 85, 114–15; Antony Black, *Guild and State: European Political Thought from the Twelfth Century to the Present* (Transaction 2003), pp. 18–20, 49–53, 68–9, 73, 80; Kantorowicz, op. cit., pp. xviii–xix, 3–24, 42–3, 57, 60, 94–7, 218–32, 358–64, 446–50; Harold J. Laski, "The Early History of the Corporation in England," 30 *Harvard Law Review* 561, 563–68 (1917); Frederic Maitland, "The Crown as Corporation," in *The Collected Papers of Frederic William Maitland* (H.A. L. Fisher ed.) (Cambridge University Press 1911), vol. 3, pp. 244–70.

[96] Conard, op. cit., p. 136.

whole interests belong also to the government. If, therefore, the foundation be private, though under the charter of the government, the corporation is private, however extensive the uses may be to which it is devoted, either by the bounty of the founder, or the nature and objects of the institution. For instance, a bank created by the government for its own uses, whose stock is exclusively owned by the government, is, in the strictest sense, a public corporation. [Compare contemporary financial institutions maintained by the government, such as the U.S. Federal Reserve.].... But a bank, whose stock is owned by private persons, is a private corporation, although it is erected by the government, and its objects and operations partake of a public nature. The same doctrine may be affirmed of insurance, canal, bridge and turnpike companies. In all these cases, the uses may, in a certain sense, be called public, but the corporations are private; as much so, indeed, as if the franchises were vested in a single person.[97]

Justice Story's opinion emphasizes the importance of the corporation as "an artificial person, existing in contemplation of law, and endowed with certain powers ... which, though they must be exercised through the medium of its natural members, are yet considered as subsisting in the corporation itself, as distinctly as if it were a real personage."[98] Story's view is therefore consistent with the emphasis in the institutional theory of the firm advanced here both with respect to the salience of the public/private distinction and the importance of the recognition of firms as "persons."

If one focuses on Justice Story's concurrence, the outcome of this landmark case turned largely on whether Dartmouth College was deemed to be a "public" or "private" corporation. As one commentator has argued, "a major issue in *Dartmouth College* was whether the institution should be treated as a public corporation" (as the New Hampshire court had held) or "a private one" (as the U.S. Supreme Court held).[99] Updating the case in modern jurisprudential terms, the government could not execute a takeover of a privately organized institution endowed with privately contributed funds without agreeing to pay a fair value in compensation for the "taking" of the private property.[100] The outcome of the case would also have been different if Dartmouth College had been deemed to be a "public" corporation under the direct authority of the government.[101]

Dartmouth College has had very large implications for the long-term development of the law of private business enterprises.[102] One implication has been political. The nineteenth-century constitutional scholar Thomas Cooley recognized the implications of the public/private distinction in *Dartmouth College* and warned

---

[97] Id., pp. 668–9.   [98] Id., p. 668.   [99] See Woolhandler, op. cit., p. 1029.

[100] On "takings" law, see Chapter 1, page 20 and accompanying notes 50–3.

[101] See Woolhandler, op. cit., p. 1029 (noting that "[i]t was widely acknowledged that later state laws could freely amend or even rescind municipal charters").

[102] See, e.g., David J. Barron, "The Promise of Cooley's City: Traces of Local Constitutionalism," 147 *University of Pennsylvania Law Review* 487, 497–505 (1999); William W. Bratton, Jr., "The New Economic Theory of the Firm: Critical Perspectives from History," 41 *Stanford Law Review* 1471, 1505 (1989); Ron Harris, "The Transplantation of the Legal Discourse on Corporate Personality Theories: From German Codification to British Political Pluralism and American Big Business," 63 *Washington and Lee Law Review* 1421, 1459 (2006); Paul M. Schoenhard, "A Three-Dimensional Approach to the Public–Private Distinction," 2008 *Utah Law Review* 635, 640–1 (2008).

that empowering private corporations too much would threaten to corrupt the public political process.[103] (This important political dimension of the public/private distinction is not addressed at length in this book, though Chapter 7 touches on this issue in connection with *Citizens United*.)

Dartmouth College also recognized that once private institutions were established and recognized, they could not be nationalized or taken over by the government (at least not without paying compensation). Following the famous language favoring of the "concession theory" (describing the corporation as "an artificial being, invisible, intangible, and existing only in contemplation of law"), the Court emphasized that once such a corporation is created for private purposes it becomes "no more a state instrument . . . than a natural person exercising the same powers would be."[104] In other words, the Court's substantive result, forbidding New Hampshire's takeover, followed the outlines of the participant theory. The Court recognized an exception (still often followed today) for corporations or other organizations created for "the purpose" of "shar[ing]" in the civil government of the country," which qualify as "public institutions."[105]

Probably the most important part of the *Dartmouth College* decision with respect to understanding the legal development of the public/private distinction and business firms appears in another part of Justice Story's concurring opinion. Although agreeing with the majority opinion's holding in favor of the legal independence of Dartmouth College as a private institution, Justice Story emphasized that governments nevertheless had the ability to "reserve powers" to change the rules of the game for the organizations that it established or allowed to be established going forward.[106] Within some specified legal limits (such as the constitutional prohibition against taking private property without paying just compensation), governments can change the background legal rules for business firms as long as they "reserve" the power to do so constitutionally. (States universally did so after *Dartmouth College*.) Changing the rules of the game going forward, however, is much different than permitting an institutional takeover by government in violation of participants' legitimate expectations. Although modern legal frameworks bend toward adopting "enabling rules" that empower private participants to set their own law, the "reserved powers" of government mean that these enabling rules may be changed. And new "mandatory rules" may be imposed (or relaxed) in response to various competing understandings of the public interest. Antitakeover statutes passed by various state legislatures in the United States to prevent hostile out-of-state takeover threats to in-state corporations provide an example.[107]

---

[103] Barron, op. cit., pp. 512–15.   [104] *Dartmouth College*, op. cit, p. 636.
[105] Id., p. 638.
[106] *Dartmouth College*, op. cit., p. 712 (Story concurring). See also Herbert Hovenkamp, *Enterprise and American Law, 1836–1937* (Harvard University Press 1991), p. 27; Ely, op. cit., pp. 373–4; Eric W. Orts, "Beyond Shareholders: Interpreting Corporate Constituency Statutes," 61 *George Washington Law Review* 14, 68–9 (1992).
[107] See, e.g., Orts, "Beyond Shareholders," op. cit., 23–6; Mark J. Roe, "A Political Theory of American Corporate Finance," 91 *Columbia Law Review* 10, 45–7, 63–4 (1991); Roberta Romano, "The Political Economy of Takeover Statutes," 73 *Virginia Law Review* 111, 120–41 (1987).

Justice Story's concurrence in *Dartmouth College* set the stage for the expansion of enabling statutes, including especially general incorporation laws that extended the right to incorporate to all citizens (who met the necessary qualification of having property to do so), which encouraged the establishment of many private business firms in the United States.[108] General incorporation statutes had been first enacted in the United States for non-business associations such as religious congregations (e.g. in New York in 1784) and for other charitable or literary groups such as libraries (e.g. in Pennsylvania in 1791). The first general incorporation statute for business enterprises had been enacted by New York in 1811, only eight years prior to the *Dartmouth College* decision. Connecticut followed in 1837, and then the movement gathered steam in other states in the 1840s and 1850s.[109] Broadly similar and parallel legal evolution occurred in Europe and other countries as well, with the general result that private forms of business enterprise became legally recognized as corporate "persons" that could assert institutional rights against governments.

Once established, these *private* firms must follow the *public* rules of the game. At the same time, *public* constitutional foundations protect *private* firms from direct government takeovers and other overreaching.

* * *

In summary, modern business enterprises have two faces: public and private. They are recognized and regulated by public authorities. And they are composed in most cases of self-organized private interests. Normative debates then follow along various dimensions about how far public responsibilities should intrude on privately defined purposes—and vice versa, that is, how far privately defined rights and purposes should influence or restrict public regulation. In other words, the public/private distinction describes an ongoing and contested balance of rights and responsibilities surrounding the social institution of the firm.

---

[108] See James Willard Hurst, *The Legitimacy of the Business Corporation in the Law of the United States, 1780–1970* (University Press of Virginia 1970), pp. 62–4, 70–1, 73 (describing this development beginning in *Dartmouth College* with respect to corporate law in the United States).

[109] Hurst, op. cit., p. 134. See also Chapter 1, page 13 and accompanying note 22.

4

Enterprise Liability, Business Participant Liability, and Limited Liability

Among the most important responsibilities of firms and their participants are those relating to the general category of legal liability for wrongful acts or omissions that cause harm to other persons (both firms and people). In some cases, firms and their participants may also be held liable for damage to other species and the natural environment, such as under statutes allowing for "natural resource damages" for pollution.[1]

Legally recognized harm to others is redressed through various means, including private lawsuits for breach of contract and a broad range of wrongful actions or omissions known as torts. A "tort" is a general term for legal liability for actions or omissions that are deemed wrongful and allow a legal right of recovery by a victim, usually paid in money damages. The word derives from the Latin *tortum*, which means "wrong" or "injustice."[2]

In addition, governments may designate particular actions or responsibilities in business as important enough to establish regulatory sanctions to prohibit and punish (or encourage and reward), usually through statutes. As the legal scholar Christopher Stone has observed, government may employ "two fundamental techniques" to control or direct the conduct of business firms and other organizations. One method employs "enterprise liability," as well as the liability of individual business participants, to deter and compensate for wrongful behavior. Another approach is to set specified "standards" of behavior for firms to follow through a method of "interventionism."[3] Interventionist methods include setting performance standards or requiring the production of information.[4] In environmental law, for example, maximum pollution levels may be specified for a firm or an industrial site (a performance

---

[1] In the United States, federal statutes with "natural resource damages" provisions include the Clean Water Act and the Oil Pollution Act. For statutory details and critical discussion of methodologies for calculating these kinds of damages, see Frank B. Cross, "Natural Resource Damage Valuation," 42 *Vanderbilt Law Review* 269 (1989); Itzchak E. Kornfeld, "Of Dead Pelicans, Turtles, and Marshes: Natural Resources Damages in the Wake of the BP Deepwater Horizon Spill," 38 *Boston College Environmental Affairs Law Review* 317 (2011); James Peck, "Measuring Justice for Nature: Issues in Evaluating and Litigating Natural Resources Damages," 14 *Journal of Land Use and Environmental Law* 275 (1999).

[2] *Oxford English Dictionary* (Oxford University Press 2011) (online version).

[3] Christopher D. Stone, "The Place of Enterprise Liability in the Control of Corporate Conduct," 90 *Yale Law Journal* 1, 8 (1980).

[4] Id., p. 36.

standard) or disclosure of data regarding pollution by a firm may be required (an informational regulation).[5] A recent example of the latter in the United States is the requirement for firms to report greenhouse gas emissions deemed to cause global climate change without setting mandatory performance limits for these emissions.[6]

Governments may also impose criminal responsibility on business entities (though taking this step has often been conceptually controversial), as well as on individual business participants who make decisions as agents within firms, such as corporate managers and other employees.[7] As Stone has also noted, significant ethical and pragmatic issues arise when using criminal penalties aimed at individual people as agents in order to control or channel organizational behavior.[8] Assessing criminal liability on business entities rather than individuals is therefore sometimes recommended as a viable alternative. Doing so assumes (though controversially) that business entities are "moral actors" with identifiable intentions and purposes, which may therefore "deserve" criminal punishment in appropriate cases.[9]

In this context, the legal recognition of the firm as an "entity" and "person" is again foundational.[10] It provides the conceptual framework for legal analysis to determine liability (or not) for both the enterprise itself and its business participants. The recognition of a relevant entity allows for four possibilities with respect to any particular cognizable harm: (1) enterprise liability; (2) business participant liability (i.e. liability of an individual business participant or group of participants); (3) both enterprise liability and business participant liability; or (4) neither enterprise liability nor liability of any business participant. I will refer to these possibilities as Options 1, 2, 3, and 4.

Note that liability under Options 1, 2, or 3 assumes that a cognizable harm is adequately proven under the applicable law to have occurred and traced in some causal fashion to the business entity, the business participant (or group of participants), or both. Legal standards of culpability range from *intentional harm* (often used as a standard for criminal liability) to *recklessness* (another standard used for criminal liability and often used for tort liability) to *negligence* (sometimes used as a standard for criminal liability and the most common standard for tort liability) to *strict liability* (i.e. no-fault liability requiring proof only of a causal connection without a culpability or state of mind requirement, which is only very rarely the standard for criminal liability and sometimes used for tort liability).

Option 1 (business entity liability) and Option 2 (business participant liability) may use the business entity to protect either the enterprise itself or some of its

---

[5] See Paul R. Kleindorfer and Eric W. Orts, "Informational Regulation of Environmental Risks," 18 *Risk Analysis* 155 (1998). See also Daniel C. Esty, "Environmental Protection in the Information Age," 79 *New York University Law Review* 115 (2004).

[6] See Mandatory Reporting of Greenhouse Gases, Final Rule, 74 Fed. Reg. 56260 (October 30, 2009). See also Andrew Schatz, Note, "Regulating Greenhouse Gases by Mandatory Information Disclosure," 26 *Virginia Environmental Law Journal* 335 (2008).

[7] See Chapter 1, pages 50–1 and accompanying notes 196–201.

[8] Stone, op. cit., pp. 28–35.

[9] See, e.g., William S. Laufer and Alan Strudler, "Corporate Intentionality, Desert, and Variants of Vicarious Liability," 37 *American Criminal Law Review* 1285 (2000).

[10] See Chapter 1.

individual participants. Option 3 (joint liability) imposes liability on both the enterprise entity and at least some group (or groups) of individual participants. Option 4 (no liability) provides for the possibility that the complexity of a firm's organization may permit an otherwise legally wrongful and cognizable harm to find no available target for liability, compensation, or punishment.

Option 4 is more common than one might think, given the complexity of modern business organization and the difficulty of tracing some kinds of harm to a clearly wrongful cause or act by a specific legal person (either an individual or an entity). In other words, organizational complexity can obscure the necessary lines of legal proof and evidence gathering. The relative paucity of litigation (especially criminal litigation) following the Great Credit Crash of 2008 provides an example. Some kinds of complex situations produce harmful large-scale consequences, but the very complexity of social organization may make it difficult to trace causal responsibility to individual people or entities. This social fact of modern life suggests that regulatory alternatives departing from the traditional models of tort-based or fault-based liability are needed. The "interventionist" regulatory approaches mentioned above rely on mandating performance standards or altering market incentives, rather than assessing fault and apportioning damages only through the law of contracts and torts.

From the perspective of potential victims and prospective plaintiffs, the mix of the four options described above determine the financial resources available (or not) for the payment of claims for wrongful harms suffered. From the perspective of the firm and its participants, the options represent the degree of exposure of business persons to liability. The options outline the potential of limited liability that business entities can confer to themselves and their participants.

An initial question is why the law would have developed to allow fictional entities and organizational persons ever to limit the available recovery for wrongful harms and injuries that they may cause. A general answer appeals to various policy justifications based on ethics, economics, and politics.

Ethical responsibility for any person (either individual or entity) ordinarily requires a causal connection to the wrongful behavior. Lines of authority become attenuated within large and complex business firm structures, thus making it difficult to fix ethical responsibility for particular wrongful harms on particular business persons (individuals or entities).

Economic policy judgments involve the extent to which taking business risks should be promoted (or not). Limited liability in particular instances may promote business values of risk-taking, investment, and economic growth—which should be balanced (in a general welfare calculation) against values of economic compensation required for any resulting wrongful harm (or the deterrence of any prospective and foreseeable wrongful harm).

Political arguments include extending limited liability to protect business enterprises in an egalitarian manner, such as extending the privilege of limited liability to protect promoters of small businesses as well as large corporations. Less sanguinely, recognizing limited liability in some instances may amount simply to a hidden subsidy paid to those who benefit from the rule, which redistributes the burden for a wrongful harm suffered to victims rather than perpetrators.[11]

Assuming that business entities are in fact often allowed to limit liability (which is the prevailing general rule and practice followed throughout the world today), a legal analysis of limited liability and the firm may be usefully divided into a consideration of the following categories: (1) "enterprise liability" imposed on the firm as a whole (and its aggregated assets and property); (2) "business participant liability" imposed on various groups and categories of individuals within the firm (e.g. managers, employees, or owners); and (3) "limited liability" afforded to both business entities and various business participants. These analytical categories track the liability options discussed above. Option 1 is enterprise liability only. Option 2 is business participant liability only. Option 3 combines enterprise and business participant liability. Option 4 allows for no liability of either the business entity or its participants.

Recall that though limited liability for business participants is often understood to refer primarily to the limited liability of shareholders in corporations (and other equity investors in limited liability firms), it applies also to protect other business participants. These other protected participants include a firm's creditors (e.g. banks), a firm's employee-agents (e.g. corporate managers and other employees), and a firm's quasi-principals (e.g. chief executive officers and boards of directors).[12] Courts have also held principles of limited liability to shield business entities themselves, most notably in complex firm organizations involving parent–subsidiary structures, franchising arrangements, or other multiple-entity business structures.

Within the categories of enterprise liability, business participant liability, and various forms of limited liability, it is also useful to distinguish further between liability for contracts and liability for torts. The American Law Institute's *Restatement of Agency* divides its coverage of the liability of principals (including organizational principals) and agents in this manner.[13] However, the two fields often interrelate. For example, exculpatory or indemnifying agreements (contracts) may affect the attribution of liability to various participants for personal injuries (torts). And the seriousness of some kinds of intentional wrongful harm (torts) may limit the allocation of risks among participants by agreements (contracts).

Neither people nor firms can "contract around" risks of criminal behavior, though organizational layers may sometimes shelter high-level agents or quasi-principals (and the enterprise itself) from liability. Organizational layers may make it difficult for prosecutors to link criminal behavior of low-level agents to their superiors. In addition, practices such as "reverse whistleblowing" and "scapegoating" may allow

---

[11] See, e.g., David Millon, "Piercing the Corporate Veil, Financial Responsibility, and the Limits of Limited Liability," 56 *Emory Law Journal* 1305, 1307 (2007) [hereinafter "Limits of Limited Liability"] (arguing "the best way to understand the purpose of limited liability is as a subsidy designed to encourage business investment"). But see Robert C. Clark, *Corporate Law* (Aspen 1986), p. 35 (arguing that "it is not correct to see [limited liability for shareholders] as a mere device for subsidizing business" because of its "substantial economic benefits" for society as a whole).

[12] On limited liability and "asset partitioning," see Chapter 1, pages 34–6 and accompanying notes 115–22; Chapter 2, pages 58–9 and accompanying notes 28–32.

[13] American Law Institute, *Restatement (Third) of Agency* (2006), ch. 6 (contracts) and ch. 7 (torts).

high-ranking executives and the firm itself to pin the blame on lower-level employees, even though the true situation may warrant a broader finding of liability if the larger organizational truth could be fully understood and adequately proven.[14] Or complex incentive structures may encourage lower-level employees to violate the law in order to increase economic performance but provide for a bureaucratic shield for those at higher levels who may have created the high-powered incentives, but did not directly order or condone criminal acts. For the most part, I omit detailed coverage here of criminal liability, though recognizing that it is an important feature of a theory of the business enterprise. Note that criminal liability is usually "joint" (Option 3), allowing for the potential prosecution of both the enterprise itself and individual participants who commit criminal acts with the requisite intent.

Enterprise liability, business participant liability, and principles of limited liability for business persons are important to include in a theory of the firm because the consequences of these concepts are more significant from a social point of view than many people realize. The legal recognition of firms as entities and persons confers on them panoplies of power to organize and coordinate economic activity. Much of this activity is beneficial, producing and supplying the goods and services of everyday economic life. At the same time, business activity often results in unintended side effects that cause wrongful harm to others, and legal theory is needed to conceptualize these social problems and to allocate their costs and burdens in practice.

Enterprise liability

At the enterprise level, contractual liability for firms is relatively straightforward. Given that firms are recognized as "persons" with the capacity to make contracts with other legal persons (both firms and individual people), it stands to reason that firms-as-persons should answer for the harm or damage caused by their contractual violations. As organizational principals, firms may sue and be sued on the authorized contracts made by their agents.[15] The property and assets owned by the firm as an entity are available to cover any substantiated claims for contractual liability. The principles of enterprise liability for authorized contracts made by agents and quasi-principals of firms are uncontroversial. The laws of agency and enterprise organization describe the lines of authority required to find a firm liable to perform or pay damages for authorized contracts. The creation of this authority in firms occurs through the interaction of the law of agency, contracts, and property elaborated in Chapter 2.

A more difficult set of questions arises with respect to *unauthorized* contracts made by a firm's agents. Generally speaking, under the legal doctrine of "apparent authority," a firm is also liable at the enterprise level for unauthorized contracts, but only if the circumstances of the transaction indicate that it was reasonable for a

---

[14] See William S. Laufer, "Corporate Prosecution, Cooperation, and the Trading of Favors," 87 *Iowa Law Review* 643 (2002).

[15] *Restatement (Third) of Agency*, op. cit., sect. 6.01.

third party who contracted with an agent ostensibly representing a firm to believe that the agent was in fact authorized to enter into the contract.[16] The test of reasonableness focuses on "the principal's manifestations" to the third party as well as the "usual authority" structures and "industry customs" in a specific case.[17] Even other actors who are not agents may bind the firm as a principal under circumstances in which the firm allowed these other actors to *appear* to have authorization.[18] Undisclosed or unidentified principals can be also liable for contracts made by their agents and apparent agents in appropriate circumstances.[19]

The general rationale for contractual liability based on apparent authority is that a business firm should be responsible for public "manifestations" that are "traceable" to the firm and induce others to believe that they are dealing with authorized agents of the business.[20] In addition, an economic justification for the liability of firms in apparent authority situations emphasizes that firms are usually in a better position to reduce the risks of mistakes or misrepresentations than third parties (e.g. individual consumers) who would otherwise have to incur significant costs to investigate the organizational credentials of agents. One commentator explains: "A principal who is in business often uses agents routinely, and thereby learns about the risk of losses and the ways to avoid such risks. That knowledge reduces the costs to the principal of maintaining loss-avoidance incentives by contract."[21] Another common-sense rationale for imposing enterprise liability in these cases attributes legal responsibility for the foreseeable consequences of using the property, premises, and name of a firm when it holds itself out to the public as doing business with potential customers.

A default rule that entitles third parties to trust and rely on the public manifestations and representations made by a business firm thus seems to be both efficient and fair. In general, no finding of fault or negligence is required for the attribution of contractual liability for apparent authority in modern cases.[22]

When torts and various personal injuries to third parties are considered, the standards for enterprise liability differ. In contrast to contracts, third parties in tort cases usually have had no previous interactions with the firm and its agents (or apparent agents) prior to an accident or other incident causing the harm. These victims would therefore have had no opportunity to negotiate allocations of risks for potential harm or injury. In torts situations, the law follows principles of "causation" and "control" to find liability for the firm as an organizational principal

---

[16] On apparent authority, see *Restatement (Third) of Agency*, op. cit., sect. 2.03; sect. 6.01.

[17] Id., sect. 2.03, cmts. b and d. See also *The Unauthorised Agent: Perspectives from European and Comparative Law* (Danny Busch and Laura J. Macgregor eds.) (Cambridge University Press 2009).

[18] *Restatement (Third) of Agency*, op. cit., sect. 2.03.

[19] Id., sect. 2.03, cmt. f.

[20] *Restatement (Third) of Agency*, op. cit., sect. 2.03, cmts. b, c, and d.

[21] See, e.g., Alan O. Sykes, "The Economics of Vicarious Liability," 93 *Yale Law Journal* 1231, 1263 (1984). See also J.A.C. Hetherington, "Trends in Enterprise Liability: Law and the Unauthorized Agent," 19 *Stanford Law Review* 76 (1966).

[22] *Restatement (Third) of Agency*, op. cit., sect. 2.03, cmt. c.

for many of these non-contractual wrongful harms inflicted by the firm's agents (or apparent agents).

Under the long-standing doctrine of "vicarious liability," for example, firms are held strictly liable as principals for the actions (or material omissions) of their agents who qualify as "employees" and who cause wrongful harm to third parties when acting (or failing to act) "within the scope of their employment."[23] The general principle of vicarious liability has been present in the Anglo-American legal tradition for at least 300 years.[24] Although modern formulations have dropped older legal terms referring to "master" and "servant," the older terms highlight the fact that legal allocations of power and authority are involved in the formulation of principles regarding responsibility and liability in organizations.[25] In turn, these principles reflect policy considerations of both fairness and economic efficiency.[26]

One common situation of vicarious liability involves an employee's negligence resulting in physical injury to a person or property. Certain kinds of injuries may also have contract-like features such as fraudulent misrepresentations (i.e. lies told when the representative of a firm is selling something).[27] The rationale for vicarious liability under these circumstances is that firms as organizational principals exercise effective control over the employees who cause the legally cognizable harm while doing their work. Responsibility should follow organizational control. This is known as the "control test" for vicarious liability.[28]

Under the control test, a number of "factual indicia" are used to determine whether an agent qualifies as an employee for the purpose of imposing vicarious liability, including "the extent of control" exerted by the principal over the details of the agent's work. Other factors include whether an agent is engaged in "a distinct occupation or business."[29] According to one legal commentator, vicarious liability for firms should follow an "enterprise control" test based on justifications of (1) "employer control"; (2) "risk reduction"; (3) "employer benefit"; and (4) "cost internationalization."[30]

An exception applies when an agent acts outside "the scope of employment." As an illustration, consider the case of a pizza delivery driver employed by a business. If the driver causes an accident and injures a third party when delivering a pizza, then the firm will be vicariously liable for any harm and damage. Vicarious liability for the firm is in the form of "strict liability" once the underlying liability of the employee is established and as long as the agent acted "within the scope of

---

[23] Id., sect. 2.04.; sect. 7.07.

[24] Glanville Williams, "Vicarious Liability and the Master's Indemnity," 20 *Modern Law Review* 220, 221 (1957).

[25] See *Restatement (Third) of Agency*, op. cit., sect. 2.04, cmt. a.

[26] For a review of different justifications for vicarious liability, finding economic-based arguments for "deterrence" the most persuasive, see Gary T. Schwartz, "The Hidden and Fundamental Issue of Employer Vicarious Liability," 69 *Southern California Law Review* 1739, 1749–64 (1996).

[27] *Restatement (Third) of Agency*, op. cit., sect. 2.04.

[28] See, e.g., Sykes, op. cit., pp. 1261–3.

[29] *Restatement (Third) of Agency*, op. cit., sect. 7.07, cmt. f.

[30] Robert Flannigan, "Enterprise Control: The Servant-Independent Contractor Distinction," 37 *University of Toronto Law Journal* 25, 31–7 (1987).

employment."[31] However, if the pizza driver decides to take an unauthorized detour after a delivery to visit a lover, and an accident happens when driving to or from the unauthorized tryst, then the accident occurs "outside of the scope of employment," and the firm will not be responsible under a vicarious liability theory. The technical legal term for this exception is a "frolic."[32]

Note that the pizza delivery driver is also potentially liable in both circumstances, but low-level employees are often not sufficiently solvent to pay damages when severe injuries or deaths occur. As lawyers say, they are "judgment proof" by virtue of having little or no assets. Note also that the examples here assume tort systems based on private schemes of tort liability. Some countries, such as New Zealand, have entirely preempted this field with a national scheme of administration to compensate personal injuries caused by accidents. In this interventionist scheme, costs to business firms are allocated partly as a function of the costs of the overall number of accidents caused by them in order to provide incentives to decrease these costs. New Zealand's precedent, however, may have limitations with respect to the potential scope of the system (given that New Zealand is comparatively small). In any event, this scheme has not yet been widely followed elsewhere.[33]

More broadly speaking, enterprise liability can apply whenever an agent acts with actual or apparent authority and commits a tort.[34] In Canada and Great Britain, the standard for "enterprise liability" appears to be expanding to include any cases of "close connection" between an agent and principal, at least in cases of intentional torts caused by agents.[35] The legal recognition of the business enterprise as an entity in these cases allows also for a "risk-shifting" analysis that may justify broad-based enterprise liability on economic grounds.[36] (Curiously, most economic theories of the firm tend to ignore the large-scale risk-shifting features of the business enterprise and its governing law, at least in the context of enterprise liability.[37])

Enterprise liability also obtains if a firm is directly "negligent in selecting, training, retraining, supervising, or otherwise controlling" an agent.[38] Returning to the pizza delivery illustration, suppose that the pizza business and its managers fail to run background checks on its drivers and negligently hire someone with a

---

[31] See, e.g., Gregory C. Keating, "The Idea of Fairness in the Law of Enterprise Liability," 95 *Michigan Law Review* 1266, 1267 (1997).

[32] *Restatement (Third) of Agency*, op. cit., sect. 7.07, cmt. e ("An employee's travel during the work day that is not within the scope of employment has long been termed a 'frolic' of the employee's own. De minimis departures from assigned routes are not 'frolics' [but rather 'detours']"). For an early history of the distinction, see Young B. Smith, "Frolic and Detour," 23 *Columbia Law Review* 444 (1923).

[33] See Peter H. Schuck, "Tort Reform, Kiwi-Style," 27 *Yale Law and Policy Review* 187 (2008).

[34] *Restatement (Third) of Agency*, op. cit., sects. 7.04, 7.08.

[35] See, e.g., Douglas Brodie, "Enterprise Liability: Justifying Vicarious Liability," 27 *Oxford Journal of Legal Studies* 493 (2007).

[36] See Simon Deakin, "'Enterprise-Risk': The Juridical Nature of the Firm Revisited," 32 *Industrial Law Journal* 97 (2003); Reinier H. Kraakman, "Corporate Liability Strategies and the Costs of Legal Controls," 93 *Yale Law Journal* 857, 858–62 (1984). Cf. also Glanville Williams, "Vicarious Liability and the Master's Indemnity (Continued)," 20 *Modern Law Review* 437, 440–8 (1957) (arguing in favor of vicarious liability on grounds of social distribution of economic risk).

[37] See Deakin, op. cit, p. 112.

[38] *Restatement (Third) of Agency*, op. cit., sect. 7.05.

history of drunk driving. Or suppose that a speeding pizza delivery driver has an accident because of a dangerous policy of guaranteeing fast deliveries.[39] These situations would result in findings of enterprise liability on grounds that are independent of the vicarious liability of the firm. Liability for the firm would follow, for example, even if the driver had an accident when on a "frolic." Because these policies of the firm are set by higher level agents who are authorized to "speak" and "act" for the firm, the concepts of quasi-principals, subagency, and agency chains apply—and enterprise liability would follow when the policies demonstrate negligence.[40]

This independent source of tort liability for the firm is important because in some countries and in various legal contexts an affirmative defense against vicarious liability is available. This defense is often allowed if a firm can demonstrate that it was not negligent (i.e. not at fault), had undertaken the "utmost care" to avoid the wrongful harm, or had adopted other proactive measures within the enterprise to prevent or mitigate the wrongful harm. Although strict vicarious liability rules apply in Great Britain and France as well as the United States, Germany and Japan allow for these kinds of employer defenses to vicarious liability.[41] A similar defense appears to be emerging in Canada as well.[42]

In the United States, the Supreme Court has recognized an affirmative defense to enterprise liability against claims of statutory sexual harassment in the workplace if a firm has previously adopted effective internal measures to prevent or respond promptly to allegations of misbehavior by employees or other organizational agents.[43] There is no defense, however, if the alleged discrimination "culminates in a tangible employment action" against the employee.[44] "These cases offer employers an affirmative defense to a hostile environment harassment claim," one scholar observes, "if the employer has shown that it took reasonable steps to prevent harassment and to eliminate it when it does occur." The approach "encourages proactive steps to produce information and build capacity to problem solve by rewarding effective results with reduced liability."[45]

Agency-related cases of enterprise liability can generate very large financial exposure. For example, the pizza delivery case discussed above is not entirely hypothetical. Domino's Pizza dropped its enterprise-level guarantee of delivery within thirty minutes in the wake of a $79 million verdict for damages in a vehicle accident case.[46]

---

[39] See Deborah A. DeMott, "Organizational Incentives to Care About the Law," 60 *Law and Contemporary Problems* 39, 45–6 (1997).

[40] See *Restatement (Third) of Agency*, op. cit., sect. 7.03, cmt. c. See also Chapters 1 and 2 above.

[41] Schwartz, op. cit., pp. 1745–6.

[42] See Attila Ataner, "How Strict Is Vicarious Liability? Reassessing the Enterprise Risk Theory," 64 *University of Toronto Faculty of Law Review* 63, 67 (2006).

[43] See, e.g., *Burlington Industries, Inc. v. Ellerth*, 524 U.S. 742 (1998).

[44] Id., p. 765. See also *Faragher v. City of Boca Raton*, 524 U.S. 775 (1998) (vicarious liability for sexual harassment upheld given failure of an affirmative defense).

[45] Susan Sturm, "Second Generation Employment Discrimination: A Structural Approach," 101 *Columbia Law Review* 458, 481, 483 (2001).

[46] DeMott, op. cit., p. 46 n. 31.

Moreover, non-agency-based laws, such as strict liability for defective products and statutory liability for employment discrimination or environmental pollution, extend a firm's responsibilities and potential financial exposure even further.[47] (This is not to say that legal agency relationships are not involved in these cases, but only that the statutes making firms specifically liable for these violations do not require an agency-based analysis to find sufficient grounds for liability.) In general, enterprise liability has expanded significantly in recent decades through legislation in many areas, requiring business firms to take responsibility (and bear the resulting costs) not only for any defective food, drugs, or other products, but also for occupational safety, toxic waste disposal, and other large-scale social "externalities."[48]

My account here is based mainly on legal developments in the United States, though enterprise liability is recognized in other countries as well. Increasingly, as the legal scholar George Priest has demonstrated, strict liability standards have been applied to business enterprises. In his words:

Modern strict liability is more than a single legal standard. It comprises a complex regime of legal doctrines and categories.... Modern tort law generates complicated legal and economic issues—of industrywide apportionment of liability, probabilistic causation, and retroactive liability.... These developments [extend to] not only the law of products liability, but also problems as diverse as toxic waste disposal, occupational safety, recovery for all forms of cumulative injury, and indeed the effects of all by-products of industrial activity, however remote.[49]

In addition to vicarious liability, strict enterprise liability often follows for various statutory harms and injuries, as well as for harms and injuries deriving from defectively designed products or "ultrahazardous" activities (such as using explosives in construction or mining).[50]

This overview of modern enterprise liability shows that important legal boundaries of the firm concern the scope of liability of a firm for actions taken by the firm's agents (and apparent agents). Firms can often manage these boundaries through creative legal architecture.

For example, a finding of vicarious liability often depends on whether or not an agent is determined to be an "employee." To hire "independent contractors" instead has been used as a method to limit a firm's potential tort exposure.[51] The

---

[47] See, e.g., *Restatement (Third) of Agency*, op. cit., sect. 7.01, cmt. c and notes.

[48] See Keating, op. cit. On externalities, see also Preface pages xvii–xviii; Chapter 1, pages 22, 47, and accompanying notes 61, 179.

[49] George L. Priest, "The Invention of Enterprise Liability: A Critical History of the Intellectual Foundations of Modern Tort Law," 14 *Journal of Legal Studies* 461, 462 (1985).

[50] See Steven P. Croley and Jon D. Hanson, "Rescuing the Revolution: The Revived Case for Enterprise Liability," 91 *Michigan Law Review* 683 (1993); William K. Jones, "Strict Liability for Hazardous Enterprise," 92 *Columbia Law Review* 1705 (1992); Keating, op. cit.

[51] The *Restatement of Agency* abjures the use of independent contractor because the term is ambivalent in the following way: some independent contractors are agents and some are not. *Restatement (Third) of Agency*, op. cit., sect. 1.01, cmt. c. Nevertheless, the line between an "employee" and a separate business relationship appears implicitly in the "factual indicia" used to determine whether a relationship of "employment" exists for purposes of vicarious liability. See pages 139 and accompany-

definition of employee also matters with respect to enterprise-level liability in labor law. "Employees" are usually covered, and "independent contractors" are often not.[52]

The organization of FedEx Ground illustrates the management of this legal boundary. FedEx Ground is a network of truck drivers organized by FedEx Corporation as "independent contractors," even though FedEx Corporation exercises significant contractual control with respect to the branding of trucks and the physical appearance of drivers for FedEx Ground. For example, FedEx Corporation requires FedEx Ground drivers to wear FedEx uniforms, hide any tattoos, and restrict their hair length. At least one purpose of this organizational design is to avoid labor law definitions of "employee," thus avoiding potential liability under labor laws. FexEx Corporation would probably inherit responsibility for any accidents or contract damages involving FedEx Ground drivers under actual or apparent authority principles. The main financial motive for FedEx Corporation here is therefore to avoid liability under federal and state labor laws that use definitions of "employee" imported from agency law.[53] Some commentators have argued against interpreting labor law in this fashion.[54] At least in the United States, however, the law has not moved in this direction, thus allowing for considerable managerial play at the employment boundaries of the firm.

More generally, the extent that a firm limits its control over agents and acts appropriately with respect to their selection and oversight determines the firm's overall exposure for torts committed against third parties. Again, the use of an independent contractor may not fully eliminate potential enterprise liability, but it can often shift the legal standard from strict vicarious liability (for the actions of an employee or closely supervised agent) to a more forgiving negligence or "fault" standard (for the actions of a non-employee agent with sufficient independence of action and judgment). Structuring a commercial relationship entirely as an arm's-length business-to-business agreement may even eliminate the risk of a finding of any agency relationship and hence any risk of enterprise liability under legal agency theories.

"Outsourcing"—that is, moving from business structures of internal employment to contractual arrangements for services outside of the firm—describes another method by which different business architectures seek to manage a firm's

ing notes 29–30. On a possible intermediate category of a "dependent contractor" in Canadian law, see Brian A. Langille and Guy Davidov, "Beyond Employees and Independent Contractors: A View from Canada," 21 *Comparative Labor Law and Policy Journal* 7 (1999).

[52] See Lewis L. Maltby and David C. Yamada, "Beyond 'Economic Realities': The Case For Amending Federal Employment Discrimination Laws To Include Independent Contractors," 38 *Boston College Law Review* 239 (1997).

[53] See Todd D. Saveland, Note, "FedEx's New 'Employees': Their Disgruntled Independent Contractors," 36 *Transportation Law Journal* 95, 99, 101–19 (2009).

[54] See, e.g., Richard R. Carlson, "Why the Law Still Can't Tell an Employee When It Sees One and How It Ought to Stop Trying," 22 *Berkeley Journal of Employment and Labor Law* 295 (2001); Langille and Davidov, op. cit.; Maltby and Yamada, op. cit.

boundaries in order to insulate the firm from potential enterprise liability. Outsourcing occurs when a firm fires its employees and replaces them with either non-employee agents or arm's-length service providers. Outsourcing has many economic motivations, perhaps most prominently reducing labor costs and increasing access to global labor markets which have been enabled by cost reductions in communications and transportation. The legal limitation of enterprise liability afforded by outsourcing provides a strong economic incentive as well.[55]

There are other methods to manage the boundaries of the firm with respect to enterprise liability. Business decisions to insure or indemnify its employees or other agents also have boundary-line implications in terms of the financial liability of the firm. Insurance is one standard method for firms to hedge uncertainties about enterprise liability, including legal uncertainties about boundary issues. It is often more efficient and fair, for example, for two or more business firms to negotiate terms of potential enterprise liability and then allocate and insure against these risks in advance, rather than to litigate about mutual liability ex post. Courts will generally respect these allocations as long as the liability does not exceed the coverage, which may then require an assessment of whether the "entity" barrier in a particular case should be respected or disregarded (an issue discussed further in this chapter). Legally requiring or encouraging insurance is therefore another possible regulatory response to increase risk-spreading through policies oriented towards enterprise liability. In a sense, mandatory insurance is a hybrid method of regulation combining enterprise liability for torts and governmental interventionism. Indemnification provisions are also usually considered legitimate topics for internal bargaining among participants in a firm within the limits of any statutory limitations (such as prohibitions against indemnification or insurance for intentional torts or crimes). In general, any determination by a business to hire an employee, engage a non-employee agent, or enter into an agreement with an independent business for a particular service will have boundary-line implications for potential enterprise liability.

Complex firms that multiply entities and tie them together in ownership-and-control structures may also be used to limit enterprise liability. Parent–subsidiary structures and franchising structures are leading examples. These complex enterprises link a number of legal entities together in control-and-ownership structures that are designed to contain primary liability in a subsidiary or franchisee, thus

---

[55] On outsourcing, see, e.g., Ravi Aron, Eric K. Clemons, and Sashi Reddi, "Just Right Outsourcing: Understanding and Managing Risk," 22 *Journal of Management Information Systems* 37 (2005); Jagdish Bhagwati, Arvind Panagariya, and T.N. Srinivasan, "The Muddles Over Outsourcing," 18 *Journal of Economic Perspectives* 93 (2004); Amitava Dutta and Rahul Roy, "Offshore Outsourcing: A Dynamic Causal Model of Counteracting Forces," 22 *Journal of Management Information Systems* 15 (2005); George S. Geis, "Business Outsourcing and the Agency Cost Problem," 82 *Notre Dame Law Review* 955 (2007); Ann E. Harrison and Margaret S. McMillan, "Dispelling Some Myths About Offshoring," 20 *Academy of Management Perspectives* 6 (2006); Justin Kent Holcombe, "Solutions for Regulating Offshore Outsourcing in the Service Sector: Using the Law, Market, International Mechanisms, and Collective Organization as Building Blocks," 7 *University of Pennsylvania Journal of Labor and Employment Law* 539 (2005). See also Chapter 2, page 61 and accompanying note 38.

shielding the parent or franchisor firm from enterprise liability.[56] The U.S. Supreme Court has recognized parent–subsidiary structures to shield the potential liability of a parent corporation, for example, in the context of interpreting federal environmental liability statutes.[57] Corporate pyramids fall into the same category, though with perhaps increased reasons for skepticism about allowing subordinate entity structures to shield apex firms from enterprise liability.[58]

Franchising is a method of business organization described as "a distribution technique that integrates the distribution system by contract instead of by a centrally controlled chain of ownership."[59] It usually involves an organizing business enterprise (the franchisor), which develops branding, business processes, and standards for the delivery of products and services through licensing arrangements with other business enterprises (the franchisees).[60] Because the franchisor often exercises significant "control" in setting the terms of business for franchisees, boundary-line agency issues are often raised with respect to enterprise liability, including claims of vicarious liability and apparent authority.[61] Again, as with outsourcing and other decisions about business architecture, there are other economic considerations involved in decisions to organize a business enterprise as a franchise. Limiting potential enterprise liability, however, is surely one of these considerations.

Parent–subsidiary and franchise structures are also sometimes combined and managed as one integrated enterprise. The Hertz rental car enterprise and the Hilton global hotel chain illustrate this organizational approach.[62] Hertz, Hilton, and other complex firms might respond that true managerial "control" lies to a significant extent with the franchisees rather than the franchisor in these corporate structures. If so, then most of the relevant legal liability with respect to everyday operations should remain with the franchisees, if one follows the principle of responsibility following control. However, at least some aspects of "control" may remain with the franchisors, and to the extent that this control leads to traceable cognizable harm to others, then the franchisors and parents should arguably bear responsibility as well.

In general, business enterprise conducted through the use of multiple entities requires an updating of principles of enterprise liability to focus on the nature of

---

[56] On parent–subsidiary structures designed to limit enterprise liability, see Chapter 1, pages 37–8 and accompanying notes 131–5. See also Robert B. Thompson, "Unpacking Limited Liability: Direct and Vicarious Liability of Corporate Participants for Torts of the Enterprise," 47 *Vanderbilt Law Review* 1, 5 (1994) (concluding that "there remains a perplexing judicial reluctance to hold a corporate parent liable for the obligations of its subsidiaries when the parent possesses both the opportunity to control and the potential to share in residual earnings of a subsidiary").

[57] *United States v. Bestfoods*, 524 U.S. 51 (1998). For a critical discussion, see Robert B. Thompson, "Agency Law and Asset Partitioning," 71 *University of Cincinnati Law Review* 1321, 1331–9 (2003).

[58] On pyramids, see Chapter 2, pages 91–5 and accompanying notes 192–222.

[59] Robert W. Emerson, "Franchising and the Collective Rights of Franchisees," 43 *Vanderbilt Law Review* 1503, 1508 (1990).

[60] Id., pp. 1506–9.

[61] See Robert W. Emerson, "Franchisors' Liability When Franchisees Are Apparent Agents: An Empirical and Policy Analysis of 'Common Knowledge' About Franchising," 20 *Hofstra Law Review* 609 (1992).

[62] Phillip I. Blumberg, "The Transformation of Modern Corporation Law: The Law of Corporate Groups," 37 *Connecticut Law Review* 605, 613 n. 34 (2005).

firms operating at this level of complexity and integration. This field has been called "the law of corporate groups."[63] It involves entities other than corporations in various business structures, however, and one may refer more accurately to "the law of business groups" or "the law of complex firms."

One sensible policy response to the multiplication of entities in business groups has been to recommend a focus on "the business enterprise as a whole, not on its fragmented components."[64] This approach would trace enterprise liability according to features of "control" and "integration" of the entire enterprise, rather than to allow the construction of a complex of entities to undermine the overall legal and ethical responsibility for organizational behavior.[65] A number of statutes in the United States and Europe adopt versions of these kinds of "control" or "integration" tests in particular fields, such as antitrust and securities regulation.[66] More generally, the legal scholar Philip Blumberg recommends that enterprise liability should be attributed to large business enterprises when they exhibit the following features: (1) "a common public persona featuring a common trade name, logo, and marketing plan"; (2) "financial interdependence"; (3) "administrative interdependence"; and (4) "group identification of employees."[67] Along these lines, German and European Union law have recognized broader and more realistic "enterprise law" principles to cover corporate groups than current law in the United States, Great Britain, and elsewhere.[68] India may have the strictest regime (at least on paper), responding in part to the Bhopal disaster and Union Carbide's shielding of its liability through a parent–subsidiary structure.[69] And an interesting case decided by the United States Supreme Court addressed whether U.S.-based multinational corporations may be held liable for international human rights violations.[70] The case highlights a more general issue for the future concerning the potential enterprise liability of very large firms operating in an increasingly small world of globally integrated production and distribution.

Limited liability of business participants

Entities of the firm allow for the dedication of specific assets to support enterprise liability and to shield enterprise entities from liability within complex firms. In

---

[63] Id., p. 605; see also Philip I. Blumberg et al., *Blumberg on Corporate Groups* (Aspen 2005); Janet Dine, *The Governance of Corporate Groups* (Cambridge University Press 2000), pp. 37–66.

[64] Blumberg, "The Transformation of Modern Corporation Law," op. cit., pp. 605.

[65] Id., pp. 608–10. See also Chapter 1, page 37 and accompanying note 133.

[66] Blumberg, "The Transformation of Modern Corporation Law," op. cit., pp. 608–10 and n. 18.

[67] Id., p. 610.

[68] See, e.g., Dine, op. cit., pp. 38, 55–9; Yitzhak Hadari, "The Structure of the Private Multi-national Enterprise," 71 *Michigan Law Review* 729, 793–7 (1973) (describing the German Law of Related Companies or *Konzernrecht*). See also *Regulating Corporate Groups in Europe* (David Sugarman and Gunther Teubner eds.) (Nomos 1990); Meredith Dearborn, Comment, "Enterprise Liability: Reviewing and Revitalizing Liability for Corporate Groups," 97 *California Law Review* 195 (2009).

[69] Dearborn, op. cit, pp. 226–9.

[70] *Kiobel v. Royal Dutch Petroleum Co.*, 133 S. Ct. 1659 (2013) (rejecting a claim brought by foreign citizens against a foreign-based corporation under the Alien Tort Statute of 1789 and adopting a presumption against extraterritorial application). See also Preface to the Paperback Edition, page x and accompanying note 7.

addition, business entities can protect individual business participants from personal liability.[71] Business participants for these purposes include (a) executives, managers, and employees who act as agents of the firm, (b) equity owners of the firm, and (c) creditors of the firm. Each of these categories is considered in turn.

Executives, managers, and employees

Again to begin with liability for contracts, business managers and other employees who are authorized through a firm's legal organizational structure to negotiate and enter into contracts on behalf of the firm are usually immunized from personal liability on these contracts. In other words, a firm's authorized agents bind the firm itself to contracts but not themselves personally, as long as they are acting in their representative capacities on behalf of their firm and within their actual authority.[72] The *Restatement (Third) of Agency* states: "An organizational executive does not become subject to personal liability on a contract as a consequence of executing a document in the executive's organizational capacity or as a consequence of holding that office."[73] One commentator describes this principle of "limited liability for managers" as follows:

> An individual who signs a contract on behalf of the corporation is cloaked in the mantle of the enterprise and is not personally liable for action taken in the corporate name. If the enterprise defaults on an obligation under the contract, the creditor normally cannot proceed against the individual.[74]

In other words, enterprise liability translates into limited liability for the firm's agent managers and employees in most ordinary contract situations.

This is a default rule, however, which means that a contracting third party may ask for a personal guarantee from the manager or another business participant (such as a majority shareholder or even a major creditor of the firm).[75] Personal guarantees of this kind are common and highly recommended when third parties enter into contracts with small firms organized as limited liability entities and when these firms may not possess sufficient capital to pay expected damages for a contractual breach or nonperformance.[76] Similarly, creditors of firms with complex corporate structures often ask for "intragroup guarantees" to counter attempts to insulate the overall enterprise from liability through the multiplication of subsidiaries (as

---

[71] See Henry Hansmann and Reinier Kraakman, "The Essential Role of Organizational Law," 110 *Yale Law Journal* 387, 390–8, 423–8, 439–40 (2000); Henry Hansmann, Reinier Kraakman, and Richard Squire, "Law and the Rise of the Firm," 119 *Harvard Law Review* 1333, 1336–43, 1354–5 (2006). See also Chapter 1, pages 34–6 and accompanying notes 115–23.

[72] See *Restatement (Third) of Agency*, op. cit., sect. 6.01.

[73] Id., sect. 6.01, cmt. d(2).

[74] Thompson, "Unpacking Limited Liability," op. cit., p. 7.

[75] Note that the default rule is reversed with respect to an "unidentified principal." In these cases, the agent is contractually bound to the third party, unless the agent and third party agree otherwise. *Restatement (Third) of Agency*, op. cit., sect. 6.02. In the case of an "undisclosed principal," both the agent and the principal are liable unless agreed otherwise. Id., sect. 6.03.

[76] See, e.g., Clark, op. cit., p. 9. See also David W. Leebron, "Limited Liability, Tort Victims, and Creditors," 91 *Columbia Law Review* 1565, 1630–2 (1991).

described above). These guarantees usually aim to bind other entities within the firm, however, rather than executives, managers, or individual owners personally.[77]

In apparent authority contract situations, a different rule of liability governs agency relationships of managers and employees within the firm. Although organizational principals are liable to third parties in these cases, they may then turn around and recover from the unauthorized agent (e.g. an executive, manager, or other employee) who entered into the contract in violation of an internal governance contract or policy.[78] In these cases, courts tend to defer to business participants and the internal arrangements of authority within the firm. For prudential reasons, firms often choose to forgo the legally available option of recovering from a manager or employee who simply made a mistake in exceeding his or her authority. Rather than suing their own agents, most firms prefer self-help remedies, such as dismissing, demoting, or otherwise internally sanctioning the offending agent.

With respect to torts and statutory violations, managers and employees usually share joint liability with the firm under legal agency principles. There is an exception in some cases of enterprise liability imposed by statute, such as employment discrimination laws that designate only "employers" or organizational principals as potentially liable, or environmental statutes that impose liability only on the "owners" or "operators" of an enterprise rather than lower-level agents.[79]

Firms may act to protect executives, managers, and employees by allocating the risks of liability primarily to the enterprise entity through indemnification agreements and insurance. In corporations, the board of directors is the usual source of authority for these arrangements. Although indemnification and insurance often travel together in practice, providing a double layer of protection, they deserve separate treatment conceptually.

Indemnification reimburses executives, managers, or other employees for damages assessed and expenses incurred for actions taken on behalf of the firm. The indemnification of agents is sometimes mandatory and sometimes permissive. In general, agents have a right to reimbursement for expenses and other costs incurred when acting on behalf of an organizational principal, including coverage of litigation expenses. The scope of mandatory indemnification differs with the business form selected (e.g. a partnership or a corporation) and legal jurisdiction. Usually, there is no mandatory right to indemnification if an agent acts without authorization and in a manner that does not benefit the principal.[80]

Many jurisdictions also provide for the extensive *permissive* indemnification of agents. In Delaware, for example, a corporation may indemnify any "director, officer, employee or agent of the corporation" for "any threatened, pending or completed action, suit or proceeding, whether civil, criminal, administrative or investigative." The only exclusion is for "an action by or in the right of the

---

[77] See Phillip I. Blumberg, "Intragroup (Upstream, Cross-Stream, and Downstream) Guaranties under the Uniform Fraudulent Transfer Act," 9 *Cardozo Law Review* 685 (1987); Richard Squire, "Strategic Liability in the Corporate Group," 78 *University of Chicago Law Review* 605 (2011).

[78] *Restatement (Third) of Agency*, op. cit., sect. 8.07.

[79] Id., sect. 7.01 and cmt. c (citing relevant statutes).

[80] Id., sect. 8.14 and cmts. b, c, and d.

corporation" brought by shareholders.[81] Even with respect to this exclusion, Delaware allows a firm to adopt an exculpatory charter provision for the benefit of corporate directors. This exculpatory provision grants an "opt out" from personal liability for violations of fiduciary duties of care that directors otherwise owe to shareholders.[82] The cumulative effect of Delaware's legal structure is to permit extensive protection of corporate agents, especially directors and officers, from threats of personal liability.[83]

Insurance, such as director and officer (D&O) insurance in corporations, is another liability-avoidance mechanism or, more precisely, a risk-of-liability spreading mechanism that protects directors and officers. D&O insurance spreads the risks of liability outside of the firm in return for premiums paid by the firm.[84] It therefore provides another level of immunization for directors and officers against personal liability. Scholars debate whether D&O insurance premiums reflect the degree of governance risk in firms and, if so, whether mandatory rules should be adopted to require disclosure of these premiums.[85] In any event, the decision whether or not to buy D&O insurance lies within the discretion of firms. In the case of corporations, for example, boards of directors have this discretion.

In extreme and very rare cases of large tort liabilities that cause the insolvency and bankruptcy of the firm, indemnification and insurance coverage may not provide full protection. Joint liability would then attribute the balance of damages to responsible agents after the resources of the firm are exhausted. Also, though most indemnification agreements and insurance contracts favor top-level executives, general insurance policies covering accidents and other routine injuries often shield lower-level employees from personal liability as well.

---

[81] Delaware Code Ann., tit. 8, sect. 145 (2010).

[82] Delaware Code Ann., tit. 8, sect. 102(b)(7) (2010).

[83] See Joseph P. Monteleone and Nicholas J. Conca, "Directors and Officers Indemnification and Liability Insurance: An Overview of Legal and Practical Issues," 51 *Business Lawyer* 573 (1996); Karl E. Stauss, Note, "Indemnification in Delaware: Balancing Policy Goals and Liabilities," 29 *Delaware Journal of Corporate Law* 143 (2004). See also James J. Hanks, Jr., "Evaluating Recent State Legislation on Director and Officer Liability Limitation and Indemnification," 43 *Business Lawyer* 1207 (1988).

[84] For an overview of D&O insurance in the United States, see, e.g., Monteleone and Conca, op. cit., pp. 584–621. See also Joseph Warren Bishop, Jr. et al., *The Law of Corporate Officers and Directors: Indemnification and Insurance* (Clark Boardman Callaghan 2010); John F. Olson et al., *Director and Officer Liability: Indemnification and Insurance* (Clark Boardman Callaghan 2010). For a rare comparative study, see Jun Sun Park, "A Comparative Study of D&O Liability Insurance in the U.S. and South Korea: Protecting Directors and Officers from Securities Litigation," 10 *Chicago-Kent Journal of International and Comparative Law* 1 (2010).

[85] For evidence that premiums increase to reflect governance risk, see Tom Baker and Sean J. Griffith, "Predicting Corporate Governance Risk: Evidence from the Directors' & Officers' Liability Insurance Market," 74 *University of Chicago Law Review* 487 (2007). See also John E. Core, "The Directors' and Officers' Insurance Premium: An Outside Assessment of the Quality of Corporate Governance," 16 *Journal of Law, Economics & Organization* 449 (2000) (using Canadian data). For a potential reform recommending mandatory public disclosure of insurance policies and their premiums, see Sean J. Griffith, "Uncovering a Gatekeeper: Why the SEC Should Mandate Disclosure of Details Concerning Directors' and Officers' Liability Insurance Policies," 154 *University of Pennsylvania Law Review* 1147 (2006).

Indemnification agreements and D&O insurance policies often exclude coverage of the following: crimes, violations of fiduciary duties of loyalty (i.e. self-dealing against the interests of the firm), and serious violations of federal law (such as securities fraud, insider trading, and false public reporting).[86] However, it is an indication of the effectiveness of these methods to limit liability—and an indication of the lack of their reviewability—that high-level business executives have been indemnified and insured by their firms even after having been convicted of crimes.[87] A related issue concerns indemnification agreements to advance expenses to defend against criminal charges, which are also generally allowed.[88]

Prison sentences for individuals, however, remain neither indemnifiable nor insurable. An unintended consequence of increasing indemnification and insurance protection for executives and managers may therefore have been to increase the incentives of government to resort to the criminal law, against which individuals cannot indemnify or insure.[89]

According to an early observer, the legal scholar Joseph Bishop, the strategies of indemnification and insurance within firms "virtually . . . immunize management from personal liability."[90] In his words, penned presciently over forty years ago:

> In sum, I think that the practice of protecting corporate executives against litigation and liability has now been carried about as far as it ought to be carried and perhaps a little farther. Corporate directors and officers should eschew efforts to protect themselves, by direct indemnification or insurance, from the consequences of breach of their duty not to enrich themselves at the corporation's expense and from the consequences of their gross negligence in the management of its affairs. And if directors and officers do not show such self-restraint, then legislatures and courts should supply the deficiency.[91]

It is now fair to conclude that requests for executive self-restraint on this score have been in vain, and legislatures and courts (at least in the United States) have not stepped up their oversight either. Legislative action has gone, if anything, in the other direction. "Current legal doctrine," one contemporary legal commentator writes, "should satisfy no one but the pragmatists who seek advantage in fribbles rather than the concepts that give life to legal strategies." Instead, "the outline of a general program of regulation" in this area is needed.[92]

In the future, perhaps some new legal reforms will begin to readjust the balance between enterprise liability and managerial liability. One intriguing suggestion proposes an extension of vicarious liability (formerly allocated only to the firm as

---

[86] See, e.g., Monteleone and Conca, op. cit., pp. 583–4, 600–3; Stauss, op. cit., pp. 160–2.

[87] See Pamela H. Bucy, "Indemnification of Corporate Executives Who Have Been Convicted of Crimes: An Assessment and Proposal," 24 *Indiana Law Review* 279 (1991).

[88] For a case setting forth the historical and scholarly background justifying enforcement of this kind of indemnification, see *United States v. Stein*, 435 F. Supp. 2d 330, 353–6 (S.D.N.Y. 2006).

[89] On the interaction of enterprise liability and individual liability in criminal law, see Samuel W. Buell, "Criminal Procedure Within the Firm," 59 *Stanford Law Review* 1613 (2007); Laufer, op. cit.

[90] Joseph W. Bishop, Jr., "Sitting Ducks and Decoy Ducks: New Trends in the Indemnification of Corporate Directors and Officers," 77 *Yale Law Journal* 1078, 1079 (1968).

[91] Id., p. 1103.

[92] Dale A. Oesterle, "Limits on a Corporation's Protection of Its Directors and Officers from Personal Liability," 1983 *Wisconsin Law Review* 513, 582 (1983).

an entity) to the highest ranking officers of an enterprise in appropriate cases.[93] For now, however, the ability of business enterprises to shield their directors, managers, and other employees from potential liability for contracts, torts, and other civil statutory damages remains very strong and relatively unconstrained.

Equity owners

Equity owners of limited liability business firms, such as corporations and limited liability companies, are also shielded from both contractual and tort liability by the entity of the firm. (The different kinds of limited liability firms are described further below and in Chapter 5.)

Limited liability for equity owners of firms is one of the best-known features of enterprise law. It became well established in the Western world beginning in the nineteenth century and had precursors even earlier. Firms with limited liability for their owners had arisen in Europe by the 1820s: limited companies in Britain, *sociétés anonymes* in France, and *Aktiengesellschaft* in Germany.[94] France recognized a principle of limited liability in 1807, and it spread throughout continental Europe via Napoleon's conquests.[95] Rudimentary forms of limited liability for owners of firms can be detected centuries earlier. Shareholders in the Dutch East India Company, for example, tasted an implicit recognition of limited liability.[96] A form of limited liability even appeared in the ancient Roman institution of the *peculium*, but this slave-based organizational form is not relevant to modern circumstances.[97]

Even after limited liability became recognized as the general rule for equity owners of many firms, variations on the scope of the principle survived for many years. In the United States, for example, some state statutes maintained that equity shareholders were liable for "double" or "triple" the amount of their capital investments. Double and triple liability for shareholders of private banks continued until after the Great Depression.[98] (Some contemporary commentators have argued for a resurrection of double liability for equity owners of banks.[99]) Interestingly with

---

[93] See Timothy P. Glynn, "Beyond 'Unlimiting' Shareholder Liability: Vicarious Tort Liability for Corporate Officers," 57 *Vanderbilt Law Review* 329 (2004).

[94] See Norman Davies, *Europe: A History* (Oxford University Press 1996), p. 768; Eric Hobsbawm, *The Age of Empire: 1875–1914* (Vintage ed. 1989) (1987), p. 10. See also Phillip I. Blumberg, "Limited Liability and Corporate Groups," 11 *Journal of Corporation Law* 573, 577–95 (1986).

[95] Blumberg, "Limited Liability and Corporate Groups," op. cit., pp. 595–6.

[96] Niall Ferguson, *The Ascent of Money: A Financial History of the World* (Penguin Press 2008), p. 12.

[97] See Hansmann, Kraakman, and Squire, op. cit., pp. 1358–60 (describing limited liability features of the *peculium*, in which slave-agents conducted business on behalf of master-owners who were allowed to claim limited liability against creditors of the *peculium*).

[98] Blumberg, "Limited Liability and Corporate Groups," op. cit., pp. 599–601. See also John R. Vincens, "On the Demise of Double Liability of Bank Shareholders," 75 *Banking Law Journal* 213 (1958) (surveying state statutes and their supervention by federal banking law).

[99] See Jonathan R. Macey and Geoffrey P. Miller, "Double Liability of Bank Shareholders: History and Implications," 27 *Wake Forest Law Review* 31 (1992).

respect to the boundaries of the firm and its various categories of participants, some early statutes even provided for shareholder liability for employee wages.[100]

Prominent academics have long hailed the rule of limited liability for equity owners as a revolutionary breakthrough in legal technology equivalent in social impact to other major inventions in the physical sciences. President Nicholas Butler of Columbia University, for example, declared in 1912 that "the limited liability corporation is the greatest single discovery of modern times." Even the invention of "steam and electricity," he said, "are far less important than the limited liability corporation, and they would be reduced to comparative impotence without it." His contemporary, President Charles Eliot of Harvard University, concurred. He described limited liability as "the corporation's most precious characteristic" and "the most effective legal invention for business purposes made in the nineteenth century."[101] The context of these early assessments is illuminating. For Butler, the "social," "ethical," and "political" institutional consequences of the advent of the corporation were as important as the economic consequences. He described the limited liability corporation as "a device by which a large number of individuals may share in an undertaking without risking in that undertaking more than they voluntarily and individually assume." This form of enterprise, Butler continued, had advantages of scale that made possible "huge economy in production and in trading," leading to "steadier employment of labor at an increased wage" and "the modern provision of industrial insurance, of care for disability, old age and widowhood."[102] For Eliot, limited liability for shareholders "enables" business corporations and their managers "to mass and direct capital." "Therefore corporations multiply and have become indispensable."[103] In other words, the social advantages and consequences of limited liability have been seen to be central. The principle of limited liability has never been justified merely to protect investors.

Today, the basic principle of limited liability for equity owners in business organizations has spread throughout the world. "Most nations offer limited liability to some, if not all, of their juridical entities," writes one comparative legal scholar, though different rules govern the availability and extent of limited liability in different countries.[104]

Limited liability for equity owners encourages investors to venture their capital in firms without worrying about the downside risk of personal liability in

[100] Blumberg, "Limited Liability and Corporate Groups," op. cit., pp. 601–2.

[101] See id., p. 577 n. 5; Bernard F. Cataldo, "Limited Liability with One-Man Companies and Subsidiary Corporations," 18 *Law and Contemporary Problems* 473, 473 (1953) (quoting both Butler and Eliot). See also James Willard Hurst, *The Legitimacy of the Business Corporation in the United States, 1780–1970* (University Press of Virginia 1970), p. 9. For the original quotations, see Nicholas Murray Butler, *Why Should We Change Our Form of Government? Studies in Practical Politics* (Charles Scribner's Sons 1912), p. 82; William W. Cook, "'Watered Stock'—Commissions—'Blue Sky Laws'—Stock Without Par Value," 19 *Michigan Law Review* 583, 583 n. 4 (1921) (quoting Eliot directly).

[102] Butler, op. cit., pp. 82–3.

[103] Cook, op. cit., p. 583 n. 4 (quoting Eliot).

[104] Sarah C. Haan, "Federalizing the Foreign Corporate Form," 85 *St. John's Law Review* 925, 952 (2011).

the low-probability but high-consequence event of a firm's bankruptcy. As one early observer of the phenomenon writes:

> Th[e] exemption of stockholders from personal liability for corporate debts has worked wonders in the industrial world. If such freedom from liability did not exist the public would not dare to buy stocks, because they would be liable for corporate debts. With that exemption from liability, however, the risk is reduced to the risk of the money actually paid for the stock.[105]

Other scholars have observed the "potent influence" that limited liability entities have had "in the expansion of industry and in the growth of trade and commerce."[106] A primary policy justification for granting limited liability to equity owners has therefore been the significant economic benefits that accrue through the encouragement of investment by risk-averse individuals. Investments by many individuals in a society encourage the large aggregations of capital that characterize many big business firms today.

Although rare, the potential for significant liability exists for equity investors even in very large firms. Companies in the asbestos industry supply a relatively recent historical example.[107] Eighty-five companies went bankrupt through asbestos-related litigation, and many individual shareholders would have been liable for substantial amounts of damages without limited liability, given the total estimated costs of over $200 billion.[108] Although asbestos damages and litigation costs were largest in the United States, many European companies were also put out of business.[109] The principle of limited liability protected investors from personal exposure of their assets to satisfy claims in these cases. Tobacco and fast-food related illnesses suggest possible future scenarios in which large liabilities may obtain for large firms and, in the absence of a rule of limited liability, their investors.[110] Even if the actual probabilities of large bankruptcies and resulting exposure of equity owners to losses are relatively low, the fear of even a small chance of large personal liability is sufficient to deter many individual investors.

In financial terms, limited liability for equity owners means that the total financial liability of the investor-owner is limited or capped at the amount actually invested in the limited liability firm. If the company goes bankrupt, then the equity owner loses only the capital invested and cannot be sued for more, even in egregious cases of mass torts or huge frauds committed by managers.

---

[105] Cook, op. cit., p. 584.

[106] William O. Douglas and Carrol M. Shanks, "Insulation from Liability Through Subsidiary Corporations," 39 *Yale Law Journal* 193, 193 (1929).

[107] See Michelle J. White, "Asbestos and the Future of Mass Torts," 18 *Journal of Economic Perspectives* 183 (2004).

[108] Id., p. 183 (total costs estimated to fall between $200 and $265 billion, including legal expenses).

[109] Id., pp. 189–91.

[110] Id., pp. 194–5. Cf. Lynn M. LoPucki, "Virtual Judgment Proofing: A Rejoinder," 107 *Yale Law Journal* 1413 (1998) (listing these and other large potential corporate liability cases, though arguing that "judgment proofing" methods such as the increased use of limited liability entities reduce exposure for many firms and their investors).

Limited liability for equity owners is usually accomplished by statute. Equity owners could themselves create a kind of "limited liability" by requiring all contracts made with a firm to include standard-form provisions that specifically exclude the equity owners from potential liability. In other words, all contracts made by the firm would designate specifically that only the assets dedicated to the firm will be available to meet contractual obligations.[111] In fact, some English "limited companies" followed this approach prior to the adoption of statutes allowing for limited liability corporations.[112] However, the transaction costs of this approach are high, and many parties to the firm's contracts may ask for negotiated exceptions (such as personal guarantees from owners). Legal interpretations of individual contract provisions are also more uncertain than a uniformly applied rule of limited liability. The self-help contractual alternative to statutory limited liability is therefore "cumbersome, expensive, and risky to the investors" in the firm.[113] An additional major weakness is that a purely self-organized contracting approach cannot limit the firm's liability with respect to potential tort victims or statutory violations, such as liability for defective products or for damage caused by environmental pollution.[114]

The statutory limitation of liability for downside risk beyond the amount of capital invested in firms has allowed for a great and continuing enlargement of the capital markets for the ownership of firms. The combination of a formal separation of business assets and limited personal liability for owners who contribute capital to a business enterprise engendered the revolutionary fragmentation of private property described in Chapter 2. In turn, this revolution in corporate property has financed the construction and ongoing maintenance of very large corporate enterprises.[115] Large capital aggregations in limited liability ownership structures fueled new business technologies and methods, increasing both the scale and scope of business activities and leading to the growth of large multinational firms and the spread of global capital markets.[116] Limited liability for shareholders contributed also to the emergence, beginning in earnest also in the nineteenth century, of "the free alienability of shares" and "free transfer" of ownership interests in limited liability firms in public securities markets, which further expanded the availability of capital and lowered the cost of capital to firms.[117]

---

[111] See Hansmann, Kraakman, and Squire, op. cit., p. 1341.

[112] See id.; Blumberg, "Limited Liability and Corporate Groups," op. cit., pp. 581–2.

[113] Clark, op. cit., p. 9.

[114] See id., pp. 9–10.

[115] On the economic justifications for limited liability for individual shareholders of large firms, see Frank H. Easterbrook and Daniel R. Fischel, *The Economic Structure of Corporate Law* (Harvard University Press 1996), pp. 41–4; Frank H. Easterbrook and Daniel R. Fischel, "Limited Liability and the Corporation," 52 *University of Chicago Law Review* 89 (1985). See also Millon, "Limits of Limited Liability," op. cit., pp. 1312–17; Robert B. Thompson, "Piercing the Corporate Veil: An Empirical Study," 76 *Cornell Law Review* 1036, 1039–41 (1991).

[116] On the economies of scale and scope of large business enterprises, see Chapter 2, pages 83–4, 102, and accompanying notes 149–51, 258.

[117] See, e.g., Clark, op. cit., pp. 10–15; Hansmann, Kraakman, and Squire, op. cit., p. 1396. On the importance of limited liability for the development of securities markets, see also Paul Halpern, Michael Trebilcock, and Stuart Turnbull, "An Economic Analysis of Limited Liability in Corporation Law," 30 *University of Toronto Law Journal* 117 (1980).

Limited liability firms include not only the widely traded "public" shareholder structures of corporations, but also closely held corporations, limited liability companies, and limited liability partnerships (which are reviewed further in Chapter 5). Rough approximations of these basic legal forms of business enterprise appear in most countries.

Reference to "public" shareholders or corporations in this context refers to the open or public trading of shares on securities markets. These ownership interests remain "private" in the sense of individual personal ownership (though often aggregated today into institutional investors who manage funds on behalf of individual beneficiaries). The "public" securities markets of shareholders who hold "private" ownership claims in firms provide another example of how the public–private distinction discussed in Chapter 3 works in practice.

Limited liability firms are authorized by specific statutes tailored to specific business needs and sizes. In the United States, each individual state has separate statutes governing corporations, partnerships, limited liability companies, and other business forms. Most other countries have unified statutes at the national level.[118] Corporations are usually divided into "close" and "public" forms. Close corporations are "closely held" with only private, non-publicly traded shares. Public corporations trade their shares on public markets. In limited liability companies (another special legal form), equity owners are called "members."[119] And in limited liability partnerships, the equity owners are of course called "partners." In all of these statutory firms, the members, partners, or shareholders qualify for limited liability as equity owners.

Limited liability has also been extended to more informally organized and often smaller businesses, even single proprietors and one-person corporations. In 1897, for example, the early landmark English case, *Salomon v. Salomon & Co.*, recognized a shield of limited liability in favor of a sole proprietor who incorporated.[120] China had been an outlier for many years in disallowing one-person limited liability firms.[121] But in 2006, the new Chinese company law formally authorized one-person limited liability firms.[122]

Over time, the legal privilege of limited liability has become gradually "democratized" in the sense that anyone going into business may choose a legal form that allows for a segregation of business assets from personal assets and a corresponding protection of personal assets from business-related risks. At least, this general trajectory has been followed in the United States and other countries that follow a substantially similar model. Historically, advocates of egalitarian democracy in the

---

[118] See, e.g., Company Law of the People's Republic of China (revised 2005), <http://www.fdi.gov.cn/pub/> (accessed September 14, 2012). See also Partnership Enterprise Law of the People's Republic of China (President's Order 2007), <http://www.fdi.gov.cn/pub/> (accessed September 14, 2012).

[119] See Revised Uniform Limited Liability Company Act, sect. 102(11) (2006).

[120] [1897] A.C. 22, HL. See also Chapter 1, page 51, note 202. Cataldo, op. cit., pp. 474–5.

[121] See Donald C. Clarke, "How Do We Know When an Enterprise Exists? Unanswerable Questions and Legal Polycentricity in China," 19 *Columbia Journal of Asian Law* 50 (2005).

[122] Company Law of the People's Republic of China, op. cit., sect. 3, arts. 58–64.

United States argued that principles of limited liability should give "the corporation held by small shareholders the same status as the one held by the wealthy, provided that the corporations themselves were equally creditworthy."[123] General incorporation statutes replaced the earlier "concession" method that allowed for the creation of new corporations only by special government-issued charters.[124]

The legal historian James Willard Hurst aptly described this historical change as moving from "special privilege" to "general utility."[125] One additional contemporaneous argument given for general incorporation statutes was that the "special" incorporation decisions by legislatures were inherently corrupt.[126] When the British Parliament adopted a model statute of general incorporation in 1869, one commentator described it as a "master-work of legislation" having as its "main object" to "throw open to everyone, on the same terms and conditions, the coveted privilege of incorporation." It also aimed at eliminating "the discrimination, favoritism, and oftentimes the corruption" of the special incorporation system.[127] Similarly, France adopted a general incorporation statute in 1867.[128]

This historical perspective on what may be called *the democratization of limited liability* explains some of the conceptual ambiguity regarding whether business firms are "top-down" creations of government or "bottom-up" creations of self-organizing business participants, as posed in Chapter 1. At an earlier period in history—and perhaps continuing today in some societies—the top-down or "concession" theory is accurate. The theory of the firm elaborated in this book assumes the historical and institutional development discussed here, which emphasizes the bottom-up perspectives of business participants as well as the top-down perspective of governments—and recognizes as well the differences respecting the relative weight assigned to top-down and bottom-up perspectives in different jurisdictions.

Entity piercing

Although there are significant exceptions, the general rule is that unless an equity owner in a limited liability firm is cavalier about respecting legal formalities or uses the entity to commit fraud (or its equivalent) on a third party, the enterprise entity will be respected and not "pierced" or "disregarded" to hold the equity owner personally liable for business commitments and debts.

The unfortunate mixed metaphor of "piercing the corporate veil" appears to have resulted from a cultural miscommunication: the combination of the delicate British

---

[123] Herbert Hovenkamp, *Enterprise and American Law, 1836–1937* (Harvard University Press 1991), pp. 50–1.

[124] See, e.g., John Steele Gordon, *An Empire of Wealth: The Epic History of American Economic Power* (HarperCollins 2004), pp. 228–9; Hurst, op. cit., pp. 13–33, 134–5. See also Chapter 1, page 13 and accompanying note 22, and Chapter 3, page 131 and accompanying note 109.

[125] Hurst, op. cit., pp. 13–57.

[126] See John Joseph Wallis, "Constitutions, Corporations, and Corruption: American States and Constitutional Change, 1842 to 1852," 65 *Journal of Economic History* 211, 238–9, 248 (2005).

[127] I. Maurice Wormser, *Frankenstein, Incorporated* (McGraw-Hill 1931), p. 26.

[128] Blumberg, "Limited Liability and Corporate Groups," op. cit., pp. 595–6.

metaphor of "lifting the veil" of an entity (to see the real individual person beneath) and the stronger "piercing" of business entities advocated by an American academic who was generally skeptical of limited liability for corporations, having titled his best known book *Frankenstein, Incorporated*.[129] "Piercing" is a rather aggressive way of stating the issue, but the image is colorful, entrenched in current usage, and relatively accurate. But I will leave aside the "veil" here. "Piercing veils" travels too far into the realm of mixed metaphors where conceptual monsters lurk: academics and judges turn back! "Piercing entities" is sufficient to describe what is actually happening in these cases from a legal point of view.

With respect to large corporations of many public shareholders, the business entity is pierced to find individual equity owners liable only very rarely, if ever. Empirical studies in the United States confirm that courts "never hold shareholders of publicly held corporations personally liable for corporate obligations"[130]

Corporate groups with parent–subsidiary or pyramid structures present occasional exceptions to the no-piercing rule as applied to large corporations, though these cases are usually better analyzed as claims of "enterprise liability." Despite arguments from commentators to the contrary, empirical evidence demonstrates that courts "seldom" pierce entities within corporate groups in the United States.[131] And in the rare cases of piercing entities within corporate groups, some showing of "misuse" of the corporate forms is usually required.[132] As discussed above, there is a strong case for the enterprise liability of corporate groups when effective control is exercised by a parent or apex entity. Also as mentioned above, courts in Europe find liability under these circumstances more frequently than in the United States.[133] British courts, for example, have begun to follow a "single economic unit theory" to pierce entities within groups.[134]

With respect to smaller firms—or, more precisely, firms with fewer individual equity owners (such as closely held corporations, limited liability family firms, or other small business enterprises)—the rule of limited liability for equity owners is much less reliable. These kinds of firms can also grow quite large in terms of economic size and scope of operations, rivaling large public corporations. Nevertheless, piercing

---

[129] See Alfred F. Conard, *Corporations in Perspective* (Foundation Press 1976), p. 425; I. Maurice Wormser, "Piercing the Veil of Corporate Entity," 12 *Columbia Law Review* 496 (1912). See also Wormser, *Frankenstein, Incorporated*, op. cit.

[130] See Millon, "Limits of Limited Liability," op. cit., p. 1326. See also Peter B. Oh, "Veil-Piercing," 89 *Texas Law Review* 81, 110 (2010); Thompson, "Piercing the Corporate Veil," op. cit., p. 1047.

[131] John H. Matheson, "The Modern Law of Corporate Groups: An Empirical Study of Piercing the Corporate Veil in the Parent-Subsidiary Context," 87 *North Carolina Law Review* 1091, 1097 (2009).

[132] Robert B. Thompson, "Piercing the Veil Within Corporate Groups: Corporate Shareholders as Mere Investors," 13 *Connecticut Journal of International Law* 379, 380 (1999).

[133] See page 146 and accompanying notes 64–70.

[134] See Thomas K. Cheng, "The Corporate Veil Doctrine Revisited: A Comparative Study of the English and the U.S. Corporate Veil Doctrines," 34 *Boston College International and Comparative Law Review* 329, 388–93 (2011). But see René Reich-Graefe, "Changing Paradigms: The Liability of Corporate Groups in Germany," 37 *Connecticut Law Review* 785 (2005) (noting some retrenchment in Germany).

the entity to hold equity owners personally liable in these kinds of firms is much more frequent. In the United States, empirical studies find that plaintiffs seeking to pierce these corporate entities succeed almost half of the time.[135] When interpreting these studies, though, one must remember that they involve reported cases that have been fully litigated, which have a significant selection bias.[136] Many "easy cases" in which limited liability entities are respected do not get litigated or, if they do, are settled without a final reported judicial decision.[137] Still, an empirical chasm divides the "no-liability" rule for individual equity owners of public corporations and a "sometimes-liability" rule for cases involving entities with only a few equity owners.

In general, entity-piercing risks tend to be inversely correlated to the size of the firm both in terms of the number of equity owners and the number of employees. Piercing the entities of one-person firms, for example, is much more likely than piercing the entities of larger firms. According to one study, piercing becomes more difficult as the number of shareholders in a closely held corporation increases. Cases involving firms with a single shareholder stand at least a 50 percent chance of piercing. Firms with three or more shareholders face only a 35 percent chance.[138] Another study finds that the likelihood of entity piercing decreases with firm size as measured by number of employees—a finding driven in part by the fact that large public corporations, which are almost never pierced, tend to have larger numbers of employees.[139]

The economic and ethical arguments that support limited liability for equity owners of very large corporate enterprises become less convincing for smaller firms (or large firms in economic size with only a few equity owners). These firms do not depend on large numbers of investors who participate in public stock markets. And management responsibility tends to coincide with ownership interests much more directly than in large firms. The organizational distance between owners and managers in smaller firms is considerably lessened and sometimes completely eliminated. In other words, there is often no "separation of ownership and control." Arguments adduced for limited liability to protect small, widely dispersed share-holders in order to encourage their participation in capital markets are therefore less persuasive if not entirely inapposite. For example, business structures that result from strategies to "close" the separation of ownership and control, such as in a private equity leveraged buyout of public shareholders, would appear to deserve less protection from entity-piercing claims.

With respect to large firms with many shareholders, the ethical argument is that remote equity owners do not participate in management and therefore do not have responsibility for the actions of management. Because remote equity owners do not

---

[135] Oh, op. cit., p. 107 (finding entity pierced in 49 percent of cases). See also Thompson, "Piercing the Corporate Veil," op. cit., p. 1048 and tbl.1 (finding entity pierced in 40 percent of cases); Thompson, "Piercing the Veil Within Corporate Groups," op. cit., p. 387 (roughly the same finding).
[136] See, e.g, Oh, op. cit., pp. 104–6.
[137] See Frederick Schauer, "Easy Cases," 58 *Southern California Law Review* 399 (1985).
[138] Thompson, "Piercing the Corporate Veil," op. cit., p. 1054–5 and tbl. 7.
[139] Christina L. Boyd and David A. Hoffman, "Disputing Limited Liability," 104 *Northwestern University Law Review* 853, 857, 893 and fig. 12 (2010).

directly control managers and have little or no knowledge of the details of managerial activities, their liability should be limited to the amount of capital committed to the enterprise. This argument reduces to the vanishing point, however, in smaller or more closely held firms where equity owners and managers are the same people. It is difficult to see how the conceptual imposition of the legal "entity" of the firm should justify a shift or change of ethical responsibility for an action by the same individual person playing the roles of both owner and manager simultaneously. To justify this legal position requires an appeal to other economic or political arguments, such as social efficiency or a principle of equal legal treatment of both large and small firms.

Consider the one-person firm. If it is free or trivial to create an entity, then it is not clear why a single individual person should be allowed to conjure the bubble of a legal entity, place into the bubble whatever personal assets are deemed by the person to have a business purpose, and then claim limited liability with respect to these newly segregated "business" assets against all possible "personal" creditors. This example explains some of the cases allowing for "reverse piercing" of entities when they are designed specifically to avoid existing or expected personal liability. In these cases, assets that a person places in an entity are often made available for recovery by personal creditors upon a showing of an intention to use the creation of the entities specifically for this purpose, namely, to avoid these creditors.[140] At least, firms with only one equity owner should face greater scrutiny to show that the assets and liabilities in a case belong to the business firm itself and not the individual owner. The current rule for one-person limited liability companies in China makes sense in this connection. Under Chinese law, a one-person equity owner bears the legal burden to prove that assets at issue are business rather than personal assets, placing a strong emphasis on a need to maintain legal formalities in a small business.[141]

One might even argue on these grounds in favor of abolishing limited liability for smaller enterprises (including large firms with few equity owners), but as indicated above the historical trend has been in the opposite direction: toward an expansion of rights for everyone to have the option to choose a limited liability form of doing business. An egalitarian argument supports this expansion, namely: *equal protection of limited liability* for small as well as big firms, ranging from the solo entrepreneur to the large corporate conglomerates. However, when faced with difficult cases in which business entities are raised as formalistic defenses to what otherwise may appear to be straightforward cases of contractual liability, tort liability, or even fraudulent schemes that employ legal entities purely as instruments of deception,

---

[140] See, e.g., Elham Youabian, "Reverse Piercing of the Corporate Veil: The Implications of Bypassing 'Ownership' Interest," 33 *Southwestern University Law Review* 573 (2004) (reviewing cases). See also Larry E. Ribstein, "Reverse Limited Liability and the Design of Business Associations," 30 *Delaware Journal of Corporate Law* 199 (2005) (noting increase in use of personal "asset protection" devices).

[141] "Company Law of the People's Republic of China," op. cit., sect. 3, art. 64 ("If the shareholder of a one-person limited liability company is unable to prove that the property of the one-person limited liability company is independent from his own property, he shall bear joint liabilities for the debts of the company.") See also Haan, op. cit., p. 985.

courts have carved out exceptions to the rule of limited liability for equity owners. Ad hoc tests are applied to pierce the entities of small and otherwise closely held business enterprises.

Unfortunately, the legal doctrine informing entity-piercing cases is murky and unpredictable. One legal scholar describes these cases as "notoriously incoherent" and based on "conclusory references to criteria of doubtful relevance" leading to "unpredictable" results.[142] Another laments that entity-piercing doctrine remains "mangled and muzzy."[143] Most famously, as Frank Easterbrook and Daniel Fischel describe the legal situation in the United States: "'Piercing' seems to happen freakishly. Like lightning, it is rare, severe, and unprincipled."[144]

The law in this area is not much clearer elsewhere in the world.[145] British law has fluctuated historically, sometimes "pro" and sometimes "anti" piercing.[146] German law has been comparatively "liberal" with respect to ease of entity piercing, but it is also very uncertain.[147]

Relying on reported cases in the United States and following the work of legal scholars who have examined the problem both theoretically and empirically, it is nevertheless possible to draw several generalizations.[148] First, most courts apply broad-gauged tests to specific circumstances with respect to enumerated factors such as (1) respecting and observing the formalities of the entity (e.g. separate accounting, legal procedures, and governance practices); (2) inadequate capitalization for incurred or expected business risks (as judged prior to the actual harm alleged); and (3) fraud or fraud-like features with respect to the use of legal entities.[149]

The justifications for each of these factors are relatively straightforward, but each of them also raises questions. (1) If the organizers themselves fail to respect the formalities required to create and maintain a business entity (such as separate accounts, appointments of officers, and mandatory meetings), then it stands to reason that courts should disallow reliance on the entity to protect them. If the organizers themselves do not respect the entity, why should a court? In the real world of business, however, it asks a lot of business people, especially those in small enterprises, to risk massive personal liability as a result of formalistic failures to have dotted an "i" or crossed a "t." (2) Adopting a standard to require a business entity to

---

[142] See, e.g., Millon, "Limits of Limited Liability," op. cit., p. 1381.

[143] Oh, op. cit., p. 145.

[144] Easterbrook and Fischel, "Limited Liability and the Corporation," op. cit., p. 89.

[145] See, e.g., Karen Vandekerckhove, *Piercing the Corporate Veil* (Kluwer Law International 2007).

[146] Cheng, op. cit., pp. 334–42.

[147] See Sandra K. Miller, "Piercing the Corporate Veil Among Affiliated Companies in the European Community and in the U.S.: A Comparative Analysis of U.S., German, and U.K. Veil-Piercing Approaches," 36 *American Business Law Journal* 73, 79–84 (1998).

[148] Piercing cases are a form of judge-made law, though some state statutes have attempted to constrain judicial flexibility. See, e.g., Thompson, "Piercing the Corporate Veil," op. cit., p. 1042 (discussing a Texas statute restricting contractual liability in entity-piercing cases to situations of "actual fraud" causing a "direct personal benefit"). See also Texas Business Organization Code, sect. 21.223 (2007).

[149] See, e.g., Conard, op. cit., pp. 429–31; Millon, "Limits of Limited Liability," op. cit., pp. 1334–9.

maintain "adequate capitalization" to cover expected or foreseeable business risks also seems reasonable in principle. In practice, however, this test may be difficult to meet, especially given a tendency toward twenty-twenty hindsight after a major accident, injury, or fraud has occurred. This standard may provide incentives for responsible business firms to acquire insurance, however, and to take other precautionary measures to manage ex ante estimated risks economically and fairly. (3) Fraud presents perhaps the easiest case for strong and clear standards. But even here, allegations that business entities are used "fraudulently" to prevent creditors from recovering funds otherwise owing to them often appear to be based on conclusory or vague arguments.[150] As a result, a common approach has been for courts to apply "a number of different tests" to see if a situation is "acid or alkaline," referring to multiple factors when deciding whether or not to pierce a business entity.[151] One scholar criticizes this approach as comprising an "unweighted laundry list" of unrelated factors.[152]

Responding at least in part to the vagueness and unreliability of multi-factor tests, some cases have held that a serious "legal wrong" equivalent to fraud, tax evasion, or some other illicit end is needed to support piercing the entity.[153] The legal wrong cannot, of course, simply amount to an injustice or "wrong" claimed by an unpaid contract or tort creditor, which if recognized would defeat business entities in almost any situation. At least, fraud or fraud-like circumstances appear to be a leading reason given by courts today when piercing a business entity.[154]

Fraud is defined as a misrepresentation (or omission) of a material fact relied on by a party to a contract.[155] Entity-piercing cases often raise the question of "who" exactly made a particular representation (e.g. agents speaking on behalf of the entity or the entity's owners with respect to representations about the purposes of the entity's construction and use): hence the characterization of some of these cases as "fraud-like" rather than directly fraudulent. A recent empirical study found that most entity-piercing cases were either "grounded" in claims of fraud or "supported by specific evidence of fraud or misrepresentation."[156] A federal court applying Delaware law has stated simply that piercing a corporate entity "is appropriate only upon a showing of fraud or something like fraud."[157]

Taking this argument to its logical extreme, at least one legal commentator proposes to bite the bullet and forbid entity-piercing entirely. Stephen Bainbridge recommends that fraud and other tort-defined remedies should be applied to find

---

[150] Cf. Clark, op. cit., pp. 36–7 (criticizing the received tests as "vague").

[151] Conard, op. cit., p. 431.

[152] Millon, "Limits of Limited Liability," op. cit., pp. 1327–30.

[153] See, e.g., *Sea-Land Services, Inc. v. Pepper Source*, 941 F.2d 519, 524 (7th Cir. 1991) (holding that "some 'wrong' beyond a creditor's inability to collect" must be established to allow piercing).

[154] See Oh, op. cit., p. 95.

[155] See E. Allan Farnsworth, *Contracts* (Little, Brown, 2d ed., 1990), pp. 246–69.

[156] Oh, op. cit., p. 90. See also Stephen B. Presser, *Piercing the Corporate Veil* sect. 1:1, pp. 1–7 (Clark Boardman Callaghan 2004) (entity piercing "often incorporates and bears a strong resemblance to fraud" cases).

[157] *Mobil Oil Corp. v. Linear Films, Inc.*, 718 F. Supp. 260, 268 (D. Del. 1989).

liability (or not) directly.[158] However, this approach would put great pressure on doctrines of fraud and other tort-related concepts to evolve in a manner that would address the complex and creative use of entities that may not meet present legal definitions of "fraud," "negligence," or other legal wrongs. Also, it does not address the question of unequal treatment of small and large business firms with respect to the privilege of limited liability for equity owners.

Entity-piercing cases do not appear to observe a distinction between contracts and torts situations, contrary to the recommendations of some commentators. However, it is still helpful for analysis to consider the theory of entity piercing in these two contexts.[159]

With respect to contracts, there is a general consensus that business entities should be pierced less easily, all things considered, than in torts or statutory liability cases, because the injured party has had an opportunity to protect itself at the time of contracting.[160] As mentioned above, it is possible in contracting situations to ask for a personal guarantee from the principal owner or manager of a firm (or guarantees from other entities within a complex corporate group). In a world characterized by the existence of many business entities, one can argue that a failure to engage in these kinds of self-protective contracts is negligent and careless—or at least implicitly accepts the risks of limited liability entities interfering with legal claims.[161]

Even so, there are some contracts cases in which business entities appear to be used essentially to commit fraud, and these situations call for piercing. In particular, making a misrepresentation (or material omission) to a counter-party regarding the very existence of the entity in question would seem to justify piercing. The law of fraudulent conveyances supports piercing a legal entity when it is used to siphon assets from preexisting or imminent claims.[162] Borderline cases that use an entity for fraud-like or misleading purposes justify piercing as well.

Many piercing cases seem to follow principles that motivate laws against fraudulent conveyances designed to protect creditors against the misuse of business

---

[158] See Stephen M. Bainbridge, "Abolishing Veil Piercing," 26 *Journal of Corporation Law* 479 (2001); Stephen M. Bainbridge, "Abolishing LLC Veil Piercing," 2005 *University of Illinois Law Review* 77 (2005).

[159] See, e.g., Douglas and Shanks, op. cit., pp. 195–218 (early study dividing analysis in this fashion).

[160] See, e.g., Thompson, "Unpacking Limited Liability," op. cit., p. 13.

[161] Self-help may be more difficult in some complex corporate group settings, given that earlier-stage creditors may not easily predict future changes in the firm's capital structure which may put them at a financial disadvantage at later stages. Shareholders and managers in complex corporate groups may use entity-splitting and unequal loan guarantees in a manner prejudicial to corporate creditors. See Squire, op. cit. The doctrine of "substantive consolidation" of assets of a corporate group in bankruptcy is sometimes used as a remedy. See id., pp. 616, 647–9. See also William H. Widen, "Corporate Form and Substantive Consolidation," 75 *George Washington Law Review* 237 (2007) (favoring substantive consolidation in bankruptcy and finding that approximately half of large bankruptcy decisions use this principle). For purposes here, one may understand "substantive consolidation" as a form of entity piercing of corporate groups in the context of bankruptcy law, which is left mostly outside the scope of this book.

[162] See Clark, op. cit., p. 39 (arguing that cases of entity-piercing "are often applications of the same basic principles that underlie fraudulent conveyance law").

entities (and individuals) to hide assets that creditors could otherwise reach. According to Robert Clark, these principles include "truth, primacy, evenhandedness, and nonhindrance."[163] Clark argues also that certain cases of inadequate capitalization support an expanded "affirmative duty of cooperation with creditors."[164] One might also understand some severe cases of inadequate capitalization as involving material omissions with respect to capital structure and therefore a "constructive fraud" on creditors. (A "constructive fraud" is another example of a legal fiction discussed in Chapter 1. It expands the traditional legal elements of fraud to reach analogous situations.)

In torts cases, there is ordinarily no opportunity for the victim to engage in self-help or protection before the fact of injury. Some legal scholars have therefore argued strongly for a significant reduction—and even the elimination—of limited liability for equity owners with respect to torts, even in large public corporations. Legal scholars Henry Hansmann and Reinier Kraakman favor the elimination of limited liability for shareholders in torts cases, with distributions of the resulting costs apportioned "pro rata" to each shareholder.[165] David Leebron argues on economic grounds that pro rata unlimited liability for shareholders in public corporations may be justified if the transaction costs of enforcement and burdens on shareholder diversification investment strategies are not too high, though he admits that this argument is "tenuous" and dependent on economic analysis of the costs and benefits of the approach.[166] Nina Mendelson proposes an agency-like application of a "control test," proposing that unlimited liability for torts should fall on "controlling shareholders" or shareholders who have "the capacity to control" the firm.[167] And another proposal has been made to eliminate limited liability for torts in closely held corporations.[168]

However, serious legal reform efforts along these lines have not as yet followed from these academic recommendations. Again, if anything, the historical trend seems to be toward an increase in the recognition of limited liability entities that immunize equity owners in business activities from tort liability. The adoption and expansion of limited liability companies and limited liability partnerships in the United States offer the main current example of this trend toward more limited liability for equity owners rather than less. Probably, the general rule of limited liability for shareholders (and other equity owners) has become too strongly entrenched in organizational law and business practice to be easily dislodged. As two early commentators observed:

Limited liability is now accepted in theory and in practice. It is ingrained in our economic and legal systems. The social and economic order is arranged accordingly. Our philosophy

---

[163] Id., pp. 41, 71–81.   [164] Id., p. 81.

[165] Henry Hansmann and Reinier Kraakman, "Toward Unlimited Shareholder Liability for Corporate Torts," 100 *Yale Law Journal* 1879 (1991).

[166] Leebron, op. cit., pp. 1569, 1574–612.

[167] Nina A. Mendelson, "A Control-Based Approach to Shareholder Liability for Corporate Torts," 102 *Columbia Law Review* 1203, 1203, 1206–7, 1247–58, 1271–303 (2002).

[168] Note, "Should Shareholders Be Personally Liable for the Torts of Their Corporations?" 76 *Yale Law Journal* 1190 (1967).

accepts it. It is legitimate for [an individual or group of individuals] to stake only a part of their fortune on an enterprise. Legislatures, courts and business usage have made it so.[169]

Academics proposing major changes with respect to limited liability for equity owners, especially for shareholders in large corporations, have tended not to discuss the practical hurdles of actually adopting these ideas. In the United States, for example, this kind of reform would probably require a federal corporation statute, given that limited liability is currently recognized as a feature of corporations in the law of fifty different states. In addition, large corporations have the option today of reincorporating in another country, and most countries in the rest of the world recognize the principle of limited liability for shareholders.

In addition, the capital markets today are probably sophisticated and nimble enough to counter any attempt at expanding liability for shareholders by inventing new financial instruments that would recreate limited liability for those individual investors who want it.[170] Many individual investors most likely would remain risk-averse with respect to the prospect of very large personal losses, even if there is a low probability of them occurring.[171] (Note that this tendency of risk aversion may provide another possible explanation for the equity premium puzzle with respect to the divergent historical performance of stocks and bonds.[172] On this view, loss aversion may combine with relatively frequent assessments of investment performance and the higher volatility of stocks compared with bonds to yield the difference. In other words, more risk-averse investors purchase bonds, driving down returns compared with stocks.[173]) Another unanticipated consequence of adopting some form of unlimited liability regime for shareholders may be to drive more risk-averse investors (such as average individuals who are not very wealthy) out of the public securities markets, thus increasing trends towards unequal distributions of wealth.

In any event, it is unlikely from an historical and economic perspective that the genie of limited liability for equity owners for torts will be forced back into its bottle. At least, this is true of large public corporations where the economic

---

[169] Douglas and Shanks, op. cit., pp. 193–4.

[170] See Joseph A. Grundfest, "The Limited Future of Unlimited Liability: A Capital Markets Perspective," 102 *Yale Law Journal* 387 (1992). But see Henry Hansmann and Reinier Kraakman, "Do the Capital Markets Compel Limited Liability? A Response to Professor Grundfest," 102 *Yale Law Journal* 427 (1992) (suggesting regulatory responses to various capital market avoidance strategies).

[171] On the general tendency toward risk aversion (and loss aversion), see, e.g., Daniel Kahneman and Amos Tversky, "Prospect Theory: An Analysis of Decision Under Risk," 47 *Econometrica* 263 (1979); Nathan Novemsky and Daniel Kahneman, "The Boundaries of Loss Aversion," 42 *Journal of Marketing Research* 119 (2005).

[172] See Chapter 2, pages 79–80, 87–8, and accompanying notes 136–7, 172–6.

[173] Shlomo Benartzi and Richard H. Thaler, "Myopic Loss Aversion and the Equity Premium Puzzle," 110 *Quarterly Journal of Economics* 73 (1995). For a statement of the traditional rationale with respect to public shareholders, see also Mendelson, op. cit., pp. 1217–19. Mendelson argues also that the average tort victim is more risk- averse than the typical shareholder. Id., pp. 1220–7. This may be true (though the comparison has an "apples and oranges" quality). But if limited liability for shareholders of large corporations is too well established to allow for change from the current path of economic development, then the option of expanding enterprise liability to cover tort victims may prove more effective than attempting to reform the rules of individual shareholder liability.

arguments favoring limited liability are strongest (and path dependence also the most difficult to reverse). Entity-piercing of small or closely held businesses for torts is more common despite "equal treatment" arguments for them.

Reforms to protect tort victims are more likely to occur at the level of enterprise liability. A focus on enterprise liability may follow several different routes. One option is to abolish limited liability for complex corporate groups, including parent corporations and their wholly-owned or "controlled" subsidiaries, with respect to tort victims.[174] This reform would require only the re-interpretation of the emerging law of corporate groups, rather than a major change with respect to individual shareholder liability. A second option would require that business enterprises carry mandatory insurance to compensate for potential or possible costs of tort-related injuries.[175] Standard "business owners policies" currently cover liability risks as well as other risks of loss, and they could be expanded.[176] A third option analogous to mandatory insurance would require enterprises to carry mandatory bonds to finance compensation funds for the benefit of potential tort victims.[177] All of these solutions have the advantage of focusing attention at the enterprise level rather than peeling back legal protection for individual investors.

Creditors

Creditors who commit capital to an enterprise through loans and other debt instruments also enjoy limited liability in most circumstances with respect to the activities of the funded enterprise.

One exception arises if creditors use their financial position to exert effective managerial "control" in a firm. In the United States, courts have held that a creditor steps into a role of "principal" with respect to another enterprise as "agent" when the creditor exercises a sufficient degree of control over the firm's operational activities.[178] In these circumstances, creditors may be found liable for the debtor firm's obligations under basic agency law principles.[179] A bank, for example, may be found liable for the actions of a borrower firm if it exercises managerial control over the borrower. According to the court deciding one of these cases, the "key issue" for determining the existence of an agency relationship in this situation is "control and domination."[180] Other cases have found that a creditor who "takes

---

[174] See Leebron, op. cit., pp. 1612–23. See also page 146 and accompanying notes 64–70.

[175] See, e.g., Easterbrook and Fischel, "Limited Liability and the Corporation," op. cit., pp. 114–17 (suggesting this alternative, but noting that it may impose significant barriers to entry for new firms).

[176] See, e.g., David Millon, "The Still-Elusive Quest To Make Sense of Veil-Piercing," 89 *Texas Law Review See Also* 15, 25–6 (2010). For lengthy list of examples of mandatory insurance in various industries, see James J. White, "Corporate Judgment Proofing: A Response to Lynn LoPucki's *The Death of Liability*," 107 *Yale Law Journal* 1363, 1410 and n. 175 (1998).

[177] See Robert J. Rhee, "Bonding Limited Liability," 51 *William and Mary Law Review* 1417, 1417–18, 1422–3, 1450–88 (2010).

[178] See Chapter 1, pages 34–5 and accompanying notes 116–19 (discussing this principle as enunciated in the famous *Cargill* case and the role of "asset partitioning" in protecting creditors).

[179] See *Restatement (Third) of Agency*, op. cit., sect. 1.01, cmt. f(1), Reporter's Notes.

[180] *Citibank, N.A. v. Data Lease Financial Corp.*, 828 F.2d 686, 691 (11th Cir. 1987).

over the management of the debtor's business" may exercise "de facto control" sufficient to find liability on an agency theory. These cases often recite a general list of "factors" reminiscent of entity-piercing doctrine.[181]

As discussed in Chapter 2, modern financial theory recognizes an essential equivalence between debt and equity ownership of a firm, at least with respect to valuation and capital structure. Overall control in some modern firms therefore often lies more in "financial structural control" than "managerial operational control."[182] In these situations, following the principle that the liability of business participants should follow effective control of the firm, creditors should shoulder greater legal risks of liability in proportion to exercising greater control, as some commentators have suggested and at least a few cases have held.[183]

Lenders have been found liable under agency principles in various contexts. One example is home construction financing. In one case in California, a court found a creditor bank which had negligently financed the construction of homes to be responsible under a theory of enterprise liability.[184] This decision was quickly superseded by a statute.[185] In the aftermath of the Great Credit Crash of 2008 and the contributing role of mortgage financing, perhaps enterprise liability for negligently promoting financial products and defectively designing financial instruments will be revisited.[186] The Consumer Financial Protection Bureau created under the Dodd–Frank statute in the United States may move law reform in this direction.[187]

Lenders have also been found responsible as an "owner" or "operator" of a toxic landfill under a statute imposing environmental liability.[188] Although this statute was also subsequently amended to clarify a "safe harbor" for bank loans, lenders still risk liability if they exercise operational control over a toxic site.[189]

Traditionally, banks made loans to firms in arm's-length transactions: sums of capital invested in return for a series of repayments with interest. This traditional "separation" between banks and commercial ownership militated against lender liability in most circumstances.[190] Today, however, corporate finance has grown

---

[181] J. Dennis Hynes, "Lender Liability: The Dilemma of the Controlling Creditor," 58 *Tennessee Law Review* 635, 638–9 (1991) (quoting *Restatement (Second) of Agency*, sect. 14O).

[182] See Chapter 2, pages 85–90 and accompanying notes 155–87 and Table 2.6.

[183] See, e.g., G. Mitu Gulati, William A. Klein, and Eric M. Zolt, "Connected Contracts," 47 *UCLA Law Review* 887, 930 (2000) (finding it "interesting and surprising that no one seems to have considered the possibility of applying the arguments for shareholder personal liability to other participants such as creditors"); see also Hynes, op. cit. (discussing cases finding creditors liable for exercising control).

[184] Note, "The Expanding Scope of Enterprise Liability," 69 *Columbia Law Review* 1084, 1090–6 (1969) (discussing *Connor v. Great Western Savings & Loan Ass'n*, 447 P.2d 609 (Cal. 1968)).

[185] California Civil Code, sect. 3434 (adopted in 1969).

[186] See, e.g., Oren Bar-Gill and Elizabeth Warren, "Making Credit Safer," 157 *University of Pennsylvania Law Review* 1 (2008).

[187] See, e.g., Laureen E. Galeoto, Karen Y. Bitar, and Gil Rudolph, "The Consumer Financial Protection Bureau: The New Sheriff in Town," 129 *Banking Law Journal* 702 (2012).

[188] See *United States v. Fleet Factors Corp.*, 901 F.2d 1550 (11th Cir. 1990).

[189] See Michael P. Vandenbergh, "The Private Life of Public Law," 105 *Columbia Law Review* 2029, 2052 n. 101 (2005).

[190] See Adam Feibelman, "Commercial Lending and the Separation of Banking and Commerce," 75 *University of Cincinnati Law Review* 943 (2007).

much more sophisticated and influential with respect to business management. Under these circumstances, legislators and courts should reconsider whether new financial arrangements warrant the traditional arm's-length approach taken to grant creditors limited liability with respect to the firm.[191] If "control" is the primary justification for finding liability for wrongful harm caused by a firm, then piercing the entity of the firm to find debt owners as well as equity owners responsible should occur more frequently in appropriate situations today than in the past.

It is not easy to define the concept of "control" to govern in these situations. According to one scholar, "defining what is meant by control is one of the most frustrating questions one faces in agency law."[192] But various legal sources can provide guidance.[193] The concept of control to determine legal responsibility is used in a number of different contexts in various areas of enterprise law. For example, "controlling shareholder" and "controlling person" are important concepts in securities regulation. Organizational control is also used to assess agency in employment relationships. There is no reason similar legal standards cannot be developed for financial and managerial control exercised by creditors.[194]

Reform with respect to creditor liability for the mass torts of large public corporations may provide a more effective approach than proposals to expand shareholder liability. David Leebron recognizes a number of possible arguments in favor of recognizing "lender liability" with respect to torts, especially in public corporations. For example, he agrees that "any control distinction between debt and equity becomes blurred in the context of the public corporation," and "institutional lenders can exercise significantly greater control over the enterprise than public shareholders." "Unlimited liability for lenders," he continues, "would also encourage lenders to monitor and control risk that shareholders and managers could otherwise externalize."[195] Despite these arguments, Leebron concludes that disruptions to bank financing and public debt markets would be too severe to move in this direction.[196] He does not explain why economic worries about disrupting or inconveniencing the world of high finance, however, prove to be sufficient reason to allow the burden of mass torts, including major frauds as well as personal injuries by defective products, to fall instead on innocent tort victims who do not participate in the economic gains from these wrongful activities.

Another possible reform to benefit tort victims would change the priority rule of recovery in bankruptcy to give tort creditors preference over unsecured creditors (and perhaps secured creditors as well). Currently in bankruptcy law in the United States, secured creditors have preference over tort creditors, and unsecured creditors

---

[191] For an argument along these lines, see Note, "Investor Liability: Financial Innovations in the Regulatory State and the Coming Revolution in Corporate Law," 107 *Harvard Law Review* 1941 (1994).

[192] Hynes, op. cit., p. 638.

[193] See, e.g., Chapter 2 above, page [92], note [19] (definition used by the *Restatement (Third) of Agency*).

[194] Cf. Mendelson, op. cit., pp. 1271–8 (discussing different definitions of "capacity to control" a corporation for purposes of attribution of liability).

[195] Leebron, op. cit., pp. 1641–2.

[196] Id., pp. 1642–3.

have equal status with tort creditors (i.e. they share in any recovery pro rata).[197] A compromise would give tort victims priority at least over unsecured non-tort creditors on the theory that contractual creditors are in a better position than tort victims to demand appropriate insurance, risk-management measures, and other precautions to avoid catastrophic liability.[198] The priority order of creditors in bankruptcy, however, is a large and controversial topic which I will not attempt to deal with at length here.[199] At a minimum, resolving this issue would require engaging with the "competing interests and norms" informing both tort law and bankruptcy.[200] At present, and at least with respect to financing a firm as a going concern, the law generally recognizes limited liability for creditors, as long as they do not step over the line of exerting direct managerial control.

The social balance of the liability and limited liability of business persons

The persons of business enterprise, both organizational and individual, are responsible for significant social costs and harms as well as significant social benefits and contributions. The goods and services produced by business firms make the economic world go around, and the mere fact that many people pay for these goods and services provides a measure of the value of these firms. The costs and benefits of business also include what economists refer to as negative and positive externalities, however, and the questions addressed in this chapter have focused primarily on the negative externalities that firms impose on others.

As explored throughout this book the specific boundaries of the entities and persons of business firms are not always easily identified. For purposes of assessing responsibility and liability, the boundaries of the firm are not settled. Instead, the boundaries of what is "inside" and "outside" a particular business enterprise are always moving and often contested, especially when significant legal liability turns on the answers given.

The legal rules of liability apportion the responsibility for the costs and harms wrongfully caused to others. Organizational rules that accord "limited liability" to business persons—whether to individual business participants or organized business entities—therefore affect the overall social balance of how the risks of various kinds of harms and losses are allocated in society. In some situations, the legal privilege of limited liability given to one person (or group of persons) may be offset by liability imposed on another person. For example, the traditional rule of limited liability bestowed on individual shareholders of large enterprises is generally bal-

---

[197] See, e.g., Leebron, op. cit., pp. 1637, 1643 (citing relevant statutes); see also Douglas G. Baird, "The Importance of Priority," 82 *Cornell Law Review* 1420 (1997).

[198] Leebron, op. cit. 1643–9 (suggesting this possibility).

[199] For a collection of sources, see Yair Listokin, "Is Secured Debt Used To Redistribute Value from Tort Claimants in Bankruptcy? An Empirical Analysis," 57 *Duke Law Journal* 1037, 1038 n. 2 (2008).

[200] Charles W. Mooney, Jr., "Judgment Proofing, Bankruptcy Policy, and the Dark Side of Tort Liability," 52 *Stanford Law Review* 73, 75 n. 10 (1999).

anced by the imposition of enterprise liability on large organizational persons for their actions. As long as the business enterprise itself is solvent or otherwise hedged against risk (such as through adequate insurance), then the responsibility shouldered by the entity of the business enterprise for the wrongful harms that it may cause will offset the social costs of limited liability for shareholders (who in fact will pay indirectly for these costs over the long term by a reduced valuation of the firm). At the margins, however, or in a society that may become characterized by a very high turnover of business firms (i.e. a high rate of new formations and failures of firms), this social balance of enterprise liability and limited liability may become distorted. Bankruptcies mean that the enterprises themselves cannot pay all of their debts, including compensation to unpaid tort claimants. In these situations or others in which defenses to liability are raised, many individual people who are wrongfully harmed by business activities will find no legal recourse. Those who may have profited from the wrongful activity (e.g. shareholders at the time) may claim limited liability, and the business enterprise itself which might otherwise have been found liable may have disappeared into bankruptcy, insolvency, or another untraceable fate. Other such fates may include a merger, acquisition, sale of assets, or other business reorganization under legal rules that may not allow successor liability.

From a social perspective, increasing the availability of limited liability for business participants, including managers and owners/investors (in both debt and equity), has played an important role in encouraging the aggregation of capital in firms and the expansion of capital markets. At the same time, the increased use and size of these entities creates new risks and harmful externalities for third parties, especially for people who do not make contracts with these firms. Wrongful harm to third parties who may not have the opportunity to negotiate contracts in advance about these risks and harms raises particularly sympathetic concerns.

The rise of enterprise liability can be understood within this larger picture as a rational and fair response to the increased risks of wrongful harm that the increasing size and presence of large limited liability firms impose on society. Enterprise liability requires business entities to take responsibility as legal persons for these risks through the expansion of principles of agency, contract, property, and torts to cover organizations. In addition, specialized statutes of the regulatory state encompass new areas of concern, such as securities trading, employment discrimination, and environmental protection. These statutes often directly impose enterprise liability in contravention of preexisting legal rules and principles because these older rules and principles are inadequate to complex modern circumstances.[201]

Cutting back radically on enterprise liability as well as continuing to expand protections of limited liability through various recognized entities could eventually result in what the legal scholar Lynn LoPucki has forbiddingly called "the death of liability."[202] Individuals as well as firms may use the proliferation of limited liability entities to immunize or "judgment proof" themselves from legal risks. In this

---

[201] For a listing of a number of relevant federal statutes in antitrust, tax, banking, bankruptcy, labor, and environmental law in the United States, see Dearborn, op. cit., pp. 231–43.

[202] Lynn M. LoPucki, "The Death of Liability," 106 *Yale Law Journal* 1 (1996).

world, many ordinary people would become increasingly vulnerable to the harmful activities of other people who are best protected by legal entities.[203] Most likely and most commonly, the beneficiaries in this world would be the wealthiest and most powerful people in society who have secured positions within large business entities or who can otherwise afford good lawyers to manipulate legal entities for their own personal protection.

At present, these fears are probably somewhat overblown. Even if one agrees with some aspects of LoPucki's general thesis, there are many types of everyday liability described above—such as liability for most kinds of routine business contracts or accidents—that he does not have in mind. LoPucki's concern lies mostly with judgment-proofing against large or personally catastrophic risks of liability, such as mass torts or business failures.[204] The same seems to be true for the concern about the judgment-proofing of individuals, which is probably limited to some protection against torts liability.[205] In general, then, "liability lives" and will continue to evolve.[206] One indication that "the death of liability" has not yet arrived appears in the size of the insurance industry covering both business and individuals for potential legal exposure. Insurance payments amount to approximately two percent of gross domestic product in the United States.[207] The expenditure on insurance by business firms has also been increasing and exceeds $100 billion annually.[208]

Despite some ideological calls for radical deregulation, it seems unlikely that governments and their citizens will yield the regulatory field entirely to the world of business entities and those who control them. If nothing else, those at the helm of large business enterprises realize that governments and regulation are indispensable partners. The legal infrastructure that serves as the foundation of modern business enterprises cannot exist without governments and their courts, legislators, and administrators. One may therefore expect the social balance of enterprise liability and business participant liability, on one hand, and limited liability for both enterprises and individuals, on the other, to continue. This balance will also continue to be assessed as it applies in various situations and adjusted into the foreseeable future.

It is not my purpose here to argue exactly where the lines of liability and limited liability should be drawn in the many complex instances in which questions arise in the business context (though I have given some hints along the way of my own views of possible directions for law reform). Instead, my main point in this chapter has been that recognition of business entities and persons allows for (1) holding firms themselves responsible and accountable for the wrongful harm that they cause

---

[203] See Stephen G. Gilles, "The Judgment-Proof Society," 63 *Washington and Lee Law Review* 603 (2006). See also Ribstein, op. cit.

[204] See James J. White, op. cit., pp. 1365–6 (1998) (criticizing LoPucki on this ground).

[205] See Gilles, op. cit., pp. 605–7 (discussing "the myth of personal tort liability").

[206] See James J. White, op. cit.; Stephen L. Schwarcz, "The Inherent Irrationality of Judgment Proofing," 52 *Stanford Law Review* 1 (1999).

[207] Kent D. Syverud, "On the Demand for Liability Insurance," 72 *Texas Law Review* 1629, 1629 (1994).

[208] Gilles, op. cit., p. 662 and n. 262. See also James J. White, op. cit., pp. 1380–2 and chart 6.

(enterprise liability); (2) holding individual business participants responsible and accountable for the wrongful harm that they cause (business participant liability); and (3) sometimes allowing for limitations on this responsibility and accountability by the judicious extension of limited liability for specific moral reasons (such as limitations with respect to causation) and social purposes (such as encouraging the accumulation of capital or the start-ups of new business enterprises).

This endeavor—the legal assessment of the liability (and limited liability) of firms and their participants—provides a significant part of the answer to theoretical questions about the boundaries of the firm. Legal answers to these questions are important because they help to determine the size, shape, scope, and purposes of firms, as well as to establish behavioral constraints and incentives for individual business participants. The legal rules of liability for firms and their participants determine both (1) how the "internalities" of firms work (including setting incentives for managers, employees, and other agents) and (2) how the "externalities" of the actions of firms and their agents (particularly negative wrongful harm to third parties) are deterred, mitigated, and compensated (or not). The default alternative when neither enterprise liability nor participant liability covers a particular wrongful harm is that the costs of this injury or other harm remains where it falls: on often-innocent people who are injured or otherwise harmed. From a political and ethical perspective, a society that condones a radically unequal distribution of risks of accidents, injuries, and other harms is unjust.[209]

Overall, a complex mosaic of legal rules governing enterprise liability, participant liability, and limited liability describes and conditions the modern world of business firms. Metaphorically and impressionistically, firms constructed as organizational persons are like planets and other astronomical bodies acting within the competing gravitational forces of legal liability rules.[210] Increasing enterprise liability along various dimensions will encourage firms to shrink, break apart, or reconfigure themselves into forms that elude legal liability. Increasing limited liability for participants can encourage firms to grow and expand. The dark matter of this metaphorical universe surrounding business firms consists in the ubiquitous markets for their goods and services, which includes demand from other firms and governments, as well as an undifferentiated mass of individual consumers. (The next chapter describes this interaction of firms and markets more concretely.)

Other forces described by economic theories of the firm act also within this larger gravitational field of the legal construction and management of liability rules for firms.[211] These other economic forces include the economics of transaction costs, that is, the balance of the "transaction costs" of making contracts and exchanges

---

[209] See, e.g., Ulrich Beck, *Risk Society: Towards a New Modernity* (Sage 1992) (original edition in German 1986). See also Stephen Breyer, *Breaking the Vicious Circle: Toward Effective Risk Regulation* (Harvard University Press 1995) (arguing for regulatory attention to be paid to this issue).

[210] Cf. Laurence H. Tribe, "The Curvature of Constitutional Space: What Lawyers Can Learn From Modern Physics," 103 *Harvard Law Review* 1 (1989).

[211] A treatment of the details of these economic theories lies outside the scope of this book. But see Preface, pages xiii–xv and accompanying notes 1–10; Chapter 1, page 27 and accompanying notes 80–1; Chapter 2, pages 64–5, 74, and accompanying notes 46–52, 105.

across markets (or *inter*firm costs) and the "organization costs" of internalizing various economic activities within a firm's legal structure (or *intra*firm costs). Two economists, Ronald Coase and Oliver Williamson, won Nobel Prizes in part based on their work describing these dynamics of transaction and organization costs in their theories of the firm.[212] Principal–agent or "agency costs" economic analysis plays a role as well, adding well-known calculations of the costs of hiring agents (and their potential to "shirk" or "slack off") versus the benefits of organization in terms of economies of scale and scope, specialization, and political influence.[213] Firms take different shapes, grow or shrink to different sizes and configurations, and select different legal forms in response to these economic pressures and opportunities as well as legal rules.

But economics is not the full story. The rules of law set the stage and also provide for significant incentives through political and governmental processes, rather than economic markets. It is also important to remember that economic theories of transaction costs and agency costs are descriptive theories, at least in their original forms. Although many scholars and practitioners tend today to use these theories normatively and prescriptively, this approach is often mistaken or at least unclear, as the business philosopher Thomas Donaldson has pointed out.[214] Donaldson recommends considering "bundled or integrated identity" as a potential solution to normative problems of the orientation of firms, and this idea has interesting parallels to an emphasis here placed on understanding firms as legal entities and persons.[215] Business participants often have the capacity to craft their own normative "identity" within a firm structure. Many varieties of legal forms of firms are currently available in most countries, which allow a selection of different normative orientations. Legal rules to encourage or discourage particular features of a firm's "identity" relates also to policy questions such as those regarding liability rules and social responsibilities of firms.

---

[212] See Preface page xiv and accompanying notes 5–8. On transaction costs, see also *The Economics of Transaction Costs* (Oliver E. Williamson and Scott E. Masten eds.) (Edward Elgar 1999). In his Nobel Prize acceptance speech, Williamson recognized the influence of Coase, as well as John R. Commons and Kenneth Arrow. Oliver E. Williamson, "Transaction Cost Economics: The Natural Progression," 100 *American Economic Review* 673, 673–6, 680, 686 (2010).

[213] For a sample of this extensive literature, see James S. Ang, Rebel A. Cole, and James Wuh Lin, "Agency Costs and Ownership Structure," 55 *Journal of Finance* 81 (2000); Kathleen M. Eisenstadt, "Agency Theory: An Assessment and Review," 14 *Academy of Management Review* 57 (1989); Eugene F. Fama, "Agency Problems and the Theory of the Firm," 88 *Journal of Political Economy* 288 (1980); Eugene F. Fama and Michael C. Jensen, "Agency Problems and Residual Claims," 26 *Journal of Law and Economics* 327 (1983); Michael C. Jensen and William H. Meckling, "Theory of the Firm: Managerial Behavior, Agency Costs and Ownership Structure," 3 *Journal of Financial Economics* 305 (1976); Daniel Levinthal, "A Survey of Agency Models of Organizations," 9 *Journal of Economic Behavior and Organization* 153 (1988); Stephen A. Ross, "The Economic Theory of Agency: The Principal's Problem," 63 *American Economic Review* 134 (1973).

[214] Thomas Donaldson, "The Epistemic Fault Line in Corporate Governance," 37 *Academy of Management Review* 256 (2012).

[215] Id., pp. 267–9; see also Chapter 1.

Previous chapters have mentioned that the legal menu of options for business participants to choose from is rather rich. The next chapter turns to describe and assess the forms of enterprise that emerge in organizational law. It builds on the basic foundations of the construction, management, financing, and liability of firms, which have been described in this book so far.

5

The Nomenclature of Enterprise: A Taxonomy of Modern Business Firms

The names used for business firms roughly correlate with their legal forms, such as "partnership" or "corporation." As previous chapters have shown, however, the enabling rules for the construction, management, and financing of modern business enterprises are broad and flexible. They allow for a great variety of business forms, types, and combinations. Recognition of the "entities" and "persons" of business provides one key to the taxonomy of the varieties of firms, but the forms of enterprise are not limited to a short menu of recognized legal templates. Modern firms range from one-person enterprises without the benefit of an entity to highly complex groups of entities using many kinds of legal linkages, including corporate groups, parent–subsidiary structures, franchises, and cooperatives.[1]

From a sociological point of view, it is also important to distinguish between formally recognized firms and informally organized social groups. Elsewhere, I discuss the relationship between firms and social groups in greater detail.[2] For purposes here, it is sufficient to recognize that almost all firms are composed of organized groups of people who are linked together through the various legal forms and processes described in this book. (The only exceptions are rare one-person firms with no employees or equity capital contributors.)

To describe a modern taxonomy of business enterprises, it makes sense to follow an analytical method of moving from the smallest and simplest firms to those that are largest and most complex. As a framework for this analysis, it also helpful to reflect first on the general organizational and market environment in which firms exist, compete, and evolve.

In general terms, modern firms are actors in *production metamarkets*, that is, they are organized to produce goods and services to sell to consumers. These consumers include private individuals, other firms as purchasers of goods and services, and governments. Consumers constitute the demand side of these transactions with firms, namely, *consumption markets*.

The legal scholar Adolf Berle makes a similar distinction in connection with the modern "revolution" in the structure of private property described in Chapter 2.

---

[1] For an earlier account of a "taxonomy" and "typology" of business firms, though focused mostly on corporations, see Alfred F. Conard, *Corporations in Perspective* (Foundation Press 1976), pp. 124–74.

[2] See Eric W. Orts, "The Business Enterprise as a Social Institution" (unpublished manuscript, available on request from the author).

Table 5.1 Business enterprises and commercial markets

Production metamarkets (goods, services, and information)	Consumption markets (goods, services, and information)
For-profit business enterprises	*Private individuals and groups*
(firms of different types and sizes competing with each other)	(including informal consumer groups, consumer cooperatives, families, etc.)
	Business enterprises as consumers
	(purchasers of inputs of goods, services, and information for the production of other goods, services, and information)
Government firms	*Governments as consumers*
(e.g. state-owned banks, oil companies, airlines, railroads, utilities, etc.)	(purchasers of military supplies and equipment, as well as other goods, services, and information for infrastructure, etc.)
Private individuals and groups acting in private, non-business productive capacities	Private individuals and groups consuming non-commercially produced goods, services, and information.

According to Berle: "My thesis is that 'property' is now divided into two categories: (1) consumption property on the one hand; and (2) productive property on the other—property devoted to production, manufacture, service or commerce, and designed to offer, for a price, goods or services to the public from which a holder expects to derive a return."[3] Note that this distinction or its equivalent is also essential for the analytical operation of economic theories of the firm that compare the transactional and organizational costs of "markets" versus "firms."[4]

Table 5.1 gives a graphical depiction of this distinction between production metamarkets of firms and their corresponding consumption markets.

This depiction requires some further explanation to elucidate the limits of the legal theory of the firm given here. The cells in the table identified as *non-commercial* production and consumption refer to the fact that many goods, services, and information that are produced and consumed in modern societies fall outside of the commercial markets mediated by money exchange and transfer by purchase or sale. Much internet production and consumption, for example, is non-commercial. A great deal of work within families, personal relationships, and homes may also be described as services that are performed within non-payment denominated systems

---

[3] Adolf A. Berle and Gardiner C. Means, *The Modern Corporation and Private Property* (Transaction Publishers 1991) (rev. ed. 1968) (1932), p. xxiii. See also Eric W. Orts, "Shirking and Sharking: A Legal Theory of the Firm," 16 *Yale Law and Policy Review* 265, 287–9 (1998) (using slightly different terms).

[4] See Chapter 4, pages 171–2 and accompanying notes 211–13.

of social cooperation. The main point here is that the *commercial business firms* described in this book participate in *production metamarkets* (in which economic as well as legal considerations determine the shapes, sizes, and legal structures of the firms) in the process of serving *consumer markets* for goods, services, and information. Illegal "black markets" are excluded from consideration. Illegal organizations such as criminal gangs and pirates are excluded as well.[5]

As described in Chapters 1 and 2, firms are relationships of property with internal agency relationships of authority and power constructed through organizational contracts and recognized as having legal personality. In this sense, Berle correctly describes firms as the modern *proprietus* (or relational structures of property, management, and labor) which are organized for the purpose of producing goods and services to sell for economic gain.[6] Firms act as the principal producers in generalized markets for goods and services demanded by consumers, namely, individual people, government entities, nonprofit organizations, and other firms.

Starting from this basic understanding, the world's marketplace looks very different from the a priori view adopted by some economists of a sea of undifferentiated individual people who are endowed with items of personal property and connected by an anarchical mess of contracts. The institutional legal theory of the firm attempts to square the circle with respect to the contemporary debate between "methodological individualism" (which focuses its analysis only on individual human beings) and "methodological holism" (which focuses only on institutions or organizations). As one scholar describes this deep methodological divide:

> There has been in the history of social thought a constant battle over the true nature of society and about the best way to understand and explain it. A major divide [separates] those who see society as an aggregate, collection, or complex of individuals and those who see society as some kind of ordered whole and/or unitary collective. The former try to explain social phenomena in terms of individuals and their interaction, while the latter maintain that this is not possible without essential reference to the social wholes of which they are a part and/or the collectives to which they belong.[7]

Similarly, the sociologist James Coleman describes the difference between individualism and holism as "two modes of explanation of the behavior of social systems" focusing on either the "component parts" or "units" within a social system or "the behavior of the system as a whole over a period of time."[8] Elsewhere, I set forth an argument in favor of combining the methods of individualism and holism in an institutional approach.[9] And the combined top-down and bottom-up institutional theory of the firm advanced in Chapter 1 is consistent with this methodology. Here, I simply assume that this methodological combination can work, following the economist Vilfredo Pareto who argued that taking an extreme view

---

[5] I thank Ryan Burg for encouraging me to clarify the scope of my "legal" theory of firm to exclude criminal enterprises and markets.

[6] Berle and Means, op. cit., p. xxiii (Berle's preface to revised edition).

[7] Lars Udehn, *Methodological Individualism: Background, History and Meaning* (Routledge 2001), p. 1.

[8] James S. Coleman, *Foundations of Social Theory* (Harvard University Press 1990), p. 2.

[9] See Orts, "The Business Enterprise as a Social Institution," op. cit.

that human beings are either "individual" or "social" is simply wrong. In his words: "The man who does not live in society is a very unusual man, one who is almost, or rather entirely, unknown to us. And a society distinct from individuals is an abstraction which does not correspond to anything real."[10]

Following an institutional approach, then, it is helpful to think of firms metaphorically as "islands of conscious power" acting within an "ocean of unconscious cooperation."[11] In other words, firms are organizations of production that compete to supply general and usually decentralized consumption markets. I say consumption markets are "usually decentralized" because they are sometimes but not often centralized, such as the demand for highly specialized and expensive military weaponry (e.g. nuclear aircraft carriers, submarines, or transcontinental missiles). Business monopolies constitute another exception to the rule of competition and are left outside of the scope of the discussion here. Within these limitations, however, the legal theory of the firm advanced in this book provides an understanding of how the islands of conscious power of business enterprise become established, recognized, and active in society. The law also sets up the menu of organizational forms that people may select when creating, maintaining, and changing these islands of conscious power in the global commercial ocean.

The entrepreneur and the pure sole proprietorship

To begin with the smallest and simplest possible productive unit, consider the solo entrepreneur. An individual person may have a good idea, a new angle on an old one, or simply decide to go into business for oneself. A classic example is a child's lemonade stand (allowing for the parental provision of the supplies).[12] With the exception of supplies provided by a well-meaning parent, the enterprise, namely, the making of the lemonade, marketing it with a sign, serving it to customers, and making money from the sales—all of the basic business functions that can become very complex in large firms—are carried out in the lemonade stand by one person.[13]

The one-person eBay entrepreneur is another recent and more economically consequential example of a pure sole proprietor. eBay specifically encourages entrepreneurial businesses, and total annual sales in eBay auctions are over $60

---

[10] Vilfredo Pareto, *Manual of Political Economy* (1909) (Macmillan 1972) p. 71, quoted in Udehn, op. cit., p. 37.

[11] D.H. Robertson, *The Control of Industry* (Nisbet and Co. 1923), p. 83. Others have found this metaphor helpful as well. See, e.g., R.H. Coase, "The Nature of the Firm," 4 *Economica* (n.s.) 386, 388 (1937); Edward B. Rock and Michael L. Wachter, "Islands of Conscious Power: Law, Norms, and the Self-Governing Corporation," 149 *University of Pennsylvania Law Review* 1619, 1621 (2001).

[12] See, e.g., Theresa A. Gabaldon, "The Lemonade Stand: Feminist and Other Reflections on the Limited Liability of Corporate Shareholders," 45 *Vanderbilt Law Review* 1387, 1388–9, 1455–6 (1992).

[13] See also William A. Klein, John C. Coffee, Jr., and Frank Partnoy, *Business Organization and Finance: Legal and Economic Principles* (Foundation Press, 11th ed., 2010), p. 5 (defining "sole proprietorship" as "a business owned directly by one individual"). These authors state also that because sole proprietorships have "no formal elements of co-ownership" they are "usually not thought of as a 'business organization' in the legal sense." Id. For the reasons given in the text, however, I count sole proprietorships as the most basic kind of firm.

billion.[14] (eBay's business itself is perhaps best described as supplying the purchased infrastructure of communications and marketing for one-person or otherwise very small firms.) One-person entrepreneurs have also become increasingly common even in societies characterized by state capitalism and the presence of many large state-owned firms, such as in China. Alibaba and its vast network of small enterprises provide a prominent example.[15] Total annual sales through Alibaba now approximate those of eBay and Amazon combined.[16]

An apparent paradox regarding the one-person firm has troubled social theorists over the years. It can be briefly stated as follows. How can one individual person act both as a regular person (e.g. consumer and citizen) and as a business firm (i.e. producer for commercial markets)? The answer and the resolution of the paradox are given by understanding the different social roles that people adopt in modern societies. Given a social and legal system in which an individual person may elect to go into business oneself (with some exceptions and regulatory hurdles, such as professional licensing requirements), and given the existence of formally organized and open markets, there are a number of social roles that emerge for individuals. In modern societies, individuals play different roles in different institutions. With respect to business firms, an individual plays twinned roles in production metamarkets and consumption markets: on one hand acting in a business role as a producer (e.g. as a sole proprietor or one-person corporation) and on the other hand acting in private life as an individual consumer and citizen.[17] Social roles track a number of modern differentiated institutions, including not only business enterprises but also nation-states and other governmental bodies (e.g. the role of "citizen"), nonprofit and religious organizations (e.g. the role of "member" or "donor"), educational institutions (e.g. the roles of "teacher," "administrator," and "student"), and families (e.g. the roles of "parent" and "grandparent" as well as "son" and "daughter").

Even though it is relatively easy to create one-person firms, they are very rare in business life. Much more often, a prospective businessperson needs or wants to recruit allies to provide financing for a new business idea or friends to help with the work of putting an idea into action. On my block in West Philadelphia, for example, summer lemonade stands are usually launched and managed by a group of neighborhood children rather than lone entrepreneurs. Even one-person start-ups, if and when they are successful, usually grow by adding more people to the business along the dimensions of ownership (e.g. investors) or labor (e.g. employees).

The one-person firm is nevertheless a cogent analytical starting point for examining the available types of business enterprise. Even though they are not the most

---

[14] "eBay Sellers Challenge to Spark Entrepreneurial Spirit," *Marketing Business Weekly*, June 28, 2009, p. 619.

[15] "Entrepreneurship in China: Let a Million Flowers Bloom," *Economist*, March 10, 2011, <http://www.economist.com> (accessed September 16, 2012).

[16] See Thomas L. Friedman, "In China We (Don't) Trust," *New York Times*, September 12, 2012, p. A31.

[17] On the complexity of different social roles, see Erving Goffman, *The Presentation of Self in Everyday Life* (Doubleday Anchor 1959). See also Joseph Vining, *Legal Identity: The Coming Age of Public Law* (Yale University Press 1978), pp. 59–60, 148–50 (discussing "occupational identity" in modern societies).

common or influential form of enterprise, one-person firms exist, and they do not require the creation of a formal legal "entity" for their creation. "A natural person," as two legal scholars write, "can—and very frequently does—serve as a firm, in the form of a sole proprietorship."[18] Given the material means to do so, an individual person in most modern societies may simply decide to go into a business to produce a good or service for sale and *voilà*: an entrepreneur is born!

The individual entrepreneur figures prominently in a number of early theories of business enterprise.[19] Jean-Baptiste Say seems to have been one of the first to introduce the idea of the "entrepreneur" in economics.[20] The idea is also prominent in Joseph Schumpeter's work.[21] Entrepreneurship today has become a central topic and popular "major" in business schools (for budding entrepreneurs, of course).[22]

In more theoretical terms, the firm of a solo entrepreneur acting alone is a *pure sole proprietorship*.[23] It is the simplest firm: self-owned, self-employed, self-financed, and self-directed. But it is rare because it often makes sense to expand or specialize along each of these dimensions of ownership, employment, finance, and management.

Pure sole proprietorships are especially rare in some countries that impede the creation of new business firms. According to one study of seventy-five countries, registering a new business remained "extremely cumbersome, time-consuming, and expensive" in many places. The same study emphasizes that cultures of bribery and corruption of government officials raise the costs of forming new business enterprises.[24] Countries that wish to encourage entrepreneurship should therefore focus greater attention on easing regulatory requirements for business registration and otherwise establishing clear and trustworthy institutional procedures for the creation of firms, including the legal recognition of them as persons and the legal protection of the private property and organizational contracts that constitute firms.[25]

---

[18] Henry Hansmann and Reinier Kraakman, "The Essential Role of Organizational Law," 110 *Yale Law Journal* 387, 392 (2000).

[19] See William J. Baumol, "Entrepreneurship in Economic Theory," 58 *American Economic Review* 64 (1968); George Heberton Evans, Jr., "A Theory of Entrepreneurship," 2 *Journal of Economic History* 142 (Supp. 1942); Frank H. Knight, "Profit and Entrepreneurial Functions," 2 *Journal of Economic History* 126 (Supp. 1942); Harvey Leibenstein, "Entrepreneurship and Development," 58 *American Economic Review* 72 (1968); August Marx, "Entrepreneur et Entreprise," 3 *Management International* 105 (1963); James H. Soltow, "The Entrepreneur in Economic History," 58 *American Economic Review* 84 (1968).

[20] See G. Koolman, "Say's Conception of the Role of the Entrepreneur," 38 *Economica* (n.s.) 269 (1971).

[21] See, e.g., Joseph A. Schumpeter, "The Creative Response in Economic History," 7 *Journal of Economic History* 149 (1947).

[22] See, e.g., Mark Casson and Nigel Wadeson, "The Discovery of Opportunities: Extending the Economic Theory of the Entrepreneur," 28 *Small Business Economics* 285 (2007).

[23] For elaboration, see Orts, "Shirking and Sharking," op. cit., pp. 289, 299–301.

[24] Robert J. Samuelson, "Book Review: The Spirit of Capitalism" 80 *Foreign Affairs* 205, 208 (January–February 2001).

[25] For an argument along these lines, see Hernando de Soto, *The Mystery of Capital: Why Capitalism Triumphs in the West and Fails Everywhere Else* (Basic Books 2003).

Horizontal and vertical expansion:
the dimensions of ownership and control

Most firms involve more than a single individual person. Enabled by the combination of organizational law recognizing the practical unity of a business entity or "person" as well as the laws of agency, contracts, and property as described in Chapters 1 and 2 above, the growth of firms occurs mainly along two dimensions.

First, firms can expand "horizontally" in terms of ownership. In the simplest example: a pure sole proprietorship may add a partner (equity ownership) or negotiate a loan (secured or unsecured debt). Adding more partners and more loans adds complexity as well as economic size and organizational power for those in authority.

Second, firms can expand "vertically" in terms of agency authority. Again in the simplest case: a pure sole proprietorship may hire an employee or a manager. Adding more employees and more managers adds complexity, size, and organizational power.

Along these dimensions, people create and configure a great variety of sizes and shapes of business firms. See Figure 5.1 for a depiction of the "horizontal" and "vertical" dimensions of the ownership and control of firms.

The horizontal and vertical dimensions of the firm depicted in Figure 5.1 are schematic and meant for purposes of illustration only. In real life, ownership interests are indeed often horizontal in the sense that they are shared and made equal (such as in the valuation of corporate shares of common stock traded on public exchanges), but they can also become quite unequal and heavily weighted in terms of either equity or debt ownership. Consider, for example, two capital structures. Firm *A* has $99 million of equity and $1 million of debt. Firm *B* has $1 million of equity and $99 million in debt.[26] Obviously, these structures are not balanced horizontally as portrayed in Figure 5.1. Instead, the horizontal line tilts like a seesaw in these examples: first one way favoring equity in Firm *A* and then the other favoring debt in Firm *B*. Moreover, in Firm *A* the equity owners call the shots in terms of the "vertical" or hierarchical control of the structures of agency authority. In contrast, Firm *B* is heavily leveraged, and its debtors exercise a substantial degree of de facto control over management decisions. In addition, the debtors of Firm *B* are likely to be compensated by much higher than usual interest rates or provided other incentives such as "equity kickers" (i.e. profit-sharing). Higher and riskier leverage exerts implicit control on managers, even if indirectly, in terms of their incentives.[27]

My point here is not to recapitulate the arguments made in Chapter 2 concerning the fragmentation of ownership in many modern firms (and the ability of debt as well as equity ownership to exert a controlling influence). Instead, the point is to show more broadly how variations in ownership structure affect the balance of authority

---

[26] I adapt this example from James J. White, "Corporate Judgment Proofing: A Response to Lynn LoPucki's *The Death of Liability*," 107 *Yale Law Journal* 1363, 1397–9 (1998).

[27] See id. See also Chapter 2, pages 84–90 and accompanying Tables 2.5 and 2.6.

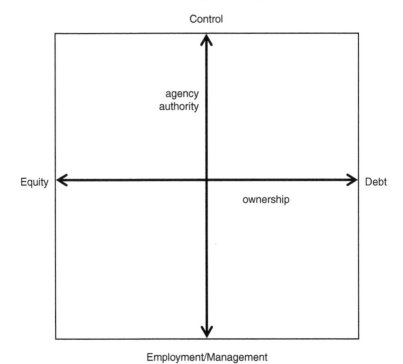

Fig. 5.1 The legal boundaries of the firm (schematic)

and control in firms. It makes sense analytically (and schematically) to depict the dimensions of "ownership" and "control" separately, but in the real world these dimensions intersect and interact with each other in a highly flexible and ever-changing manner.

Rather than a "black box" (as suggested by Figure 5.1), the firm is better conceptualized geometrically as a highly variable structure with several interactive dimensions, including those of capital ownership, managerial governance, and agency authority. In other words, imagine Figure 5.1 as a highly changeable and flexible shape: shrinking into a single dot in a one-person firm or expanding along several dimensions with the addition of owners and agents of different kinds. Replicate the number of "boxes" and configure them into various patterns to visualize the lines of ownership and authority in corporate groups and other complex business structures.

The general partnership provides an example of how a sole proprietor—who is now more accurately called an *enterprise-organizer*—can act to expand a firm along the dimensions of both ownership and control simultaneously.[28] A plain vanilla

---

[28] See Chapter 2, page 63 and accompanying note 43. Other theorists of the firm refer to "entrepreneur-coordinator" or "entrepreneur-organizer." See Coase, "The Nature of the Firm," op. cit., pp. 388–9; Armen A. Alchian and Harold Demsetz, "Production, Information Costs, and Economic Organization," 62 *American Economic Review* 777, 789 n. 14 (1972). I prefer *enterprise-organizer* because the term is broader. See also R. H. Coase, "The Nature of the Firm: Meaning," 4

partnership is created when two enterprise-organizers join forces to create a business firm. General partners agree to pool their capital and labor, and they agree to share any profits and risks of loss. They share in the equity ownership of the firm, and they share in the management. Sharing profits and losses, as well as managerial control, is the *sine qua non* of a general partnership, as compared with other business arrangements.[29] In terms of authority and control, general partners become agents of each other.[30] Adding partners or adding employees expands the firm along the dimensions of ownership, agency authority, or both. Partnerships can also incur debt, altering their ownership and managerial incentives accordingly, just like any other business.[31]

The default rules of partnership are variable by mutual agreement.[32] For example, one partner may provide only capital and another only labor, though both would have to agree to share some portion of profits and losses to maintain a partnership relationship. In addition, considerable variation is possible in terms of partnership management and distributions. For example, many law firms have adopted a "two-tier" governance structure of "equity partners" (profit-sharing) and "non-equity partners" (not profit-sharing, but participating in governance).[33]

Other legal forms of business offer alternative avenues for expansion along the lines of both capital ownership (including decisions about different types, amounts, and relative weights of equity and debt) and agency authority (including choices about layers of management and divisions of operations). The primary, most powerful alternative organizational form remains the business corporation, either closely held or with broad public share ownership.[34] Other organizational forms are also available, such as limited liability companies, private business trusts, and cooperatives.[35]

Cooperatives present a somewhat complicated case for a theory of the firm because they can be organized as either *producer cooperatives* (which count as a business firm under the theory advanced here) or *consumer cooperatives* (which count as an organized group of consumers rather than a firm). Hybrid versions of

---

Journal of Law, Economics, & Organization 19, 31–2 (1988) (suggesting a revised preference for a broader term). It encompasses managers as well as entrepreneurs, and it covers the general responsibility of organizing a business, including not only coordination and oversight, but also the occasional reorganization of the entire structure of a firm in the "shapeshifting" situations described in Chapter 1.

[29] See Klein, Coffee, and Partnoy, op. cit., pp. 62–3.

[30] See Chapter 2, pages 57–8 and accompanying notes 22–3.

[31] For an introduction to basic partnership law, see Stephen M. Bainbridge, *Agency, Partnerships & LLCs* (Foundation Press 2004), pp. 100–77.

[32] On default rules, see Chapter 2, page 68 and accompanying notes 72–4.

[33] See William D. Henderson, "An Empirical Study of Single-Tier Versus Two-Tier Partnerships in the Am Law 200," 84 *North Carolina Law Review* 1691 (2006).

[34] On corporations, see Chapter 3, pages 127–8 and accompanying notes 92–6. On the distinction between "close" and "public" corporations, see Chapter 4, pages 151–6 and accompanying notes 94–128.

[35] See Henry Hansmann, Reinier Kraakman, and Richard Squire, "The New Business Entities in Evolutionary Perspective," 2005 *University of Illinois Law Review* 5 (2005); Larry E. Ribstein, "Why Corporations?" 1 *Berkeley Business Law Journal* 183 (2004). See also Symposium, "LLCs, LLPs and the Evolving Corporate Form," 66 *University of Colorado Law Review* 855 (1995). On modern business trusts, see Thomas E. Rutledge and Ellisa O. Habbart, "The Uniform Statutory Trust Entity Act: A Review," 65 *Business Lawyer* 1055 (2010).

co-ops can act as both firms (e.g. selling food retail to the public) and consumer groups (e.g. purchasing food wholesale for co-op members).[36]

All of these business forms, however, may be analyzed legally in terms of their organization of capital ownership, entity governance, and agency authority. The combination of these features gives each business form the identity and unity of a recognized legal "firm."

Limited liability entities

As discussed in Chapter 4, limited liability is a feature that any business may now choose (at least in the United States and most other jurisdictions in the world). Even a pure sole proprietorship may choose to transform into a one-person corporation in most places. An individual simply needs to fill out the paperwork, file a registration statement, pay a small fee, and follow the required formalities.[37] The easy availability of limited liability forms does not mean that an enterprise-organizer should always choose an entity of this kind as a practical matter. Often, the foreseeable risks involved for a small business are easily insurable, and the costs of the limited liability form (including government fees and other transactional costs of creation and maintenance) outweigh the benefits of limited liability to the enterprise-organizers and any other participants in the firm.[38]

In the last few decades in the United States, new statutes have been passed to authorize general partnerships to convert easily into limited liability partnerships.[39] This option allows for retaining the general partnership form of organization while extending an umbrella of limited liability over the equity partners (in return for a registration fee and other required formalities). Enterprise-level liability insurance is sometimes mandated by statute for these forms of business, but this is often a small price to pay for the peace of mind afforded by limited liability.[40] The United Kingdom has also adopted a limited liability partnership statute, responding to political pressure from the accounting and legal professions.[41] If history is a guide,

---

[36] For a different but informed account of the diversity of cooperatives in many sectors, including agriculture and housing, see Henry Hansmann, *The Ownership of Enterprise* (Harvard University Press 1996), pp. 12–15, 66–181, 195–223. See also Lewis D. Solomon and Melissa B. Kirgis, "Business Cooperatives: A Primer," 6 *DePaul Business Law Journal* 233 (1994) (reviewing the use of corporate forms for cooperatives).

[37] See Chapter 4, page 155 and accompanying notes 120–2.

[38] For an overview of some of these issues, see Judith Freedman, "Small Businesses and the Corporate Form: Burden or Privilege?" 57 *Modern Law Review* 555 (1994).

[39] See, e.g., Klein, Coffee, and Partnoy, op. cit., p. 104; Robert R. Keatinge, Allan G. Donn, George W. Coleman, and Elizabeth G. Hester, "Limited Liability Partnerships: The Next Step in the Evolution of the Unincorporated Business Organization," 51 *Business Lawyer* 147 (1995).

[40] See Klein, Coffee, and Partnoy, op. cit., p. 104.

[41] See, e.g., Joseph A. McCahery and Erik P.M. Vermeulen, "The Evolution of Closely Held Business Forms in Europe," 26 *Journal of Corporation Law* 855, 866 (2001). See also Judith Freedman, "Limited Liability Partnerships in the United Kingdom—Do They Have a Role for Small Firms?" 26 *Journal of Corporation Law* 897 (2001) (describing the U.K. law passed in 2000, but warning of limitations).

following a long-term trend of "democratization" of limited liability business forms, then limited liability partnerships are likely to spread elsewhere in Europe and the world.[42]

Limited liability companies (LLCs) provide another statutory option with flexibility to choose among the traditional features of partnerships and corporations.[43] In other words, LLCs are a legislatively created hybrid of partnerships and corporations. On one hand, like partnerships in the United States, LLCs are granted "pass-through" treatment to avoid enterprise-level taxes that are assessed on many corporations. (The United States, unlike many other jurisdictions in the world, often taxes corporate profits at the enterprise level and then taxes dividends again at the shareholder level. "Pass-through" tax treatment refers to the avoidance of this "double tax" for equity investors in a firm.) On the other hand, like corporations, LLCs may exercise an option for centralized management and the creation of passive equity investors (i.e. "members" with rights and powers similar to shareholders).[44]

As a highly flexible, tax-advantaged business form with built-in limited liability, the LLC has become the fastest growing choice of legal entity for new business firms in the United States. In 1977, Wyoming enacted the first LLC statute in the United States at the request of a company that acquired a Panamanian *limitada*. In a special ruling, the Internal Revenue Service permitted partnership-like pass-through taxation of the entity, but the explosion of LLC statutes and entities did not occur until 1988 when a general tax ruling blessed pass-through treatment of LLCs.[45] All fifty states have now adopted LLC statutes of slightly different varieties. As one legal scholar observes, "the number of LLCs is skyrocketing," and the LLC "has become the organizational form of choice for most small businesses."[46] Several other scholars describe the LLC as "the dominant form of organization for new closely held businesses" in the twenty-first century.[47] According to one estimate, approximately half of new businesses formed annually in the United States choose the LLC form.[48]

Following Germany, which deserves credit as the first country to authorize a version of this business form in 1892, many other countries have adopted statutes authorizing limited liability companies.[49] The German limited liability company

---

[42] On the historical "democratization" of limited liability, see Chapter 4, pages 155–6 and accompanying notes 123–8.

[43] For an introduction to the basic law of LLCs, see Bainbridge, op. cit., pp. 178–99.

[44] See, e.g., Klein, Coffee, and Partnoy, op. cit., pp. 102–4; Howard M. Friedman, "The Silent LLC Revolution—The Social Cost of Academic Neglect," 38 *Creighton Law Review* 35, 40–4 (2004).

[45] See Carol R. Goforth, "The Rise of the Limited Liability Company: Evidence of a Race Between the States, But Heading Where?" 45 *Syracuse Law Review* 1193, 1198–206, 1220–62 (1995); Howard M. Friedman, op. cit., pp. 44–9.

[46] Bainbridge, op. cit., p. 180.

[47] Klein, Coffee, and Partnoy, op. cit., p. 103. See also Thomas Earl Geu, "A Single Theory of Limited Liability Companies: An Evolutionary Analysis," 42 *Suffolk University Law Review* 507 (2009).

[48] Howard M. Friedman, op. cit., pp. 35–40.

[49] See Ingrid Lynn Lenhardt, "The Corporate and Tax Advantages of a Limited Liability Company: A German Perspective," 64 *University of Cincinnati Law Review* 551 (1996).

(*Gesellschaft mit beschränkter Haftung* or GmbH) was authorized in response to legislative reforms that restricted the German corporate form (*Aktiengesellschaft* or AG).[50] There are about one million limited liability companies (GmbH) in Germany.[51] By the 1960s, the following countries subsequently adopted versions of the German statute (in chronological order): Portugal, Austria, Poland, Brazil, Chile, Bulgaria, France, Liechtenstein, Turkey, Hungary, Cuba, Argentina, Luxembourg, Uruguay, Mexico, Belgium, Switzerland, and Spain.[52] The GmbH statute has therefore been described as Germany's "most successful export" of law.[53]

As discussed in Chapter 4, the expansion of the variety and availability of limited liability firms has major social policy implications for the general balance of enterprise liability, business participant liability, and limited liability. An important topic left largely outside the scope of this book is that the global mobility of capital and choice of business registration may also bring political pressure on governments to "liberalize" organizational law to include greater protection from liability for both enterprise entities and business participants. One can already perceive this tendency, for example, in the European Union.[54] In addition, a long-term trend appears to be developing toward allowing greater protection of specialized firms of attorneys, accountants, and other traditional "gatekeepers" of good governance practices. This trend raises significant policy concerns about the credibility and reliability of these professional groups in detecting and preventing fraudulent and other illegal behavior in the business firms that they serve.[55]

All limited liability entities in the United States and most other countries are required to register with the sponsoring government and pay an annual fee for the privilege. These fees are usually relatively small. The traditional justification for this registration requirement has been to give legal notice to potential creditors and anyone who deals with a limited liability entity.[56] Today, the registration requirement counts mostly as a fee-generating service for governments, though the general statutory "concession" of limited liability to an entity allows governments also to "reserve" the right to alter the rules by which these firms are organized (and self-organized).[57]

Limited liability firms have become the rule rather than the exception. Although it may have made sense in the past to divide the world of business firms into those

---

[50] Henry P. De Vries and Friedrich K. Juenger, "Limited Liability Contract: The GmbH," 64 *Columbia Law Review* 866, 869 (1964).

[51] See Klaus J. Hopt, "American Corporate Governance Indices as Seen From a European Perspective," 158 *University of Pennsylvania Law Review PENNumbra* 27, 37 (2009).

[52] Id., p. 869 n. 19.

[53] Lenhardt, op. cit., p. 552 (quoting German commentators Marcus Lutter and Peter Hommelhoff).

[54] See William W. Bratton, Joseph A. McCahery, and Erik P.M. Vermeulen, "How Does Corporate Mobility Affect Lawmaking? A Comparative Analysis," 57 *American Journal of Comparative Law* 347 (2009).

[55] See John C. Coffee, Jr., *Gatekeepers: The Professions and Corporate Governance* (Oxford University Press 2006).

[56] For a deeper theoretical argument favoring business registrations, see Benito Arruñada, "Institutional Support of the Firm: A Theory of Business Registries," 2 *Journal of Legal Analysis* 525 (2010).

[57] See Klein, Coffee, and Partnoy, op. cit., pp. 112–14; Roberta Romano, *The Genius of American Corporate Law* (AEI Press 1993). On the "reserved powers" of legislatures regarding firms, see Chapter 3, page 130 and accompanying notes 106–7.

with limited liability (e.g. corporations) and those without (e.g. partnerships), the feature of limited liability is better conceived today as simply another important attribute of many types of firms. As discussed in Chapter 4, it is an attribute with shifting boundaries both within and outside of the firm for the purposes of assessing enterprise liability and the liability of business participants. In the taxonomy of firms, however, limited liability is only one feature among many that distinguishes different types of modern firms.

The corporation

For various reasons, many of which have been discussed in previous chapters, the corporation has become the largest and most powerful organizational form of business enterprise in the world. The traditional strength and flexibility of the legal entity of the corporation to protect business participants (as described in Chapters 1 and 4) and the advantages of fragmented corporate ownership (as described in Chapter 2) are two major reasons for the historical and continuing success of this business form.

In addition, the corporate institution of the board of directors acts as an effective "organizational principal."[58] Elected by shareholders and responsible for the selection of top managers and other major organizational decisions, the corporate board has proven useful for centuries and has been adopted by firms worldwide. The historical antecedents of corporate boards of directors trace back at least as far as the English East India Company and the Dutch East India Company, which were founded in the early seventeenth century as hybrid public–private enterprises.[59] One legal scholar aptly describes the corporate board today as "the most prominent actor in corporate governance" and "regulated in the corporation laws of virtually all countries."[60] Disagreement continues about the effectiveness of corporate boards for various purposes, such as whether they provide effective monitoring of executives.[61] Note also that small or closely held corporations may usually waive the requirement of a board of directors, given that their shareholders and top managers are effectively the same people (or, in the case of the one-person corporation, the same individual).[62] In any event, corporate boards appear to provide organizational advantages to many business enterprises and are likely to continue in popularity.

---

[58] See Chapter 2, page 59 and accompanying notes 29–30.

[59] See Harold J. Cook, *Matters of Exchange: Commerce, Medicine, and Science in the Dutch Golden Age* (Yale University Press 2007), pp. 62–4; Ronald Findlay and Kevin H. O'Rourke, *Power and Plenty: Trade, War, and the World Economy in the Second Millennium* (Princeton University Press 2007), pp. 177–8; John Keay, *The Honourable Company: A History of the English East India Company* (HarperCollins 1991), pp. 25–8.

[60] Klaus J. Hopt, "Comparative Corporate Governance: The State of the Art and International Regulation," 59 *American Journal of Comparative Law* 1, 19 (2011). See also id., pp. 19–44 (describing differences in the structure and operations of corporate boards in different countries).

[61] Compare, for example, Melvin Aron Eisenberg, *The Structure of the Corporation: A Legal Analysis* (1976), pp. 139–211, with Victor Brudney, "The Independent Director—Heavenly City or Potemkin Village?" 95 *Harvard Law Review* 597 (1982).

[62] See, e.g., Franklin A. Gevurtz, *Corporation Law* (West Group 2000), p. 186.

Corporations also have advantages of organizational flexibility in the multiplication of entities, parent–subsidiary structures, and franchising, as discussed in Chapters 1, 2, and 4. The invention and recognition of holding companies opened the door for a number of different corporate structures, including the home-parent and foreign-subsidiary divisions used within multinational corporations. Corporate structures allow for the construction of pyramids and cross-shareholding arrangements in some countries.

Another hallmark of the corporate form lies in the combination of limited liability and the free transferability of shares. Only corporations can offer public shares traded on public stock markets.[63] In addition to listed companies, there are also many "potentially public" corporations that hope to mature sufficiently to meet listing requirements for public stock exchanges.[64]

Corporate "shapeshifting" can also occur relatively easily to allow small growing firms to "go public" (though initial public offerings of shares), as well as the reverse: "going private" transactions to reorganize public companies.[65] In this connection, corporate shapeshifting is essential in supporting venture capital start-up enterprises (though partnerships and LLCs are also sometimes used at first) and providing "exits" for successful ventures to public securities markets or acquisition by established corporate enterprises. The United States has developed venture capital funding and shapeshifting institutions that appear to work relatively well.[66] Other countries have attempted to emulate this institutional success, such as in Brazil's *Novo Mercado* and Germany's *Neuer Markt*.[67]

Related to its shapeshifting capabilities, the corporate form possesses advantages in terms of the legal mechanics of the mergers and acquisitions of business firms and other organizational control transactions.[68] An example of the creative uses of corporate entities in control transactions is the triangular merger.[69] An advantage of corporations in this context, as well as others, is that corporate law has worked out many organizational rules that allow lawyers to plan with relative certainty based on assessments of prior case decisions and detailed statutes (as compared with, for example, newer LLCs or modern business trusts).

Because of these various organizational advantages, corporations far outweigh any other legal form of business enterprise in terms of their economic activity and overall wealth. In the United States, for example, census data reveal that corporations account for more than four times the total receipts of sole proprietorships

---

[63] See, e.g., Robert C. Clark, *Corporate Law* (Aspen 1986), pp. 1–4, 13–14; Conard, op. cit., pp. 163–5.

[64] Conard, op. cit., pp. 162–3.

[65] On corporate "shapeshifting," see Chapter 1, pages 39–40 and accompanying notes 139–45.

[66] See Ronald J. Gilson, "Engineering a Venture Capital Market: Lessons from the American Experience," 55 *Stanford Law Review* 1067 (2003).

[67] See Ronald J. Gilson, Henry Hansmann, and Mariana Pargendler, "Regulatory Dualism as a Development Strategy: Corporate Reform in Brazil, the United States, and the European Union," 63 *Stanford Law Review* 475 (2011) (estimating Brazil's innovation as successful and Germany's not).

[68] On the basic legal ground rules, see Clark, op. cit., pp. 401–592; Gevurtz, op. cit., pp. 630–746.

[69] See Chapter 1 above, pages **38–9** and Figure 1.1.

Table 5.2 Business firms in the United States: population and income (2007)

	Number of firms	Total receipts
Proprietorships	23.1 million	$1.3 trillion
Partnerships	3.1 million	$4.5 trillion
Corporations[a]	5.9 million	$27.3 trillion

[a] Excludes "S" corporations (i.e. closely held corporations that do not have to file federal tax returns).
Source: compiled from U.S. Census Bureau, Statistical Abstract of the United States (2011), p. 491, table 743.

Table 5.3 Business firms in the United States: size and employment[a] (2007)

	Number of firms	Total employment	Total payroll
Under 20 employees	6.6 million	30.1 million	$1.07 trillion
20 to 100 employees	892,000	35.6 million	$1.31 trillion
100 to 500 employees	161,000	30.5 million	$1.31 trillion
500 to 1000 employees	12,000	8.28 million	$428 billion
1000-plus employees	7,000	16.2 million	$910 billion

[a] Employment figures do not include government employees, the self-employed, and (for some obscure historical reason) railroad employees.
Source: compiled from U.S. Census Bureau, Statistical Abstract of the United States (2011), p. 500, table 757.

and partnerships combined. In terms of the total number of firms, however, proprietorships and partnerships outpace corporations. In the United States, there are more than four times as many firms organized as proprietorships and partnerships than corporations. See Table 5.2. Also, though corporations are usually much wealthier than other kinds of firms, smaller firms including proprietorships and partnerships employ many more people in the aggregate than corporations. See Table 5.3.

Up-to-date, complete, and reliable comparative data are difficult to find, but the available evidence suggests that the general proportions and capitalizations of small and large firms are roughly similar in other developed rich countries.[70] Germany, for example, appears to track the United States in terms of the relative number of corporations (AGs) to limited liability companies (GmbH): with 3,400 AGs compared with 600,000 GmbHs in 1994. But the relative economic weight of total share capitalization falls in favor of the GmbH form: with $104 billion in AGs compared with $160 billion in GmbHs. Note, however, that the flexibility of the GmbH structure makes it the preferred form for foreign subsidiaries of multinational corporations, such as IBM Deutschland GmbH, so this fact may account in part for this difference in capital.[71]

In developing poor countries, one might expect that the ratio would skew toward smaller enterprises given a lack of capital for large ones, but the prevalence of

[70] See, e.g., Freedman, "Small Businesses and Corporate Form," op. cit., p. 574.
[71] Lenhardt, op. cit., p. 553.

corporate pyramids and similar structures discussed in Chapter 2 may lead to different empirical findings. The optimal "mix" of different sizes and kinds of firms for different societies is an important question, but one that is left outside the scope of this book.[72]

In summary, the economic size of corporations varies widely. They range from small one-person "minicorporations" to huge global "supercorps" or "megafirms" with annual revenues of hundreds of billions of dollars.[73]

The number of multinational corporations has been rising fast in the last several decades. From 1982 to 2004, foreign direct investment jumped twenty-five fold from $27 billion to $730 billion. During the same period, sales of foreign subsidiaries of multinational firms increased from $2.8 trillion to $18.7 trillion, and their assets expanded from $2.1 trillion to $36 trillion. Reflecting this increased economic activity, the number of multinational enterprises—defined as business enterprises that have significant operations in more than one country—exploded by a factor of ten from around 7,000 in 1970 to approximately 77,000 by 2005.[74]

The "home" parent countries of multinational firms have also begun to diversify. As late as 1970, half of the world's largest multinational corporations were based in either the United Kingdom or the United States.[75] By 2012, the Fortune Global 500 list of the largest business enterprises had expanded to include multinational companies based not only in Europe (151) and the United States (132), but also China (seventy-three), Japan (sixty-eight), South Korea (thirteen), Canada (eleven), Australia (nine), Brazil (eight), India (eight), Russia (seven), Taiwan (six), Mexico (three), Singapore (two), and one multinational firm each in Columbia, Hungary, Malaysia, Poland, Saudi Arabia, Thailand, Turkey, United Arab Emirates, and Venezuela.[76]

Census data and annual reports give only a small window into the overall picture, however.[77] Firms are structured in much more complex ways than an easy separation of "proprietorship, partnerships, and corporations" would lead one to believe.[78] And large firm corporate structures are often complicated. A modern typology of business firms must therefore expand beyond a simple list of the basic

---

[72] For discussion along these lines, see William J. Baumol, Robert E. Litan, and Carl J. Schramm, *Good Capitalism, Bad Capitalism, and the Economics of Growth and Prosperity* (Yale University Press 2007). More empirical studies of the types and sizes of firms in different societies would be very useful.

[73] See Conard, op. cit., pp. 154–9; Randall S. Thomas, Stewart J. Schwab, and Robert G. Hansen, "Megafirms," 80 *North Carolina Law Review* 115 (2001).

[74] Stephen D. Cohen, *Multinational Corporations and Foreign Direct Investment: Avoiding Simplicity, Embracing Complexity* (Oxford University Press 2007), pp. 47–8 (citing U.N. statistics).

[75] "Back in Fashion," *Economist*, March 27, 1993, pp. 5–6.

[76] CNN/Money, "Global 500," <http://money.cnn.com/magazines/fortune/global500/> (accessed December 27, 2012).

[77] A useful global data research project would collect better statistics about the legal forms of business enterprise and their attributes around the world. Data with respect to nation-states as a primary methodological lens is much more common than data focusing on business enterprises themselves.

[78] The U.S. census data are distilled from federal tax returns. There are many uncertainties in it as a result. Many firms are structured specifically with variables of federal tax liability in mind. LLCs are probably reported as either "partnerships" or "proprietorships," for example, for this reason. Better data at the national level on types of firms and their attributes would also be helpful for future policy making.

legal forms to include a variety of more complex firms that are created with these basic entities as legal building material.

Complex relational firms

A large number of integrated business enterprises belong to the category of complex relational firms.[79] Corporate groups, including parent–subsidiary, conglomerate, and pyramid structures, count as one subset of complex relational firms. These groups, as described in Chapters 1 and 2, use holding companies and other legal techniques to combine a number of different entities together into an integrated business operation. Other techniques of legally linking a number of business entities together in terms of ownership and control structures include franchising, licensing, marketing alliances, manufacturing joint ventures, research partnerships, distribution networks, and long-term supply contracts.[80]

Some complex arrangements are difficult to classify, such as corporate cross-shareholding (*keiretsu*) that does not amount to effective operational control or integration. As in other situations, however, the best answer lies in considering the context of a particular legal claim or question of "control" or "integration" (such as enterprise liability, agency authority, an antitrust or securities law violation, or other issue), and then examining the particular circumstances of the business organization involved. Again, the legal answers to questions of firm integration, ownership, and control should depend on the specific policy contexts.

Take franchises for example. The growth of franchise enterprises has been particularly robust in recent years. According to one estimate, the United States hosted more than 900,000 franchise businesses in 2010, which accounted for more than one-third of total retail sales.[81] As discussed in Chapter 4, franchises raise difficult questions of enterprise liability and agency authority, which should turn largely on whether parent franchisors exercise effective "control" over the operations of franchisees. The law of franchises appears to be evolving comparatively slowly, supplying an example of how new forms of business organization can emerge and grow much faster than the law and policy governing them.[82] Given continuing uncertainty in the law, perhaps legislative solutions should be adopted that take into account the complexity of the legal structure as well as relevant policy principles. Statutory imposition of vicarious liability for franchisors in specified circumstances and mandatory insurance are two policy options.[83]

---

[79] See also Orts, "Shirking and Sharking," op. cit., pp. 312–13 (using slightly different terminology).

[80] For basic descriptions of some of these legal "ties that bind," see Conard, op. cit., pp. 167–73.

[81] Robert W. Emerson, "Franchise Encroachment," 47 *American Business Law Journal* 191, 196–7 (2010); Joseph H. King, Jr., "Limiting the Vicarious Liability of Franchisors for the Torts of Their Franchisees," 62 *Washington and Lee Law Review* 417, 421 (2005).

[82] See King, op. cit., pp. 419–20.

[83] See Robert W. Emerson, "Franchisors' Liability When Franchisees Are Apparent Agents: An Empirical and Policy Analysis of 'Common Knowledge' About Franchising," 20 *Hofstra Law Review*

Cooperatives of various kinds present a related example. Agricultural cooperatives process and market such well-known products as Ocean Spray cranberries, Sunkist oranges, Sun Maid raisins, Land O'Lakes butter, Organic Valley milk, and Welch's grape juice. True-Value, Ace, and Servistar are retailer-owned hardware wholesale cooperatives. Associated Press is run as a complex cooperative of news networks. Visa and Mastercard are organized as cooperatives of member banks.[84] These cooperatives are complex arrangements, and one can follow the outlines of governing documents and organizational contracts to address most conflicts that may arise among cooperative members. It is not always clear, however, how cooperatives should be treated in various areas of the law (such as antitrust, environmental, or securities regulation). Like franchises, cooperatives can also raise difficult issues of "control" and "integration" for purposes of finding enterprise liability and agency authority for wrongful harm to others.

Although the many available techniques for coordinating and integrating business operations may lead some commentators to throw up their hands and declare that "all is contracts," this approach does not do justice to the legal and practical realities of these enterprises.[85] One implication of an "all is contracts" approach is to avoid the tough legal questions of responsibility, accountability, and enterprise liability. By failing to examine questions of whether an arrangement of ownership and control amounts to "integration" sufficient to perceive a coherent enterprise (which may then be found to have legal responsibility for a particular action or behavior), an "all is contracts" approach tends to default to the market rather than to potential regulation. At least implicitly, this hands-off approach encourages the manipulation of legal entities to avoid responsibility, accountability, and liability. Instead, "economic integration" when "a firm unites groups of assets under common control" is an important feature of the modern business world that deserves to be taken seriously in contemporary legal and economic analysis.[86]

As discussed in Chapters 1 and 4, motivations for forming complex business relationships often stem from a desire to lessen or eliminate potential liability for the firm itself or business participants for the wrongful harms that they may impose on others. Similar economic reasoning often drives decisions to organize various business relationships "inside" or "outside" of the firm, such as in "outsourcing" decisions.[87] But an economic decision to structure a business enterprise to avoid potential liability should not dispose of questions about whether the method of avoidance should be legally respected as a matter of public policy.

609 (1992) (suggesting a legislative solution imposing vicarious liability on franchisors); King, op. cit. (suggesting a legislative solution requiring effective notice and insurance coverage).

[84] Hansmann, *The Ownership of Enterprise*, op. cit., pp. 121, 157–8. See also Eric W. Orts, "The Future of Enterprise Organization," 96 *Michigan Law Review* 1947, 1956 (1998) (book review). For Organic Valley, see <http://www.organicvalley.coop/> (accessed September 29, 2012).

[85] See Chapter 2, pages 64–8 and accompanying notes 51–69.

[86] See Edward M. Iacobucci and George G. Triantis, "Economic and Legal Boundaries of Firms," 93 *Virginia Law Review* 515, 569 (2007).

[87] See Chapter 2, page 61 and accompanying note 38, and Chapter 4, pages 143–4 and accompanying note 55. See also George Baker, Robert Gibbons, and Kevin J. Murphy, "Relational Contracts and the Theory of the Firm," 117 *Quarterly Journal of Economics* 39 (2002).

Again, the policy argument here is one that depends on choice of normative orientation as well as the execution of one's analysis. Too many economic arguments in the law of business enterprise today rely on an assumption that various self-organization techniques should be presumed "efficient" given generally competitive markets. Empirically, however, this assumption is often not supported. One might as easily assume that any organizational arrangement is anti-competitive and "inefficient." At least, assumptions about the presumed efficiency of business organization structures should be tested empirically as well as analytically. Moreover, the discipline of economics is not the only normative perspective that should be consulted. Non-economic moral principles are often relevant. Political judgments expressed in legislation convey other values that should have a legitimate place as well.

In any event, the primary legal attributes of business firms—namely, the combination of ownership, control, and agency authority—do not disappear with increasing organizational complexity. Instead, it is likely that wealthy individuals and business enterprises who can afford high-priced legal and financial talent may often fall into the temptation to increase organizational complexity as a ploy to avoid regulatory coverage and evade potential liability. This kind of "avoision" is common in tax law and other areas, and there is no reason to think that enterprise law is immune. The legal scholar Leo Katz coined the term "avoision" to refer to questionable legal practices "hovering in the limbo between legitimate avoidance and illegitimate evasion."[88] If the creation of complexity in enterprise organization is used to avoid and evade the policy purposes of the law, then it stands to reason that judges and legislators should endeavor to pierce through this often "fraud-like" if not actually fraudulent pettifoggery. Analogies might be drawn to the "entity-piercing" arguments discussed in Chapter 4 to apply to complex relational firms.

Even within complex enterprises, one can trace key elements of "control" (including governance and agency authority) as well as "ownership" (including dedicated assets and financial interests).[89] Like any good mystery, the key to determining control is often to "follow the money" or, in more precise business terms, to discover who is taking the greatest financial risks and receiving the greatest economic gains. Often, those with the most at stake are those who also pull the strings of organizational power and authority. "Stripped to the fundamentals," as one legal scholar observes, "participants in a business organization are concerned about two things—wealth and power."[90]

Determining the legal boundaries of complex relational firms for various purposes is often difficult. The boundaries will often shift, again to invoke H.L.A. Hart, depending on the question being asked.[91] Answers about the boundaries

---

[88] Leo Katz, *Ill-Gotten Gains: Evasion, Blackmail, Fraud, and Kindred Puzzles of the Law* (University of Chicago Press 1996), p. x.

[89] One contribution usefully refers to these kinds of agreements as "control bargains." G. Mitu Gulati, William A. Klein, and Eric M. Zolt, "Connected Contracts," 47 *UCLA Law Review* 887, 918–29 (2000). However, this contribution misses the importance of how these bargains actually result in unified and integrated firms. See Chapter 2, page 67 and accompanying notes 64–5.

[90] Cf. Gevurtz, op. cit., p. 179.

[91] H.L.A. Hart, "Definition and Theory in Jurisprudence," in *Essays in Jurisprudence and Philosophy* (Oxford University Press 1983), pp. 21–3, 31–3, 40–5.

of the firm may differ for some questions (such as enterprise liability) compared to others (such as managerial authority). Difficulty of practical application does not mean, however, that complex relational firms do not exist.

As discussed above, business participants use the law to create the various forms of enterprise organization. These legal structures of property, power, and control are discoverable. The financial contributions and expectations of investors in these enterprises are usually delineated clearly, and the resulting capital structures are understandable, even if they are often highly detailed and complex. With sufficient knowledge and investigation, one may discern the curves of control and the bodies of ownership that compose the shapes of complex relational firms. Legal lenses reveal the structural details of firm organization. And social policies chosen by lawmakers to hold business enterprises and their participants responsible can then be applied accordingly, with eyes wide open about the nature of the business organization in question.

As I have argued throughout this book, the normative principles used to determine these policies may come from a variety of perspectives. Often, economic considerations may predominate. The determination of a corporate default rule, for example, might rely mostly on economic analysis. Sometimes a moral principle may take precedence. Criminal violations such as intentional fraud or embezzlement call for applications of a basic ethical principle (i.e. a moral prohibition of commercial dishonesty and theft). For the purposes of this book, I am agnostic about which values or policies should prevail in specific cases. I insist, however, that there are choices to be made about competing values and policies in law. And any theory of the firm that hides or obfuscates these choices is not socially useful or truthful.

Government and state-owned enterprises

Government corporations and other state-owned enterprises constitute an important additional category of firms. In societies characterized as following a version of state capitalism, state-owned enterprises are dominant (by definition).[92] However, state-owned and -operated enterprises appear also in societies that follow an ideal of market capitalism, especially in sectors such as transportation (e.g. airlines or railroads), communications (e.g. postal services), and utilities (e.g. electricity and water services).[93] Most societies exhibit a mix of state capitalism and market capitalism. According to one observer, "real-world forms of capitalism" are arrayed along a spectrum from "state capitalism" to "free-market capitalism."[94]

---

[92] For the concept of "state capitalism," see Introduction, page 4 and accompanying note 13; Chapter 1, pages 12–13, 19, 21–2, and accompanying notes 20–1, 46, 54–9; and Chapter 3, pages 110–12, 114, and accompanying notes 6–23, 32–3.

[93] See Chapter 3, page 111 and accompanying notes 11–12.

[94] Ian Bremmer, *The End of the Free Market: Who Wins the War Between States and Corporations?* (Portfolio 2010), pp. 43–4.

China is the leading example of state capitalism today (though Russia and other countries also exhibit strong tendencies in this direction).[95] Business managers in China are advised to work directly with government officials.[96] Although much of the economic growth in contemporary China has been fed by small enterprises as well as foreign partnerships with private companies, large state-owned enterprises still play an outsized role, especially in the banking and energy sectors.[97] State-owned firms account for an estimated 80 percent of total business capitalization in China. (The figure is 60 percent in Russia and 35 percent in Brazil.)[98] Chinese state-owned firms account for half of the total industrial output, receive half of government loans and subsidies, and employ about 35 percent of urban workers in China.[99] According to one survey, PetroChina is the second largest business enterprise in the world (trailing only ExxonMobil) with an estimated market value of more than $300 billion and more than 500,000 employees. The two largest Chinese banks also rank in the top ten largest firms in the world.[100]

Other state-owned enterprises in the oil and gas industry qualify as among the twenty largest companies in the world. They include Petrobras in Brazil and Gazprom in Russia.[101] On an aggregated basis, state-owned oil companies currently account for three-quarters of the world's petroleum reserves.[102] Other large state-owned energy companies are based in Abu Dhabi, Algeria, Kuwait, Iran, Malaysia, Mexico, Nigeria, Norway, and Venezuela.[103]

State-owned firms fit uneasily into the general template provided here for understanding the business enterprise. As described in Chapter 3, these companies are part of state capitalist systems answering to government masters, and yet they also have the advantage of plugging into a market-capitalist global infrastructure of privately organized trade and commerce. They qualify as firms, then, in the sense that they are producers of goods and services for global consumer markets. At the same time, they are owned by governments, and any profits made are returned to government coffers (with losses also imposed on governments). State-owned firms therefore fall heavily on the "public" side of the public–private divide, but they nevertheless qualify as a variation of business enterprise.

State-owned firms also do not fit easily within received "socialist" frameworks, whether in China or elsewhere. Because these firms participate in global commercial

---

[95] See id., pp. 128–45; Stefan Helper, *The Beijing Consensus: How China's Authoritarian Model Will Dominate the Twenty-First Century* (Basic Books 2010), pp. 3, 9–10, 68–72, 103–8; David Brooks, "The Larger Struggle," *New York Times*, June 15, 2010, at A25; "The State and the Economy: Re-enter the Dragon," *Economist*, June 3, 2010, <http://www.economist.com> (accessed September 16, 2012).

[96] See Lynn S. Paine, "The China Rules," *Harvard Business Review* (June 2010), pp. 103–5.

[97] See Chapter 3, pages 111–12 and accompanying notes 13–23.

[98] Mariana Pargendler, "State Ownership and Corporate Governance," 80 *Fordham Law Review* 2917, 2918–19 (2012) (citing statistics reported in the *Economist*).

[99] Leng Jing, *Corporate Governance and Financial Reform in China's Transition Economy* (Hong Kong University Press 2009), pp. 22–3.

[100] FT Global 500 (Financial Times 2011), <http://media.ft.com> (accessed September 29, 2012).

[101] Id.   [102] Bremmer, op. cit., p. 56.   [103] Id., pp. 56–60, 121–2.

markets, they often operate relatively independently from government bureaucracies in terms of their everyday management.[104]

Another important example of ownership and investment in firms by political states appears in the form of sovereign wealth funds. These are government-based funds, and they have grown quite large. The sixty largest funds control over $5 trillion in assets worldwide. (More than half of these assets derive their original capital from the oil and gas business.) Four of the top twelve funds are Chinese. Other countries represented in the top twelve funds are Kuwait, Norway, Russia, Saudi Arabia, Singapore, Qatar, and the United Arab Emirates.[105]

Some legal scholars argue that sovereign wealth funds illustrate the dangers of a "new mercantilism" and maintain that countries that adhere generally to a market capitalism approach should regulate state-owned sovereign wealth fund investments.[106] Ronald Gilson and Curtis Milhaupt, for example, propose legislation in the United States that would strip sovereign wealth funds of voting rights in U.S.-based privately held firms unless the investments are converted to "non-state ownership." They anticipate that U.S.-based sovereign wealth funds might become the targets of reciprocal regulation.[107] Sovereign wealth funds based in Alaska, Texas, New Mexico, and Wyoming also qualify as among the top fifty largest funds in the world.[108] State pension funds, such as the California Public Employees' Retirement System (Calpers) and the California State Teachers' Retirement System (Calsters), probably qualify as well. If combined, Calpers and Calsters would form the second largest sovereign wealth fund in the world.[109]

Another regulatory proposal focusing on foreign sovereign wealth funds would allow for "safe harbors" for good practices (such as passive investment strategies) and grant exemptions to funds based in market-oriented societies (such as Norway).[110] In addition, the United States, Australia, and some other market-oriented countries have taken some steps in the direction of greater regulation at the international level.[111] In response to heightened scrutiny, China, Russia, and other sponsors of sovereign wealth funds have begun to increase surveillance of incoming foreign investments into their countries as well.[112]

Other legal scholars claim that attempts to regulate sovereign wealth funds would be counterproductive or, at least, that the case has not yet been made of a need for

---

[104] See Bremmer, op. cit., pp. 59–60, 90, 124–5 (citing various state-owned energy companies in this category).

[105] Sovereign Wealth Fund Institute, Sovereign Wealth Fund Rankings (updated September 2012), <http://www.swfinstitute.org/fund-rankings/> (accessed September 29, 2012).

[106] See Ronald J. Gilson and Curtis J. Milhaupt, "Sovereign Wealth Funds and Corporate Governance: A Minimalist Response to the New Mercantilism," 60 *Stanford Law Review* 1345 (2008).

[107] Id., pp. 1352–3, 1362–5, 1369.

[108] See Sovereign Wealth Fund Institute, op. cit.

[109] Benn Steil, "California's Sovereign Wealth Fund," *Wall Street Journal*, March 7, 2008, p. A14.

[110] See Jennifer Cooke, Survey, "Finding the Right Balance for Sovereign Wealth Fund Regulation: Open Investment vs. National Security," 2009 *Columbia Business Law Review* 728 (2009).

[111] "The Changing International Economic Balance of Power," 102 *Proceedings of the Annual Meeting (American Society of International Law)* 293, 295–6 (2008) (remarks of Faryar Shirzad).

[112] Id.

regulation. They argue that most sovereign investment funds have not been "aggressive" in terms of seeking controlling interests in private firms.[113] Another commentator agrees that it is not yet known whether sovereign wealth funds will "mix political considerations with their investment-value-maximizing tactics" and, if so, to what extent.[114] It appears, however, that conflict is brewing on the horizon in this area internationally.

An intermediate position supports enhanced disclosure reporting and "standards of transparency" to govern sovereign wealth fund investments.[115] Mandatory disclosure of this kind is common in securities regulation. International organizations of nation-states have endorsed "best practices" for sovereign wealth funds to include transparency of investments and the intentions behind them.[116]

If international investment practices do not raise direct conflicts between systems of state capitalism and market capitalism (or at least not yet), one cannot treat international mergers and acquisitions with as much sanguinity. State-owned enterprises based in China have recently targeted private companies elsewhere for acquisitions. In 2005, a bid by a state-owned Chinese company (China National Offshore Oil Corporation) to take over a private U.S.-based company (Unocal) with low-cost debt financing supplied by state-owned Chinese banks caused a political stir. Close and negative attention from the U.S. Congress scotched the deal.[117] Chinese deals for the acquisition of overseas companies have nevertheless increased. In 2012, total global mergers and acquisitions slumped, but Chinese-sponsored deals increased by 28 percent. Most Chinese buyers were state-owned companies financed by state-owned banks.[118]

There is irony and, more deeply, a structural contradiction with respect to state-owned firms participating in and gaining economic benefits from an international trade regime of freely organized business enterprises and a global consumer market-place. This structural contradiction puts implicit limits on the extent to which state-owned enterprises can expand without spawning an adverse political reaction from countries that support the global regime of free markets and business competition. A long-term institutional choice between two possible future directions is therefore likely: (1) greater movement toward market capitalism in China, Russia, and other countries that sponsor large state-owned businesses; or (2) increasing international political conflict between the national sponsors of state capitalism and those of market capitalism. (A third possibility of greater entrenchment of state capitalism everywhere is possible but not likely, because it would undermine the global markets on which all countries currently depend.)

---

[113] See Richard A. Epstein and Amanda M. Rose, "The Regulation of Sovereign Wealth Funds: The Virtues of Going Slow," 76 *University of Chicago Law Review* 111 (2009).

[114] Detlev F. Vagts, "The Financial Meltdown and Its International Implications," 103 *American Journal of International Law* 684, 688 (2009).

[115] Evan Bayh, "Time for Sovereign Wealth Rules," *Wall Street Journal*, February 13, 2008, p. A26.

[116] See Epstein and Rose, op. cit., pp. 120–2 (describing these initiatives and recommendations).

[117] See, e.g., Gilson and Milhaupt, op. cit., p. 1349.

[118] See Keith Bradersher and Michael J. de la Merced, "China Woos Overseas Companies, Looking for Deals," *New York Times*, December 12, 2012, at B1.

The general tension between state capitalism and market capitalism implicates political values. Countries that fall generally into the camp of state capitalism tend to have relatively authoritarian regimes, while countries adhering to an ideal and general practice of market capitalism tend to follow more open and democratic government. These political issues related to enterprise organization and theories of the firm are very important and unavoidable, and I hope to deal with them more directly in future work, but not here.

Even in countries characterized mostly by an orientation toward market capitalism, government corporations play a large and business-like role in the economy. In the United States, for example, government corporations operate the postal service, the passenger rail system, and a number of public utilities for electricity (such as the Tennessee Valley Authority (TVA)).[119] As one legal scholar has described the situation:

> The federal government has entered business areas in a variety of ways. With the creation of the TVA, it created a new enterprise. With Amtrak, it took over a formerly private enterprise. With the Postal Service, it separated what was formerly a government department into a separate corporation. All of these institutions present questions as to how far they should be ruled by a set of principles established by instruments of government, and how far by the rules developed for other entities which perform essentially economic services.[120]

A more recent study counts forty-five government charters and more than 6,000 individual government corporations in the United States.[121] Another legal scholar, Michael Froomkin, identifies ownership variations among these government corporations as including the following: "wholly owned" by the government, "mixed [public–private] ownership," and "private."[122] Government-owned firms are also common in other parts of the world in business sectors such as banking, postal services, telecommunications, and transportation. Postal services are government-owned almost everywhere, and telecommunications, transportation, and public utilities are very commonly monopolized or dominated by government-owned entities.[123] Great Britain, France, Germany, and Spain have gone through relatively recent historical phases during which they "nationalized" other major business sectors—such as coal, steel, and other large-scale industries—into state-owned enterprises.[124] As recently as 1982 in France, the national government controlled more than one-third of the total value of manufacturing, and "the main channels

---

[119] See Chapter 3, page 111 and accompanying notes 11–12. On the mixed record of the TVA, see Erwin C. Hargrove, *Prisoners of Myth: The Leadership of the Tennessee Valley Authority, 1933–1990* (Princeton University Press 1994); Thomas K. McCraw, "Book Review: The Hubris of the Engineers," 36 *Technology and Culture* 1007 (1995).

[120] Conard, op. cit., p. 141.

[121] Pargendler, op. cit., p. 2926.

[122] A. Michael Froomkin, "Reinventing the Government Corporation," 1995 *University of Illinois Law Review* 543, 546–57 (1995).

[123] See Louis Galambos, "State-owned Enterprises in a Hostile Environment: The U.S. Experience," in *The Rise and Fall of the State-Owned Enterprise in the Western World* (Pier Angelo Toninelli ed.) (Cambridge University Press 2000), p. 275, fig. 12.1.

[124] See *The Rise and Fall of the State-Owned Enterprise in the Western World*, op. cit., pp. 103–27, 157–236 (providing historical overviews of each of these countries).

for industrial credit were state-directed."[125] The state ownership and operation of banks and other financial institutions has been and remains common in the world, given a perceived link to economic development and financial stability.[126]

An unusual variant of the state-owned firm is the treaty-chartered corporation, which is formed through a partnership of sovereign nation-states. For example, the United Arab Shipping Company was created by a treaty among Bahrain, Saudi Arabia, Kuwait, Qatar, United Arab Emirates, and Iraq. An incorporated subsidiary of the firm operates in the United States. Gulf Air is a "joint stock company with limited liability" created by a treaty among the Emirate of Abu Dhabi, Bahrain, Qatar, and Oman.[127] Treaty-chartered firms are quite rare, however, because of the intrinsic complications of the formal treaty-making process.

All of these examples of state-owned enterprises present similar questions with respect to the source of their institutional discipline: government administration, market competition, or both? If one cannot answer this question regarding the responsibility and accountability of one or more of these enterprises convincingly, then the ambiguity in the sources of monitoring and oversight signals potential trouble.

The Great Credit Crash of 2008 and the ensuing recession highlighted one example of how public–private hybrid organizations can cause major problems. Fannie Mae and Freddie Mac are the nice and friendly-sounding names given to the two main government-sponsored enterprises (GSEs) responsible for housing mortgage financing in the United States. The "government-sponsored" feature of these hybrid firms referred to the fact that they were subsidized by receiving access to low-interest guaranteed government loans, as well as an implicit guarantee of a government bailout, as events would later show.[128] (Sallie Mae, another nice-sounding name, reminding one of a kindly aunt, was a GSE for student loans, but its special government sponsorship was withdrawn after it appeared that little benefit from this GSE actually transferred to its intended beneficiaries, namely, students.[129])

Most observers agree that the failures of Fannie Mae and Freddie Mac were a significant cause of the collapse of credit that led to a global financial crisis, though some debate remains about which part of the financial system failed most severely.[130] At least one root cause of the Great Credit Crash of 2008 has been traced to low credit standards applied to the authorization and approval of housing mortgages (which were then also widely securitized by investment banks) and

---

[125] Bob Hancké, "Revisiting the French Model: Coordination and Restructuring in French Industry" in *Varieties of Capitalism: The Institutional Foundations of Comparative Advantage* (Peter A. Hall and David Soskice eds.) (Oxford University Press 2001), p. 308.

[126] See Rafael La Porta, Florencio Lopez-de-Silanes, and Andrei Shleifer, "Government Ownership of Banks," 57 *Journal of Finance* 265 (2002).

[127] See Sarah C. Haan, "Federalizing the Foreign Corporate Form," 85 *St. John's Law Review* 925, 954–5 (2011).

[128] For an overview of the regulatory issues and their context, see, e.g., Dale Arthur Oesterle, "The Collapse of Fannie Mae and Freddie Mac: Victims or Villains?" 5 *Entrepreneurial Business Law Journal* 733 (2010); David Reiss, "Fannie Mae and Freddie Mac and the Future of Federal Housing Finance Policy: A Study of Regulatory Privilege," 61 *Alabama Law Review* 907 (2010).

[129] See, e.g., Reiss, op. cit., p. 953.

[130] See Preface, pages xix–xx and accompanying note 25, and Chapter 1, page 25 and accompanying note 72.

enabled at least in part by Fannie Mae and Freddie Mac. Both majority and dissenting views of the official report of the Financial Crisis Inquiry Commission found that Fannie Mae and Freddie Mac played a major part by overleveraging themselves and encouraging irresponsible lending to "subprime" borrowers.[131]

Economic and other policy arguments have characterized these organizations as unholy hybrids that lacked effective oversight and discipline from either government or markets.[132] The two clearest options to public–private hybrids are either privatization or government integration. Dangerous public–private hybrids may illuminate the practical consequence for some who refuse to recognize the importance of maintaining a distinction between public and private institutions, as discussed in Chapter 3. The social mechanisms of discipline are very different for private firms and administrative agencies. One problem that contributed to the meltdown of Fannie and Freddie was that government sponsorship led to cozy connections with politicians. From 1999 to 2008, Fannie and Freddie executives spent $164 million on lobbying.[133]

Going forward, the lessons from the past suggest that greater clarity is needed with respect to state-owned firms. In the case of housing mortgage financing in the United States, one option would privatize Fannie and Freddie fully, and then subject them to appropriate regulation.[134] A second option would allow for the government to continue to run Fannie and Freddie directly, but now on a fully nationalized post-bailout basis. As of this writing, however, neither option has been adopted.[135]

In general, private–public hybrids of this kind should be avoided. At a minimum, some manner of special regulatory treatment is necessary for government corporations that both provide goods and services for public consumption like a business and at the same time remain owned and operated by a government. Reforms should consider accountability mechanisms, options of either full privatization or full nationalization, and other relevant considerations.[136]

Charitable and nonprofit enterprises

Another borderline category with respect to a general taxonomy of firms is found in enterprises intended to pursue charitable and other nonprofit purposes. In general,

---

[131] See Financial Crisis Inquiry Commission, *The Financial Crisis Inquiry Report* (Public Affairs 2011); Financial Crisis Inquiry Commission, Dissenting Statement of Peter J. Wallison (January 2011), <http://fcic-static.law.stanford.edu/cdn_media/fcic-reports/fcic_final_report_wallison_ dissent.pdf>, pp. 444–5, 451–533 (accessed September 29, 2012). See also Gretchen Morgenson and Joshua Rosner, *Reckless Endangerment: How Outsized Ambition, Greed, and Corruption Led to Economic Armageddon* (Times Books 2011).

[132] For a prescient warning about the conflicting objectives, confused internal incentives, and ineffective oversight of government corporations, including private–public hybrids, see Froomkin, op. cit., pp. 546–57, 560–1, 577, 582–614.

[133] Financial Crisis Inquiry Commission, op. cit., p. xxvi.

[134] See, e.g., Reiss, op. cit.

[135] See, e.g., David Zaring, "The Post-Crisis and Its Critics," 12 *University of Pennsylvania Journal of Business Law* 1169, 1177–9 (2010).

[136] See Froomkin, op. cit., pp. 618–33.

this book excludes treatment of these organizational forms because their purpose is not primarily business, namely, the pursuit of profit and economic gain. Instead, the typical nonprofit organization is devoted to charitable or philanthropic purposes, such as religion, political activities, social causes, or education. Nonprofit organizations are also often committed to leisurely pursuits, such as social clubs or amateur sporting leagues—the modern heirs to the informal, socially oriented Greek and Roman *collegia*.[137]

One might dispute this philosophical distinction between philanthropy and business. It is possible to argue that the overall objective of business enterprises acting in markets is to benefit humanity generally in material and economic terms, albeit through the institution of profitable exchanges and the beneficent effects of markets and the "invisible hand." But here I follow the traditional distinctions among (1) *philanthropy* understood as private nonprofit initiatives and institutions for the public good; (2) *business* understood as private profit-oriented initiatives and institutions for private economic gain; and (3) *government* understood as publicly organized institutions established for the public good. See Table 5.4.

As the last section discussing government enterprises and this section discussing nonprofit enterprises demonstrate, these categories are not hermetically sealed in the real world. For example, some government-sponsored enterprises are expressly devoted to nonprofit purposes. In the United States, these include the Smithsonian Institution and the National Park Foundation.[138] The field of education is also especially complicated, with some private for-profit ventures competing with traditional private nonprofit colleges and universities, as well as state colleges and universities.[139] Nevertheless, philanthropic, educational, and religious organizations of various stripes are accurately described in general as in the "nonprofit sector."[140]

Table 5.4 Social institutions and the public/private distinction

	Private/public organization	Private/public purpose
Philanthropy	Private	Public
Business	Private	Private
Government	Public	Public

---

[137] See also Chapter 1, pages 9–10 and accompanying note 3. On the ancient *collegia*, see John S. Kloppenborg, "*Collegia* and *Thiasoi*: Issues in Function, Taxonomy and Membership" in *Voluntary Associations in the Graeco-Roman World* (John S. Kloppenborg and Stephen G. Wilson eds.) (Routledge 1996).

[138] See Froomkin, op. cit., p. 580.

[139] See Henry Hansmann, "The Evolving Economic Structure of Higher Education," 79 *University of Chicago Law Review* 159, 159 (2012) (noting an increase in "market share" of new for-profit educational ventures).

[140] On the development of modern philanthropic ideas and organizations in the United States, see, e.g., Peter Dobkin Hall, *Inventing the Nonprofit Sector and Other Essays on Philanthropy, Voluntarism, and Nonprofit Organizations* (Johns Hopkins University Press 1992); Olivier Zunz, *Philanthropy in America: A History* (Princeton University Press 2012).

Charitable or otherwise nonprofit organizations often make business-like administrative decisions, but these decisions are usually related to an overall nonprofit objective. In terms of the production metamarkets/consumption markets dichotomy described above, nonprofit organizations act as producers and consumers, but the central aim of their work lies outside of commercial markets.[141] For example, a city church purchases supplies, enters into contracts with staff, and pays for maintenance of its building. But one does not think of the ultimate objective of the church as providing "services" to its members in a business sense. The same example can be repeated, of course, for a mosque, synagogue, or other religious gathering place or organization.

If one responds that churches and other religious organizations conduct "services," which shows that they are economically oriented, this response itself demonstrates a misunderstanding of the aim of religious organizations. These kinds of "services" are commonly thought to be directed to an objective greater than the commercial interests of the members themselves, that is, their spiritual well-being, the well-being of the community, or other non-economic objectives. To classify religious "services" in economic terms entirely misses the point of most religions. At the same time, this is not to say that religions do not have significant implications for business activity in terms of providing connections among people who may go into business together or do business with each other in various capacities. These business connections, however, are separate from the nonprofit religious institutions themselves.

Because the main objectives of charitable, religious, and other nonprofit organizations are explicitly *not* business and profits, the traditional approach has been to exclude them from classification as business firms. In general, I follow this common-sense view and exclude most nonprofit enterprises from coverage here. Some of the same basic legal rules and principles of organizational law—such as the ability of an organization to hold property, to make contracts, and to be held legally responsible for enterprise liability—may nevertheless apply to nonprofit organizations. Fiduciary duties with respect to agency and governance are also often applicable. But this book does not examine these principles in this context.

One indication of the institutional separation of nonprofit and profit organizations is that different statutes and laws apply to them. In the United States and many European countries, major nonprofit organizations are usually established under general nonprofit corporation statutes. In Anglo-American legal systems, the roots of nonprofit organizations trace to the English legal form of charitable trusts.[142] The etymological origin of the word "corporation" to describe both nonprofit and profit organizations attests to a common heritage of the institutions, but this does not mean that no institutional differentiation has occurred.[143]

---

[141] See page 176 and Table 5.1. In terms of Table 5.1, the primary activities of nonprofit organizations occur in the lower two cells representing noncommercial production and consumption.

[142] See American Law Institute, Principles of the Law of Nonprofit Organizations, Council Draft No. 6 (September 2009) [hereinafter Principles of the Law of Nonprofit Organizations (Draft No. 6)], introductory note, pp. 3–4.

[143] See Chapter 3, pages 127–8 and accompanying notes 91–6.

In some countries, charitable organizations are specifically and separately registered with the government.[144] The American Law Institute is currently undertaking a major project on *The Principles of the Law of Nonprofit Organizations*.[145] Other countries tend also to follow this pattern of separate legal treatment.[146]

Tax laws exemplify this conceptual separation. Tax treatment is usually more forgiving toward nonprofit organizations than business firms. Perhaps the largest of these tax benefits is the exemption of charitable and philanthropic organizations from income taxes in Anglo-American legal systems.[147] This separate legal treatment provides another indication that nonprofit organizations are not ordinarily considered as a type of business firm.

Some legal scholars dispute this view that nonprofits are not business firms. They consider most charitable or nonprofit enterprises to be "operating" nonprofits that provide "goods and services" to their members and to general customers as well.[148] Examples of operating nonprofit enterprises are said to include "colleges, hospitals, day care centers, nursing homes, research institutes, publications, symphony orchestras, social clubs, trade associations, labor unions, churches, and organizations for the relief of the needy and distressed."[149] According to these scholars, all of these nonprofits should be considered business firms because they are "producers of services."[150]

These scholars tend to use a tax-based and accounting definition as a starting point for analysis, namely, that nonprofit organizations may not distribute "net earnings" in the form of profits to its directors, officers, and other employees as owners or investors.[151] Nonprofit organizations are not legally allowed to have owners who receive returns on their investments in the same sense as business firms. This restriction is known as "the nondistribution constraint." Although most large nonprofits are incorporated under special nonprofit statutes, they cannot have shareholders or other equity investors (though they may get loans).[152]

---

[144] See, e.g., Principles of the Law of Nonprofit Organizations (Draft No. 6), op. cit., introductory note, pp. 8–9, 12–14 (describing registration process for nonprofits under the Charity Commission in England and Wales); see also Richard Fries, "The Charity Commission for England and Wales," in *Comparative Corporate Governance of Non-Profit Organizations*, (Klaus J. Hopt and Thomas Von Hippel eds.) (Cambridge University Press 2010), pp. 896–914.

[145] This project was approved to proceed in 2000, though it is not yet completed as of this writing. See American Law Institute, "Current Projects: Principles of the Law of Nonprofit Organizations," <http://www.ali.org/> (accessed September 16, 2012).

[146] See essays collected in *Comparative Corporate Governance of Non-Profit Organizations*, op. cit.

[147] See Rob Atkinson, "Theories of the Federal Income Tax Exemption for Charities: Thesis, Antithesis, and Syntheses," 27 *Stetson Law Review* 395 (1997); Boris I. Bittker and George K. Rahdert, "The Exemption of Nonprofit Organizations from Federal Income Taxation," 85 *Yale Law Journal* 299 (1976); Henry Hansmann, "The Rationale for Exempting Nonprofit Organizations From Corporate Income Taxation," 91 *Yale Law Journal* 54 (1981).

[148] See Henry B. Hansmann, "The Role of Nonprofit Enterprise," 89 *Yale Law Journal* 835, 837 (1980); Hansmann and Kraakman, op. cit., pp. 390, 392, 395, 405, 432–6.

[149] Hansmann, "The Role of Nonprofit Enterprise," op. cit., p. 837.

[150] See id., p. 872.

[151] Hansmann, "The Role of Nonprofit Enterprise," op. cit., p. 838. See also Henry B. Hansmann, "Reforming Nonprofit Corporation Law," 129 *University of Pennsylvania Law Review* 497, 501–4 (1981); Anup Malani and Eric A. Posner, "The Case for For-Profit Charities," 93 *Virginia Law Review* 2017, 2024–6 (2007).

[152] See Hansmann, "Reforming Nonprofit Corporation Law," op. cit., pp. 501–2.

As any business lawyer for close corporations knows, however, the nondistribution constraint for earnings does not stop a legally savvy business person from creating various entities and other mechanisms by which to funnel revenues (with appropriate accounting treatment) to corporate executives or managers as compensation (e.g. raises or bonuses) leaving nothing for distribution as "profits." The same legerdemain occurs in nonprofit organizations. Many leaders of large nonprofit corporations are in fact compensated very generously with funds deriving from the continued operations of the organization. Some presidents of leading private nonprofit universities in the United States, for example, as well as some professors and sports coaches are paid handsomely compared with most of the population. Thirty of the top-earning university presidents in the United States pull down annual compensation of over $1 million, and some other staff, most notably football coaches and medical school administrators, often earn considerably more than university presidents.[153]

Despite large salaries paid to university presidents or professors, the overall objective of universities and colleges should remain education and research. To the extent that some universities and colleges have tilted their objective toward a pecuniary "business" purpose (yes, even in business schools), the tilt should be corrected by those who administer, govern, and fund these institutions.[154] Otherwise, it is not apparent why special treatment, such as under federal tax laws, should apply.

It is true that an economic approach to analyzing nonprofit organizations reveals borderline cases in which purportedly "nonprofit" organizations have adopted essentially a "business purpose," at least with respect to some of their major activities. To capture these cases, Henry Hansmann introduces the useful concept of a "commercial nonprofit."[155] Closer analysis, however, reveals the idea of a "commercial nonprofit" to be potentially oxymoronic as a category of classification. To the extent that the principal objective of a nonprofit organization is to make profits, then the organization should count as a business firm at least for some purposes of analysis and legal treatment. Good examples of borderline cases in the United States include some nursing homes, some hospitals and other health care organizations, and some educational institutions.[156] Some of these enterprises establish themselves straightforwardly as for-profit firms. But others attempt to maintain their nonprofit status even when their operations and records show a clear for-profit orientation. These cases raise difficult questions under tax laws in some countries, including the United States, with respect to whether the tax-free status of a nonprofit organization should be removed if the organization is shown to act essentially as a for-profit business rather than as a nonprofit. A general "commerciality doctrine" applies to deny tax exemptions when "the operation of the charity in

---

[153] See Tamar Lewin, "Private-College Chiefs See Rise in Pay," *New York Times*, November 15, 2010, p. A14; Tamar Lewin, "Many Specialists at Private Universities Earn More Than Presidents," *New York Times*, February 22, 2009, p. A17.

[154] For a critical examination, see Derek Bok, *Universities in the Marketplace: The Commercialization of Higher Education* (Princeton University Press 2003).

[155] Hansmann, "The Role of Nonprofit Enterprise," op. cit., pp. 840–1, 862–73.

[156] See id., pp. 863–8.

question was more in the nature of a commercial business operating in competition with for-profit companies" than a true nonprofit organization with non-commercial objectives.[157]

So-called "commercial nonprofits" that fail this test should be included in a theory of the firm because they compete with other business firms, and their legal structures are essentially similar to those of other business firms, with the exception of the nondistribution constraint. In other words, the objectives of these enterprises are more "commercial" than "nonprofit." At the same time, nonprofit organizations that do not have commercial objectives and do not slide into becoming concerned principally with making money should be excluded from the category of business firms—and the burdens, obligations, and sometimes privileges of business firms. A conceptual bifurcation separates true "charities," which adopt an "other-regarding orientation" toward mission and "group governance," and for-profit business firms.[158]

In terms of the theory of the firm presented here, nonprofit organizations that follow purely noncommercial objectives are excluded from coverage as firms. True nonprofit organizations focus on noncommercial markets and other kinds of human activity, including "other-regarding" efforts that lie outside of markets. The donation of one's money or labor to help build housing for people who have been impoverished by a natural disaster such as a hurricane in Haiti, for example, is a noncommercial activity, even though it may use social infrastructure (such as money, transportation, food, and tools) to pursue the noncommercial end.

The current draft proposal of the *Principles of the Law of Nonprofit Organizations* provides a list of charitable and other noncommercial purposes to help to determine whether an organization has a legitimate "nonprofit" purpose. The list includes: "(1) the relief of poverty; (2) the advancement of knowledge or education; (3) the advancement of religion; (4) the promotion of health; (5) governmental or municipal purposes; and (6) other purposes that are beneficial to the community."[159] (The inclusion of "government or municipal purposes" implicates the boundary between business firms and government entities discussed previously.) Specifically excluded are organizations that aim to provide an "impermissible private benefit."[160]

To illustrate, consider a case in the United States in which a group of restaurants and health food stores claimed nonprofit status on grounds of strictly following religious principles.[161] The group was denied nonprofit tax exempt status. The overall "commercial hue" of the group's primary activities, its "competition with commercial firms," and "the existence and amount of annual or accumulated profits" led the court to conclude that the group operated with a "substantial

---

[157] Marion R. Fremont-Smith, *Governing Nonprofit Organizations: Federal and State Law and Regulation* (Harvard University Press 2004), pp. 247–8. See also Dana Brakman Reiser, "Charity Law's Essentials," 86 *Notre Dame Law Review* 1, 18–25 (2011) (referring to a general "anticommerciality" principle governing nonprofits).

[158] Reiser, "Charity Law's Essentials," op. cit., pp. 2–5.

[159] Principles of the Law of Nonprofit Organizations (Draft No. 6), op. cit., sect. 100(a), p. 20.

[160] Id., sect. 100(b).

[161] *Living Faith, Inc. v. Commissioner of Internal Revenue*, 950 F.2d 365, 372, 376 (7th Cir. 1991).

commercial purpose."[162] In other words, it was shown to be operating really as a business firm rather than a nonprofit enterprise—and therefore did not deserve the privileged tax treatment accorded to a nonprofit organization.

The general criteria used to distinguish nonprofit organizations and business firms are somewhat vague, and borderline cases can cause problems. As one scholar in this field observes correctly, "the boundary between nonprofits and for-profits" has been "undertheorized."[163] But this does not mean that the legal boundary is unimportant.

Analogously to the public–private distinction examined in Chapter 3, the nonprofit–profit distinction has social value and reflects the different intentions and purposes that people have when they form and participate in different kinds of organizations. For example, people may often join a nonprofit organization for the purpose of developing a "social identity" rather than pursuing a particular economic goal.[164] Their motivations for joining may also be religious, political, educational, or informally "social" (e.g. private clubs or gaming associations). On this view, as one scholar observes, the "entity form can itself create meaning, by creating a type of good incompatible with the profit motive."[165]

Reducing all organizations to the rationalizing measurements of economic analysis used for business does not do justice to the plurality of different organizational forms and associational purposes in most contemporary societies. Legal theorizing and boundary-marking along the lines of nonprofit organizations and business firms should therefore continue.[166]

Hybrid social enterprises

An issue related to the nonprofit–profit divide concerns the extent to which business firms can or should follow nonprofit *and* profit objectives in the course

---

[162] Id., pp. 372, 376.

[163] Dana Brakman Reiser, "For-Profit Philanthropy," 77 *Fordham Law Review* 2437, 2471–3 (2009).

[164] Usha Rodrigues, "Entity and Identity," 60 *Emory Law Journal* 1257 (2011).

[165] Id., p. 1322. See also James R. Hines, Jr., Jill R. Horwitz, and Austin Nichols, "The Attack on Nonprofit Status: A Charitable Assessment," 108 *Michigan Law Review* 1179 (2010) (defending the maintenance of the profit–nonprofit distinction based on entities with respect to tax law).

[166] For a contrary argument for the abolition of the distinction at least with respect to the federal nonprofit tax exemption, see Malani and Posner, op. cit. They expose or cash out (depending on one's perspective) the consequences of beginning one's analysis of nonprofit organizations from an economic perspective. If one begins with a definition of nonprofit organizations in economic terms alone, then differential treatment of them can be justified only in economic terms. Malani and Posner show how this analytical approach can result in a conclusion to eliminate the difference between nonprofit and profit organizations, at least with respect to taxation exemptions for charitable activity. Malani and Posner, op. cit., pp. 2020–52. But this approach doesn't work if one adopts a different normative starting point, namely, that nonprofit organizations aim at non-economic objectives that at least to some extent cannot be measured in economic terms (such as economic measurements of social welfare, "public goods," or the consequential value of "altruism"). Beginning from a non-economic normative understanding, the differential treatment of nonprofit organizations with non-business purposes retains persuasive force. For a critique of Malani and Posner's thesis on different grounds, see also Benjamin Moses Leff, "The Case Against For-Profit Charity," 42 *Seton Hall Law Review* 819 (2012).

of doing business. Examples include the following. The Acumen Fund supports entrepreneurs in developing countries to address social problems in agriculture, education, energy, health, housing, and water. Aurolab manufactures intraocular lenses for cataracts and sells them to poor people in poor countries at low prices. The Ghana Sustainable Aid Project and Open Capital Advisors aid economic development in Africa by providing local start-up companies with access to capital. In 2009, the Bill and Melinda Gates Foundation set up a kickstarter fund of $400 million to support these kinds of hybid social enterprises.[167] Note also a further legal complication: the Gates Foundation's funding in this situation is classified as a "program-related investment" under U.S. tax law, which permits a nonprofit foundation to invest in for-profit enterprises as long as its purpose is charitable and related to its nonprofit mission.[168]

Unlike purely charitable or philanthropic organizations, these hybrid social enterprises count as firms because part of their main purpose is to make a profit for their owners and investors. As one student of this new kind of firm has argued, four core features distinguish hybrid social enterprises from pure for-profit business firms, on one hand, and charitable non-profit organizations, on the other: (1) a "governing social mission that guides organizational decisions and behavior"; (2) a "sophisticated business model (which is typically associated with traditional, purely for-profit companies)" and which "serves as the primary tool to achieve the mission"; (3) the ability to attract a mixture of "grant, debt, and equity financing," the sources of which often conflict in terms of traditional legal forms; and (4) the ability to "balance the mission and profit motives of the various managers, investors, and stakeholders."[169] These qualities define what has also been called "social entrepreneurship."[170]

The advent of hybrid social enterprises and the financing and management issues that they face has led to the creation of new legal forms to accommodate them. These business forms include "low-profit limited liability companies" (L3Cs) in the United States and "community interest companies" (CICs) in the United Kingdom. Another innovation in the United States goes by the name of the "benefit corporation."[171] Traditional business forms may also be used to achieve "social enterprise" objectives.[172]

Another organizational form called an "Economy of Communion," which has been recognized in some countries in Europe and South America, has been categorized by some observers as a hybrid social enterprise.[173] The fact that this

---

[167] See Keren G. Raz, "Toward an Improved Legal Form for Social Enterprise," 36 *New York University Review of Law & Social Change* 283, 284–6 (2012) (giving these examples).

[168] Id., p. 286 n. 13. This issue is discussed further in the text below.

[169] Raz, op. cit., p. 277.

[170] See J. Gregory Dees, "Taking Social Entrepreneurship Seriously," 44 *Society* 24 (2007).

[171] See Raz, op. cit., pp. 297–307; Dana Brakman Reiser, "Benefit Corporations—A Sustainable Form of Organization?" 46 *Wake Forest Law Review* 591, 591–5 (2011).

[172] See Susan Manwaring and Andrew Valentine, "Canadian Structural Options for Social Enterprise," 23 *Philanthropist* 399 (2010).

[173] See Heather Sertial, Note, "Hybrid Entities: Distributing Profits with a Purpose," 17 *Fordham Journal of Corporate & Financial Law* 261, 273–9 (2012). See also Lorna Gold, *New Financial Horizons: The Emergence of an Economy of Communion* (New City Press 2010).

organizational form does not allow for the distribution of profits to investors suggests that it may be better classified as a pure nonprofit organization rather than a business firm. But at least some of them seem to allow returns of profits to employee-owners, in which case they could be classified as worker cooperatives. If allocations to social objectives are added on to a cooperative for-profit structure, then this form may count as another hybrid social enterprise option. A number of European countries appear to allow for this sort of hybrid cooperative organizational form, though strong constraints on profit distributions may disqualify many of them as social hybrid enterprises.[174] In this book, I focus mainly on options available in the United States and the United Kingdom.

L3Cs have been formally adopted by statute in a number of U.S. states beginning in 2008. The statutes aim specifically to allow an expanded social objective for a limited liability company, in addition to the pursuit of profit and economic gain.[175] Essentially, the L3C "tweaks the LLC form of organization" in order to allow the firm "to pursue traditionally charitable activities, but also contemplates making some, albeit likely low, profit."[176] The primary goal of the L3C structure relates to its financing. Basically, L3Cs establish two tranches of funding: one for regular for-profit investors (debt and equity) and one for nonprofit grants.[177] In this manner, the L3C form aims to pursue twin objectives: (1) to make profits for its owners and investors; and (2) to address social problems by raising funds from nonprofit organizations through grants or other charitable support. The L3C purports to be "a for-profit with a nonprofit soul."[178]

One primary purpose of the L3C form is to allow a firm to accept "program-related investments" (PRIs) from nonprofit foundations from the perspective of the tax treatment of the foundations.[179] (See the example of the Gates Foundation fund mentioned at the start of this section.) Under current tax law in the United States, a PRI "must meet three criteria: (1) the foundation must be motivated solely by a desire to further its exempt charitable purpose; (2) the production of income or the appreciation of property may not be a significant factor behind the foundation's investment; and (3) only limited lobbying purposes, and no electioneering, may be served by the investment."[180] Advocates have also pressed for a liberalization of the tax laws to allow for the expansion of nonprofit foundation investments in hybrid

---

[174] For legal forms available in various European countries, see Jacques Defourny and Marthe Nyssens, "Social Enterprise in Europe: Recent Trends and Developments," 4 *Social Enterprise Journal* 202 (2008).

[175] See Raz, op. cit., p. 297 (counting nine states by 2012); see also Reiser, "Charity Law's Essentials," op. cit., pp. 35–6; Rodrigues, op. cit., p. 1314.

[176] Reiser, "Charity Law's Essentials," op. cit., p. 36.

[177] See Dana Brakman Reiser, "Governing and Financing Blended Enterprise," 85 *Chicago-Kent Law Review* 619, 628–9 (2010); Rodrigues, op. cit., p. 1316.

[178] Elizabeth Schmidt, "Vermont's Social Hybrid Pioneers: Early Observations and Questions To Ponder," 35 *Vermont Law Review* 163, 197 (2010).

[179] Raz, op. cit., p. 297.

[180] J. Haskell Murray and Edward I. Hwang, "Purpose with Profit: Governance, Enforcement, Capital-Raising and Capital-Locking in Low-Profit Limited Liability Companies," 66 *University of Miami Law Review* 1, 24 (2011) (citing U.S. Treasury regulations).

social enterprises.[181] Without the recognition of the appropriateness of the L3C business model under tax law, the nondistribution constraint imposed on nonprofit organizations may limit this hybrid method of financing and management. The Internal Revenue Service does not recognize L3C as a nonprofit organization, and it is not yet clear whether or how exactly PRIs by nonprofit foundations will be authorized.[182] Note also that the organizational flexibility of traditional LLCs may be exploited to create hybrid purpose business firms in the founding documents, even in the absence of a special L3C statute.[183]

Similar to how the L3C is a variation on preexisting LLC statutes, the community interest company piggybacks on regular company law in the United Kingdom. First established by statute in 2004, CICs express a similar hybrid profit-and-nonprofit purpose.[184] In order to maintain the nonprofit portion of the organizational commitment, two statutory requirements restrict distributions of profits in CICs. First, an "asset lock" forbids the transfer of the firm's assets to any business participants and, in the event of liquidation or dissolution, requires a CIC to transfer its assets only to another CIC or a charitable organization.[185] Second, "dividend caps" limit the amount of profits that equity investors may receive. Statutory dividend caps are set on a per share basis (5–20 percent of profits), on an overall basis (35 percent of profits), and with a time-based limit (four years). Similar limitations are placed on performance-based interest rates for debt which might otherwise be used to end-run the dividend caps.[186]

CICs must register with a government regulator who determines whether the "community interest" test is met, and more than 4,000 CICs have been registered.[187] The CIC regulator also has authority to assure that CICs follow the financial requirements regarding asset locks and dividend caps. CICs must submit a public annual report on its conduct to the CIC regulator.[188] As one commentator has emphasized, reliable disclosure and reporting are necessary to assure the "mission accountability" of CICs and other hybrid social enterprises.[189]

---

[181] Id., p. 25.

[182] See, e.g., Raz, op. cit., pp. 297–9. For an optimistic assessment, see Thomas Kelley, "Law and Choice of Entity on the Social Enterprise Frontier," 84 *Tulane Law Review* 337, 366–77 (2009). For more skeptical views, see J. William Callison and Allan W. Vestal, "The L3C Illusion: Why Low-Profit Limited Liability Companies Will Not Stimulate Socially Optimal Private Foundation Investment in Entrepreneurial Ventures," 35 *Vermont Law Review* 273 (2010); Daniel S. Kleinberger, "A Myth Deconstructed: The 'Emperor's New Clothes' on the Low-Profit Limited Liability Company," 35 *Delaware Journal of Corporate Law* 879, 879 (2010).

[183] See Robert R. Keatinge, "LLCs and Nonprofit Organizations—For-Profits, Nonprofits, and Hybrids," 42 *Suffolk University Law Review* 553 (2009).

[184] See Stephen Lloyd, "Transcript: Creating the CIC," 35 *Vermont Law Review* 31, 34 (2010).

[185] See Reiser, "Governing and Financing Blended Enterprise," op. cit., pp. 634–5.

[186] See Raz, op. cit., p. 307; Reiser, "Governing and Financing Blended Enterprise," op. cit., pp. 635–6; Lloyd, op. cit., pp. 36–8.

[187] See Lloyd, op. cit., pp. 36–9. See also Raz, op. cit., p. 307; Sertial, op. cit., p. 286.

[188] See Lloyd, op. cit., pp. 38–9; Sertial, op. cit., p. 286.

[189] Briana Cummings, Note, "Benefit Corporations: How to Enforce a Mandate to Promote the Public Interest," 112 *Columbia Law Review* 578 (2012). For a review of a sample of CIC reports and recommendations concerning the "light touch" regulation of CICs, see also Alex Nicholls,

An open question remains whether the oversight of social reporting is best left to the government, market-oriented third parties, or a combination. Some commentators argue in favor of voluntary market-oriented solutions in this context.[190] Another view counters that enforceable legal standards are required to assure that voluntary reporting does not amount to the false claims, overstatements, and misdirections known as "greenwashing."[191]

Also in the category of hybrid social enterprises are the relatively recent "benefit corporations" or "B corporations."[192] (Unfortunately, the B corporation designation sounds similar to the designations of "C corporation" and "S corporation," which are terms used in the United States to refer to tax status. In a nutshell, C corporations are subject to federal taxation at the entity level; S corporations are not.[193] "B corporation" is completely unrelated to the tax status of the business entity, though perhaps some may hope for an eventual specific tax exemption to be issued.)

In the United States, B corporations come in two distinct flavors. First, beginning in 2006, a nonprofit group called B Lab created a new extra-legal standard and labeling scheme called "Certified B Corporations."[194] B Lab provides independent third-party certification through reporting and monitoring requirements, testifying that a firm combines business and social objectives in its practices. After completing and passing a "B Lab impact assessment," a Certified B Corporation may then market itself as combining these objectives.[195] B Lab provides this service as a third-party certifier to any firm that applies, qualifies, and pays a fee. (The fee is reported to be one tenth of 1 percent of annual revenue.[196]) By 2011, the number of Certified B Corporations had increased to over 500 (including forty-four in Canada and one in Europe).[197]

The Certified B *Corporation* is a misnomer legally, because B Lab invites not only corporations but any legal form of business, including sole proprietorships, partnerships, LLCs, and cooperatives, to petition for certification. (Notably, nonprofit corporations may not apply.[198]) B Lab provides an interactive tool for various kinds

---

"Institutionalizing Social Entrepreneurship in Regulatory Space: Reporting and Disclosure By Community Interest Companies," 35 *Accounting, Organizations and Society* 394 (2010).

[190] See, e.g., Cummings, op. cit.

[191] See William S. Laufer, "Social Accountability and Corporate Greenwashing," 43 *Journal of Business Ethics* 253 (2003).

[192] See Cummings, op. cit.; Raz, op. cit., pp. 300–6; Reiser, "Benefit Corporations," op. cit.; Reiser, "Governing and Financing Blended Enterprise," op. cit., pp. 637–43. See also Steven J. Haymore, Note, "Public(ly Oriented) Companies: B Corporations and the Delaware Stakeholder Provision Dilemma," 64 *Vanderbilt Law Review* 1311 (2011).

[193] See Klein, Coffee, and Partnoy, op. cit., pp. 237–9.

[194] See, e.g., Keatinge, op. cit., pp. 579–80; Reiser, "Benefit Corporations," op. cit., p. 594.

[195] Cummings, op. cit., p. 594.

[196] See Hannah Clark Steiman, "A New Kind of Company: A 'B' Corporation," *Inc.* (July 1, 2007), <http://www.inc.com/> (accessed September 29, 2012).

[197] See B Corporation Annual Report (2012), <http://www.bcorporation.net/>, p. 8 (accessed September 29, 2012); Certified B Corporation, "B Corp Community, <http://www.bcorporation.net/> (accessed September 29, 2012).

[198] See Haymore, op. cit., p. 1314 n. 13.

of firms to apply with different web-based links for different legal forms.[199] Certified B *Business* would have been a less confusing label.

In a second and more legally important variation, a number of U.S. states have passed legislation establishing formal benefit corporations or "B Corporations." Maryland passed the first statute in 2010, and twenty-eight other states and the District of Columbia have followed as of this writing, including the commercially large and important states of California, Delaware, Illinois, and New York.[200] Statutes have also been passed in Arkansas, Arizona, Hawaii, Louisiana, Massachusetts, New Jersey, Nevada, Oregon, Pennsylvania, South Carolina, Vermont, and Virginia. And legislation has been introduced in ten more states.[201] These statutes are relatively new, and data is lagging, but one report suggests that at least several hundred firms in various states have formally registered as statutory benefit corporations.[202]

Like British CICs, registered benefit corporations are a specific form of corporation (not a partnership, LLC, or other legal option). Statutes in different states include varying provisions, but in general the statutes allow for both new incorporations and the amendment of charters of preexisting corporations to become benefit corporations. In addition, when specific benefit corporation provisions do not apply to a particular situation, then the default rules from regular corporate law are assumed to apply as "gap-fillers."[203]

Statutory benefit corporations are entirely distinct from the Certified B Corporations promoted by B Lab, but a statutory benefit corporation may become certified if desired. Patagonia, the outdoor apparel company, for example, was the first firm to register under California's benefit corporation statute, and it has also elected to follow the Certified B Corporation standard.[204]

Also similar to British CICs, statutory benefit corporations usually require an annual report on the "general public benefit" of their mission.[205] They must select third-party standards to measure and assess their performance on this dimension. More precisely, a benefit corporation must report on "its overall social and environmental performance as assessed against a comprehensive, credible, independent, and transparent third-party standard."[206] The standard selected may be the one promulgated by B Lab, but a firm may choose another standard developed by

---

[199] See Certified B Corporation, "Legal Roadmap," <http://www.bcorporation.net/> (accessed September 29, 2012).

[200] See Reiser, "Benefit Corporations," op. cit., p. 594.

[201] For a continually updated list of the statutes, see Benefit Corp. Information Center, "State By State Legislative Status," <http://www.benefitcorp.net/> (accessed May 28, 2015).

[202] See B Corps: Firms with Benefits," *Economist*, January 7, 2012, <http://www.economist.com> (accessed September 16, 2012).

[203] Reiser, "Benefit Corporations," op. cit., pp. 595–6.

[204] See "B Corps: Firms with Benefits," op. cit. See also Yvon Chouinard and Vincent Stanley, *The Responsible Company: What We've Learned from Patagonia's First 40 Years* (Patagonia Books 2012).

[205] Reiser, "Benefit Corporations," op. cit., p. 597. Delaware's statute, however, requires only a report to shareholders. Public reporting is permissive, but not mandatory. Delaware Code Ann., tit. 8, sect. 366 (2013).

[206] William H. Clark, Jr. and Elizabeth K. Babson, "How Benefit Corporations Are Redefining the Purpose of Business Corporations," 38 *William Mitchell Law Review* 817, 838–9 (2012).

another independent nonprofit group instead. Other standards include those developed by the Global Reporting Initiative, Good Guide, Green Seal, the International Standards Organization, and Underwriters Laboratories.[207] There are at least a dozen recognized third-party standards.[208]

Again like British CICs, then, benefit corporations must provide annual reporting on their "social mission". Unlike CICs, however, benefit corporations do not report directly to a government regulator. A benefit corporation is required only to select a third-party "standard." No third-party verification of the reports is generally required.[209] This raises a policy question outside the scope of discussion here about whether third-party certification should be required of these reports similar to third-party auditing of financial reports by accountants.[210]

A telling feature of both benefit corporations and Certified B Corporations is that they both require the equivalent of a corporate constituency statute for their governance and management. Constituency statutes have been enacted in most U.S. states (more than thirty of them) beginning in the late 1980s and early 1990s to clarify that the scope of corporate directors' and managers' fiduciary duties included interests and considerations "beyond shareholders."[211] A typical statute provides that corporate directors and officers, when making decisions, may consider the effects on "shareholders, employees, suppliers, customers and creditors of the corporation, and upon communities in which offices or other establishments of the corporation are located."[212] In addition, they may consider the "short-term and long-term interests of the corporation."[213]

The United Kingdom adopted a version of a corporate constituency statute with broadly similar provisions in 2006.[214] This statute provides that a corporate director must act "in good faith" in a manner "most likely to promote the success of the company for the benefit of its members as a whole." It specifically authorizes consideration of "long-term" consequences; "the interests of the company's employees"; "relationships with suppliers, customers, and others"; "impact of the company's operations on the community and the environment"; "maintaining a reputation for high standards of business conduct"; and "the need to act fairly."[215]

---

[207] Cummings, op. cit., p. 594; Reiser, "Benefit Corporations," op. cit., pp. 600–4.

[208] See Benefit Corp Information Center, "List of Standards," <http://benefitcorp.net/> (accessed September 29, 2012).

[209] Benefit Corp Information Center, "Selecting a Third Party Standard," <http://benefitcorp.net/> (accessed September 29, 2012). Delaware's statute is exceptional and requires neither a third-party standard nor third-party verification. Both are optional. Delaware Code Ann., tit. 8, sect. 366(c) (2013).

[210] For an introduction to this issue, see Lesley K. McAllister, "Regulation by Third-Party Verification," 53 *Boston College Law Review* 1 (2012).

[211] See Eric W. Orts, "Beyond Shareholders: Interpreting Corporate Constituency Statutes," 61 *George Washington Law Review* 14 (1992). See also Lawrence E. Mitchell, "A Theoretical and Practical Framework for Enforcing Corporate Constituency Statutes," 70 *Texas Law Review* 579 (1992). For the count of more than thirty statutes (though, importantly, not yet including Delaware), see Barnali Choudhury, "Serving Two Masters: Incorporating Social Responsibility into the Corporate Paradigm," 11 *University of Pennsylvania Journal of Business Law* 631, 644 (2009); Haymore, op. cit., p. 1340.

[212] 15 Pennsylvania Consolidated Statutes Ann., sect. 1715(a)(1) (2012).

[213] Id., sect. 1715(a)(2).

[214] Companies Act 2006 (UK), sect. 172(1) (effective in 2007).

[215] Id. See also Andrew Keay, "Tackling the Issue of the Corporate Objective: An Analysis of the United Kingdom's 'Enlightened Shareholder Value Approach,'" 29 *Sydney Law Review* 577 (2007).

Constituency statutes appear to be unnecessary in some other parts of the world. In at least some countries, nonshareholder business participants are accorded consideration and protection under preexisting legal frameworks.[216]

Consistent with the legal theory of the firm developed here, constituency statutes reflect the fact that large modern corporations do not break down into a simple agency problem of shareholders versus managers (or a simple conception of the separation of ownership and control—see Chapter 2). Instead, large corporations are usually composed of complex constellations of different business participants, including not only boards of directors, managers, and shareholders, but also creditors and employees of various kinds and levels. Corporate groups and other complex relational firms further complicate these interests. Constituency statutes extend discretion to corporate directors and managers to take this wide array of interests into account in their decision making—and to include in their deliberations other non-economic normative considerations of corporate ethics and social responsibility as well.

In my view, corporate constituency statutes are best interpreted to reinforce the traditional interpretation of fiduciary duties given to corporate managers and directors under the business judgment rule, namely, a broad discretion to make decisions in good faith on policy matters regarding the best interests of the corporation and its shareholders.[217] Shareholders have a degree of "primacy" in a corporation because they carry voting rights to elect directors as the governing authority.[218] Only shareholders, after all, can elect and replace corporate boards through voting procedures (i.e. proxy fights or tender offers). (Germany is exceptional in this respect with its codetermination laws mandating employee representation on some large corporate boards.) Directors retain broad latitude to make decisions about capital structure, executive compensation, and most other major business matters. This traditional view came under assault in the late 1980s and early 1990s by economic and legal theorists who favored judicial enforcement of "shareholder maximization" norms, particularly in the context of hostile takeovers financed with high-yield bonds. Constituency statutes were one of a number of state antitakeover statutes designed to reject the view that corporate control offers were superior to the status quo simply on financial grounds that compared current trading prices of shares.[219] This policy debate continues to be played out, including under the influential law of Delaware and its "duty to auction" standard, which requires a strict shareholder maximization test in some hostile takeover situations.[220] One general alternative to a free market in corporate takeovers is to allow competition in the production and consumer markets (more so than in

---

[216] See Mark J. Loewenstein, "Stakeholder Protection in Germany and Japan," 76 *Tulane Law Review* 1673 (2002).

[217] See Orts, "Beyond Shareholders," op. cit., pp. 41–8, 83–105.

[218] For sources on the "shareholder primacy" debate, see Chapter 2, page 88, note 180.

[219] Orts, "Beyond Shareholders," op. cit., pp. 23–6, 35–44, 44–8, 92–115.

[220] The leading case remains *Revlon, Inc. v. MacAndrews and Forbes Holdings, Inc.*, 506 A.2d 173 (Del. 1986). See also Troy A. Paredes, "The Firm and the Nature of Control: Toward a Theory of Takeover Law," 29 *Journal of Corporation Law* 103, 138–78 (2003).

financial markets) to determine winners and loser among firms over time. Although an important issue, however, further detailed treatment of corporate takeover policy lies outside the scope of this book.[221]

Benefit corporation statutes reenact and track the language of constituency statutes in new provisions, though with the significant difference that they frame consideration of other corporate interests as mandatory rather than permissive.[222] New York's benefit corporation statute, for example, requires directors and officers to consider the following: (a) "the ability for the benefit corporation to accomplish its general and any specific public benefit purpose," (b) "the shareholders," (c) "the employees and workforce," (d) "the interests of customers," (e) "community and societal considerations," (f) "the local and global environment," and (g) "the short-term and long-term interests of the benefit corporation."[223] Many benefit corporation statutes provide for a "benefit enforcement proceeding," but limit standing to directors, officers, or substantial shareholders (i.e. those with a greater than 5 percent stake).[224] However, these litigation provisions (or the absence of them in some statutes) could become traps for the unwary, with the potential to subject board-level and managerial discretion to second-guessing by other business participants.[225]

Certified B Corporations require either incorporation in a jurisdiction with a constituency statute or the adoption of what might be called a "constituency bylaw" or similar governance provision in the founding documents of a firm.[226] The reason for this requirement is obvious: a hybrid social enterprise cannot deliver on its twin objectives of "general public benefit" and making money if it focuses only on maximizing profits for shareholders to the exclusion of either "social benefit" or "community interest."

An interesting legal question in the United States concerns how the courts, including Delaware courts, will treat benefit corporations and Certified B Corporations in hostile takeover situations. One student who has examined the issue with respect to Certified B Corporations and "stakeholder bylaws" adopted pursuant to certification concludes that a Delaware court would strike down such a bylaw as a violation of the "duty to auction" standard.[227] I am not so sure. Directors and officers exercising their statutory authority with the consent of shareholders who

---

[221] One might nevertheless hazard to suggest that the *Revlon* standard might not survive an analysis that provides reason to doubt the centrality of shareholders in corporate governance. Cf. Orts, "Beyond Shareholders," op. cit., pp. 104–8 (arguing against a "duty to auction" under constituency statutes).

[222] See Reiser, "Benefit Corporations," op. cit., pp. 598–9; Clark and Babson, op. cit., pp. 828–33, 838–41; Christopher Lacovara, Note, "Strange Creatures: A Hybrid Approach to Fiduciary Duty in Benefit Corporations," 2011 *Columbia Business Law Review* 815, 835 n. 82 (2011). Delaware's statute, however, is permissive rather than mandatory. It allows directors to "balance[] the pecuniary interests of the stockholders, the best interests of those materially affected by the corporation's conduct, and the specific public benefit or public benefits identified in its certificate of incorporation." Delaware Code Ann., tit. 8, sect. 365 (2013). It is also subject to the exculpatory "opt out" provision for fiduciary duties. Id. See also Chapter 4, page 149 and accompanying note 82.

[223] New York Business Corporation Law, sect. 1707(a) (2012).

[224] See Lacovara, op. cit., pp. 828–9.

[225] See id., pp. 868–72.

[226] Reiser, "Governing and Financing Blended Enterprise," op. cit., pp. 637–40.

[227] Haymore, op. cit., pp. 1323–5, 1345–6.

have notice that they are purchasing shares in a benefit corporation or Certified B Corporation would seem to be legally compelled to reject a standard that focuses only on a "duty to auction" to maximize shareholder value. In any event, a holding that a constituency bylaw or registration as a benefit corporation could serve as an antitakeover device in Delaware would certainly increase the popularity of these options! Benefit corporations and Certified B Corporations in other states seem to be in an even stronger position to withstand hostile takeover bids under their governing statutes.

The connection between benefit corporations and constituency statutes is also illustrated by the newest kid on the block: California's "flexible purpose corporation." Adopted in 2011, the statute creating this new business form is essentially a composite of a constituency statute and a benefit corporation statute.[228] It allows for a new or existing California corporation to "opt in" to either a benefit corporation provision or a constituency governance provision or both.[229] Even if not unique, California's statute highlights a commonality of all statutes that authorize hybrid social enterprises: an allowance for a broader statement of business purposes than maximizing the economic returns for financial investors.[230]

The diversity of purposes, interests, sizes, and values in firms

As this chapter has shown, business enterprises come in many varieties, and they expand and contract along a number of different dimensions. Business enterprises can grow from one person who supplies all of the capital and all of the labor into much larger entities that expand the capital ownership structure of the firm and increase the number of its agents (including managers and employees). Most firms have the option of selecting limited liability. Many of the largest firms in the world select the corporation as a preferred form of organization given its flexibility in terms of multiplying entities internally (including parent–subsidiary or pyramid structures), as well as other advantages (such as in mergers, acquisitions, and other business combinations). Different types of firms are inscribed with different levels of complexity with respect to the economic interests of their business participants. A great deal of legal complexity is possible, particularly when one considers corporate groups and other complex relational firms, such as wide-ranging franchises and cooperative groups of firms. Even in complex firms, however, one can decipher their legal structures in terms of capital ownership, agency authority, and internal governance arrangements. All are described as entities or organizational collections of entities. All act as "persons" in commercial markets with legal rights of recognition and representative action.

---

[228] Corporate Flexibility Act, California Legislative Service (S.B. 201) (Westlaw 2011) (effective 2012).

[229] California Corporations Code Ann., sect. 2602 (2013).

[230] See Christen Clarke, Note, "California's Flexible Purpose Corporation: A Step Forward, a Step Back, or No Step At All?" 5 *Journal of Business, Entrepreneurship and the Law* 301, 315–21 (2012); Angelica Salceda, "Flexible Purpose Corporation: California's New Corporate Form," BerkeleyLaw (December 13, 2011), <http://thenetwork.berkeleylawblogs.org/> (accessed September 29, 2012).

Firms also vary in terms of their collectively intended purposes and value orientations.[231] California's "flexible purpose corporation" makes this choice explicit, but differences in purpose and value orientation appear in other firms too. State-owned firms are likely to have a much different objective than independent privately organized firms. Political agendas are important within state-owned firms virtually by definition, though this is not to say that politics is irrelevant to privately organized firms.[232] Hybrid social enterprises link the objective of making money with the objective of addressing social or environmental problems at the same time.

Difficult boundary-drawing along the nonprofit–profit frontier will be required with respect to hybrid social enterprises, as well as with respect to true "nonprofit" institutions as compared with for-profit business firms.[233] Social hybrid enterprises will also face managerial difficulties of competing disciplinary "logics" of the "market" (profit-making) and "charity" (advancing a social good or environmental objective). This difficulty of "twin objectives" will no doubt often result in organizational failure, but some enterprises are likely to demonstrate creative resolutions that will lead to new innovations and "success" measured in hybrid terms.[234]

As the connection to constituency statutes suggests with respect to hybrid social enterprises and California's flexible purpose corporation, general issues of "corporate social responsibility" remain on the agenda for ordinary for-profit firms as well. Questions about the social responsibility of for-profit firms, as well as the ethical scope permitted for their top executives when making decisions and setting policies, have been on the public agenda for many decades—and remain there today.[235]

In the United States, corporate governance debates about social responsibility are often traced to the well-known Berle–Dodd debate in the 1930s.[236] But there are other sources around the same time and before.[237] Older intellectual antecedents may be found in Europe, such as in the writings of the Weimar-era industrialist and politician Walther Rathenau.[238] More recently, a resurgence of discussions of

---

[231] On collective purposes, see also Chapter 1, pages 45–6 and accompanying notes 173–5.

[232] I leave the large but important topic of right relations between business and politics (including such issues as bribery, corruption, lobbying, and campaign finance) mostly outside of the scope of this book.

[233] For some suggested principles to follow, see J. Gregory Dees and Beth Battle Anderson, "Sector-Bending: Blurring Lines Between Nonprofit and For-Profit," 40 *Society* 16 (2003). See also Ken Peattie and Adrian Morley, "Eight Paradoxes of the Social Enterprise Research Agenda," 4 *Social Enterprise Journal* 91 (2008).

[234] See Jason Jay, "Navigating Paradox as a Mechanism of Change in Hybrid Organizations," 56 *Academy of Management Journal* 137 (2013).

[235] See Janet E. Kerr, "The Creative Capitalism Spectrum: Evaluating Corporate Social Responsibility Through a Legal Lens," 81 *Temple Law Review* 831 (2008). See also J.E. Parkinson, *Corporate Power and Responsibility: Issues in the Theory of Company Law* (Oxford University Press 1993), pp. 260–346.

[236] Adolf A. Berle, Jr., "For Whom Corporate Managers Are Trustees: A Note," 45 *Harvard Law Review* 1365 (1932); E. Merrick Dodd, Jr., "For Whom Are Corporate Managers Trustees?" 45 *Harvard Law Review* 1145 (1932). See also Harwell Wells, "The Cycles of Corporate Social Responsibility: An Historical Retrospective for the Twenty-First Century," 51 *University of Kansas Law Review* 77 (2002).

[237] For an overview of some sources, see Harwell Wells, "The Birth of Corporate Governance," 33 *Seattle University Law Review* 1247 (2010).

[238] See Bernhard Grossfeld and Werner Ebke, "Controlling the Modern Corporation: A Comparative View of Corporate Power in the United States and Europe," 26 *American Journal of Comparative Law* 397, 431–3 (1978).

corporate social responsibility has occurred, at least rhetorically if not also substantively.[239] One may add to the mix concerns about "business sustainability," which may refer to both responsibility for natural environmental impacts and management for long-term adaptation and survival.[240]

Just as different firms perform better or worse in financial terms, they also differ in their ethical, environmental, social, and legal performance. In terms of stated objectives, an organizational continuum stretches from pure nonprofit organizations to hybrid social enterprises to pure for-profit firms. Among these types of firms, including for-profit firms, differences will appear in terms of actual performance—both financial performance and performance with respect to nonfinancial criteria, such as legal compliance, business ethics, and environmental responsibility. Nonfinancial performance measurements have become increasingly important to for-profit business firms as well as nonprofit organizations and hybrid social enterprises that certify themselves to chosen external standards.[241] Motivations for adopting nonfinancial measurements may include economically rational calculations regarding risk assessment and management, as well as non-economic motivations such as "following the law" and ethical or environmental concerns. According to one recent empirical study, a "culture of sustainability" in large firms correlated with measurable long-term improvements in financial performance, especially for companies in particular sectors.[242] (As a practical note, "making the business case" for a legal compliance, ethical, or environmental decision or project as a "win–win" proposition is usually the easiest course of action for an employee or manager acting within a for-profit firm. However, this does not mean that top-level executives in firms do not sometimes have to make hard choices between "doing the right thing" and maximizing economic returns.)

It is impossible for any firm (or any individual person) to get a perfect score on all of the dimensions of financial performance, legal compliance, good ethics, and environmental sustainability. (Note that nonprofit organizations can score as poorly on organizational ethics and failure to comply with the law as any for-profit firm, as the Catholic Church and Penn State University have demonstrated.[243])

---

[239] See John M. Conley and Cynthia A. Williams, "Engage, Embed, and Embellish: Theory versus Practice in the Corporate Social Responsibility Movement," 31 *Journal of Corporation Law* 1 (2005).

[240] See John Elkington, *Cannibals with Forks: The Triple Bottom Line of 21st Century Business* (Wiley 1999); Paul Hawken, *The Ecology of Commerce: A Declaration of Sustainability* (Harper Business, rev. ed., 2010) (1993); James Gustave Speth, *The Bridge at the End of the World: Capitalism, the Environment, and Crossing from Crisis to Sustainability* (Yale University Press 2008).

[241] For an overview of some research trends, see, e.g., Robert G. Eccles, Michael P. Krzus, Jean Rogers, and George Serafeim, "The Need for Sector-Specific Materiality and Sustainability Reporting Standards," 24 *Journal of Applied Corporate Finance* 65 (2012).

[242] Robert G. Eccles, Ioannis Ioannou, and George Serafeim, "The Impact of Corporate Sustainability on Organizational Processes and Performance," 60 *Management Science* (forthcoming 2014). But see Joshua Daniel Margolis and James Patrick Walsh, *People and Profits? The Search for A Link Between A Company's Social and Financial Performance* (Lawrence Earlbaum Associates 2001) (finding in an review of many empirical studies no clear causal relationship between corporate social responsibility practices and financial performance).

[243] See, e.g., "Roman Catholic Church Sex Abuse Cases," *New York Times*, (survey of developments) (updated September 6, 2012), <http://www.nytimes.com/pages/topics/index.html> (accessed September 29, 2012); "Report of the Special Investigative Counsel Regarding the Actions of Pennsylvania State

Even the goal of legal compliance, which may appear at first glance quite basic, is not easy for large and complex firms to achieve with confidence. Although most major firms devote significant resources to legal compliance, it is not an easy goal to achieve. One survey of general counsels of large U.S. firms, for example, found that only 30 percent of them believed that their firms could fully comply with the matrix of environmental law alone, not to mention various other legal areas.[244] "Ascertaining whether a company is in full compliance with all applicable laws at any one point in time," according to another scholarly examination, "is nearly unattainable."[245] If legal trouble can be expected and even assumed, though, a general value of "following the law" nevertheless remains important.[246]

Other ethical considerations are important too. In the United States, for-profit corporate executives and directors are counseled to "take into account ethical considerations that are reasonably regarded as appropriate to the responsible conduct of business" and to "devote a reasonable amount of resources to public welfare, humanitarian, educational, and philanthropic purposes."[247] Leaders of U.K. companies are similarly admonished to consider the "impact of the company's operations on the community and the environment," to maintain "a reputation for high standards of business conduct," and "to act fairly."[248] These provisions encourage for-profit corporations to consider hybrid social purposes in their decisions at least to some extent.

Again, a range of business attitudes and practices should be expected. Corporate philanthropy may be viewed by some companies as part of "good corporate citizenship," especially with respect to communities in which they operate, while other companies may treat corporate giving as justified only if an immediate advertising or marketing benefit obtains. Different firms entertain different sensibilities and judgments about which ethical principles or priorities are sufficiently "appropriate" to the "responsible conduct" of their business as well (to echo the American Law Institute's formulation). Ethical considerations may often go beyond the legal minimum, that is, "beyond compliance."[249] Sometimes a firm

---

University Related to the Child Sexual Abuse Committed by Gerald A. Sandusky" (July 12, 2012), <http://thefreehreportonpsu.com/> (accessed September 29, 2012).

[244] Marianne Lavelle, "Environmental Vise: Law, Compliance," *National Law Journal*, 1993 Corporate Counsel Survey, August 30, 1993, p. S1.

[245] David Monsma and John Buckley, "Non-Financial Corporate Performance: The Material Edges of Social and Environmental Disclosure," 11 *University of Baltimore Journal of Environmental Law* 151, 151 and n. 1 (2004).

[246] See American Law Institute, *Principles of Corporate Governance: Analysis and Recommendations* (1994), sect. 2.01 (describing the requirement "to act within the boundaries set by law" as a constraint on the overall economic "objective" of the for-profit business corporation). For an argument that the obligation to follow the law is often deeper than a concern for the interests of business participants or "stakeholders," see Eric W. Orts and Alan Strudler, "The Ethical and Environmental Limits of Stakeholder Theory," 12 *Business Ethics Quarterly* 215, 221–2 (2002).

[247] *Principles of Corporate Governance*, op. cit., sect. 2.01.

[248] Companies Act 2006 (UK), sect. 172(1).

[249] See Bruce Smart, *Beyond Compliance: A New Industry View of the Environment* (World Resources Institute 1992).

(like an individual person) may even find itself compelled morally to violate an unjust law in an act of corporate civil disobedience.[250]

Given globalization, ethical conduct has also become more complex for business firms based in different countries and crossing national borders in their management, financing, and operations. Globalization means that different sets of values and philosophical traditions become involved for many firms.[251] People in different countries and regions of the world often have different views of ethics and different ethical priorities. For example, a Confucian ethical tradition may lead to different views of business ethics in certain situations than in the Western tradition. Values relating to community often take precedence over individual rights.[252]

Google, the global internet giant, has articulated a vision of business responsibility that illustrates the normative diversity among for-profit firms. In its founding documents for its initial public offering in 2004, Google's enterprise-organizers implanted a corporate social responsibility proviso that reflected its motto: "Don't be evil." Specifically, Google included the following in its letter to shareholders (and also in formal securities law filings):

Google is not a conventional company. We do not intend to become one.... Our goal is to develop services that significantly improve the lives of as many people as possible. In pursuing this goal, we may do things that we believe have a positive impact on the world, even if the near term financial returns are not obvious.... We will live up to our "don't be evil" principle.... [253]

Some observers interpreted Google's later decision to exit the Chinese market rather than submit to intrusive government censorship of its internet services and customers as an example of this ethical principle in action.[254] Previously, Google and other internet companies had been strongly criticized on this score, and many companies continue to abide by censorship requirements in China that many business scholars regard as unethical.[255]

---

[250] Cf. Frederick A. Elliston, "Civil Disobedience and Whistleblowing: A Comparative Appraisal of Two Forms of Dissent," 1 *Journal of Business Ethics* 23 (1982).

[251] See Richard T. De George, *Competing with Integrity in International Business* (Oxford University Press 1993); Thomas Donaldson and Thomas W. Dunfee, *Ties that Bind: A Social Contracts Approach to Business Ethics* (Harvard Business School Press 1999); *International Business Ethics: Challenges and Approaches* (George Enderle ed.) (University of Notre Dame Press 1999); Thomas Donaldson, "Values in Tension: Ethics Away From Home, *Harvard Business Review* (September–October 1996), pp. 29–36.

[252] See Tae Wan Kim and Alan Strudler, "Workplace Civility: A Confucian Approach," 22 *Business Ethics Quarterly* 557 (2012); Alan Strudler, "Confucian Skepticism About Workplace Rights," 18 *Business Ethics Quarterly* 67 (2008).

[253] Google, Inc., "An Owner's Manual for Google's Shareholders," from Amendment No. 9 to Form S-1 Registration Statement, <http://investor.google.com/corporate/2004/ipo-founders-letter. html>, quoted in Erika George, "See No Evil? Revisiting Early Visions of the Social Responsibility of Business: Adolf A. Berle's Contribution to Contemporary Conversations," 33 *Seattle University Law Review* 965, 1003 (2010).

[254] See, e.g., George, op. cit., p. 1003 n. 181; see also Miguel Helft and David Barboza, "Google Shuts China Site in Dispute Over Censorship," *New York Times*, March 22, 2010, p. A1.

[255] See, e.g., George G. Brenkert, "Google, Human Rights, and Moral Compromise," 85 *Journal of Business Ethics* 453 (2009).

Google does not, of course, rely on the general good will of a majority of public shareholders trading on Wall Street to follow up on this promise with respect to the potential "sacrifice" of shareholder value to social or ethical considerations.[256] It is generally known that most public shareholders prefer higher immediate economic returns to "doing good," even though there are a large and apparently increasing number of socially responsible investors who aim to invest in companies that "don't do evil" and, perhaps more positively, "aim to do good."[257] Instead, Google's founders and executive team have retained a controlling interest in the company.[258] Google's public shareholders (and other investors) must then set their expectations accordingly.

Google made another splash when it went further to found Google.org, a hybrid form that was specifically focused on socially beneficial projects and yet had the potential of a "profit default" if socially positive investments proved economically successful. This example indicates the potential for the entity-within-entity creations in complex relational firms to expand at the level of larger corporate enterprises.[259] Google.org may be a pioneer of hybrid social corporate subsidiaries. (Other large corporations have acquired "sustainable" smaller firms, though their long-term intentions are unclear. Examples include Unilever's acquisition of Ben & Jerry's ice cream, Colgate's acquisition of Tom's of Maine toothpaste, Clorox's acquisition of Burt's Bees natural personal care products, and Coca-Cola's purchase of a 40 percent stake in organic Honest Tea.[260])

Google is not alone among large companies in focusing on the larger social good as well as profits. At the turn of the twentieth century, Henry Ford advocated for lower short-term profits and higher employee wages than some shareholders may have wished in order to advance his vision of mass-produced, high-quality, and inexpensive automobiles. Ford's arguments are highlighted in the famous teaching

---

[256] On the managerial discretion to "sacrifice" profits for principles, see Einer Elhauge, "Sacrificing Corporate Profits in the Public Interest," 80 *New York University Law Review* 733 (2005).

[257] See John Tozzi, "New Legal Protections for Social Entrepreneurs," *Bloomberg Businessweek*, April 22, 2010, <http://www.businessweek.com/> (accessed September 16, 2012) (estimating value of socially responsibility investment at about $2.7 trillion in 2007). Note, however, that "vice funds" trade in the other direction, and some empirical evidence suggests that they may have a general advantage. See Harrison Hong and Marcin Kacperczyk, "The Price of Sin: The Effects of Social Norms on Markets," 93 *Journal of Financial Economics* 15 (2009); Meir Statman and Denys Glushkov, "The Wages of Social Responsibility," 65 *Financial Analysts Journal* 33 (2009). In general, empirical evidence continues to be mixed about whether corporate responsibility (by different measures) correlates with financial performance and, if so, whether a direction of causation can be ascertained.

[258] See Reiser, "Charity Law's Essentials," op. cit., pp. 46–7.

[259] See Michael D. Gottesman, Comment, "From Cobblestones to Pavement: The Legal Road Forward for the Creation of Hybrid Social Organizations," 26 *Yale Law and Policy Review* 345, 345–6 (2007); Kelley, op. cit., pp. 344–5; Reiser, "Charity Law's Essentials," op. cit., pp. 34–5, 60.

[260] See Rakhi I. Patel, "Facilitating Stakeholder-Interest Maximization: Accommodating Beneficial Corporations in the Model Business Corporation Act," 23 *Saint Thomas Law Review* 135, 144 (2010). On the Ben and Jerry's acquisition, see Antony Page and Robert A. Katz, "Freezing Out Ben & Jerry: Corporate Law and the Sale of a Social Enterprise Icon," 35 *Vermont Law Review* 211 (2010).

case of *Dodge v. Ford Motor Co.*[261] Merck, the global pharmaceutical giant, defines its business objective as "preserving and improving human life."[262]

These expressions of what Robert Clark called "high idealism" in corporate law appear to have resulted in large business successes in at least some cases. As Clark describes this approach:

High idealism holds that the business corporation's residual goal, and not just its specific, externally imposed legal obligations, should be defined to include a much wider set of interests than those of the shareholders. One variation is that the purpose of the corporation, and the general residual duty of those who hold decision making power over its activities, is to achieve a reasonable accommodation of the interests of all groups affected by the corporation.[263]

It stands to reason, after all, that if a firm can produce goods and services that many people want to buy, then there is probably some correlation to "social good" that results. This is not to say that a "dark side" to business success does not also often appear. For example, the internet expands the availability of obscenity, cars cause air pollution, and drugs often produce horrific side effects. In response, customers may change their preferences, shareholders may sell their stock, creditors may refuse to lend, and citizens may demand increased regulation.

From the point of view of business participants, the flexible legal framework that enables the founding, growth, and organizational change of business firms allows for a wide range of choice of values that firms may embrace, as well as a range of choice about what specific goods and services are produced—and how they are produced and sold. Nothing in the basic legal framework of business firms mandates a particular orientation to making money over all other possible values. Instead, the decentralized legal framework that exists in most parts of the world allows for a number of different kinds of firms to develop with different mixtures of profit–nonprofit value orientations.[264]

---

[261] 170 N.W. 668 (Mich. 1919). Although this case is often cited for the court's expression in favor of "shareholder primacy" in granting a special dividend request, the court also upheld Ford's decisions with respect to investments in employees and plant expansion based on a long-term planning rationale. *Dodge*, op. cit., pp. 684–5. One may also interpret the court's order to pay dividends to the Dodge brothers (as shareholders) as an antitrust case rather than one impinging on managerial prerogatives. See Clark, op. cit., pp. 602–4, 678–9; Edward B. Rock, "Corporate Law through an Antitrust Lens," 92 *Columbia Law Review* 497, 519–23 (1992). One scholar argues that the case should not be taught as a foundation of the "shareholder value" argument for corporate purpose. Lynn A. Stout, "Why We Should Stop Teaching *Dodge v. Ford*," 3 *Virginia Law & Business Review* 163 (2008). However, I find in my own teaching that Ford's larger vision of his business objective (including concern for motivating employees, strategic investments in plant and equipment, and a focus on increasing long-term market share) presents an interesting contrast to strategies that focus only on short-term shareholder returns.

[262] Merck, "Our Values," <http://www.merck.com/about/our-values/home.html> (accessed September 29, 2012).

[263] Clark, op. cit. pp. 688. Clark himself is somewhat skeptical of high idealism. But he argues correctly that "no one knows with certainty that corporations transformed in accord with some leading version of high idealism would fail to make a net improvement in the overall welfare of our society" and that measures of success are ultimately "empirical." Id., p. 694. One must also be careful to distinguish true motivations of "high idealism" from rhetorical, insincere "greenwashing."

[264] Although the principle of "shareholder value maximization" has been taught as dogma in many business and law schools in the United States for the last several decades (perhaps spreading to a

In a legal theory of the firm, however, one does not need to take a normative position with respect to what kind of business firm is best. Perhaps different legal forms are better for different kinds of businesses. Perhaps national culture and politics matter. And no doubt some business firms will prove to be more resilient and successful over time than others for many different reasons. For purposes here, it is sufficient to point out the many variations of firms and to appreciate that there is a great deal of freedom available with respect to the organizational structure of enterprise: both in the "bottom-up" sense of business participants' choices of business form and in the "top-down" sense of legislation that provides for different modes of responsibility and accountability for different kinds of firms.

number of other countries as well), there are signs that dissenting voices may be gaining influence. See, e.g., Lynn Sharp Paine, *Value Shift: Why Companies Must Merge Social and Financial Imperatives to Achieve Superior Performance* (McGraw-Hill 2003); Lynn Stout, *The Shareholder Value Myth: How Putting Shareholders First Harms Investors, Corporations, and the Public* (Berrett-Koehler Publishers 2012); Joe Nocera, "Down with Shareholder Value," *New York Times*, August 11, 2012, p. A15. Note also that shareholders are too often conceived as having the same fungible interests, when in fact there are many kinds of shareholders. See Daniel J.H. Greenwood, "Fictional Shareholders: For Whom Are Corporate Managers Trustees, Revisited," 69 *Southern California Law Review* 1021 (1996) (criticizing the tendency in the academic literature to treat all shareholders as "uniform" rather than as different people with different interests, values, and investment objectives).

6

Managing and Regulating the Shifting Boundaries of the Firm

The taxonomy of modern firms presents a large menu of organizational choices from the point of view of business participants. These choices confront both those in a position to decide issues of business form and structure (mostly enterprise-organizers, high-level managers, or major investors) and those deciding to participate in one business firm or another (whether as employees, investors, or otherwise). The diversity of types of firms also presents a complex institutional tapestry from the point of view of external regulators.

The legal boundaries of firms shift in response to different questions asked about the authority, ownership, power, responsibility, and liability of a firm and its partici-pants. In other words, the boundaries of the firm depend on the question asked and the purpose of asking the question.[1] One may refer to an *uncertainty principle in the law of business organization* that is roughly analogous to Heisenberg's uncertainty principle in physics.[2] The boundaries of a particular firm will often change when different inquires are made about (1) the firm's authority and power (and the authority and power of its legal agents); (2) the firm's capital ownership structure; (3) the potential liability of the firm itself for harmful wrongs (i.e. enterprise liability); or (4) the potential liability of various of the firm's participants for harmful wrongs (i.e. business participant liability).

Questions of internal organization refer to private agreements made among business participants to adjust the patterns of management and ownership. Questions of external regulation refer to the recognition of the business enterprise as having particular powers and rights to act as an entity or "person" in markets and society generally, as well as deciding whether attributions of liability are appropriate in particular circumstances and, if so, the scope or extent of this liability (i.e. enterprise liability, business participant liability, or both).

Answers to these questions may also lead to changes, both internally and exter-nally. Internal reorganizations of firms may restrict authority, change ownership structure, or restructure operations to avoid or reduce liability risks. External

---

[1] See Reprise on Foundations, pages 107–8 and accompanying notes 5–6; and Chapter 5, pages 193–4 and accompanying note 91 (citing H.L.A. Hart).

[2] This analogy to the Heisenberg principle is only illustrative; it's dangerous to push the comparison too far. See Jim Holt, "Uncertainty About the Uncertainty Principle," *Slate*, March 6, 2002, <http://www.slate.com/articles/arts/egghead/2002/03/uncertainty_about_the_uncertainty_principle.html> (accessed September 30, 2012).

regulation can change as well (and sometimes in response to developments among firms). Policy makers, including legislators and judges, decide whether to strengthen, relax, or otherwise adapt applicable legal rules in light of changing circumstances and knowledge. From a macro-social point of view, one can perceive an iterative dialectical process of "bottom-up" changes in firm organization responding to "top-down" regulatory changes—and vice versa. This evolutionary process reflects the cumulative policy determinations and organizational adaptations by both firms and governments over time.

The public–private distinction both creates and reinforces this duality of perspective: (1) the "bottom-up" view of private business participants who are accorded organizational freedom to construct and manage their own firms; and (2) the "top-down" view of the public legal system and government which establish, interpret, enforce, and revise the rules of the game of business organization and competition. The institutional theory of the firm presented in Chapter 1, encompassing both bottom-up and top-down perspectives, thus depends conceptually and historically on the public–private distinction discussed in Chapter 3.

From both internal and external points of view, the law recognizes firms and draws the formal boundaries by which firms are distinguished from other social institutions, such as economic markets (of various kinds), political states (and their various parts), nonprofit organizations (such as religious, charitable, and politically oriented groups), and individual people.

I omit labor unions from this generic list of other institutions because they are another example of an important borderline organization with respect to firms. On one hand, labor unions or European-style "works councils" organized among employees within a firm (or a complex corporate group) may be described as part of the firm, namely, an organized group of employee participants. On the other hand, labor unions are often organized on a broader scale according to the type or sector of work (e.g. steelworkers, miners, or municipal employees) with the primary objective of influencing politics and the development of labor- and employment-related laws. A firm-level union or works council counts as an organized group of employees who are recognized as a legitimate component of the theory of the firm advanced here. A union organized primarily at an industrial level for political influence would fall outside of the legal boundaries of the firm described here, akin to other nonprofit political groups advocating for particular legal changes or goals. Large politically organized labor unions (such as the AFL-CIO or the Teamsters) seem analogous organizationally to large organized groups of business owners and managers (such as the U.S. Chamber of Commerce). As discussed at various points in this book, employment and labor laws—and the political forces determining them—have significant influence on the answers to questions regarding the boundaries of the firm for various purposes. See Chapter 1 (describing different treatment of employees in firms under different legal regimes of the world), Chapter 2 (describing employees as agents of firms), Chapter 3 (discussing employees' rights of various kinds both within and outside of the workplace), Chapter 4 (examining the liability of both employees and firms, as well as limitations to their liability), and Chapter 5 (discussing managers' and directors' prerogatives to consider employees' interests under corporate constituency and benefit corporation statutes). Labor unions of various kinds cut across these different points of intersection with firms.

The role of law in recognizing firms and marking their boundaries is important from both the internal perspective of business participants and the external perspective of governments. I adapt this method of looking at "internal" and "external" perspectives from an approach used by H.L.A. Hart to examine the nature of legal rules and legal systems. For Hart, the "internal" point of view of legal rules is one taken by lawyers and judges who participate in and accept the overall legitimacy of the legal system. The "external" point of view considers the legal system and its rules from the point of view of a society (or an outsider observer of the society).[3]

I adapt Hart's distinction and apply it here to business firms as follows. (1) The internal point of view refers to business participants looking at legal rules and principles from the point of view of their own firms and their own interests and values. (2) The external point of view adopts the perspective of policy makers and citizens looking at legal rules and principles that govern firms from the point of view of society as a whole (and what is best for all of the members of the society collectively).

The internal point of view looks at the legal structures and boundaries of the firm from the perspective of business participants: managers, owners, investors, and employees. A better understanding of the rules of the game will allow business participants to negotiate the legal "matrix" to advantage in their own activities.[4]

The external point of view considers the firm from the perspective of government and society as a whole. A better understanding of the rules of the game from this perspective will allow for more informed discussions and decisions about whether the status quo makes sense or requires reform—and, if reform is recommended, what shape it should take and in what direction it should go.

From an internal perspective, it is essential for business participants to understand how the legal rules of the game work in theory and practice. These rules will often determine whether participants succeed or fail within their firms (as they negotiate with other internal business participants), as well as in their collective competition with other firms. As one of my Wharton colleagues argues, the business world is highly competitive, and it is therefore often the case that a firm and its participants must either "make the rules" or their "rivals will."[5] One might add that it is important to take care to observe legal and ethical limitations on these strategies, especially in the political domain, with hard constraints with respect to bribery and corruption in most modern societies, even if history is replete with counterexamples. (Again, a full treatment of the limitations of business firms with respect to politics is left outside the scope of this book.)

At least, the regulatory rules of the game are critical for everything from negotiating executive compensation packages and collective bargaining agreements to adjusting potential organizational and personal exposure to liability. In addition,

---

[3] See H.L.A. Hart, *The Concept of Law* (Oxford University Press, 2nd ed., 1994), pp. 100–5.
[4] For the analogy to *The Matrix*, see Chapter 2, page 73 and accompanying note 103.
[5] G. Richard Shell, *Make the Rules or Your Rivals Will* (Crown Business 2004).

the legal framework of modern firms allows for enormous flexibility in terms of selecting different business forms, as well as making choices about the basic authority and ownership structures of the firm. It is essential for managers and investors to understand the flexibility of the overall legal framework as well as the potential pitfalls of different options. There is a great deal of technical as well as normative complexity in the law, and the basic theoretical knowledge that I attempt to impart in this book is intended to put business participants of every stripe in a position to understand the legal infrastructure of firms.[6] They can then proceed to bargain with other business participants with an appreciation of the relevant background of organizational law, including specialized applications of agency, property, contracts, and liability rules. Contracting around various legal obstacles or sticking points is broadly encouraged in most legal systems and often respected by other business participants and the courts, but one needs to know the landscape first if only to avoid the potential minefields hidden within it.

From an external perspective, the regulation of firms is important for several reasons, but near the top of the list are questions of liability for wrongful harm to third parties—including both enterprise liability and the liability of business participants who may have been involved directly (or indirectly) in causing the wrongful harm. The radical flexibility of modern firms with respect to organizational forms means that legislative and judicial crafting of standards and principles should evolve in tandem with the evolution of business realities in order to assess effective "control" and interested "ownership" in firms for the purposes of attributing responsibility and liability under general legal principles. External explication is needed as well of legal responsibility and liability under specific statutes and regulations that address these issues, often in response to increasing business complexity.[7] The expanding number of limited liability firms raises questions in terms of legal response: a need to match policy justifications with the increasingly creative use and combination of legal forms. The narrowing scope of enterprise liability through organizational methods of avoidance and evasion most likely leaves a greater percentage of the damage and costs imposed by high-technology societies on their relatively poorer, less powerful members.[8] Fast-changing, shape-shifting organizational forms, with the added complexities of globalization, may well mean that newer methods of comprehensive regulation are needed—such as mandatory insurance or administrative regimes—rather than continuing to rely on outmoded litigation solutions that are likely to bog down in legal complexity and pettifoggery. New procedural methods such as class actions or multidistrict litigation may

---

[6] This book is not, of course, intended as a primer on all relevant issues of business law. It should nevertheless help business participants to ask the right questions of lawyers, politicians, and others with responsibility for creating and applying the relevant legal rules and principles in various substantive areas.

[7] See *Juridification of Social Spheres: A Comparative Analysis in the Areas of Labor, Corporate, Antitrust and Social Welfare Law* (Gunther Teubner ed.) (Walter de Gruyter 1987). See also Chapter 2.

[8] See Chapters 1, 2, and 4. On the problem of risk distributions in society (in contradistinction to distributions of wealth), see, e.g., Ulrich Beck, *Risk Society: Towards a New Modernity* (Sage 1992). On the comparative risks and costs of different kinds of regulation, see, e.g., Stephen Breyer, *Breaking the Vicious Circle: Toward Effective Risk Regulation* (Harvard University Press 1995).

represent advancements in some situations, but it is also possible that the transactional costs of these adaptations may exceed the economic and other benefits for third-parties who have been wrongfully harmed.[9]

One particularly difficult problem in complex litigation involving organizations is also the "time lag" between wrongful event and legal consequence. With respect to organizational dynamics, increasing the time between the wrongful event and the legal consequence means that many of the actual human beings responsible for a particular set of wrongful harms caused by an organization are no longer associated with the enterprise when the legal consequence arrives, and they therefore escape responsibility, which instead is imposed on another less culpable set of current business participants.

Indirect methods of regulation used to "nudge" business firms and their participants in the right direction may work better in these situations than more direct traditional methods. One approach of these indirect methods focuses on cognitive biases revealed by studies in behavioral economics and suggests changes in terms of regulatory "choice architectures."[10] Required disclosure of information is one indirect method of regulation. Mandatory reporting of information has become standard in various areas of securities regulation (such as the requirement of audited annual reports) and environmental law (such as reporting major chemical accidents or discharges of pollution). For this method to work, of course, people must actually read or otherwise process the information disclosed. Two legal scholars have recently challenged the usefulness of mandatory disclosure in many areas on strong empirical grounds.[11] Even these authors give a pass, however, to some forms of mandatory disclosure "aimed directly at sophisticated intermediaries," including "securities disclosures to investors" and "environmental disclosures that government entities can use."[12]

Perhaps informational disclosure and other methods of indirect or "reflexive" regulation can be adapted as alternative approaches in various other areas of business regulation. "Reflexive" regulation refers to legal methods that aim to influence the internal decision-making of business firms (and other organizations) through indirect approaches, rather than direct regulating of specific behavior or performance.[13]

---

[9] See, e.g., Deborah R. Hensler, "As Time Goes By: Asbestos Litigation after *Amchem* and *Ortiz*," 80 *Texas Law Review* 1899, 1924 (2002) ("It is generally accepted that compensating injury victims through tort is less efficient than compensating victims through 'no fault' or other administrative systems, because of the relatively high dollar and time costs to deliver tort compensation, by comparison to delivering compensation through an administrative scheme.")

[10] See Richard H. Thaler and Cass R. Sunstein, *Nudge: Improving Decisions about Health, Wealth, and Happiness* (Yale University Press 2008). See also Dan Ariely, *Predictably Irrational: The Hidden Forces That Shape Our Decisions* (HarperCollins 2009); *The Irrational Economist: Making Decisions in a Dangerous World* (Erwann Michel-Kerjan and Paul Slovic eds.) (PublicAffairs 2010).

[11] Omri Ben-Shahar and Carl E. Schneider, "The Failure of Mandated Disclosure," 159 *University of Pennsylvania Law Review* 647 (2011).

[12] Id., p. 732.

[13] See Sanford E. Gaines, "Reflexive Law as a Legal Paradigm for Sustainable Development," 10 *Buffalo Environmental Law Journal* 1 (2002–03); David Hess, "Regulating Corporate Social Performance: A New Look at Social Accounting, Auditing, and Reporting," 11 *Business Ethics Quarterly* 307 (2001); Dennis D. Hirsch, "Green Business and the Importance of Reflexive Law: What Michael Porter Didn't Say," 62 *Administrative Law Review* 1063 (2010); Eric W. Orts, "Reflexive Environmental Law," 89 *Northwestern University Law Review* 1227 (1995); Richard B. Stewart, "A New

The affirmative defense given to firms that adopt proactive internal processes to address sexual harassment claims provides an example.[14] Proposals for "responsive regulation" share similarities with those favoring indirect or "reflexive" law as well.[15]

My main purpose in this book, however, is not to make detailed recommendations about how business firms should be regulated. I have undertaken to argue only that regulation is necessary—both (1) minimally, in terms of setting up the basic enabling legal structure for firms to exist, grow, and evolve; and (2) broadly, in terms of a general need to regulate in a manner that aims to reduce or compensate for the wrongfully harmful externalities imposed by firms and their participants.

I refer to "wrongful harm" here and elsewhere in this book because some kinds of harms or costs imposed by business activity on third parties in society are tolerated or condoned by collective decisions via the processes of law and government. For example, it is inevitable that serious accidents will occur when heavy automobiles capable of driving at high speeds are produced and widely used. Yet the vast majority of the costs of these accidents are not borne by the automobile manufacturers. Instead, a social judgment is made implicitly that only "wrongful harm" (such as those caused by a "defective design" of a vehicle) will support liability for injuries. Similarly, many business activities cause air pollution, and yet a certain amount of pollution is "permitted" (often explicitly in a legal "permit"). Any harm to others caused by this "permitted" pollution is not deemed "wrongful," and the costs are borne by the harmed third parties (e.g. lung cancer patients and asthma sufferers), unless otherwise mitigated by governmental health insurance mechanisms or other social safety nets.

External regulatory questions about the recognition and boundaries of firms will depend in part on normative assessments by governmental and legal policy makers (and the citizens who influence them). The legal theory of the firm advanced here is therefore compatible with an array of normative orientations and approaches. For example, some may argue (as many scholars do currently in the United States) that the laws of enterprise organization should follow the god of economic efficiency.[16] Others may argue that the normative principles of democracy and political equality should take precedence. For example, an advocate of democratic equality may argue in favor of "one share one vote" requirements for public shareholding

---

Generation of Environmental Regulation?" 29 *Capital University Law Review* 21 (2001); Cynthia A. Williams, "The Securities and Exchange Commission and Corporate Social Transparency," 112 *Harvard Law Review* 1197 (1999). See also Gunther Teubner, "Substantive and Reflexive Elements in Modern Law," 17 *Law and Society Review* 239 (1983).

[14] See Chapter 4, page 141 and accompanying notes 43–5 (discussing U.S. Supreme Court cases on this issue). See also Jean L. Cohen, *Regulating Intimacy: A New Legal Paradigm* (Princeton University Press 2002).

[15] See, e.g., Ian Ayres and John Braithwaite, *Responsive Regulation: Transcending the Deregulation Debate* (Oxford University Press 1992); Philippe Nonet and Philip Selznick, *Law and Society in Transition: Toward Responsive Law* (Harper & Row 1978).

[16] See Chapters 1 and 2. Note that even scholars who adopt a strong version of this approach usually adhere to a social measure of economic utility or general welfare. They do not simply assume that economic efficiency for individual business firms will inevitably yield social efficiency.

of corporations or in favor of the legal recognition and protection of labor unions.[17] The theory of the firm advanced here countenances both enthusiasts of law-and-economics and advocates of democratic equality, as well as a number of other normative points of view.

Although the institutional theory of the firm described here is compatible with most normative orientations, there are exceptions at the extremes. Because my theory of the firm assumes government as a source of legitimate law, normative theories advocating anarchy or an extreme libertarianism which eschews any central role for government are excluded. At the other extreme, because my theory of the firm assumes some degree of private ownership of property (and one's own labor), it is inconsistent with Marxist views advocating government expropriation of all private property.

My own intuition is that competing values—including economic efficiency, democracy, deontological duties (such as honesty and loyalty), and distributive justice—will prove more or less compelling in different situations. At least descriptively, it is inaccurate to say that any one particular value (such as overall social welfare maximization as determined from an economic perspective) is dominant in current legal practice. Some legal determinations are driven by considerations of moral or political principles instead of economic analysis. Examples include fiduciary duties of *care* and *loyalty* (emphasis added), as well as conflict-of-interest rules. Fraud, theft, and its variants such as insider trading are also best understood as violations of ethical norms rather than principles derived from economic calculations.[18] Legal principles themselves may also control results, such as the value of fidelity to the proper textual interpretation of authoritative rules.[19] Normatively, perhaps a pluralistic approach to values in the making of law and policy makes sense. Political democracy is sometimes described as involving a pluralism of values as well as interests.[20]

In any event, the main point here is not to argue for any particular normative framework. Instead, it is to stress that government acting through law has the ability—and uses it—to set the boundary conditions for business enterprise. In the final analysis, government creates the rules of the game for business, and the legal rules can be changed in light of different normative objectives and changing social circumstances. In democratic societies, at least in theory, individual citizens possess the final say on these objectives. In practice, governments (including legislatures

---

[17] See Gar Alperovitz, *America Beyond Capitalism: Reclaiming Our Wealth, Our Liberty, and Our Democracy* (John Wiley & Sons 2005). See also Kent Greenfield, *The Failure of Corporate Law: Fundamental Flaws and Progressive Possibilities* (University of Chicago Press 2006).

[18] See Ian B. Lee, "Fairness and Insider Trading," 2002 *Columbia Business Law Review* 119 (2002); Kim Lane Scheppele, "'It's Just Not Right': The Ethics of Insider Trading," 56 *Law and Contemporary Problems* 123 (1993); Alan Strudler and Eric W. Orts, "Moral Principle in the Law of Insider Trading," 78 *Texas Law Review* 375 (1999).

[19] See Frederick Schauer, *Playing By the Rules: A Philosophical Examination of Rule-Based Decision-Making in Law and in Life* (Oxford University Press 1993).

[20] For a philosophical defense of this general point of view focusing on the integrative capacity of law as well as democratic government, see Jürgen Habermas, *Between Facts and Norms: Contributions to a Discourse Theory of Law and Democracy* (William Rehg trans.) (MIT Press 1998). See also James Bohman, "Complexity, Pluralism, and the Constitutional State: On Habermas's *Faktizität und Geltung*," 28 *Law and Society Review* 897 (1994).

the final say on these objectives. In practice, governments (including legislatures and courts) are influenced not only by the preferences of individual citizens but also organized interests and views of various collective groups—including firms themselves (such as through lobbying, political campaign contributions, and litigation). Even in state capitalist societies such as China or Russia, business firms are likely to have an increasing influence over governments, though nondemocratic governments have the potential to impose harsh limits on business influence in particular cases.[21]

This book also does not propose to give detailed advice to business participants about how best to manage the internal legal frameworks of the firm to their advantage or to recommend what ends and objectives to set for themselves. Different business participants in different situations with different personal philosophies of life will have very different ideas about their goals and how to achieve them. Some business participants may pursue an objective devoted only to Mammon. Others may find motivation beyond economic gain in terms of other ethical principles and social objectives. The theory of the firm here is broad enough (and neutral enough) to embrace these different motivations, objectives, and values of business participants.

In the previous chapters of this book, I have endeavored to provide a general understanding of the legal underpinnings of modern business enterprise to inform both internal and external perspectives. Modern business firms are sometimes simple in construction, but more often they grow into complex structures of aggregated property and contracts within organized structures of authority and power. They are framed by principles of institutional responsibility, with legal boundaries drawn for enterprise liability as well as the potential liability for business participants. Different types of business firms are defined by specific statutory authorizations, including a menu of limited-liability forms as well as the ability to combine entities into very large organizational structures, the most powerful of which are multinational firms operating in global markets.

The boundary-setting issues that arise with respect to business firms are often as complex as the modern human society in which they operate. The law has helped to create this complexity and can help to manage it as well. The complex and shifting boundaries of the firm are therefore nothing to fear. They are the product of legal work and imagination—and the results of business growth and creativity. The problems of the boundaries of the firm are not easy, but they can be clarified and resolved with careful thought and attention.

---

[21] A leading example is that of Mikhail Khodorkovsky, who was once one of Russia's wealthiest citizens and founder of a leading oil company, but was then arrested and jailed (apparently on trumped up charges) when his political ambitious ran afoul of the interests of the Kremlin. See, e.g., Masha Gessen, "The Wrath of Putin," *Vanity Fair*, April 2012, <http://www.vanityfair.com> (accessed September 30, 2012); Susan Glasser and Peter Baker, "The Billionaire Dissident," *Foreign Policy*, May–June 2010, <http://www.foreignpolicy.com/> (accessed September 30, 2012).

7

Two Applications

In this final chapter, I provide two examples of how the legal theory of the firm advanced in this book may have beneficial practical value in thinking about and resolving difficult issues in business and law. The first example grapples with controversies surrounding the amounts and kinds of compensation paid to corporate executives. The second addresses the question of constitutional rights of political speech for corporate persons.

Executive compensation

Consider first the controversy surrounding current levels of corporate executive compensation. Dramatic inequality of compensation within firms is largely an Anglo-American phenomenon (perhaps replicated in some developing countries), but there are signs that other legal and economic systems that have traditionally had more egalitarian patterns of business wealth distribution, such as Germany and China, may be moving in the same general direction.[1]

Unquestionably, there has been a radical increase in the annual pay of top-level corporate executives as compared with average employees in the last few decades in the United States, though the general issue is not new.[2] In 1991, the average chief executive officer was paid about 140 times more than the average employee. By 2003, the average CEO's income had jumped to 500 times more.[3] Historically, the difference between pay for top executives

---

[1] See Brian R. Cheffins, "The Metamorphosis of 'Germany Inc.': The Case of Executive Pay," 49 *American Journal of Comparative Law* 497 (2001); Chen Lin, Wei Shen, and Dongwei Su, "Executive Pay at Publicly Listed Firms in China," 59 *Economic Development and Cultural Change* 417 (2011).

[2] For an historical perspective including a review of relevant cases in the United States, see, e.g., Detlev Vagts, "Challenges to Executive Compensation: For the Market or the Courts?" 8 *Journal of Corporation Law* 231 (1983). See also Randall S. Thomas and Harwell Wells, "Executive Compensation in the Courts: Board Capture, Optimal Contracting, and Officers' Fiduciary Duties," 95 *Minnesota Law Review* 846 (2011); Harwell Wells, "'No Man Can Be Worth $1,000,000 A Year': The Fight Over Executive Compensation in 1930s America," 44 *University of Richmond Law Review* 689 (2010).

[3] Stephen M. Bainbridge, *Corporate Governance after the Financial Crisis* (Oxford University Press 2012), p. 110; Lucian Bebchuk and Jesse Fried, *Pay without Performance: The Unfulfilled Promise of Executive Compensation* (Harvard University Press 2004), p. 1. Comparatively and historically, pay ratios have been highest in the United States. Twenty years ago, the ratio of CEO-to-average pay of 120:1 in the U.S. compared with 21:1 in Germany and 16:1 in Japan. See Graef S. Crystal, *In Search of Excess: The Overcompensation of the American Corporate Executive* (W.W. Norton 1991), pp. 27, 207–9.

compared with average workers in the United States has been accelerating. In 1960, the ratio of CEO to average employee pay was approximately 40:1, and it grew to around 70:1 in 1989, before becoming more extremely disproportionate in the 1990s and early 2000s.[4]

This general pattern, replicated also in the United Kingdom and perhaps elsewhere, has continued to the present, moderated only slightly by the economic fallout from the financial crisis of 2008.[5] In the United States, the financial crisis checked the trend of increasing inequality of pay somewhat (mostly because of falling stock market values affecting options). But in 2011, the ratio of CEO to average worker pay remained 380:1.[6] The two hundred highest paid CEOs averaged annual compensation of $14.5 million.[7] According to one academic study, "racheting" and "leapfrogging" behavior may explain continuing high levels of executive compensation even as stock markets stalled.[8] Kim Clark, the former Dean of Harvard Business School, has observed that CEO pay-ratcheting is a manifestation of the "Lake Wobegon effect" where "everybody is above average."[9]

The acceleration of executive compensation in the last several decades has direct roots in economic theories of the firm that characterize the essential problem of corporate governance as one of "the separation of ownership and control" between shareholders and top managers. See Chapter 2. From this starting point, some economists and other policy makers recommended that executive pay structures should be reformed to better align the interests of CEOs and other top executives with the interests of shareholders by paying the executives more heavily in stock and stock options rather than salary. Advocating a legally dubious principal–agent analysis, these scholars argued for the "bonding" of corporate executive compensation to share performance.[10]

Not surprisingly, given the prospect of lucrative benefits, CEOs and other top executives embraced this economic theory, and corporate boards were encouraged to follow it in practice by professional advisers and consultants, as well as CEOs themselves.[11] A massive shift in compensation resulted—from salary to stock and

---

[4] Robert B. Reich, *The Work of Nations: Preparing Ourselves for 21st Century Capitalism* (Alfred A. Knopf 1991), pp. 7, 205.

[5] On the United Kingdom, see Cheffins, op. cit., p. 506 (noting that U.K. CEO pay in the largest companies increased by over 600% from 1979 to 1994).

[6] See Leslie Kwoh, "Careers: Firms Resist New Pay-Equity Rules," *Wall Street Journal*, June 27, 2012, p. B8 (citing AFL-CIO calculations).

[7] See Nathaniel Popper, "C.E.O. Pay, Rising Despite the Din," *New York Times*, June 16, 2012, p. BU1.

[8] Thomas A. DiPrete, Gregory M. Eirich, and Matthew Pittinsky, "Compensation Benchmarking, Leapfrogs, and the Surge in Executive Pay," 115 *American Journal of Sociology* 1671 (2010).

[9] Bebchuk and Fried, op. cit., pp. 71–2 (quoting Kim Clark).

[10] See Michael C. Jensen and Kevin J. Murphy, "CEO Incentives—It's Not How Much You Pay, But How," *Harvard Business Review*, May–June 1990, p. 138; Michael C. Jensen and Kevin J. Murphy, "Performance Pay and Top-Management Incentives," 98 *Journal of Political Economy* 225 (1990). See also Chapter 2, pages 81–4 and accompanying notes 144–53.

[11] See, e.g., Bainbridge, op. cit., p. 114.

stock options. The "lion's share" of increases in executive compensation occurred through an expansion of "options-based compensation."[12]

One large error in this approach has been well-diagnosed by other scholars. Executives themselves often exercise more organizational power within corporate firms than shareholders and boards of directors, so the "pay for performance" metrics have often been unevenly administered (to put it mildly).[13] The economic theory of linking executive compensation packages to share price depends on boards negotiating honestly and at arm's length with executives. Instead, stock options have often been "reset" or "repriced" when they have not worked out favorably for executives. Executive pay in options has tended to exhibit a one-way "racheting" effect: giving rewards for stock price advances, but not imposing losses or penalties for stock price retreats. In other words, some of the original economic arguments did not account sufficiently for the prevalence of managerial power exercised within firms.[14]

The most popular proposed solution has been a "shareholder empowerment" strategy for closing the presumed "separation of ownership and control."[15] In practical terms, the primary recommendation along these lines is to reinvigorate shareholder power in elections of corporate boards, as well as paying directors in stock and stock options.[16] If the compensation packages of stock and options are better negotiated and targeted, according to this strategy, they will then work according to the original plan.

The institutional legal theory of the firm proposed here, however, suggests that the analytical problems regarding executive compensation go much deeper into firms than an analysis based only on a bilateral manager–shareholder axis of separation of ownership and control. As discussed in Chapter 2, contemporary scholarly interpretations and applications of the separation of ownership and control in business corporations have tended to be too simple. The shareholder empowerment strategy is likely to prove insufficient because its theoretical foundation is underspecified.

Other business participants beyond shareholders may have legitimate claims to the revenues of the firm. Indeed, the primary source of outcry about current levels of executive compensation derives from a comparison of executive pay and average employees' compensation.[17] A bivalent theory of the firm

---

[12] Bebchuk and Fried, op. cit., p. 1.

[13] For an influential critique along these lines, see Bebchuk and Fried, op. cit.

[14] Id., pp. 61–79 (advancing the "managerial power perspective"). See also Avinash Arya and Huey-Lian Sun, "Stock Option Repricing: Heads I Win, Tails You Lose," 50 *Journal of Business Ethics* 297 (2004). The extent of "managerial power" in this context has been contested, however. For a defense arguing that most current executive compensation packages are "efficient" and "optimal" for shareholders, see John E. Core, Wayne R. Guay, and Randall S. Thomas, "Is U.S. CEO Compensation Inefficient Pay Without Performance?" 103 *Michigan Law Review* 1142 (2005) (book review). See also Bainbridge, op. cit., pp. 116–18 (arguing that most boards negotiate executive compensation packages independently and in the best interests of shareholders).

[15] See Chapter 2, pages 80–2, accompanying notes 139–46, and Table 2.4.

[16] See, e.g., Bebchuk and Fried, op. cit., pp. 201–13.

[17] See pages 231–2 and accompanying notes 2–6.

that considers only top managers and shareholders to be relevant is myopic. An institutional theory provides corrective lenses by including other relevant business participants.

Creditors, for example, demand to be paid interest according to their legally enforceable debt contracts, but they may also have reasonable expectations of an "equity cushion" indicating good prospects of continuing to be paid in the future. If managers and boards meet these expectations, then overall benefits to the firm may accrue through a reduction in the cost of debt capital over time.[18]

Employees at many levels, including other managers, may claim that their efforts and creativity have contributed significantly to a firm's success to an extent that exceeds the legal provisions of their employment agreements. A component of good long-term management is to compensate high-performing employees in a manner that provides optimal incentives for productivity. Some evidence indicates that excessively unequal executive pay structures can have a demoralizing effect on lower-level employees and reduce their productivity.[19]

Long-term investments in the research and development of new products (and basic research that will lead to new products) may be called for strategically in particular business contexts.[20] Maximizing executive compensation to increase short-term stock price valuations may undermine the long-term perspective necessary for these investments.

Other individual participants and institutional partners in complex relational firms may have expectations of the sharing of returns to be considered as well. These relationships often cannot be reduced to questions of black-and-white contracting.[21]

The assumption of principal-agent theories of the firm is that all non-shareholder participants should be treated in terms of arm's-length contracts of one kind of another, while shareholders are different only because they have "residual claims" to leftover profits.[22] But the great diversity of different kinds of firms, business models, capital structures, and complex relations among firms (and relations within them) suggests that this one-size-fits-all economic theory will not work very well in practice, at least for many kinds of firms.[23] For instance, firms that depend on highly creative and motivated employees may need to compensate them accordingly, perhaps with high-powered profit-sharing arrangements distributed broadly within the employment structure of the firm, even if this strategy means less immediate returns for shareholders. In practice, the allocation of stock

---

[18] On debt financing and the firm, see Chapter 2, pages 84–90, accompanying notes 154–87, and Table 2.6.

[19] See Kwoh, op. cit. (citing several studies). See also Sven Kepes, John Delery, and Nina Gupta, "Contingencies in the Effects of Pay Range on Organizational Effectiveness," 62 *Personnel Psychology* 497 (2009); Concha R. Neeley and Nancy G. Boyd, "The Influence of Executive Compensation on Employee Behaviors Through Precipitating Events," 22 *Journal of Managerial Issues* 546 (2010).

[20] See, e.g., Constance E. Helfat, "Firm-Specificity in Corporate Applied R&D," 5 *Organization Science* 173 (1994).

[21] On complex relational firms, see Chapter 5, pages 191–4 and accompanying notes 79–91.

[22] Most "contractarian" theories of the firm fall into this category as well. See Chapter 2, pages 64–8 and accompanying notes 46–69.

[23] On the diversity of types and structures of firms, see especially Chapters 2 and 5.

options appears often to travel quite deep into the ranks of lower level managers and other employees.[24] And considerations of motivating employees may supply the main reason.

Note that a critique of profit-sharing with employees as suboptimal for shareholders begs the question of the purpose and overall objective of the firm.[25] A particular firm may decide that profit-sharing with key employees is *more important* than sharing profits with shareholders on grounds of relative overall contributions to the firm's long-term economic success. A decline in the firm's share value might then be expected, but it is not irrational to suggest that this decline could be offset by greater value experienced by employees, as well as the potential longer term viability and economic success of the enterprise.

A firm that sees long-term trends as critical may also decide to devote substantial resources into research and development that will not translate directly or immediately into stock price improvement. Some research and development may involve strategic secrecy. If so, then news of successful work may not immediately translate into present stock prices (at least in the absence of leaks to the stock market or insider trading). Empirical evidence appears to be mixed concerning whether stock prices accurately reflect the economic value of various kinds of research and development.[26]

Or a firm may decide to keep large reserves of retained earnings to hedge against cyclical markets that characterize its business sector. For example, the retention of a financial buffer appears to have helped Ford Motor Company remain independent of a government bailout in the recession following the Great Credit Crash of 2008.[27]

The current law in many jurisdictions allows for broad managerial discretion about the reinvestment, distribution, or retention of earnings, which supports these various options.[28] Even though allocating resources to creditors, employees, research and development, or cash reserves may not necessarily translate into maximizing current share prices, these strategies may often support legitimate business strategies aiming for long-term economic and social success.

This is not to say that top managers don't deserve to get paid well—often extremely well. Demanding jobs running large and complex enterprises focused on achieving economic results will drive competitive labor markets for managerial services. The theory of the firm advanced here casts doubt, however, on the idea that simple references to stock price performance can capture the complexity and difficulty involved in many of these top jobs.

---

[24] See Brian J. Hall and Kevin Murphy, "The Trouble with Stock Options," 17 *Journal of Economic Perspectives* 49 (2003).

[25] See id. (finding allocations to low-level managers and employees unjustified on shareholder-primacy grounds).

[26] See, e.g., Louis K. C. Chan, Josef Lakonishok, and Theodore Sougiannis, "The Stock Market Valuation of Research and Development Expenditures," 56 *Journal of Finance* 2431 (2001).

[27] See Chapter 2, pages 87–8 and accompanying notes 175–6.

[28] See Chapter 1, page 41 and accompanying notes 151–2; and Chapter 2, pages 99–104 and accompanying notes 244–71.

Even if one agrees that stock price is one good measure of a firm's economic performance, it is not at all clear that it is the best possible estimate of the current economic value of a corporate firm. Without entering this debate at length here, there are reasons to doubt that current share price provides an objectively "true" valuation that should always guide managerial decisions, including decisions about compensation. These reasons include the following. (1) Stock prices often reflect general economic conditions in the world, a geographical region, or a business sector as much as (and perhaps sometimes more than) the economic prospects and performance of a specific company. (2) Stock prices may have a bias toward short time horizons, especially if stock trading is dominated by players looking for relatively quick returns (i.e. short-term "speculators" rather than long-term "investors"). (3) Stock prices may not include confidential or secret information about long-term product development or strategies.[29]

Payment in stock and stock options is therefore likely to be a poor measure (or at least a poor single measure) of corporate managerial performance. When deciding on executive performance targets, corporate boards and their compensation committees should instead consider other factors that are specific to a particular business firm and its future needs and challenges. An example of another approach to compensation that factors in other performance variables is the "balanced scorecard."[30] A virtue of this approach is that different kinds of firms can "mix and match" performance variables depending on their overall objectives and values.

In this context, note that the complexity of firms also throws the "ballplayer analogy" into doubt. This refers to the argument that high compensation for star athletes provides a justification by analogy for high levels of CEO pay for "winning" firms. However, the measures of performance for top athletes on teams—such as Michael Jordon or LeBron James in basketball—are much more direct than for top executives.[31] Steve Jobs and Bill Gates are business geniuses, but they are perhaps exceptions that prove the rule. Although a significant part of the economic success of Apple or Microsoft owes to these visionary leaders, it is also true that many other business participants deserve credit as well for their hard work (employees and other managers) and risk-taking investments (i.e. capital providers). Moreover, a close look at the motivations of many business heroes reveals that the prospect of astronomical amounts of compensation did not drive them to higher levels of performance. They were self-motivated from other sources in addition to the prospect of material gain.[32] The psychological motivations of executives do not involve only the prospect of material rewards, and there may also be a ceiling at which the prospect of

---

[29] For an argument favoring incentive payments for executives only in restricted stock and stock options that focus on long-term performance, see Sanjai Bhagat and Roberta Romano, "Reforming Executive Compensation: Focusing and Committing to the Long-Term," 26 *Yale Journal on Regulation* 359 (2009).

[30] See Robert S. Kaplan and David P. Norton, *The Balanced Scorecard: Translating Strategy Into Action* (Harvard Business Review Press 1996); Robert S. Kaplan and David P. Norton, *The Strategy-Focused Organization: How Balanced Scorecard Companies Thrive in the New Business Environment* (Harvard Business Review Press 2000).

[31] See Bebchuk and Fried, op. cit., pp. 20–1.

[32] See, e.g., Walter Isaacson, *Steve Jobs* (Simon and Schuster 2011).

an annual monetary reward may "maximize" an executive's motivation. For example, the prospect of a $5 million annual pay target would seem sufficient to maximally motivate almost anyone.

The legal theory of the firm advanced here also opens a conceptual space for other ethical and prudential arguments favoring moderation in executive compensation. Many commentators have criticized current discrepancies in pay as "outrageous" or even "obscene," invoking ethical values of distributive justice and fairness.[33] In addition, many economists who advocated pay-for-performance practices did not anticipate that high-powered incentives for top managers to increase short-term stock price values would also significantly increase temptations to commit accounting fraud to achieve the same objective (albeit falsely). The wave of corporate fraud scandals in the United States in the 2000s is attributable at least in part to greater temptations for managers to violate the law in order to achieve false (but nevertheless profitable) short-term increases in share prices.[34]

Because of the limited liability principles for business participants discussed in Chapter 4, some of the costs of these corporate frauds often fall on those left holding the bag—after perpetrators have left the company (and sometimes left the country or gone to jail). Shareholders and other investors who profit indirectly from corporate frauds may also elude responsibility. Recent "clawback" remedies are designed in part to address this problem, but they cover only some executives. It is not clear how far these remedies can go to solve the larger problem.[35]

Once the mainstream principal-agent economic model of the firm is rejected as too narrow, simple, and naïve (at least with respect to many firms), a path toward other possible law reform opens.[36] An appreciation of the flexibility of legal structures of firms allows for an explanation of how the internal processes of executive compensation can be captured or unduly tilted toward executives. This

---

[33] See T. Leigh Anenson and Donald O. Mayer, "'Clean Hands' and the CEO: Equity as an Antidote for Excessive Compensation," 12 *University of Pennsylvania Journal of Business Law* 947 (2010); Carl T. Bogus, "Excessive Executive Compensation and the Failure of Corporate Democracy," 41 *Buffalo Law Review* 1 (1993); Jared D. Harris, "What's Wrong with Executive Compensation," 85 *Journal of Business Ethics* 147 (2009); Ella Mae Matsumura and Jae Yong Shin, "Corporate Governance Reform and CEO Compensation: Intended and Unintended Consequences," 62 *Journal of Business Ethics* 101 (2005); Jeffrey Moriarty, "Do CEOs Get Paid Too Much?" 15 *Business Ethics Quarterly* 257 (2005).

[34] See Jared Harris and Philip Bromiley, "Incentives to Cheat: The Influence of Executive Compensation and Firm Performance on Financial Misrepresentation," 18 *Organization Science* 350 (2007). See also Donald C. Langevoort, "Resetting the Corporate Thermostat: Lessons from the Recent Financial Scandals about Self-Deception, Deceiving Others and the Design of Internal Controls," 93 *Georgetown Law Journal* 285 (2004).

[35] See Amy L. Goodman and Gillian McPhee, "'Clawbacks' of Executive Compensation," 22 *Insights: Corporate and Securities Law Advisor* 7 (2008). See also Jesse Fried and Nitzan Shilon, "Excess-Pay Clawbacks," 36 *Journal of Corporation Law* 721 (2011).

[36] For the characterization that the principal–agent economic theory is "mainstream," at least with respect to debates about executive compensation, see Core, Guay, and Thomas, op. cit., pp. 1142, 1159–60 (characterizing "mainstream scholars" as espousing an "official view" known as "optimal contracting theory, which posits that contracts are [or should be] designed to maximize shareholder value net of contracting costs and transactions costs" and including Bebchuk and Fried's theory of managerial power as also within the "mainstream").

approach has also been described as the "board capture" theory.[37] An institutional theory of the firm allows also for understanding that the rules of the game can be changed to favor a broader conception of relevant interests within firms.[38]

So far, attempts to check rising levels of executive compensation in the United States (and to close the widening gap between top executive pay and the income of most regular employees) have invoked mandated disclosure techniques, which may empower other business participants as well as shareholders. The Dodd–Frank Act following the financial crisis, for example, adopted several disclosure requirements for public corporations, including: (1) disclosures about the use of compensation committees and compensation consultants; and (2) disclosures about pay-for-performance compensation and internal ratios of executive pay compared with average employee pay.[39] Recent legislation has added advisory shareholder voting on compensation to the regulatory mix.[40] One high-profile result of this new disclosure requirement was shareholder disapproval (though only advisory) of the executive compensation package of Citibank's CEO.[41]

These disclosure policies are often advanced as a "shareholder empowerment" strategy for reform. But required disclosure can allow other groups and interests beyond shareholders to exercise influence with respect to executive compensation. Employees may use the information in their own internal bargaining. And the media may galvanize public opinion, triggering possible "shaming" effects (though the prospect of significant financial gains may encourage executives to resist purely moral arguments).[42]

Stronger legal medicine is also available. For example, enhanced judicial review of the "reasonableness" of executive pay packages could be initiated under fiduciary duty standards.[43] A few recent cases in Delaware indicate a greater willingness of judges to review executive compensation arrangements rigorously.[44] Given the dangers of board capture through the exercise of managerial power, there is arguably the equivalent of an "omnipresent specter" of conflicts of interest involved

---

[37] See Thomas and Wells, op. cit, pp. 852–4, 857–64.

[38] See especially Chapters 2 and 5.

[39] As of this writing, implementing regulations have been adopted for the former but not the latter. Securities and Exchange Commission, "Corporate Governance Issues, Including Executive Compensation Disclosure and Related SRO Rules," June 29, 2012, <http://www.sec.gov/spotlight/dodd-frank/corporategovernance.shtml> [hereinafter "SEC, Corporate Governance Issues"] (discussing Dodd–Frank Act, sections 952 and 953). Substantive requirements for "independence" of compensation committees and consultants are also included. Securities and Exchange Commission, Listing Standards for Compensation Committees, Release No. 33-9330 (June 20, 2012).

[40] See SEC, Corporate Governance Issues, op. cit. (describing section 951 of the Dodd–Frank Act); Shareholder Approval of Executive Compensation and Golden Parachute Compensation, 67 Fed. Reg. 6010 (February 2, 2011).

[41] See, e.g., Steven M. Davidoff, "Citigroup Has Few Options After Pay Vote," *New York Times*, April 18, 2012, <http://dealbook.nytimes.com/2012/04/18/citigroup-has-few-options-after-pay-vote/ > (accessed September 30, 2012).

[42] See David A. Skeel, Jr., "Shaming in Corporate Law," 149 *University of Pennsylvania Law Review* 1811 (2001).

[43] For a previous version of this argument, see Eric W. Orts, "Shirking and Sharking: A Legal Theory of the Firm," 16 *Yale Law and Policy Review* 265, 320–3 (1998).

[44] See Thomas and Wells, op. cit, pp. 884–97.

in setting executive compensation, which would justify "enhanced scrutiny."[45] Courts could also revive earlier precedents which questioned "payments of sums as salaries so large as in substance and effect to amount to spoliation or waste of corporate property" under relevant corporate law standards.[46]

Another regulatory option would be to revive progressive income taxation.[47] However, this solution would address broader concerns of inequality of wealth distribution in society (including highly paid entertainers, sports stars, doctors, lawyers, university professors, and independently wealthy investors). It may therefore prove overinclusive as a solution to executive compensation in public corporations.

Constitutional rights of political speech for corporate persons

A second example of the practical applicability of the theory of the firm offered in this book appears in the controversy surrounding whether and how "corporations are persons" for purposes of legal recognition of constitutional free-speech rights. As mentioned in the preface, the *Citizens United* case is one of the most important U.S. Supreme Court cases relevant to business firms in history.[48] *Citizens United* is at least as important as *CTS Corp. v. Dynamics Corp. of America*, which upheld a state antitakeover statute against federal challenge.[49] The only other cases in United States history that rival the influence of *Citizens United* on the law of business firms are *Dartmouth College* and the cases that first held that business enterprises (including corporations) could assert constitutional rights as "persons" under the Fourteenth Amendment.[50] *Citizens United* explicitly acknowledged business corporations (and implicitly other firms) as legal persons with constitutional rights of political free speech.

Citizens United involved a legal challenge to a federal statute that restricted for-profit business firms from participating directly in political campaigns. Specifically, a nonprofit corporation, which received funding in part from for-profit corporations, wanted to distribute a political video called "Hillary" during an election cycle. The movie opposed the candidacy of Hillary Clinton. The federal statute

---

[45] Cf. *Unocal Corp. v. Mesa Petroleum Co.*, 493 A.2d 946 (Del.1985) (using this language in adopting enhanced standards for review of antitakeover defenses).

[46] *Rogers v. Hill*, 289 U.S. 582, 591–2 (1933). See also Vagts, "Challenges to Executive Compensation," op. cit., pp. 252–68; Wells, op. cit., pp. 717–37.

[47] See Derek Bok, *The Cost of Talent: How Executives and Professionals are Paid and How It Affects America* (Free Press 1993), pp. 275–80; Donna M. Byrne, "Progressive Taxation Revisited," 37 *Arizona Law Review* 739 (1995); Joseph Bankman and Thomas Griffith, "Social Welfare and the Rate Structure: A New Look at Progressive Taxation," 75 *California Law Review* 1905 (1987); Walter J. Blum and Harry Kalven, Jr., "The Uneasy Case for Progressive Taxation," 19 *University of Chicago Law Review* 417 (1952).

[48] *Citizens United v. Federal Election Commission*, 130 S. Ct. 876 (2010). See Preface, pages xviii–xix and accompanying notes 19–24.

[49] 481 U.S. 69 (1987).

[50] See Chapter 1, pages 10–12 and accompanying notes 4–16; and Chapter 3, pages 126–31 and accompanying notes 81–108.

banned this activity, and the nonprofit Citizens United challenged the law under the First Amendment.[51]

The general view that "First Amendment protection extends to corporations" is not controversial today. Justice Kennedy's majority opinion in *Citizens United* cited a long line of precedents for the proposition.[52] As discussed in Chapters 1 and 4, it is not unusual to recognize corporations and other organizations as "persons" for various purposes, including their ability to assert constitutional rights or their capacity to be held responsible for criminal acts. It is no rash or radical step, then, to argue that the First Amendment should afford some level of protection to business firms as "persons."

Dissenting in an earlier case, Chief Justice William Rehnquist had articulated a view that business corporations should not be recognized to have any constitutional rights of political speech under the First Amendment, though he agreed with previous precedents recognizing constitutional rights for the protection of corporate property and grudgingly recognized some level of protection for "commercial speech."[53] His view was not adopted, however. I focus only on "political speech" here and do not discuss the separate and expanding area of constitutional law relating to "commercial speech."[54]

In *Citizens United*, Justice Kennedy's majority opinion struck down the federal law banning for-profit corporations from participating in political elections. In expansive terms, the Court "rejected the argument that political speech of corporations or other associations should be treated differently under the First Amendment simply because such associations are not 'natural persons.'" Justice Kennedy's opinion cited only one precedent for this proposition, *First National Bank of Boston v. Bellotti*.[55]

In fact, this precedent did not go as far as Justice Kennedy's opinion suggested. *Bellotti* struck down a restriction on a business corporation's right to speak in opposition to a state referendum to establish a graduated progressive income tax. The majority opinion in *Bellotti* stated: "The proper question . . . is not whether corporations 'have' First Amendment rights and, if so, whether they are coextensive with those of natural persons." Instead, the *Bellotti* majority inquired whether the statute repressed the kind of "expression that the First Amendment was meant to protect" and found that it did.[56] Because the case involved direct political speech, *Bellotti* struck down the statute as it applied to a for-profit corporation. The majority in *Bellotti*, however, explicitly reserved the question of whether, "under different circumstances, a justification for a restriction on speech that would be

[51] *Citizens United*, op. cit., pp. 886–8.

[52] Id., p. 899.

[53] *First National Bank of Boston v. Bellotti*, 435 U.S. 765, 822–8 (1978) (Rehnquist, C.J., dissenting).

[54] For a recent case on "commercial speech," see *Sorrell v. IMS Health Inc.*, 131 S. Ct. 2653 (2011). For an argument against distinguishing between commercial and non-commercial speech, see Alex Kozinski and Stuart Banner, "Who's Afraid of Commercial Speech?" 76 *Virginia Law Review* 627 (1990).

[55] *Citizens United*, op. cit, p. 900, citing *Bellotti*, op. cit.

[56] *Bellotti*, op. cit., p. 776.

inadequate as applied to individuals might suffice to sustain the same restriction as applied to corporations, unions, or like entities."[57]

Citizens United therefore broke new and controversial ground with its assertion that the First Amendment rights for political speech of corporations are essentially indistinguishable from those of natural individual people. Justice Kennedy's majority opinion invoked "the principle that the Government lacks the power to ban corporations from speaking" and struck down the federal restriction on corporate-sponsored communications in political elections.[58] In his concurring opinion, Chief Justice John Roberts asserted the same broad principle, making it clear that the scope of the opinion applies to other formal organizations as well. "The text and purpose of the First Amendment point in the same direction: Congress may not prohibit political speech, even if the speaker is a corporation or union."[59]

Justice Kennedy's opinion refers to a number of First Amendment cases to support his conclusion. He does not, however, provide a full-fledged legal theory to explain why business corporations should have a right of political free speech equivalent to individual citizens. This is problematic because the nondiscriminatory principle that he announces in the case flies in the face of case law in other constitutional contexts in which corporations (and other business firms) are treated differently than individual people. For example, Supreme Court cases under the Fifth Amendment cut both ways, depending on the circumstance and substantive protections at issue. In a criminal case, a business corporation may invoke the Double Jeopardy Clause, asserting a right not to be tried twice for the same crime. But a corporation may not invoke the Fifth Amendment right against self-incrimination.[60]

Justice Stevens' dissenting opinion in *Citizens United* does not dig very deeply into a theory of corporate personality either. Instead, Justice Stevens simply asserts a contrast between "people" and "corporations," but he does not then elaborate the constitutional meaning of the distinction. He objects to the majority opinion's "constant reiteration" of "the proposition that the First Amendment bars regulatory distinctions based on a speaker's identity, including its 'identity' as a corporation." And he emphasizes a contrary proposition that "the distinction between corporate and human speakers" is "significant," especially in the context of political elections.[61] The complex nature of corporate organizations and the fact that human interests are represented through them, however, do not spur him to undertake further analysis of the underlying theoretical problem. With respect to questions regarding discrimination based on the "identity of the speaker," for example, the dissenting opinion focuses mostly on other cases of exceptions for natural people in the First Amendment context (such as students, members of the military, or

---

[57] Id., p. 777 n. 13.   [58] *Citizens United*, op. cit., p. 903.

[59] Id., p. 919 (Roberts, C.J., concurring).

[60] See Chapter 1, page 51 and accompanying notes 200–1. See also Susanna Kim Ripken, "Corporate First Amendment Rights After *Citizens United*: An Analysis of the Popular Movement to End the Constitutional Personhood of Corporations," 14 *University of Pennsylvania Journal of Business Law* 209, 244–6 (2011).

[61] *Citizens United*, op. cit., p. 930 (Stevens, J., dissenting).

prisoners).[62] The more relevant questions regarding the nature of the organizational "identity" of firms is left unexplored.

Justice Stevens argues in favor of three substantive policies or rationales for subjecting corporate political speech to government regulation, namely, "anti-corruption," "antidistortion," and "shareholder protection."[63] All three of these arguments supported a previous Supreme Court decision, *Austin v. Michigan Chamber of Commerce*, which upheld a state law scheme to segregate funds from corporations used for political campaigns.[64] The majority opinion in *Citizens United* rejected all three of these arguments and expressly overruled *Austin*.[65]

The *anticorruption rationale* refers to the realistic possibility that a business firm may seek financial gain in return for its support of a particular candidate, in other words, the prohibited "quid pro quo" of bribery or its indirect equivalent of "undue influence."[66] The *antidistortion rationale* refers to the fact that business firms, especially in corporate form, have grown very large and powerful, and allowing firms to participate freely and without restrictions in the political process will arguably skew the results in their favor. The fear is that the economic power of large profit-motivated firms will drown out other voices and other values.[67] The *shareholder protection rationale* refers to the concern that managers who have author-ity to decide on the allocation of company resources in political campaigns are not likely to poll their equity investors before making these political decisions. As a result, shareholders who disagree will effectively support corporate political speech without an opportunity to express a contrary opinion or to "opt out."[68] Having advanced these policy arguments favoring a government interest in regulating corporate political speech, however, Justice Stevens does not appear to admit to a limiting constitutional principle with respect to the scope or extent of regulations that may be used to achieve these ends. In oral argument, the government illustrated the problem by conceding that it might be permissible to censor the publication of a book with political purposes or themes under the antidistortion rationale.[69]

---

[62] Id., pp. 945–8.

[63] Id., pp. 961–79. Note that political speech includes making financial contributions in order to speak or disseminate speech in the media or otherwise.

[64] 494 U.S. 652, 658–63 (1990).

[65] *Citizens United*, op. cit., pp. 903–13.

[66] Id., pp. 961–8 (Stevens, J., dissenting). In another relatively recent case decided on different constitutional grounds, the Court required a state judge who had received a massive campaign donation to recuse himself from a case involving the donor. *Caperton v. A.T. Massey Coal Co.*, 556 U.S. 868 (2009).

[67] *Citizens United*, op. cit., pp. 971–7 (Stevens, J., dissenting).

[68] Id., pp. 977–9. In this connection, campaign finance law in the United States after *Citizens United* now treats labor unions differently than corporations. Employees' individual freedom of speech rights are often recognized by statutory "opt out" provisions with respect to political campaigns. But employees, shareholders, and other business participants are not given "opt out" rights in business corporations under *Citizens United*. See Benjamin I. Sachs, "Unions, Corporations, and Political Opt-Out Rights after *Citizens United*," 112 *Columbia Law Review* 800 (2012). This discrepancy highlights the need to look into the black box of firms and other organizations when deciding whether and how to apply constitutional principles.

[69] *Citizens United*, op. cit., p. 904. The dissenting opinion responded that books and print media were excluded from coverage under the text of the statutes, but this does not address the

The *Citizens United* case, a five-to-four decision, generated a great deal of rancor. As mentioned earlier, the stakes were very high in terms of the rules of the game regarding for-profit corporate contributions in the political process.[70] A telling and dramatic moment occurred during President Obama's State of the Union speech in January 2010 when he denounced the *Citizens United* opinion while the Supreme Court Justices sat silently along with other dignitaries in front of him, and Justice Alito was seen on television clips to mutter "not true, not true" in response. Debate among commentators then erupted as to whether President Obama offended the Supreme Court, whether Justice Alito offended the President, or both.[71]

Although the political and rhetorical gap between the majority and minority opinions in *Citizens United* seems wide (and the gap dividing pundits as well as politicians even wider), an analysis drawing on the institutional theory of the firm advanced here may point toward some helpful directions going forward. As one scholar has aptly summarized the current situation:

> The Supreme Court has never developed a unified theoretical justification for its conclusion that corporations are persons under the Constitution. Thus, there is no coherent, consistent way of defining corporate constitutional rights. The effect is a corporate personhood jurisprudence that often seems purely result-oriented. The Court has utilized conflicting theories of corporate personhood to support particular results, rather than as guiding principles to help reach them.[72]

The two main opinions in *Citizens United* illustrate this problem of conflicting theories of the firm in constitutional decision-making. The majority and minority opinions fall basically into two of the main categories of legal theories of the firm outlined in Chapter 1: the top-down "concession theory" and the bottom-up "participant theory."[73]

Justice Stevens' in his minority opinion implicitly adopts the top-down concession theory. He echoes a strong government-centered view of business corporations and other firms, for example, when he writes:

> [C]orporations have no consciences, no beliefs, no feelings, no thoughts, no desires. Corporations help structure and facilitate the activities of human beings, to be sure, and their "personhood" often serves as a useful legal fiction. But they are not themselves members of "We the People" by whom and for whom our Constitution was established.[74]

---

larger theoretical question of constitutional limitations of possible regulation. Id., pp. 943–4 n. 31 (Stevens, J., dissenting).

[70] See Preface, pages xviii and accompanying notes 19–21.

[71] See Robert Barnes, "Reactions Split on Obama's Remark, Alito's Response at State of the Union," *Washington Post*, January 29, 2010, <http://www.washingtonpost.com/> (accessed September 30, 2012).

[72] Ripken, op. cit., pp. 246–7. Some may be tempted to jettison the idea of corporate personality entirely, but this is not a viable position. Ignoring the organizational persons that law, government, and society create will not make them go away.

[73] See Chapter 1, pages 12–14, accompanying notes 17–24, and Table 1.1.

[74] *Citizens United*, op. cit., p. 972 (Stevens, J., dissenting).

Justice Stevens argues for various regulatory restrictions on business firms and, given that they are "creatures of the state", he sees no reason to recognize constitutional limitations on regulating them. In this sense, his dissent belongs to the rhetorical tradition of *Dartmouth College*, a case which he cites approvingly.[75] Although Justice Stevens contends in a footnote that "nothing in this opinion turns on whether the corporation is conceptualized as a grantee of a state concession" (citing *Dartmouth College*) or "any other model," the thrust of his substantive arguments puts him squarely in the camp of the concession theory as it is described in this book. Rather than develop an applicable theory to fit the constitutional problem, Stevens writes: "It is not necessary to agree on a precise theory of the corporation to agree that corporations differ from natural persons in fundamental ways, and that a legislature might therefore need to regulate them differently if it is human welfare that is the object of its concern."[76] In this last clause, however, Stevens and his dissenting colleagues indicate a strong substantive embrace of the top-down concession view of the firm favoring regulation over the rights of business participants without any constitutional limitation except for a broad and vague objective of "human welfare."

Justice Kennedy's majority opinion embraces a version of the opposite bottom-up participant theory.[77] On this view, firms are composed of people, and they represent the real interests of people when acting in the world. Therefore, constitutional protection should extend to these institutions with respect to freedom of political speech. To do otherwise would trample on the legitimate constitutional rights of business participants and accord too much power to the government.[78]

Perhaps the most theoretically interesting opinion is the concurrence by Justice Antonin Scalia (joined by Justices Thomas and Alito). Scalia adopts an originalist approach to constitutional interpretation and reviews the history of business firms around the time of the founding of the United States. He accurately describes the rise of business firms, including modern corporations, from smaller "progenitors," including "small unincorporated business associations" as well as "religious, educational, and literary corporations" that "were incorporated under general incorporation statutes, much as business corporations are today." "Were all of these [organizations] silently excluded," he asks rhetorically, "from the protections of the First Amendment?"[79] On this score, Scalia's criticism of the dissenting opinion hits home. Justice Stevens' opinion invokes some good arguments to regulate organizations, including business firms, with some legitimate government purposes in mind (such as the anticorruption principle). But he does not accede or respond effectively to Scalia's main argument that some First Amendment protection for political speech must extend to organizations, including business firms, given that people compose firms. At the same time, Stevens' dissent is probably more accurate

---

[75] Id., p. 950; see also Chapter 1, page 10 and accompanying notes 4–5.
[76] *Citizens United*, op. cit., p. 971 n. 72 (Stevens, J., dissenting).
[77] See Chapter 1, pages 10–12 and accompanying notes 6–16.
[78] *Citizens United*, op. cit., pp. 898–9, 916–17.
[79] Id., p. 926 (Scalia, J., concurring).

historically when he argues that actual business corporations (or, more precisely, their precursors) at the time of the American founding were conceived under the concession theory to be direct creatures of the state (given that the general incorporation statutes were yet to come).[80] This historical riposte, however, does not recognize that the bottom-up participant theory of the firm had already begun to gain traction by this time.[81] Scalia's invocation of the emerging rights of printing presses and small-firm publishers clinches the general historical argument in his favor.[82]

Some political free-speech rights for business firms should therefore be recognized, and the interesting and difficult question then becomes when and how legitimate regulation may be adopted to protect other compelling government interests (such as anticorruption) within this constitutional limitation. Neither absolutist position of "no regulation of rights" or "no boundaries to regulation" seems persuasive.

Applying an institutional theory of the firm combines these two perspectives and, in the process, exposes some flaws in both positions. It also suggests some possible grounds for compromise—or at least opens some conceptual space for further productive debate.

The majority's participant theory makes sense because business firms are composed of people and therefore should, derivatively, have their constitutional rights recognized. However, the majority does not grapple sufficiently with the complexity of modern firms, and in this respect Justice Stevens' dissent is right to castigate a theoretical position that draws no serious distinction between firms and individual people. Two important issues here relate to the purposes of business firms and their internal structures of representation.

With respect to purpose, it is relevant that most business firms are organized primarily to pursue profits and economic gain, rather than to bring together like-minded citizens who want to aggregate their political influence.[83] *Citizens United* would be an easy case if it only involved the funding of a nonprofit political organization through the aggregation of individual donors.[84] (This context provides another important use for the profit–nonprofit distinction regarding the overall "purpose" of an organization, by the way, as discussed in Chapter 5.) The economic objective of business firms raises legitimate concerns about their motivations for becoming involved in the political process. The anticorruption rationale is compelling. But it is also true that many individuals pursue their own economic self-interests when engaging in politics (i.e. "voting their pocketbooks"). As one commentator observes, "the threat to democracy posed by allowing corporations, with their immense aggregations of wealth, to function as political speakers" exists

---

[80] Id., p. 950 (Stevens, J., dissenting).

[81] See Chapter 1, pages 10–11 and accompanying notes 6–11.

[82] *Citizens United*, op. cit., pp. 927–8 (Scalia, J., concurring); see also id., p. 906 (discussing original coverage of printing presses and other media).

[83] Hybrid social enterprises may qualify as partial exceptions. See Chapter 5, pages 206–15.

[84] See David Shelledy, "Autonomy, Debate, and Corporate Speech," 18 *Hastings Constitutional Law Quarterly* 541, 544–5 (1991).

within "the same regime that allows individual citizens, who may also accumulate tremendous wealth, to spend as much of that wealth as they choose on political speech."[85] Therefore, simply to say that business firms have economic motivations does not justify forbidding them from engaging in political speech.

This line of argument largely counters the antidistortion rationale. One might respond that the influence of wealth in politics should be curtailed generally by placing widespread restrictions on individuals as well as firms and other organizations in terms of how much money they may devote to political purposes, but this approach has not found favor in the United States under recent First Amendment cases.[86]

Adding an understanding of the internal organizational structure of firms changes the theoretical picture. Firms are structures of authority and power, as well as economic wealth-generating machines. They select representative agents who act in the firm's name and allocate corporate funds to achieve the firm's objectives. These internal governance structures are designed with economic objectives primarily in mind.[87] To assume that these same structures will work to transmit political preferences among the different participants of the firm is fundamentally mistaken. Allowing the *economic* representatives of firms to act also as *political* representatives of the firm's business participants is to mix apples with oranges. It does not respect the different roles that individuals play in different social spheres of life: as economic business participants, on one hand, and as political citizens, on the other.[88] Acting as a single individual, one can sometimes combine or switch between these two roles of economic actor and political citizen. The specialized organization of a complex business firm cannot.

For example, an individual person may decide to work for a particular company with political motivations partially in mind, or an individual consumer may consider political as well as economic values when making purchasing decisions. However, a complex business firm that combines many people within its organization and aims at an overall economic objective does not seem to provide the same degree of normative flexibility and coherence.

One might respond that the representative agents of firms can be expected to act politically to advance the best economic interests of the firm itself. But the structural conflicts-of-interest problem reflected in the problem of executive compensation is replicated in this context as well. In other words, executives who have the authority to allocate a firm's funds to political objectives may not be sufficiently constrained by the representative structures within the firm to act only in the firm's

---

[85] Amy J. Sepinwall, "*Citizens United* and the Ineluctable Question of Corporate Citizenship," 44 *Connecticut Law Review* 575, 579 (2012).

[86] See id., p. 579 n. 10 (citing cases). This does not mean that I fully agree with this position normatively, but I leave this topic for another day.

[87] See especially Chapters 1 and 2 above.

[88] For a related argument developing the concept of a "normative citizen," see Sepinwall, op. cit. On the many different roles that individuals play in modern societies, see Chapter 1, page 28 and accompanying note 82, and Chapter 5, page 179 and accompanying note 17. For a theoretical justification of a separation between the categories of politics and economics, see also Michael Walzer, *Spheres of Justice: A Defense of Pluralism and Equality* (Basic Books 1992).

economic interests rather than to devote the firm's resources to further their own political preferences. Firms constructed for economic purposes are not designed to channel or constrain political preferences. *Citizens United* therefore reopens large questions about how decisions to engage in political speech will be made within firms and whether and how any restrictions should apply under the laws of enterprise organization.

Given that *Citizens United* protects the rights of business firms to make political donations of various kinds, questions also arise about the fiduciary standards that executives should follow when making decisions to engage in political speech or campaign financing. Political speech or contributions unrelated to a firm's business might be challenged as *ultra vires* (i.e. outside the powers of executives as agents of the firm) or as corporate waste.[89] Other commentators responding to *Citizens United* have recommended the adoption of an internal default rule against corporate political speech without shareholder approval as well as various disclosure requirements.[90] Again, however, as in the executive compensation debate, it is not clear why shareholders are the only relevant business participants in the context of this particular problem. Even if shareholders approve political speech, other business participants (including other managers and employees) may disapprove. The problem of political representation within firms travels beyond shareholders and should include other business participants who finance and work within business enterprises.

For example, consider a large and complex for-profit corporation's decision to support a candidate for President. On the theory of the firm presented here, this kind of corporation is composed of a great number of individual people who are linked together with specific organizational objectives in mind. If one Presidential candidate will clearly advance the economic interest of the firm as a whole better than another, then on one view it would be perfectly alright for the firm's representatives to devote resources toward this end. (This perspective supports the majority view in *Citizens United*.) Elections are equivalent to political lobbying, on this view, and therefore firms should be allowed to participate without constraint as long as the representatives of the firm can be trusted to follow the firm's collective economic objective rather than their own political preferences.

However, one may respond (following the institutional theory of the firm advanced in this book) that business participants in large complex corporations are quite diverse—and their interests extend considerably beyond the shareholder protection rationale advanced by Justice Stevens' dissent in *Citizens United*. Employees, different levels of managers, different kinds of creditors, and other business participants may have radically diverse views about who should be elected President based on a host of other values and considerations unrelated to their collective economic interests in the firm's prospects. If so, then the correct representative

---

[89] See Victor Brudney, "Business Corporations and Stockholders' Rights under the First Amendment," 91 *Yale Law Journal* 235, 243–52 (1981).

[90] See Lucian A. Bebchuk and Robert J. Jackson, Jr., "Corporate Political Speech: Who Decides?" 124 *Harvard Law Review* 83 (2010).

course politically would be for the corporation's agents to remain neutral in the Presidential election. (This perspective supports the minority view in *Citizens United*.)

Observe that this institutional view extends beyond the "shareholder protection" rationale to include a much broader range of relevant business participants. Justice Stevens, in his theory-doesn't-matter footnote, says that his conclusions do not depend on whether he adopts a "stakeholder" or "team production" conception of the corporation.[91] But this assertion cannot be true at least with respect to the shareholder protection rationale. A "team production" model would include employees as another category of relevant business participants to protect, and adding them (as well as the larger number of business participants embraced by an institutional theory of the firm) would have strengthened the force of Stevens' argument.

In fact, even on purely economic grounds, there are strong reasons to expect that the complexity of large firms—and the number of people and interests that they combine within them—will lead executives to avoid tendentious political disputes such as Presidential elections. As one experienced commentator observes, big firms have a tendency to adopt "prudentially pusillanimous policies" when it comes to political involvement.[92] As he observes, speaking from the perspective of a business executive:

Political statements will win a corporation many enemies—enemies who can then boycott your products. The same political statements may win you some friends, but not friends who will double their purchases just because you have taken a stand they find favorable. Hence, the last thing that you want to do as a corporation is get involved with election campaigns when it is clear that no candidate embodies all the positions—and only those positions—that are ideal for the firm. Entering this swamp presents a real danger, and no sensible corporation should take that risky step.[93]

On the theory of the firm advanced here, the "enemies" created by a firm taking controversial political positions would also include the firm's own employees. Note, however, that the opportunity to engage in political speech secretly (in the absence of a public disclosure law) may change these calculations significantly.

With respect to Justice Stevens' minority opinion, the view expressed about the nature of business firms, including corporations, is too abstracted and removed. Justice Stevens calls corporations "fictions" with "no consciences, no beliefs, no feelings, no thoughts, [and] no desires."[94] But this approach misses the social fact that firms are composed of real people with all of these attributes acting within real institutions.[95] Many of the substantive arguments that Stevens advances in favor of regulation have merit, especially the anticorruption rationale and an expanded

---

[91] *Citizens United*, op. cit., p. 971 n. 72 (Stevens, J., dissenting), citing Margaret M. Blair and Lynn A. Stout, "A Team Production Theory of Corporate Law," 85 *Virginia Law Review* 247 (1999).

[92] Richard A. Epstein, "*Citizens United v. FEC*: The Constitutional Right that Big Corporations Should Have But Do Not Want," 34 *Harvard Journal of Law and Public Policy* 639, 653 (2011).

[93] Id., pp. 656–7.

[94] *Citizens United*, op. cit., p. 972 (Stevens, J., dissenting).

[95] See Chapter 1.

version of what might be called a *business participant protection rationale*. Because Stevens' arguments are not grounded in an institutional appreciation of the nature of real firms, however, his conclusions favoring regulation are too sweeping and unequivocal. Corporations are composed of people, and people as citizens have constitutional rights of free political speech. If so, then any regulations imposed on corporations and other firms should observe some constitutional limits, though the exact nature and scope of these limits may remain for further debate and decision. At the same time and by the same token, the political rights of people and firms are not equivalent. As Stevens observes, it would be absurd to say that the fact that corporations cannot vote violates their political rights of free speech![96]

Both the majority and minority views in *Citizens United* therefore appear too extreme and uncompromising. To say that "corporations are persons" and therefore should possess the full complement of constitutional rights afforded to individual citizens is too simplistic and absolute. Yet it is also too simplistic and absolute to say that "corporations are not people" and therefore deserve no constitutional rights. (In part for this reason, the idea of a constitutional amendment to declare that "corporations are not persons" or "corporations are not people" is also a nonstarter.[97]) A better, more theoretically grounded answer to this question—namely, whether the First Amendment's protection of freedom of speech should extend to for-profit corporations and, if so, to what extent and under what available regulation—is likely to lie in a middle ground. Firms are recognized as legal persons for many purposes and in many situations (as discussed throughout this book), and this recognition should extend to protect a legitimate role in the political process. At a minimum, for example, business firms can provide helpful information about potential economic consequences of proposed regulation. At the same time, the legal persons of corporations and other business firms are also regulated in many different circumstances for the public good (also as discussed throughout this book) and in a manner appreciative of their structural complexity and considerable social power. This institutional power engenders a realistic concern for its misuse to corrupt the political processes of government.

One specific compromise to recommend is the adoption of a robust regulatory system of "disclaimers and disclosure" of the organizational and individual identities of donors to political campaigns and political media operations (including especially the producers and distributors of negative attack ads). Justice Kennedy's majority opinion in *Citizens United* upheld the "disclaimer and disclosure" provisions at issue in the case and referred favorably to the disclosure regime currently existing for political lobbying.[98] At the outset of his opinion, Justice Kennedy emphasized that government may "regulate corporate political speech through

---

[96] *Citizens United*, op. cit., p. 948 (Stevens, J., dissenting).

[97] See Kent Greenfield, "How to Make the 'Citizens United' Decision Worse," *Washington Post*, January 19, 2012, <http://www.washingtonpost.com> (accessed September 11, 2012). See also Preface, page xix and accompanying note 24.

[98] *Citizens United*, op. cit., pp. 913–17. On disclosure regimes for lobbying, see id., p. 915, citing *United States v. Harriss*, 347 U.S. 612 (1954).

disclaimer and disclosure requirements."[99] Regulatory reform in other areas of the law would be needed to achieve the objective of full disclosure about business participation in politics.[100] If a spirit of compromise can be reached to adopt these reforms then an effective indirect solution of information regulation could address at least some of the most problematic issues regarding the political speech of business firms.[101] Disinfecting sunlight may provide a better check than direct regulatory prohibitions to address the nebulous but nefarious role of too much money in politics.

Recommending a disclosure regime is also not to minimize the extent of the problem of corruption, which requires at least some direct substantive regulation, such as the prohibition of bribery.[102]

Although *Citizens United* and related issues are specific to the United States, general questions about legal regulation of the political relationship between business firms and governments appear in other parts of the world in different guises. Addressing these issues and others relating to the proper role of business firms in politics will continue for many years into the future. In the United States, *Citizens United* represents a new beginning rather than an end of legal and political debate about the scope of First Amendment rights for the business persons of the firm.[103]

---

[99] *Citizens United*, op. cit., p. 886.

[100] For a summary of the legal state of play as of this writing, see Stephen Engelberg and Kim Barker, "Flood of Secret Campaign Cash: It's Not All Citizens United," *ProPublica*, August 23, 2012, <http://www.propublica.org> (accessed September 30, 2012).

[101] See Amy Gutmann and Dennis F. Thompson, *The Spirit of Compromise: Why Governing Demands It and Campaigning Undermines It* (Princeton University Press 2012) (providing examples of successful bipartisan compromises).

[102] On the problem of corruption generally, see Elizabeth Drew, *The Corruption of American Politics: What Went Wrong and Why* (Overlook Press, reissue ed., 2000); Brooks Jackson, *Honest Graft: Big Money and the American Political Process* (Farragut, 2nd ed., 2000); Robert G. Kaiser, *So Damn Much Money: The Triumph of Lobbying and the Corrosion of American Government* (Alfred A. Knopf 2009); Robert E. Klitgaard, *Controlling Corruption* (University of California Press 1988); Susan Rose-Ackerman, *Corruption and Government: Causes, Consequences, and Reform* (Cambridge University Press 1999).

[103] For some subsequent decisions as this book goes to press, see *American Tradition Partnership, Inc. v. Bullock*, 132 S. Ct. 2490 (2012) (overturning the state of Montana's anti-corruption legislation on *Citizens United* grounds); *Bluman v. Federal Election Commission*, 800 F. Supp.2d 281 (D.D.C. 2011), *aff'd* 132 S. Ct. 1087 (2012) (upholding federal prohibition against foreign residents of the United States from making contributions to political campaigns); *Ognibene v. Parkes*, 671 F.3d 174 (2d Cir. 2012) (upholding New York City's restrictions on the participation of firms doing business with the city in making contributions to municipal election campaigns, primarily on anticorruption grounds).

Conclusion

Above all, reform requires a theory.[1]

— John C. Coffee, Jr.

We fill pre-existing forms and when we fill them we change and are changed.[2]

— Frank Bidart

According to a well-known adage, it takes a theory to beat a theory. As mentioned in the preface and alluded to throughout this book, the leading theories of the firm for the past several decades have been economic in nature. Although these theories provide valuable insights about the evolving shapes and sizes of firms—as well as the strategies that they undertake—they are insufficient for a complete understanding of the business enterprise. The main reason, as this book has argued, is that business firms are not created and cannot exist through the processes of economics alone. Law is also fundamental for understanding the nature of firms and the purposes they are intended to serve. The primary objective of this book has been to elucidate some of the most important legal conceptions that underpin and explain modern business firms.

In terms of methodology, I have followed what may be called an interpretive theoretical approach to the phenomenon of business firms, focusing on an explication of the legal rules, principles, and structures that have been used to create and shape them over time. Although my own academic and cultural background has biased my account toward sources written in English and focused mostly on the United States, I have endeavored to draw comparisons with other countries in mind and to discuss variations on enterprise structures found in other places. I hope that my account will resonate with perspectives in other jurisdictions, especially given the ever-increasing "global reach" of business firms.[3] The increasing globalization of business firms occurs through both trade (across firm boundaries) and production (within multinational firm boundaries). Further thought should be given in the future about how to better conceptualize and regulate the increasingly global dimensions of firms and the capital and labor markets that support them.[4]

---

[1] John C. Coffee, Jr., *Gatekeepers: The Professions and Corporate Governance* (Oxford University Press 2006), p. 10.

[2] Frank Bidart, "Borges and I," quoted in David Foster Wallace, *The Pale King: An Unfinished Novel* (Back Bay Books 2012), p. 3.

[3] For the original coinage, see Richard J. Barnet and Ronald E. Müller, *Global Reach: The Power of Multinational Corporations* (Simon and Schuster 1976).

[4] For steps in this direction, see, e.g., Eric W. Orts, "The Legitimacy of Multinational Corporations," *Progressive Corporate Law* (Lawrence E. Mitchell ed.) (Westview Press 1995), pp. 247–79;

Also included in my interpretation of the firm are multidisciplinary elements of history and sociology as well as jurisprudence. I have not hesitated to draw on empirical evidence, including economic evidence, when it has been relevant to my arguments. However, my method of research has not been narrowly "positive" in the sense of setting forth a scientific hypothesis and testing it by empirical fact-gathering and experiment. Instead, I have given a general theoretical interpretation of the legal reality of business firms, drawing mostly from legal sources but also from other disciplines when helpful toward the end of a better interpretation of social reality. Readers will judge for themselves whether this interpretation is convincing and useful. I hope to have provided an interpretation of the modern business firm that meets the standard of the anthropologist Clifford Geertz who wrote:

A good interpretation of anything—a poem, a person, a history, a ritual, an institution, a society—takes us into the heart of that which it is the interpretation. When it does not do that, but leads us instead somewhere else—into an admiration of its own elegance, of its author's cleverness, or of the beauties of the Euclidean order—it may have its intrinsic charms; but it is something else than what the task at hand . . . calls for.[5]

My main argument has been that in order to go "into the heart" of the nature of the business firm, one must engage with the intricacies of the law.

Although some of the legal details provided in this book have been complex, following the nature of its topic, I have tried to be straightforward in the direction of the overall argument. Business firms, which have grown in importance in the everyday lives of almost everyone in modern global society, are essentially legal creations.[6] Although firms act within a system of markets and respond to economic signals and incentives, they cannot be understood only in these terms. A resurrection of foundational elements of legal theory—including an appreciation of firms as legally constructed and empowered "entities" and "persons"—allows for a more accurate, complete, and useful understanding of the nature of the firm than economics and other non-legal theories can provide. A legal theory of the firm supplies a necessary description of the social truth of firms—both what they are and what they are not. Law is also needed to describe the real but elusive and often evanescent boundaries of the firm.

This is not to say that other disciplines in addition to law (and economics) are not important and relevant: quite to the contrary! My argument here is only that legal theory is an essential part of a basic understanding of firms. Other disciplines that have provided and promise significant insights about modern business firms include anthropology, history, philosophy, political theory (and political science), psych-

---

Detlev F. Vagts, "The Governance of the Multinational," 23 *Wisconsin International Law Journal* 525 (2005).

[5] Clifford Geertz, *The Interpretation of Cultures* (Basic Books 1973), p. 18.

[6] Some of the most impoverished people on the planet who live on a subsistence basis may be excluded, but even they live in a world that is largely dominated by the business firms, commercial markets, and nation-states that provide the basic infrastructure of the modern global economy.

ology (including social psychology), religious studies, and sociology—as well as the specialized business disciplines of accounting, finance, management, and marketing.

In this book, I have reconstructed some foundational research on the institutional nature of firms which has been too often forgotten or misinterpreted.[7] As these older debates and discussions reveal (in work, for example, by "old institutionalists" such as Max Weber, Thorstein Veblen, Friedrich Hayek, and Adolf Berle), business firms are legal constructions of authority and power, as well as economically efficient organizational engines.[8] Firms are human-created and human-managed institutional "persons" that are recognized to have legal authority to act in the world. This legal authority to act externally in markets, and society generally, as organizational persons has been accorded to modern firms because we recognize them as entities composed of internal relationships of agency, contracts (self-governance), and property (capital structure).[9] In other words, law creates the necessary conditions for the construction of organizational "identity." Any theory of the firm must therefore include law as foundational.

Although many of the arguments advanced in this book are academic as well as theoretical, the practical implications of a modern institutional legal theory of the firm are large. Because firms result from organizational activities that occur within a complex structure of legal rules and principles, they are subject to greater potential variation and change than sometimes appreciated. The legal rules regarding the liability of firms and their participants, for example, are not set in stone or dictated by economic forces of inevitability. Instead, these rules have changed over time and will continue to evolve, even though forces of historical inertia and "path dependence" are strong as well.[10] Against the status quo, there are two possible avenues for change regarding the structure and purposes of firms: (1) from the "bottom-up" in terms of the self-organizing creativity of business participants who select and constitute particular business firms; and (2) from the "top-down" in terms of the framing of the legal rules of the game, which are composed of a mix of enabling, default, and mandatory rules and principles.[11]

From a bottom-up perspective, business participants and everyday consumers have more options than may appear at first glance concerning the organizational structure of business firms. This perspective of the firm from the point of view of its participants reveals that the current structure of enterprise law in most countries of

---

[7] For a similar view that the problem of the "legal person" has been lost in modern jurisprudence and should be returned to consideration (though on somewhat different sociological grounds), see Gunther Teubner, "Enterprise Corporatism: New Industrial Policy and the 'Essence' of the Legal Person," 36 *American Journal of Comparative Law* 130 (1988). See also Preface, page xxii and accompanying note 31.

[8] See Introduction, pages 3, 5, and accompanying notes 11, 14. For consonant accounts of the social power of modern firms, see also J.E. Parkinson, *Corporate Power and Responsibility: Issues in the Theory of Company Law* (Oxford University Press 1993); Edward S. Herman, *Corporate Control, Corporate Power* (Cambridge University Press 1981).

[9] See Chapters 1 and 2.

[10] See Chapter 4. On path dependence in the law, see Lucian Arye Bebchuk and Mark J. Roe, "A Theory of Path Dependence in Corporate Ownership and Governance," 52 *Stanford Law Review* 127 (1999). See also Chapter 1, page 32 and accompanying note 104.

[11] See Chapters 1 and 2.

the world is relatively open for new experimentation and entrepreneurship. In fact, most countries embrace a principle of freedom of self-organization as fundamental and even "constitutional." In the United States, for example, the constitutional protections of freedom of speech and association, as well as private property (such as under the Takings Clause), reinforce this bottom-up view of firms. Although this organizational freedom is less pervasive in countries that emphasize state capitalism, millions of entrepreneurial flowers have been blooming and pollinating for the last several decades in these lands too.[12] Associational freedom in the construction of business enterprise means that a great deal of normative diversity is possible among firms. Although some economists counsel a strict focus on shareholders' interests in corporations, for example, the theory of the firm advanced here reveals that other alternatives focusing on a broad array of business participants (sometimes called "stakeholders") are available, and a number of experiments with different "hybrid" forms are underway.[13] From the bottom-up perspective, consumers may also make their normative preferences known through their purchasing decisions (or their opposite, namely, consumer boycotts).

Note that in this book, I have used the term "business participants" rather than "stakeholders" in order to avoid confusion. In previous work, a co-author and I set forth an argument in favor of a "narrow" version of theories of stakeholders to require that these interests have a truly relevant "stake" at risk in the business enterprise. This broadens the category of business participants to include managers, employees, and creditors of various kinds—but it rejects arguments that less concrete "interests" in the firm, such as society in general or the natural environment in the abstract, should qualify as stakeholders.[14] Given the risks of confusion in using the term "stakeholders," I refer instead to "business participants" in the legal theory of the firm developed here.

From a top-down perspective, a greater appreciation of the rules of the game of business enterprise—including the history of and reasons for various rules that have been adopted, dropped, or otherwise changed—will put everyone in society in an improved position to see and comprehend the otherwise invisible "legal matrix" of modern business.[15] Education and increased public understanding will make policy arguments about one rule or another more accessible to a wider range of citizens, academics, policy makers, judges, administrators, and legislators. Making the underlying legal matrix of firms more visible may also decrease the ability of sophisticated lobbyists and lawyers (and the influential—usually richer and more powerful—business people who control and direct them) to fix the legal rules behind the scenes and render them opaque to the rest of the world. One historical cause of the increasing complexity of large enterprises (and sometimes small ones), as well as a corresponding increase in the complexity of legislation to govern them,

---

[12] See Chapters 3 and 5.   [13] See especially Chapters 2 and 5.

[14] Eric W. Orts and Alan Strudler, "The Ethical and Environmental Limits of Stakeholder Theory," 12 *Business Ethics Quarterly* 215 (2002). See also Eric W. Orts and Alan Strudler, "Putting a Stake in Stakeholder Theory," 88 *Journal of Business Ethics* 605 (2009).

[15] Cf. *The Matrix* (Warner Bros. 1999). See Chapter 2, page 73 and accompanying note 103.

may be traced to the motivations of those who control these enterprises to obfuscate the true lineages of power, wealth, and authority involved in them.[16] A number of the financial corporate structures and transactions that caused scandals such as Enron and that characterized investment banking practices contributing to the financial crisis beginning in 2008, for example, were "facilitated by technocratic obfuscation" in the prolific misuse of legal entities to avoid regulators' or investors' oversight.[17]

Some of the most important and basic rules of the game governing firms have been touched on in this book. For example, a key variable in many areas of law concerns the shifting boundaries of the firm with respect to the imposition of organizational responsibility and liability for wrongful harms. Expanding "limited liability" for both managers and investors in firms poses practical questions about who (if anyone) takes responsibility for the behavior of business firms when their actions wrongfully harm others. Large complex firms pose particular difficulties in situations when "entities-within-entities" are shielded from responsibility and liability. Multinational business structures that cross legal jurisdictions complicate this problem still further.[18] In some cases at least, one gets the sense that the overuse of business entities creates what one of David Foster Wallace's characters calls "a fugue of evaded responsibility."[19] Diagnosing these problems of organizational responsibility and liability is the first step toward recommending legislative, judicial, self-help, or other possible solutions to them.

An institutional theory of the firm that combines "bottom-up" and "top-down" perspectives also suggests different approaches to other contemporary problems. Chapter 7 highlighted the examples of executive compensation and political free-speech rights for firms. A bottom-up perspective on these problems suggests possible action by business participants themselves: those in charge of executive pay practices and those responsible for donating to political campaigns are in a position to advance some of the lessons of business complexity advanced in this book in their everyday actions within their firms. At the same time, citizens, politicians, policy makers, and judges may take account of the arguments made here in terms of recommendations for top-down legislative reform or when deciding new legal cases. Better legal theory can improve legislative and judicial outcomes with respect to executive compensation practices, political free-speech rights for firms, and other issues.

In short, the institutional theory of the firm presented here provides a basic framework to begin further analysis leading to new business experiments, new policy recommendations, and new directions for legal reform in a world in which organizational persons are becoming increasingly powerful and influential.

* * *

Humanity has inherited a myriad of legal forms of business enterprise, and people fill these preexisting forms in various capacities over the course of their lives in

---

[16] See also Chapter 2.

[17] William W. Bratton and Adam J. Levitin, "A Transactional Genealogy of Scandal: From Michael Milken to Enron to Goldman Sachs," 86 *Southern California Law Review* 783, 864 (2013).

[18] See Chapter 4.   [19] Wallace, op. cit., p. 120.

various roles: as employees, managers, and investors. People act also as both consumers and citizens. People are changed by their engagement with the various forms of business, and at the same time they have the power to change these legal forms over time by acting with and within them. The forms and persons of business enterprise have been created through legal technologies, which have proven highly successful as well as powerful for their intended purposes. Although they are artificial fictions, business firms have become socially real through widespread practice and belief. Business firms act as persons in the world. Firms own property, make contracts, and shoulder legal rights and responsibilities. We say and mean "ExxonMobil" or "Patagonia" just as we say and mean the "United States of America" or the "People's Republic of China." Theories that disregard these social facts will be discarded into the proverbial dustbins of history.

With the perspective offered by an institutional legal theory of the firm, the organized persons of business can change—both through self-organized decisions by business participants (bottom-up change) and through reforms adopted by legal and political processes (top-down change). In various ways, the persons of business enterprise will inevitably evolve and adapt: the main question for the future is how they will change and in what direction.

Table of Cases

Bibliography

Acharya, Viral V., Thomas F. Cooley, Matthew Richardson, and Ingo Walter (eds.), *Regulating Wall Street: The Dodd–Frank Act and the New Architecture of Global Finance* (Wiley 2010).

Alchian, Armen A., and Harold Demsetz, "Production, Information Costs, and Economic Organization," 62 *American Economic Review* 777 (1972).

Alexander, Janet Cooper, "Unlimited Shareholder Liability Through a Procedural Lens," 106 *Harvard Law Review* 387 (1992).

Allen, Franklin, and Douglas Gale, *Comparing Financial Systems* (MIT Press 2000).

Allen, William T., "The Pride and Hope of Delaware Corporate Law," 25 *Delaware Journal of Corporate Law* 70 (2000).

Almeida, Heitor V., and Daniel Wolfenzon, "A Theory of Pyramidal Ownership and Family Business Groups," 61 *Journal of Finance* 2637 (2006).

American Law Institute, *Principles of Corporate Governance: Analysis and Recommendations* (American Law Institute 1994) (two volumes).

American Law Institute, *Restatement (Third) of Agency* (American Law Institute 2006) (two volumes).

American Law Institute, Principles of the Law of Nonprofit Organizations, Council Draft No. 6 (September 2009).

Anand, Anita Indira, "An Analysis of Enabling vs. Mandatory Corporate Governance: Structures Post-Sarbanes-Oxley," 31 *Delaware Journal of Corporate Law* 229 (2006).

Anenson, T. Leigh, and Donald O. Mayer, "'Clean Hands' and the CEO: Equity as an Antidote for Excessive Compensation," 12 *University of Pennsylvania Journal of Business Law* 947 (2010).

Ang, James S., Rebel A. Cole, and James Wuh Lin, "Agency Costs and Ownership Structure," 55 *Journal of Finance* 81 (2000).

Aoki, Masahiko, *Corporations in Evolving Diversity: Cognition, Governance, and Institutions* (Oxford University Press 2010).

Ariès, Philippe, and Georges Duby (gen. eds.), *A History of Private Life* (Harvard University Press 1987–91) (five volumes).

Aristotle, *Politics* (Ernest Barker ed. and trans.) (Oxford University Press 1958).

Armour, John, and Michael J. Whincop, "The Proprietary Foundations of Corporate Law," 27 *Oxford Journal of Legal Studies* 429 (2007).

Aron, Ravi, Eric K. Clemons, and Sashi Reddi, "Just Right Outsourcing: Understanding and Managing Risk," 22 *Journal of Management Information Systems* 37 (2005).

Arrow, Kenneth J., *The Limits of Organization* (W.W. Norton 1974).

Arruñada, Benito, "Institutional Support of the Firm: A Theory of Business Registries," 2 *Journal of Legal Analysis* 525 (2010).

Arthur, W. Brian, *Increasing Returns and Path Dependency in the Economy* (University of Michigan Press 1994).

Arya, Avinash, and Huey-Lian Sun, "Stock Option Repricing: Heads I Win, Tails You Lose," 50 *Journal of Business Ethics* 297 (2004).

Ataner, Attila, "How Strict Is Vicarious Liability? Reassessing the Enterprise Risk Theory," 64 *University of Toronto Faculty of Law Review* 63 (2006).

Atkinson, Rob, "Theories of the Federal Income Tax Exemption for Charities: Thesis, Antithesis, and Syntheses," 27 *Stetson Law Review* 395 (1997).

Avi-Yonah, Reuven S., "The Cyclical Transformations of the Corporate Form: A Historical Perspective on Corporate Responsibility," 30 *Delaware Journal of Corporate Law* 767 (2005).

Ayres, Ian, and John Braithwaite, *Responsive Regulation: Transcending the Deregulation Debate* (Oxford University Press 1992).

Ayres, Ian, and Robert Gertner, "Filling Gaps in Incomplete Contracts: An Economic Theory of Default Rules," 99 *Yale Law Journal* 87 (1989).

Bainbridge, Stephen M., "Abolishing Veil Piercing," 26 *Journal of Corporation Law* 479 (2001).

Bainbridge, Stephen M., "Director Primacy: The Means and Ends of Corporate Governance," 97 *Northwestern University Law Review* 547 (2003).

Bainbridge, Stephen M., *Agency, Partnerships and LLCs* (Foundation Press 2004).

Bainbridge, Stephen M., "Abolishing LLC Veil Piercing," 2005 *University of Illinois Law Review* 77 (2005).

Bainbridge, Stephen M., *The New Corporate Governance in Theory and Practice* (Oxford University Press 2008).

Bainbridge, Stephen M., *Corporate Governance after the Financial Crisis* (Oxford University Press 2012).

Baird, Douglas G., "The Importance of Priority," 82 *Cornell Law Review* 1420 (1997).

Bakan, Joel, *The Corporation: The Pathological Pursuit of Profit and Power* (Free Press 2004).

Baker, George, Robert Gibbons, and Kevin J. Murphy, "Relational Contracts and the Theory of the Firm," 117 *Quarterly Journal of Economics* 39 (2002).

Baker, Tom, and Sean J. Griffith, "Predicting Corporate Governance Risk: Evidence from the Directors' and Officers' Liability Insurance Market," 74 *University of Chicago Law Review* 487 (2007).

Bank, Steven A., and Brian R. Cheffins, "The Corporate Pyramid Fable," 84 *Business History Review* 435 (2010).

Bansal, Ravi, and Amir Yaron, "Risks for the Long Run: A Potential Resolution of Asset Pricing Puzzles," 59 *Journal of Finance* 1481 (2004).

Bar-Gill, Oren, and Gideon Parchomovsky, "Law and the Boundaries of Technology-Intensive Firms," 157 *University of Pennsylvania Law Review* 1649 (2009).

Bar-Gill, Oren, and Elizabeth Warren, "Making Credit Safer," 157 *University of Pennsylvania Law Review* 1 (2008).

Barnet, Richard J., and Ronald E. Müller, *Global Reach: The Power of Multinational Corporations* (Simon and Schuster 1976).

Barnett, Randy E., "Foreword: Four Senses of the Public Law–Private Law Distinction," 9 *Harvard Journal of Law and Public Policy* 267 (1986).

Barron, David J., "The Promise of Cooley's City: Traces of Local Constitutionalism," 147 *University of Pennsylvania Law Review* 487 (1999).

Barron, J.F., "Business and Professional Licensing: California, A Representative Example," 18 *Stanford Law Review* 640 (1966).

Baskoy, Tuna, "Thorstein Veblen's Theory of Business Competition," 37 *Journal of Economic Issues* 1121 (2003).

Baumol, William J., "Entrepreneurship in Economic Theory," 58 *American Economic Review* 64 (1968).

Baumol, William J., Peggy Heim, Burton G. Malkiel, and Richard E. Quandt, "Earnings Retention, New Capital and the Growth of the Firm," 52 *Review of Economics and Statistics* 345 (1970).

Baumol, William J., Robert E. Litan, and Carl J. Schramm, *Good Capitalism, Bad Capitalism, and the Economics of Growth and Prosperity* (Yale University Press 2007).

Bebchuk, Lucian A., "Foreword: The Debate on Contractual Freedom in Corporate Law," 89 *Columbia Law Review* 1395 (1989).

Bebchuk, Lucian A., "The Case for Increasing Shareholder Power,"118 *Harvard Law Review* 83 (2005).

Bebchuk, Lucian A., "Letting Shareholders Set the Rules," 119 *Harvard Law Review* 1784 (2006).

Bebchuk, Lucian A., "The Myth of the Shareholder Franchise," 93 *Virginia Law Review* 675 (2007).

Bebchuk, Lucian, Alma Cohen, and Allen Ferrell, "What Matters in Corporate Governance?" 22 *Review of Financial Studies* 783 (2009).

Bebchuk, Lucian, and Jesse Fried, *Pay without Performance: The Unfulfilled Promise of Executive Compensation* (Harvard University Press 2004).

Bebchuk, Lucian A., and Robert J. Jackson, Jr., "Corporate Political Speech: Who Decides?" 124 *Harvard Law Review* 83 (2010).

Bebchuk, Lucian Arye, Reinier Kraakman, and George Triantis, "Stock Pyramids, Cross-Ownership, and Dual Class Equity: The Mechanisms and Agency Costs of Separating Control from Cash Flow Rights," in *Concentrated Corporate Ownership* (Randall K. Morck ed.) (National Bureau of Economic Research 2000).

Bebchuk, Lucian Arye, and Mark J. Roe, "A Theory of Path Dependence in Corporate Ownership and Governance," 52 *Stanford Law Review* 127 (1999).

Beck, Ulrich, *Risk Society: Towards a New Modernity* (Mark Ritter trans.) (Sage 1992).

Becker, Gary S., *Human Capital: A Theoretical and Empirical Analysis, with Special Reference to Education* (University of Chicago Press, 3rd ed., 1993).

Ben-Shahar, Omri, "A Bargaining Theory of Default Rules," 109 *Columbia Law Review* 396 (2009).

Ben-Shahar, Omri, and Carl E. Schneider, "The Failure of Mandated Disclosure," 159 *University of Pennsylvania Law Review* 647 (2011).

Benartzi, Shlomo, and Richard H. Thaler, "Myopic Loss Aversion and the Equity Premium Puzzle," 110 *Quarterly Journal of Economics* 73 (1995).

Berglöf, Erik, and Enrico Perotti, "The Governance Structure of the Japanese Financial Keiretsu," 36 *Journal of Financial Economics* 259 (1994).

Berl, E. Ennalls, "The Vanishing Distinction Between Creditors and Stockholders," 76 *University of Pennsylvania Law Review* 814 (1928).

Berle, Adolf A., "For Whom Corporate Managers Are Trustees: A Note," 45 *Harvard Law Review* 1365 (1932).

Berle, Adolf A., "The Theory of Enterprise Entity," 47 *Columbia Law Review* 343 (1947).

Berle, Adolf A., and Gardiner C. Means, "Corporation," in *Encyclopedia of the Social Sciences* (Macmillan 1931).

Berle, Adolf A., and Gardiner C. Means, *The Modern Corporation and Private Property* (Transaction Publishers 1991) (rev. ed. 1968) (1932).

Berlin, Isaiah, *The Proper Study of Mankind: An Anthology of Essays* (Henry Hardy and Roger Hausheer eds.) (Farrar, Straus and Giroux 1998).

Bhagat, Sanjai, and Roberta Romano, "Reforming Executive Compensation: Focusing and Committing to the Long-Term," 26 *Yale Journal on Regulation* 359 (2009).

Bhagwati, Jagdish, Arvind Panagariya, and T.N. Srinivasan, "The Muddles Over Outsourcing," 18 *Journal of Economic Perspectives* 93 (2004).

Bishop, Joseph W., Jr., "Sitting Ducks and Decoy Ducks: New Trends in the Indemnification of Corporate Directors and Officers," 77 *Yale Law Journal* 1078 (1968).

Bishop, Joseph Warren., Jr., *The Law of Corporate Officers and Directors: Indemnification and Insurance* (Clark Boardman Callaghan 2010).

Bittker, Boris I., and George K. Rahdert, "The Exemption of Nonprofit Organizations from Federal Income Taxation," 85 *Yale Law Journal* 299 (1976).

Black, Antony, *Political Thought in Europe, 1250–1450* (Cambridge University Press 1992).

Black, Antony, *Guild and State: European Political Thought from the Twelfth Century to the Present* (Transaction 2003).

Blair, Margaret M., and Lynn A. Stout, "A Team Production Theory of Corporate Law," 85 *Virginia Law Review* 247 (1999).

Blair, Margaret M., and Lynn A. Stout, "Trust, Trustworthiness, and the Behavioral Foundations of Corporate Law," 149 *University of Pennsylvania Law Review* 1735 (2001).

Blumberg, Phillip I., "Limited Liability and Corporate Groups," 11 *Journal of Corporation Law* 573 (1986).

Blumberg, Phillip I., "Intragroup (Upstream, Cross-Stream, and Downstream) Guaranties under the Uniform Fraudulent Transfer Act," 9 *Cardozo Law Review* 685 (1987).

Blumberg, Phillip I., *The Multinational Challenge to Corporation Law: The Search for a New Corporate Personality* (Oxford University Press 1994).

Blumberg, Phillip I., "The Transformation of Modern Corporation Law: The Law of Corporate Groups," 37 *Connecticut Law Review* 605 (2005).

Blumberg, Philip I., et al., *Blumberg on Corporate Groups* (Aspen 2005).

Bogus, Carl T., "Excessive Executive Compensation and the Failure of Corporate Democracy," 41 *Buffalo Law Review* 1 (1993).

Bok, Derek, *The Cost of Talent: How Executives and Professionals are Paid and How It Affects America* (Free Press 1993).

Bok, Derek, *Universities in the Marketplace: The Commercialization of Higher Education* (Princeton University Press 2004).

Booth, Richard A., "Junk Bonds, the Relevance of Dividends, and the Limits of Managerial Discretion," 1987 *Columbia Business Law Review* 553 (1987).

Booth, Richard A., "Who Owns a Corporation and Who Cares?" 77 *Chicago-Kent Law Review* 147 (2001).

Booth, Richard A., "The Duty to Creditors Reconsidered—Filling a Much Needed Gap in Corporation Law," 1 *Journal of Business and Technology Law* 415 (2007).

Boyd, Christina L., and David A. Hoffman, "Disputing Limited Liability," 104 *Northwestern University Law Review* 853 (2010).

Brandeis, Louis D., *Other People's Money and How the Bankers Use It* (Frederick A. Stokes 1914).

Bratman, Michael A., *Faces of Intention: Selected Essays on Intention and Agency* (Cambridge University Press 1999).

Bratton William W., "The New Economic Theory of the Firm: Critical Perspectives from History," 41 *Stanford Law Review* 1471 (1989).

Bratton William W., "The 'Nexus of Contracts' Corporation: A Critical Appraisal," 74 *Cornell Law Review* 407 (1989).

Bratton William W., "The Economic Structure of the Post-Contractual Corporation," 87 *Northwestern University Law Review* 180 (1992).

Bratton William W., "Dividends, Noncontractibility, and Corporate Law," 19 *Cardozo Law Review* 409 (1997).

Bratton, William W., and Adam J. Levitin, "A Transactional Genealogy of Scandal: From Michael Milken to Enron to Goldman Sachs," 86 *Southern California Law Review* 783 (2013).

Bratton, William W., Joseph A. McCahery, and Erik P.M. Vermeulen, "How Does Corporate Mobility Affect Lawmaking? A Comparative Analysis," 57 *American Journal of Comparative Law* 347 (2009).

Bratton, William W., and Michael L. Wachter, "A Theory of Preferred Stock," 161 *University of Pennsylvania Law Review* 1815 (2013).

Braudel, Fernand, *Civilization and Capitalism, 15th–18th Century* (trans. Siân Reynolds) (University of California Press 1992) (three volumes).

Brealey, R.A., Hodges, S.D., and Capron, D., "The Return on Alternative Sources of Finance," 58 *Review of Economics and Statistics* 469 (1976).

Bremmer, Ian, *The End of the Free Market: Who Wins the War Between States and Corporations?* (Portfolio 2010).

Brenkert, George G., "Google, Human Rights, and Moral Compromise," 85 *Journal of Business Ethics* 453 (2009).

Breyer, Stephen, *Breaking the Vicious Circle: Toward Effective Risk Regulation* (Harvard University Press 1995).

Brodie, Douglas, "Enterprise Liability: Justifying Vicarious Liability," 27 *Oxford Journal of Legal Studies* 493 (2007).

Brooks, Richard R.W., "Incorporating Race," 106 *Columbia Law Review* 2023 (2006).

Brudney, Victor, "Dividends, Discretion, and Disclosure," 66 *Virginia Law Review* 85 (1980).

Brudney, Victor, "Business Corporations and Stockholders' Rights under the First Amendment," 91 *Yale Law Journal* 235 (1981).

Brudney, Victor, "The Independent Director—Heavenly City or Potemkin Village?" 95 *Harvard Law Review* 597 (1982).

Brudney, Victor, "Corporate Governance, Agency Costs, and the Rhetoric of Contract," 85 *Columbia Law Review* 1403 (1985).

Brudney, Victor, "Corporate Bondholders and Debtor Opportunism: In Bad Times and Good," 105 *Harvard Law Review* 1821 (1992).

Brudney, Victor, "Contract and Fiduciary Duty in Corporate Law," 38 *Boston College Law Review* 595 (1997).

Bucy, Pamela H., "Indemnification of Corporate Executives Who Have Been Convicted of Crimes: An Assessment and Proposal," 24 *Indiana Law Review* 279 (1991).

Buell, Samuel W., "Criminal Procedure within the Firm," 59 *Stanford Law Review* 1613 (2007).

Bunkanwanicha, Pramuan, and Yupana Wiwattanakantang, "Big Business Owners in Politics," 22 *Review of Financial Studies* 2133 (2009).

Burk, Dan L., "Intellectual Property and the Firm," 71 *University of Chicago Law Review* 3 (2004).

Busch, Danny, and Laura J. Macgregor (eds.), *The Unauthorised Agent: Perspectives From European and Comparative Law* (Cambridge University Press 2009).

Callison, J. William, and Allan W. Vestal, "The L3C Illusion: Why Low-Profit Limited Liability Companies Will Not Stimulate Socially Optimal Private Foundation Investment in Entrepreneurial Ventures," 35 *Vermont Law Review* 273 (2010).

Carlson, Richard R., "Why the Law Still Can't Tell an Employee When It Sees One and How It Ought to Stop Trying," 22 *Berkeley Journal of Employment and Labor Law* 295 (2001).

Casson, Mark, and Nigel Wadeson, "The Discovery of Opportunities: Extending the Economic Theory of the Entrepreneur," 28 *Small Business Economics* 285 (2007).

Cataldo, Bernard F., "Limited Liability with One-Man Companies and Subsidiary Corporations," 18 *Law and Contemporary Problems* 473 (1953).

Chan, Louis K. C., Josef Lakonishok, and Theodore Sougiannis, "The Stock Market Valuation of Research and Development Expenditures," 56 *Journal of Finance* 2431 (2001).

Chandler, Alfred D., Jr., *Scale and Scope: The Dynamics of Industrial Capitalism* (Harvard University Press 1990).

Chandler, Alfred D., Jr., Franco Amatori, and Takashi Hikino (eds.), *Big Business and the Wealth of Nations* (Cambridge University Press 1997).

Chang, Sea Jin, and Jae Bum Hong, "Economic Performance of Group-Affiliated Companies in Korea: Intragroup Resource Sharing and Internal Business Transactions," 43 *Academy of Management Journal* 429 (2000).

Cheffins, Brian R., "Does Law Matter? The Separation of Ownership and Control in the United Kingdom," 30 *Journal of Legal Studies* 459 (2001).

Cheffins, Brian R., "The Metamorphosis of 'Germany Inc.': The Case of Executive Pay," 49 *American Journal of Comparative Law* 497 (2001).

Cheffins, Brian R., "The Trajectory of (Corporate Law) Scholarship," 63 *Cambridge Law Journal* 456 (2004).

Cheffins, Brian R., *Company Law: Theory, Structure, and Operation* (Oxford University Press 2007).

Chen, Ronald, and Jon Hanson, "The Illusion of Law: The Legitimating Schemas of Modern Policy and Corporate Law," 103 *Michigan Law Review* 1 (2004).

Cheng, Thomas K., "The Corporate Veil Doctrine Revisited: A Comparative Study of the English and the U.S. Corporate Veil Doctrines," 34 *Boston College International and Comparative Law Review* 329 (2011).

Choudhury, Barnali, "Serving Two Masters: Incorporating Social Responsibility into the Corporate Paradigm," 11 *University of Pennsylvania Journal of Business Law* 631 (2009).

Chouinard, Yvon, and Vincent Stanley, *The Responsible Company: What We've Learned from Patagonia's First 40 Years* (Patagonia Books 2012).

Clark, Robert C., "The Four Stages of Capitalism: Reflections on Investment Management Treatises," 94 *Harvard Law Review* 561 (1981).

Clark, Robert C., *Corporate Law* (Aspen 1986).

Clark, Robert C., "Contracts, Elites, and Traditions in the Making of Corporate Law," 89 *Columbia Law Review* 1703, 1705 (1989).

Clark, Robert C., "Agency Costs Versus Fiduciary Duties," in *Principals and Agents: The Structure of Business* (John W. Pratt and Richard J. Zeckhauser eds.) (Harvard Business School Press, rev. ed., 1990).

Clark, William H., Jr., and Elizabeth K. Babson, "How Benefit Corporations Are Redefining the Purpose of Business Corporations," 38 *William Mitchell Law Review* 817 (2012).

Clarke, Christen, Note, "California's Flexible Purpose Corporation: A Step Forward, a Step Back, or No Step At All?" 5 *Journal of Business, Entrepreneurship and the Law* 301 (2012).

Clarke, Donald C., "How Do We Know When an Enterprise Exists? Unanswerable Questions and Legal Polycentricity in China," 19 *Columbia Journal of Asian Law* 50 (2005).

Coase, R.H., "The Nature of the Firm," 4 *Economica* (n.s.) 386 (1937).

Coase, R.H., *The Firm, the Market, and the Law* (University of Chicago Press 1988).

Coase, R.H., "The Nature of the Firm: Meaning," 4 *Journal of Law, Economics, & Organization* 19 (1988).

Coase, R.H., "The Institutional Structure of Production," 82 *American Economic Review* 713 (1992).

Coates, John C., IV, Note, "State Takeover Statutes and Corporate Theory: The Revival of an Old Debate," 64 *New York University Law Review* 806 (1989).

Coffee, John C., Jr., "'No Soul to Damn: No Body to Kick': An Unscandalized Inquiry into the Problem of Corporate Punishment," 79 *Michigan Law Review* 386 (1981).

Coffee, John C., Jr., "Shareholders versus Managers: The Strain in the Corporate Web," 85 *Michigan Law Review* 1 (1986).

Coffee, John C., Jr., "No Exit? Opting Out, the Contractual Theory of the Corporation, and the Special Case of Remedies," 53 *Brooklyn Law Review* 919 (1988).

Coffee, John C., Jr., "The Mandatory/Enabling Balance in Corporate Law: An Essay on the Judicial Role," 89 *Columbia Law Review* 1618 (1989).

Coffee, John C., Jr., "The Rise of Dispersed Ownership: The Roles of Law and the State in the Separation of Ownership and Control," 111 *Yale Law Journal* 1 (2001).

Coffee, John C., Jr., *Gatekeepers: The Professions and Corporate Governance* (Oxford University Press 2006).

Cohen, Morris R., "Property and Sovereignty," 13 *Cornell Law Quarterly* 8 (1927–8).

Cohen, Morris R., "The Basis of Contract," 46 *Harvard Law Review* 553 (1933).

Cohen, Stephen D., *Multinational Corporations and Foreign Direct Investment: Avoiding Simplicity, Embracing Complexity* (Oxford University Press 2007).

Coleman, James S., *Foundations of Social Theory* (Harvard University Press 1990).

Commons, John R., *Legal Foundations of Capitalism* (Augustus M. Kelly, reprint ed., 1974) (1924).

Conard, Alfred F., *Corporations in Perspective* (Foundation Press 1976).

Conley, John M., and Cynthia A. Williams, "Engage, Embed, and Embellish: Theory versus Practice in the Corporate Social Responsibility Movement," 31 *Journal of Corporation Law* 1 (2005).

Cook, William W., "'Watered Stock'—Commissions—'Blue Sky Laws'—Stock Without Par Value," 19 *Michigan Law Review* 583 (1921).

Cooke, Jennifer, Note, "Finding the Right Balance for Sovereign Wealth Fund Regulation: Open Investment vs. National Security," 2009 *Columbia Business Law Review* 728 (2009).

Core, John E., "The Directors' and Officers' Insurance Premium: An Outside Assessment of the Quality of Corporate Governance," 16 *Journal of Law, Economics, & Organization* 449 (2000).

Core, John E., Wayne R. Guay, and Randall S. Thomas, "Is U.S. CEO Compensation Inefficient Pay Without Performance?" 103 *Michigan Law Review* 1142 (2005) (book review).

Cover, Robert M., "The Supreme Court, 1982 Term—Foreword: Nomos and Narrative," 97 *Harvard Law Review* 4 (1983).

Cox, Paul N., "The Public, the Private, and the Corporation," 80 *Marquette Law Review* 391 (1997).

Croley, Steven P., and Jon D. Hanson, "Rescuing the Revolution: The Revived Case for Enterprise Liability," 91 *Michigan Law Review* 683 (1993).

Crystal, Graef S., *In Search of Excess: The Overcompensation of the American Corporate Executive* (W.W. Norton 1991).

Cummings, Briana, Note, "Benefit Corporations: How To Enforce a Mandate To Promote the Public Interest," 112 *Columbia Law Review* 578 (2012).

Cyert, Richard M., and James G. March, *A Behavioral Theory of the Firm* (Blackwell Business, 2nd ed., 1992).

Dan-Cohen, Meir, *Rights, Persons, and Organizations: A Legal Theory for Bureaucratic Society* (University of California Press 1986).

Dan-Cohen, Meir, "Between Selves and Collectivities: Toward a Jurisprudence of Identity," 66 *University of Chicago Law Review* 1213 (1994).

Dan-Cohen, Meir, "Sanctioning Corporations," 19 *Journal of Law and Policy* 15 (2010).

Deakin, Simon, "'Enterprise-Risk': The Juridical Nature of the Firm Revisited," 32 *Industrial Law Journal* 97 (2003).

Dearborn, Meredith, Comment, "Enterprise Liability: Reviewing and Revitalizing Liability for Corporate Groups," 97 *California Law Review* 195 (2009).

Dees, J. Gregory, "Taking Social Entrepreneurship Seriously," 44 *Society* 24 (2007).

Dees, J. Gregory, and Beth Battle Anderson, "Sector-Bending: Blurring Lines Between Nonprofit and For-Profit," 40 *Society* 16 (2003).

Defourny, Jacques, and Marthe Nyssens, "Social Enterprise in Europe: Recent Trends and Developments," 4 *Social Enterprise Journal* 202 (2008).

De George, Richard T., *Competing with Integrity in International Business* (Oxford University Press 1993).

DeMott, Deborah A., "Organizational Incentives to Care About the Law," 60 *Law and Contemporary Problems* 39 (1997).

DeMott, Deborah A., "The Lawyer as Agent," 67 *Fordham Law Review* 301 (1998).

DeMott, Deborah A., "Breach of Fiduciary Duty: On Justifiable Expectations of Loyalty and Their Consequences,"48 *Arizona Law Review* 925 (2006).

Demsetz, Harold, "Toward a Theory of Property Rights," 57 *American Economic Review* 347 (1967).

Demsetz, Harold, *Ownership, Control, and the Firm: The Organization of Economic Activity* (Basil Blackwell 1988).

Demsetz, Harold, "The Theory of the Firm Revisited," 4 *Journal of Law, Economics, & Organization* 141 (1988).

De Soto, Hernando, *The Mystery of Capital: Why Capitalism Triumphs in the West and Fails Everywhere Else* (Basic Books 2003).

De Vries, Henry P., and Friedrich K. Juenger, "Limited Liability Contract: The GmbH," 64 *Columbia Law Review* 866 (1964).

Dewey, John, "The Historic Background of Legal Personality," 35 *Yale Law Journal* 655 (1926).

Dickinson, Laura A., "Public Law Values in a Privatized World," 31 *Yale Journal of International Law* 383 (2006).

Dimson, Elroy, Paul Marsh, and Mike Staunton, *Triumph of the Optimists: 101 Years of Global Investment Returns* (Princeton University Press 2002).

Dine, Janet, *The Governance of Corporate Groups* (Cambridge University Press 2000).

DiPrete, Thomas A., Gregory M. Eirich, and Matthew Pittinsky, "Compensation Benchmarking, Leapfrogs, and the Surge in Executive Pay," 115 *American Journal of Sociology* 1671 (2010).

Dodd, E. Merrick, Jr., "For Whom Are Corporate Managers Trustees?" 45 *Harvard Law Review* 1145 (1932).

Donaldson, Thomas, "Values in Tension: Ethics Away From Home, *Harvard Business Review* (September–October 1996).

Donaldson, Thomas, "The Epistemic Fault Line in Corporate Governance," 37 *Academy of Management Review* 256 (2012).

Donaldson, Thomas, and Thomas W. Dunfee, *Ties that Bind: A Social Contracts Approach to Business Ethics* (Harvard Business School Press 1999).

Dore, Ronald, William Lazonick, and Mary O'Sullivan, "The Varieties of Capitalism in the Twentieth Century," 15 *Oxford Review of Economic Policy* 102 (1999).

Dorf, Michael C., "Legal Indeterminacy and Institutional Design," 78 *New York University Law Review* 875 (2003).

Douglas, Mary, and Steven Ney, *Missing Persons: A Critique of Personhood in the Social Sciences* (University of California Press 1998).

Douglas, William O., and Carrol M. Shanks, "Insulation from Liability Through Subsidiary Corporations," 39 *Yale Law Journal* 193 (1929).

Drury, Robert R., "The Regulation and Recognition of Foreign Corporations: Responses to the 'Delaware Syndrome,'" 57 *Cambridge Law Review* 165 (1998).

Dulman, Scott P., "The Development of Discounted Cash Flow Techniques in U.S. Industry," 63 *Business History Review* 555 (1989).

Durkheim, Emile, *The Division of Labor in Society* (George Simpson trans.) (Free Press 1933).

Dworkin, Ronald, "The Model of Rules," 35 *University of Chicago Law Review* 14 (1967).

Easterbrook, Frank H., "Two Agency-Cost Explanations of Dividends," 74 *American Economic Review* 650 (1984).

Easterbrook, Frank H., and Daniel R. Fischel, "Limited Liability and the Corporation," 52 *University of Chicago Law Review* 89 (1985).

Easterbrook, Frank H., and Daniel R. Fischel, "The Corporate Contract," 89 *Columbia Law Review* 1416 (1989).

Easterbrook, Frank H. and Daniel R. Fischel, *The Economic Structure of Corporate Law* (Harvard University Press 1996).

Eccles, Robert G., Ioannis Ioannou, and George Serafeim, "The Impact of Corporate Sustainability on Organizational Processes and Performance," 60 *Management Science* (forthcoming 2014).

Eccles, Robert G., Michael P. Krzus, Jean Rogers, and George Serafeim, "The Need for Sector-Specific Materiality and Sustainability Reporting Standards," 24 *Journal of Applied Corporate Finance* 65 (2012).

Edlin, Aaron S., and Joseph E. Stiglitz, "Discouraging Rivals: Managerial Rent-Seeking and Economic Inefficiencies," 85 *American Economic Review* 1301(1995).

Eisenberg, Melvin Aron, "Legal Models of Management Structure in the Modern Corporation: Officers, Directors, and Accountants," 63 *California Law Review* 375 (1975).

Eisenberg, Melvin Aron, *The Structure of the Corporation: A Legal Analysis* (Little Brown 1976).

Eisenberg, Melvin Aron, "The Structure of Corporation Law," 89 *Columbia Law Review* 1461(1989).

Eisenberg, Melvin Aron, "The Theory of Contracts," in *The Theory of Contract Law: New Essays* (Peter Benson ed.) (Cambridge University Press 2001).

Eisenstadt, Kathleen M., "Agency Theory: An Assessment and Review," 14 *Academy of Management Review* 57 (1989).

Elhauge, Einer, "Sacrificing Corporate Profits in the Public Interest," 80 *New York University Law Review* 733 (2005).

Elkington, John, *Cannibals with Forks: The Triple Bottom Line for 21st Century Business* (Wiley 1999).

Ely, James W., Jr., "The Protection of Contractual Rights: A Tale of Two Constitutional Provisions," 1 *New York University Journal of Law and Liberty* 370 (2005).

Emerson, Robert W., "Franchising and the Collective Rights of Franchisees," 43 *Vanderbilt Law Review* 1503 (1990).

Emerson, Robert W., "Franchisors' Liability When Franchisees Are Apparent Agents: An Empirical and Policy Analysis of 'Common Knowledge' About Franchising," 20 *Hofstra Law Review* 609 (1992).

Emerson, Robert W., "Franchise Encroachment," 47 *American Business Law Journal* 191 (2010).

Enderle, George (ed.), *International Business Ethics: Challenges and Approaches* (University of Notre Dame Press 1999).

Epstein, Richard A., *Takings: Private Property and the Power of Eminent Domain* (Harvard University Press 1985).

Epstein, Richard A., *Simple Rules for a Complex World* (Harvard University Press 1995).

Epstein, Richard A., "*Citizens United v. FEC*: The Constitutional Right That Big Corporations Should Have But Do Not Want," 34 *Harvard Journal of Law and Public Policy* 639 (2011).

Epstein, Richard A., and Amanda M. Rose, "The Regulation of Sovereign Wealth Funds: The Virtues of Going Slow," 76 *University of Chicago Law Review* 111 (2009).

Esty, Daniel C., "Environmental Protection in the Information Age," 79 *New York University Law Review* 115 (2004).

Evans, George Heberton, Jr., "A Theory of Entrepreneurship," 2 *Journal of Economic History* 142 (Supp. 1942).

Fama, Eugene F., "Agency Problems and the Theory of the Firm," 88 *Journal of Political Economy* 288 (1980).

Fama, Eugene F., and Michael C. Jensen, "Agency Problems and Residual Claims," 26 *Journal of Law and Economics* 327 (1983).

Fama, Eugene F., and Michael C. Jensen, "Separation of Ownership and Control," 26 *Journal of Law and Economics* 301 (1983).

Fan, Joseph P.H., T.J. Wong, and Tianyu Zhang, "Organizational Structure as a Decentralization Device: Evidence from Corporate Pyramids" (working paper, February 2007), <http://papers.ssrn.com>.

Feibelman, Adam, "Commercial Lending and the Separation of Banking and Commerce," 75 *University of Cincinnati Law Review* 943 (2007).

Ferguson, Niall, *The Ascent of Money: A Financial History of the World* (Penguin Press 2008).

Financial Crisis Inquiry Commission, *The Financial Crisis Inquiry Report* (Public Affairs 2011).

Fischel, Daniel R., "The Law and Economics of Dividend Policy," 67 *Virginia Law Review* 699 (1981).

Fischel, William A., *Regulatory Takings: Law, Economics, and Politics* (Harvard University Press 1995).

Fisher, Talia, "A Nuanced Approach to the Privatization Debate," 5 *Law and Ethics of Human Rights* 73 (2011).

Flannigan, Robert, "Enterprise Control: The Servant-Independent Contractor Distinction," 37 *University of Toronto Law Journal* 25(1987).

Flannigan, Robert, "The Economics of Fiduciary Accountability," 32 *Delaware Journal of Corporate Law* 393 (2007).

Flannigan, Robert, "The Debt–Equity Distinction," 26 *Banking and Finance Law Review* 451 (2011).

Fletcher, George P., *Basic Concepts of Legal Thought* (Oxford University Press 1996).

Fox, Merrit B., *Finance and Industrial Performance in a Dynamic Economy: Theory, Practice, and Policy* (Columbia University Press 1987).

Frankel, Tamar, "Fiduciary Law," 71 *California Law Review* 795 (1983).

Frankel, Tamar, "What Default Rules Teach Us About Corporations; What Understanding Corporations Teaches Us About Default Rules," 33 *Florida State University Law Review* 697 (2006).

Freedman, Judith, "Small Businesses and the Corporate Form: Burden or Privilege?" 57 *Modern Law Review* 555 (1994).

Freedman, Judith, "Limited Liability Partnerships in the United Kingdom—Do They Have a Role for Small Firms?" 26 *Journal of Corporation Law* 897 (2001).

Freeman, Jody, "Extending Public Law Norms Through Privatization," 116 *Harvard Law Review* 1285 (2003).

Fremont-Smith, Marion R., *Governing Nonprofit Organizations: Federal and State Law and Regulation* (Harvard University Press 2004).

Fried, Jesse, and Nitzan Shilon, "Excess-Pay Clawbacks," 36 *Journal of Corporation Law* 721 (2011).

Friedman, Howard M., "The Silent LLC Revolution—The Social Cost of Academic Neglect," 38 *Creighton Law Review* 35 (2004).

Friedman, Milton, "The Social Responsibility of Business Is to Increase Its Profits," *New York Times*, September 13, 1970 (magazine), p. 33.

Friend, Irwin, and Frank Husic, "Efficiency of Corporate Investment," 55 *Review of Economics and Statistics* 122 (1973).

Froomkin, A. Michael, "Reinventing the Government Corporation," 1995 *University of Illinois Law Review* 543 (1995).

Fu, Tingmei, "Legal Person in China: Essence and Limits," 41 *American Journal of Comparative Law* 261 (1993).

Fukuyama, Francis, *Trust: The Social Virtues and the Creation of Prosperity* (Free Press 1995).

Fuller, Lon, *Legal Fictions* (Stanford University Press 1967).

Gabaldon, Theresa, "The Lemonade Stand: Feminist and Other Reflections on the Limited Liability of Corporate Shareholders," 45 *Vanderbilt Law Review* 1387 (1992).

Galeoto, Laureen E., Karen Y. Bitar, and Gil Rudolph, "The Consumer Financial Protection Bureau: The New Sheriff in Town," 129 *Banking Law Journal* 702 (2012).

Garrouste, Pierre, and Stéphane Saussier, "Looking for a Theory of the Firm: Future Challenges," 58 *Journal of Economic Behavior and Organization* 178 (2005).

Gavison, Ruth, "Privacy and the Limits of Law," 89 *Yale Law Journal* 421 (1980).

Gavison, Ruth, "Feminism and the Public/Private Distinction," 45 *Stanford Law Review* 1 (1992).

Geertz, Clifford, *The Interpretation of Cultures* (Basic Books 1973).

Geis, George S., "Business Outsourcing and the Agency Cost Problem," 82 *Notre Dame Law Review* 955 (2007).

Geldart, W.G., *Legal Personality* (Oxford University Press 1924).

George, Erika, "See No Evil? Revisiting Early Visions of the Social Responsibility of Business: Adolf A. Berle's Contribution to Contemporary Conversations," 33 *Seattle University Law Review* 965 (2010).

Gerlach, Michael L., "Twilight of the Keiretsu? A Critical Assessment," 18 *Journal of Japanese Studies* 79 (1992).

Gerlach, Michael L., "The Japanese Corporate Network: A Blockmodel Analysis," 37 *Administrative Science Quarterly* 105 (1992).

Geu, Thomas Earl, "A Single Theory of Limited Liability Companies: An Evolutionary Analysis," 42 *Suffolk University Law Review* 507 (2009).

Gevurtz, Franklin A., *Corporation Law* (West Group 2000).

Gilbert, Margaret, *On Social Facts* (Princeton University Press 1989).

Gilbert, Margaret, *Sociality and Responsibility: New Essays in Plural Subject Theory* (Rowman and Littlefield 2000).

Gilles, Stephen G., "The Judgment-Proof Society," 63 *Washington and Lee Law Review* 603 (2006).

Gilson, Ronald J., "Engineering a Venture Capital Market: Lessons from the American Experience," 55 *Stanford Law Review* 1067 (2003).

Gilson, Ronald J., Henry Hansmann, and Mariana Pargendler, "Regulatory Dualism as a Development Strategy: Corporate Reform in Brazil, the United States, and the European Union," 63 *Stanford Law Review* 475 (2011).

Gilson, Ronald J., and Curtis J. Milhaupt, "Sovereign Wealth Funds and Corporate Governance: A Minimalist Response to the New Mercantilism," 60 *Stanford Law Review* 1345 (2008).

Gilson, Ronald J., and Mark J. Roe, "Understanding the Japanese Keiretsu: Overlaps Between Corporate Governance and Industrial Organization," 102 *Yale Law Journal* 871 (1993).

Gioia, Dennis A., Majken Schultz, and Kevin G. Corley, "Organizational Identity, Image, and Adaptive Instability," 25 *Academy of Management Review* 63 (2000).

Gleeson-White, Jane, *Double Entry: How the Merchants of Venice Created Modern Finance* (W.W. Norton & Co. 2012).

Glendon, Mary Ann, *Rights Talk: The Impoverishment of Political Discourse* (Free Press 1991).

Glickman, Murray, "A Post Keynesian Refutation of Modigliani-Miller on Capital Structure," 20 *Journal of Post Keynesian Economics* 251 (1997–98).

Glynn, Timothy P., "Beyond 'Unlimiting' Shareholder Liability: Vicarious Tort Liability for Corporate Officers," 57 *Vanderbilt Law Review* 329 (2004).

Goetz, Charles J., and Robert E. Scott, "Principles of Relational Contracts," 67 *Virginia Law Review* 1089 (1981).

Goffman, Erving, *The Presentation of Self in Everyday Life* (Doubleday Anchor 1959).

Goforth, Carol R., "The Rise of the Limited Liability Company: Evidence of a Race Between the States, But Heading Where?" 45 *Syracuse Law Review* 1193 (1995).

Gold, Lorna, *New Financial Horizons: The Emergence of an Economy of Communion* (New City Press 2010).

Gompers, Paul, Joy Ishii, and Andrew Metrick, "Corporate Governance and Equity Prices," 118 *Quarterly Journal of Economics* 107 (2003).

Gordon, Jeffrey N., "The Mandatory Structure of Corporate Law," 89 *Columbia Law Review* 1549 (1989).

Goshen, Zohar, "Shareholder Dividend Options," 104 *Yale Law Journal* 881 (1995).

Gottesman, Michael D., Comment, "From Cobblestones to Pavement: The Legal Road Forward for the Creation of Hybrid Social Organizations," 26 *Yale Law and Policy Review* 345 (2007).

Gourevitch, Peter A., and James Shinn, *Political Power and Corporate Control: The New Global Politics of Corporate Governance* (Princeton University Press 2005).

Grandy, Christopher. "New Jersey Corporate Chartermongering, 1875–1929," 49 *Journal of Economic History* 677 (1989).

Grant, Robert M., "Toward a Knowledge-Based Theory of the Firm," 17 *Strategic Management Journal* 109 (1996).

Grantham, Ross, and Charles Rickett (eds.), *Legal Personality in the 20th Century* (Hart Publishing 1998).

Gray, John, *Hayek on Liberty* (Routledge, 3rd ed., 1998).

Gray, John Chipman, *The Nature and Sources of the Law* (Macmillan, 2nd ed., 1927).

Greenawalt, Kent, *Law and Objectivity* (Oxford University Press 1992).

Greenfield, Kent, *The Failure of Corporate Law: Fundamental Flaws and Progressive Possibilities* (University of Chicago Press 2006).

Greenwood, Daniel J.H., "Fictional Shareholders: For Whom Are Corporate Managers Trustees, Revisited," 69 *Southern California Law Review* 1021 (1996).

Greenwood, Daniel J.H., "The Dividend Puzzle: Are Shares Entitled to the Residual?" 32 *Journal of Corporation Law* 103 (2006).

Griffith, Sean J., "Uncovering a Gatekeeper: Why the SEC Should Mandate Disclosure of Details Concerning Directors' and Officers' Liability Insurance Policies," 154 *University of Pennsylvania Law Review* 1147 (2006).

Grossfeld, Bernhard, and Werner Ebke, "Controlling the Modern Corporation: A Comparative View of Corporate Power in the United States and Europe," 26 *American Journal of Comparative Law* 397 (1978).

Grundfest, Joseph A., "The Limited Future of Unlimited Liability: A Capital Markets Perspective," 102 *Yale Law Journal* 387 (1992).

Guillén, Mauro, "Business Groups in Emerging Economies: A Resource-Based View," 43 *Academy of Management Journal* 362 (2000).

Gulati, G. Mitu, William A. Klein, and Eric M. Zolt, "Connected Contracts," 47 *UCLA Law Review* 887 (2000).

Gutmann, Amy (ed.), *Multiculturalism: Examining the Politics of Recognition* (Princeton University Press 1994).

Gutmann, Amy (ed.), *Freedom of Association* (Princeton University Press 1999).

Gutmann, Amy, and Dennis F. Thompson, *The Spirit of Compromise: Why Governing Demands It and Campaigning Undermines It* (Princeton University Press 2012).

Haan, Sarah C., "Federalizing the Foreign Corporate Form," 85 *St. John's Law Review* 925 (2011).

Habermas, Jürgen, *Between Facts and Norms: Contributions to a Discourse Theory of Law and Democracy* (William Rehg trans.) (MIT Press 1998).

Hadari, Yitzhak, "The Structure of the Private Multinational Enterprise," 71 *Michigan Law Review* 729 (1973).

Hager, Mark E., "Bodies Politic: The Progressive History of Organizational 'Real Entity' Theory," 50 *University of Pittsburgh Law Review* 575 (1989).

Hale, Christopher, "Addressing the Incentive for Exploitation within Business Groups: The Case of the Korean Chaebol," 30 *Fordham International Law Journal* 1 (2006).

Hall, Brian J., and Kevin Murphy, "The Trouble with Stock Options," 17 *Journal of Economic Perspectives* 49 (2003).

Hall, Peter A., and David Soskice (eds.), *Varieties of Capitalism: The Institutional Foundations of Comparative Advantage* (Oxford University Press 2001).

Hall, Peter Dobkin, *Inventing the Nonprofit Sector and Other Essays on Philanthropy, Voluntarism, and Nonprofit Organizations* (Johns Hopkins University Press 2001).

Halpern, Paul, Michael Trebilcock, and Stuart Turnbull, "An Economic Analysis of Limited Liability in Corporation Law," 30 *University of Toronto Law Journal* 117 (1980).

Hampden-Turner, Charles, and Alfons Tompenaars, *The Seven Cultures of Capitalism: Value Systems for Creating Wealth in the United States, Japan, Germany, France, Britain, Sweden, and the Netherlands* (Doubleday 1993).

Hanks, James J., Jr., "Evaluating Recent State Legislation on Director and Officer Liability Limitation and Indemnification," 43 *Business Lawyer* 1207 (1988).

Hansmann, Henry B., "The Role of Nonprofit Enterprise," 89 *Yale Law Journal* 835 (1980).

Hansmann, Henry B., "The Rationale for Exempting Nonprofit Organizations From Corporate Income Taxation," 91 *Yale Law Journal* 54 (1981).

Hansmann, Henry B., "Reforming Nonprofit Corporation Law," 129 *University of Pennsylvania Law Review* 497 (1981).

Hansmann, Henry B., *The Ownership of Enterprise* (Harvard University Press 1996).

Hansmann, Henry B., "The Evolving Economic Structure of Higher Education," 79 *University of Chicago Law Review* 159 (2012).

Hansmann, Henry, and Reinier Kraakman, "Toward Unlimited Shareholder Liability for Corporate Torts," 100 *Yale Law Journal* 1879 (1991).

Hansmann, Henry, and Reinier Kraakman, "A Procedural Focus on Unlimited Shareholder Liability," 106 *Harvard Law Review* 446 (1992).

Hansmann, Henry, and Reinier Kraakman, "Do the Capital Markets Compel Limited Liability? A Response to Professor Grundfest," 102 *Yale Law Journal* 427 (1992).

Hansmann, Henry, and Reinier Kraakman, "The Essential Role of Organization Law," 110 *Yale Law Journal* 387 (2000).

Hansmann, Henry, Reinier Kraakman, and Richard Squire, "The New Business Entities in Evolutionary Perspective," 2005 *University of Illinois Law Review* 5 (2005).

Hansmann, Henry, Reinier Kraakman, and Richard Squire, "Law and the Rise of the Firm," 119 *Harvard Law Review* 1333 (2006).

Harlow, Carol, "'Public' and 'Private' Law: Definition without Distinction," 43 *Modern Law Review* 241 (1980).

Harmon, Louise, "Falling off the Vine: Legal Fictions and the Doctrine of Substituted Judgment," 100 *Yale Law Journal* 1 (1990).

Harris, Jared D., "What's Wrong with Executive Compensation?" 85 *Journal of Business Ethics* 147 (2009).

Harris, Jared, and Philip Bromiley, "Incentives to Cheat: The Influence of Executive Compensation and Firm Performance on Financial Misrepresentation," 18 *Organization Science* 350 (2007).

Harris, Ron, "The Transplantation of the Legal Discourse on Corporate Personality Theories: From German Codification to British Political Pluralism and American Big Business," 63 *Washington and Lee Law Review* 1421 (2006).

Harrison, Ann E., and Margaret S. McMillan, "Dispelling Some Myths About Offshoring," 20 *Academy of Management Perspectives* 6 (2006).

Hart, H.L.A., "Definition and Theory in Jurisprudence," in *Essays in Jurisprudence and Philosophy* (Oxford University Press 1983).

Hart, H.L.A., *The Concept of Law* (Oxford University Press, 2nd ed., 1997).

Hart, Oliver, *Firms, Contracts, and Financial Structure* (Oxford University Press 1995).

Hart, Oliver, and John Moore, "Property Rights and the Nature of the Firm," 98 *Journal of Political Economy* 1119 (1990).

Hawken, Paul, *The Ecology of Commerce: A Declaration of Sustainability* (Harper-Business, rev. ed., 2010) (1993).

Hayek, Friedrich A., *The Constitution of Liberty* (University of Chicago Press 1960).

Hayek, Friedrich A., *Law, Legislation, and Liberty: Volume 1, Rules and Order* (University of Chicago Press 1973).

Hayek, Friedrich A., *Law, Legislation, and Liberty: Volume 2, The Mirage of Social Justice* (University of Chicago Press 1976).

Hayek, Friedrich A., *The Road to Serfdom: Text and Documents* (Bruce Caldwell ed.) (University of Chicago Press 2007) (1944).

Haymore, Steven J., Note, "Public(ly Oriented) Companies: B Corporations and the Delaware Stakeholder Provision Dilemma," 64 *Vanderbilt Law Review* 1311 (2011).

Hazard, Geoffrey C., Jr., "Ethical Dilemmas of Corporate Counsel," 46 *Emory Law Journal* 1011 (1996).

Helper, Stefan, *The Beijing Consensus: How China's Authoritarian Model Will Dominate the Twenty-First Century* (Basic Books 2010).

Henderson, William D., "An Empirical Study of Single-Tier versus Two-Tier Partnerships in the Am Law 200," 84 *North Carolina Law Review* 1691 (2006).

Herman, Edward S., *Corporate Control, Corporate Power* (Cambridge University Press 1981).

Hess, David, "Regulating Corporate Social Performance: A New Look at Social Accounting, Auditing, and Reporting," 11 *Business Ethics Quarterly* 307 (2001).

Hetherington, J.A.C., "Trends in Enterprise Liability: Law and the Unauthorized Agent," 19 *Stanford Law Review* 76 (1966).

Hines, James R., Jill R. Horwitz, Jr., and Austin Nichols, "The Attack on Nonprofit Status: A Charitable Assessment," 108 *Michigan Law Review* 1179 (2010).

Hobsbawm, Eric, *The Age of Empire: 1875–1914* (Vintage Books ed. 1989) (1987).

Hobsbawm, Eric, *The Age of Revolution: 1749–1848* (Vintage Books ed. 1996) (1962).

Hodgson, Geoffrey M., "The Legal Nature of the Firm and the Myth of the Firm-Market Hybrid," 9 *International Journal of Economics and Business* 37 (2002).

Holmes, Oliver Wendell, *The Common Law* (Legal Classics Library reprint ed. 1982) (1881).

Holmes, Oliver Wendell, "Agency," 4 *Harvard Law Review* 345 (1891).

Hong, Harrison, and Marcin Kacperczyk, "The Price of Sin: The Effects of Social Norms on Markets," 93 *Journal of Financial Economics* 15 (2009).

Honneth, Axel, *The Struggle for Recognition: The Moral Grammar of Social Conflicts* (Joel Anderson trans.) (Polity Press 1995).

Honoré, A.M., "Ownership," in *Oxford Essays in Jurisprudence: A Collaborative Work* (Anthony Gordon Guest ed.) (Oxford University Press 1961).

Hopt, Klaus J., "American Corporate Governance Indices as Seen from a European Perspective," 158 *University of Pennsylvania Law Review PENNumbra* 27 (2009).

Hopt, Klaus J., "Comparative Corporate Governance: The State of the Art and International Regulation," 59 *American Journal of Comparative Law* 1 (2011).

Hopt, Klaus J., and Thomas Von Hippel (eds.), *Comparative Corporate Governance of Non-Profit Organizations* (Cambridge University Press 2010).

Horwitz, Morton J., "The History of the Public/Private Distinction," 130 *University of Pennsylvania Law Review* 1423 (1982).

Hovenkamp, Herbert, *Enterprise and American Law, 1836–1937* (Harvard University Press 1991).

Hsieh, Nien-hê "Incommensurable Values," *Stanford Encyclopedia of Philosophy*, <http://plato.stanford.edu/entries/value-ibncommensurable/> (July 23, 2007).

Hu, Henry T.C., "New Financial Products, the Modern Process of Financial Innovation, and the Puzzle of Shareholder Welfare," 69 *Texas Law Review* 1273 (1991).

Huang, Peter H., and Michael S. Knoll, "Corporate Finance, Corporate Law, and Finance Theory," 74 *Southern California Law Review* 175 (2000).

Huang, Yasheng, *Capitalism with Chinese Characteristics: Entrepreneurship and the State During the Reform Era* (Cambridge University Press 2008).

Huang, Yasheng, "Debating China's Economic Growth: The Beijing Consensus or the Washington Consensus," 24 *Academy of Management Perspectives* 31 (2010).

Hughes, Everett C., "The Ecological Aspect of Institutions," 1 *American Sociological Review* 180 (1936).

Hurst, James Willard, *The Legitimacy of the Business Corporation in the United States, 1780–1970* (University Press of Virginia 1970).

Hynes, J. Dennis, "Lender Liability: The Dilemma of the Controlling Creditor," 58 *Tennessee Law Review* 635 (1991).

Iacobucci, Edward M., and George G. Triantis, "Economic and Legal Boundaries of Firms," 93 *Virginia Law Review* 515 (2007).

Issacharoff, Samuel, and Daniel R. Ortiz, "Governing Through Intermediaries," 85 *Virginia Law Review* 1627 (1999).

Iwai, Katsuhito, "Persons, Things and Corporations: The Corporate Personality Controversy and Comparative Corporate Governance," 47 *American Journal of Comparative Law* 583 (1997).

Jamieson, Dale, "Method and Moral Theory," in *A Companion to Ethics* (Blackwell Publishers 1993).

Jansen, Marius B., *The Making of Modern Japan* (Harvard University Press 2000).

Jay, Jason, "Navigating Paradox as a Mechanism of Change in Hybrid Organizations," 56 *Academy of Management Journal* 137 (2013).

Jensen, Michael C., "Agency Costs of Free Cash Flow, Corporate Finance, and Takeovers," 76 *American Economic Review* 323 (1986).

Jensen, Michael C., *A Theory of the Firm: Governance, Residual Claims, and Organizational Forms* (Harvard University Press 2003).

Jensen, Michael C., and William H. Meckling, "Theory of the Firm: Managerial Behavior, Agency Costs and Ownership Structure," 3 *Journal of Financial Economics* 305 (1976).

Jensen, Michael C., and Kevin J. Murphy, "CEO Incentives—It's Not How Much You Pay, But How," *Harvard Business Review* (May 1990).

Jensen, Michael C., and Kevin J. Murphy, "Performance Pay and Top-Management Incentives," 98 *Journal of Political Economy* 225 (1990).

Johnston, Jason Scott, "Strategic Bargaining and the Economic Theory of Contract Default Rules," 100 *Yale Law Journal* 615 (1990).

Jones, William K., "Strict Liability for Hazardous Enterprise," 92 *Columbia Law Review* 1705 (1992).

Kahan, Marcel, and Edward B. Rock, "When The Government Is the Controlling Shareholder," 89 *Texas Law Review* 1293 (2011).

Kahneman, Daniel, and Amos Tversky, "Prospect Theory: An Analysis of Decision Under Risk," 47 *Econometrica* 263 (1979).

Kang, Jerry, and Benedikt Buchner, "Privacy in Atlantis," 18 *Harvard Journal of Law and Technology* 229 (2004).

Kantorowicz, Ernst H., *The King's Two Bodies: A Study in Medieval Political Theology* (Princeton University Press 1957).

Kaplan, Robert S., and David P. Norton, *The Balanced Scorecard: Translating Strategy into Action* (Harvard Business Review Press 1996).

Kaplan, Robert S., and David P. Norton, *The Strategy-Focused Organization: How Balanced Scorecard Companies Thrive in the New Business Environment* (Harvard Business Review Press 2000).

Kaplow, Louis, and Steven Shavell, "Fairness Versus Welfare," 114 *Harvard Law Review* 961 (2001).

Katyal, Neal Kumar, "Architecture as Crime Control," 111 *Yale Law Journal* 1039 (2002).

Katz, Leo, *Ill-Gotten Gains: Evasion, Blackmail, Fraud, and Kindred Puzzles of the Law* (University of Chicago Press 1996).

Keating, Gregory C., "The Idea of Fairness in the Law of Enterprise Liability," 95 *Michigan Law Review* 1266 (1997).

Keatinge, Robert R., "LLCs and Nonprofit Organizations—For-Profits, Nonprofits, and Hybrids," 42 *Suffolk University Law Review* 553 (2009).

Keatinge, Robert R., Allan G. Donn, George W. Coleman, and Elizabeth G. Hester, "Limited Liability Partnerships: The Next Step in the Evolution of the Unincorporated Business Organization," 51 *Business Lawyer* 147 (1995).

Keay, Andrew, "Tackling the Issue of the Corporate Objective: An Analysis of the United Kingdom's 'Enlightened Shareholder Value Approach,'" 29 *Sydney Law Review* 577 (2007).

Keister, Lisa A., "Capital Structure in Transition: The Transformation of Financial Strategies in China's Emerging Economy," 15 *Organization Science* 145 (2004).

Keller, Simon, *The Limits of Loyalty* (Cambridge University Press 2007).

Kelley, Thomas, "Law and Choice of Entity on the Social Enterprise Frontier," 84 *Tulane Law Review* 337 (2009).

Kennedy, Duncan, "The Stages of the Decline of the Public/Private Distinction," 130 *University of Pennsylvania Law Review* 1349 (1982).

Kerr, Janet E., "The Creative Capitalism Spectrum: Evaluating Corporate Social Responsibility Through a Legal Lens," 81 *Temple Law Review* 831 (2008).

Khanna, V.S., "Corporate Criminal Liability: What Purpose Does It Serve?" 109 *Harvard Law Review* 1477 (1996).

Kim, Tae Wan, and Alan Strudler, "Workplace Civility: A Confucian Approach," 22 *Business Ethics Quarterly* 557 (2012).

King, Joseph H., Jr., "Limiting the Vicarious Liability of Franchisors for the Torts of Their Franchisees," 62 *Washington and Lee Law Review* 417 (2005).

Kirsch, Clifford E., *Investment Adviser Regulation: A Step-by-Step Guide to Compliance and the Law* (Practicing Law Institute, 3rd ed., 2011) (two volumes).

Klare, Karl E., "The Public/Private Distinction in Labor Law," 130 *University of Pennsylvania Law Review* 1358 (1982).

Klausner, Michael, "Corporations, Corporate Law, and Networks of Contracts," 81 *Virginia Law Review* 757 (1995).

Klausner, Michael, "The Contractarian Theory of the Corporate Law: A Generation Later," 31 *Journal of Corporation Law* 779 (2006).

Klein, Benjamin, "Contracting Costs and Residual Claims: The Separation of Ownership and Control," 26 *Journal of Law and Economics* 367 (1983).

Klein, William A., "The Modern Business Organization: Bargaining Under Constraints," 91 *Yale Law Journal* 1521 (1982).

Klein, William A., John C. Coffee, Jr., and Frank Partnoy, *Business Organization and Finance: Legal and Economic Principles* (Foundation Press, 11th ed., 2010).

Kleinberger, Daniel S., "A Myth Deconstructed: The 'Emperor's New Clothes' on the Low-Profit Limited Liability Company," 35 *Delaware Journal of Corporate Law* 879 (2010).

Kleindorfer, Paul R., and Eric W. Orts, "Informational Regulation of Environmental Risks," 18 *Risk Analysis* 155 (1998).

Knauer, Nancy J., "Legal Fictions and Juristic Truth," 23 *St. Thomas Law Review* 1 (2010).

Knight, Frank H., "Profit and Entrepreneurial Functions," 2 *Journal of Economic History* 126 (Supp. 1942).

Knight, Frank H., *Risk, Uncertainty, and Profit* (Signalman 2009) (1921).

Knight, Jack, *Institutions and Social Conflict* (Cambridge University Press 1992).

Kogut, Bruce, and Udo Zander, "Knowledge of the Firm, Combinative Capabilities, and the Replication of Technology," 3 *Organization Science* 383 (1992).

Kogut, Bruce, and Udo Zander, "A Memoir and Reflection: Knowledge and an Evolutionary Theory of the Multinational Firm 10 Years Later," 34 *Journal of International Business Studies* 505 (2003).

Kostant, Peter C., "Breeding Better Watchdogs: Multidisciplinary Partnerships in Corporate Legal Practice," 84 *Minnesota Law Review* 1213 (2000).

Koolman, G., "Say's Conception of the Role of the Entrepreneur," 38 *Economica* (n.s.) 269 (1971).

Kraakman, Reinier, "Corporate Liability Strategies and the Costs of Legal Controls," 93 *Yale Law Journal* 857 (1984).

Kraakman, Reinier, John Armour, Paul Davies, Luca Enriques, Henry B. Hansmann, Gérard Hertig, Klaus J. Hopt, Hideki Kanda, and Edward B. Rock., *The Anatomy of Corporate Law: A Comparative and Functional Approach* (Oxford University Press, 2nd ed., 2009).

Kramer, Roderick M., and Tom R. Tyler (eds.), *Trust in Organizations: Frontiers of Theory and Research* (Sage 1996).

Krannich, Jess M., "The Corporate 'Person': A New Analytical Approach to a Flawed Method of Constitutional Interpretation," 37 *Loyola University Chicago Law Journal* 61 (2005).

Kripke, Saul A., *Naming and Necessity* (Harvard University Press 1980).

Kroszner, Randall S., and Robert J. Shiller, *Reforming U.S. Financial Markets: Reflections Before and Beyond Dodd–Frank* (Benjamin M. Freidman ed.) (MIT Press 2011).

Lacovara, Christopher, Note, "Strange Creatures: A Hybrid Approach to Fiduciary Duty in Benefit Corporations," 2011 *Columbia Business Law Review* 815 (2011).

Ladenson, Robert F., "Free Speech in the Workplace and the Public–Private Distinction," 7 *Law and Philosophy* 247 (1988–89).

Landers, Jonathan M., "A Unified Approach to Parent, Subsidiary, and Affiliate Questions in Bankruptcy," 42 *University of Chicago Law Review* 589 (1975).

Landers, Jonathan M., "Another Word on Parents, Subsidiaries and Affiliates in Bankruptcy," 43 *University of Chicago Law Review* 527 (1976).

Landes, David S., *The Unbound Prometheus: Technological Change and Industrial Development in Western Europe from 1750 to the Present* (Cambridge University Press 1969).

Landes, William M., "The Empirical Side of Law and Economics," 70 *University of Chicago Law Review* 167 (2003).

Landes, William M., and Richard A. Posner, "The Influence of Economics on Law: A Quantitative Study," 36 *Journal of Law and Economics* 385 (1993).

Landes, David S., Joel Mokyr, and William J. Baumol (eds.), *The Invention of Enterprise: Entrepreneurship from Ancient Mesopotamia to Modern Times*, (Princeton University Press 2010).

Langevoort, Donald C., "Agency Law Inside the Corporation: Problems of Candor and Knowledge," 71 *University of Cincinnati Law Review* 1187 (2003).

Langevoort, Donald C., "Resetting the Corporate Thermostat: Lessons from the Recent Financial Scandals about Self-Deception, Deceiving Others and the Design of Internal Controls," 93 *Georgetown Law Journal* 285 (2004).

Langille, Brian A., and Guy Davidov, "Beyond Employees and Independent Contractors: A View from Canada," 21 *Comparative Labor Law and Policy Journal* 7 (1999).

La Porta, Rafael, Florencio Lopez-de-Silanes, and Andrei Shleifer, "Corporate Ownership around the World," 54 *Journal of Finance* 471 (1999).

La Porta, Rafael, Florencio Lopez-de-Silanes, and Andrei Shleifer, "Government Ownership of Banks," 57 *Journal of Finance* 265 (2002).

Laski, Harold J., "The Personality of Associations," 29 *Harvard Law Review* 404 (1916).

Laski, Harold J., "The Early History of the Corporation in England," 30 *Harvard Law Review* 561 (1917).

Laufer, William S., "Corporate Culpability and the Limits of Law," 6 *Business Ethics Quarterly* 311 (1996).

Laufer, William S., "Corporate Prosecution, Cooperation, and the Trading of Favors," 87 *Iowa Law Review* 643 (2002).

Laufer, William S., "Social Accountability and Corporate Greenwashing," 43 *Journal of Business Ethics* 253 (2003).

Laufer, William S., and Alan Strudler, "Corporate Intentionality, Desert, and Variants of Vicarious Liability," 37 *American Criminal Law Review* 1285 (2000).

Lazear, Edward P., "Economic Imperialism," 115 *Quarterly Journal of Economics* 99 (2000).

Lee, Ian B., "Fairness and Insider Trading," 2002 *Columbia Business Law Review* 119 (2002).

Leebron, David W., "Limited Liability, Tort Victims, and Creditors," 91 *Columbia Law Review* 1565 (1991).

Leff, Arthur Allen, "Economic Analysis of Law: Some Realism about Nominalism," 60 *Virginia Law Review* 451 (1974).

Leff, Benjamin Moses, "The Case Against For-Profit Charity," 42 *Seton Hall Law Review* 819 (2012).

Leibenstein, Harvey, "Entrepreneurship and Development," 58 *American Economic Review* 72 (1968).

Leng, Jing, *Corporate Governance and Financial Reform in China's Transition Economy* (Hong Kong University Press 2009).

Lenhardt, Ingrid Lynn, "The Corporate and Tax Advantages of a Limited Liability Company: A German Perspective," 64 *University of Cincinnati Law Review* 551 (1996).

Levinthal, Daniel, "A Survey of Agency Models of Organizations," 9 *Journal of Economic Behavior and Organization* 153 (1988).

Levmore, Saul, "Love It or Leave It: Property Rules, Liability Rules, and Exclusivity of Remedies in Partnership and Marriage," 58 *Law and Contemporary Problems* 221 (1995).

Liebowitz, S.J., and Stephen E. Margolis, "Path Dependence, Lock-in, and History," 11 *Journal of Law, Economics, & Organization* 205 (1995).

Lin, Chen, Wei Shen, and Dongwei Su, "Executive Pay at Publicly Listed Firms in China," 59 *Economic Development and Cultural Change* 417 (2011).

Lincoln, James R., Michael L. Gerlachand, and Christina L. Ahmadjian, "Keiretsu Networks and Corporate Performance in Japan," 61 *American Sociological Review* 67 (1996).

Lindblom, Charles E., *Politics and Markets: The World's Political-Economic Systems* (Basic Books 1977).

Lindblom, Charles E., *The Market System: What It Is, How It Works, and What To Make of It* (Yale University Press 2001).

Lipton, Martin, "Corporate Governance in the Age of Finance Corporatism," 136 *University of Pennsylvania Law Review* 1 (1989).

List, Christian, and Philip Pettit, *Group Agency: The Possibility, Design, and Status of Corporate Agents* (Oxford University Press 2011).

Listokin, Yair, "Is Secured Debt Used to Redistribute Value from Tort Claimants in Bankruptcy? An Empirical Analysis," 57 *Duke Law Journal* 1037 (2008).

Lleweyllan, Karl N., "What Price Contract?—An Essay in Perspective," 40 *Yale Law Journal* 704 (1931).

Lloyd, Stephen, "Transcript: Creating the CIC," 35 *Vermont Law Review* 31 (2010).

Loewenstein, Mark J., "Stakeholder Protection in Germany and Japan," 76 *Tulane Law Review* 1673 (2002).

LoPucki, Lynn M., "The Death of Liability," 106 *Yale Law Journal* 1 (1996).

LoPucki, Lynn M., "Virtual Judgment Proofing: A Rejoinder," 107 *Yale Law Journal* 1413 (1998).

Loss, Louis, Joel Seligman, and Troy Paredes, *Fundamentals of Securities Regulation* (Aspen, 6th ed., 2011) (two volumes).

Lowenstein, Roger, *The End of Wall Street* (Penguin Press 2010).

Luhmann, Niklas, *A Sociological Theory of Law* (Elizabeth King and Martin Albrow trans.) (Routledge and Kegan Paul 1985).

Luhmann, Niklas, *Law as a Social System* (Klaus A. Ziegart trans.) (Fastima Kastner et al., eds.) (Oxford University Press 2004).

McAllister, Lesley K., "Regulation by Third-Party Verification," 53 *Boston College Law Review* 1 (2012).

McCahery, Joseph A., and Erik P.M. Vermeulen, "The Evolution of Closely Held Business Forms in Europe," 26 *Journal of Corporation Law* 855 (2001).

McCraw, Thomas K. (ed.), *Creating Modern Capitalism: How Entrepreneurs, Companies, and Countries Triumphed in Three Industrial Revolutions* (Harvard University Press 1997).

MacNeil, Ian R., "Relational Contract: What We Do and Do Not Know," 1985 *Wisconsin Law Review* 483 (1985).

Macey, Jonathan R., "A Pox on Both Your Houses: Enron, Sarbanes–Oxley, and the Debate Concerning the Relative Efficiency of Mandatory Versus Enabling Rules," 81 *Washington University Law Quarterly* 329 (2003).

Macey, Jonathan R., *Corporate Governance: Promises Kept, Promises Broken* (Princeton University Press 2008).

Macey, Jonathan R., and Geoffrey P. Miller, "Double Liability of Bank Shareholders: History and Implications," 27 *Wake Forest Law Review* 31 (1992).

Machen, Arthur W., Jr., "Corporate Personality," 24 *Harvard Law Review* 253, 346 (1911) (two parts).

Machlup, Fritz, "Theories of the Firm: Marginalist, Behavioral, Managerial," 57 *American Economic Review* 1 (1967).

Madrick, Jeff, *Age of Greed: The Triumph of Finance and the Decline of America, 1970 to the Present* (Knopf 2011).

Mahoney, Paul G., "Contract or Concession? An Essay on the History of Corporate Law," 34 *Georgia Law Review* 873 (2000).

Maitland, Frederic, "The Crown as Corporation," in *The Collected Papers of Frederic William Maitland* (H.A.L. Fisher ed.) (Cambridge University Press 1911).

Malani, Anup, and Eric A. Posner, "The Case for For-Profit Charities," 93 *Virginia Law Review* 2017 (2007).

Maltby, Lewis L., and David C. Yamada, "Beyond 'Economic Realities': The Case For Amending Federal Employment Discrimination Laws to Include Independent Contractors," 38 *Boston College Law Review* 239 (1997).

Manning, Bayless, and James J. Hanks, Jr., *Legal Capital* (Foundation Press, 3rd ed., 1990).

Mantzavinos, Chrysostomos, *Individuals, Institutions, and Markets* (Cambridge University Press 2001).

Manwaring, Susan, and Andrew Valentine, "Canadian Structural Options for Social Enterprise," 23 *Philanthropist* 399 (2010).

Margolis, Joshua Daniel, and James Patrick Walsh, *People and Profits? The Search for a Link Between a Company's Social and Financial Performance* (Lawrence Earlbaum Associates 2001).

Mark, Gregory A., Comment, "The Personification of the Business Corporation in American Law," 54 *University of Chicago Law Review* 1441 (1987).

Masten, Scott E., "A Legal Basis for the Firm," 4 *Journal of Law, Economics, & Organization* 181 (1988).

Matheson, John H., "The Modern Law of Corporate Groups: An Empirical Study of Piercing the Corporate Veil in the Parent–Subsidiary Context," 87 *North Carolina Law Review* 1091 (2009).

Matsumura, Ella Mae, and Jae Yong Shin, "Corporate Governance Reform and CEO Compensation: Intended and Unintended Consequences," 62 *Journal of Business Ethics* 101 (2005).

Mayer, Carl J., "Personalizing the Impersonal: Corporations and the Bill of Rights," 41 *Hastings Law Journal* 577 (1990).

Mayer, Colin, "New Issues in Corporate Finance," 32 *European Economic Review* 1167 (1988).

Mayer, Colin, "Corporate Governance, Competition, and Performance," 24 *Journal of Law and Society* 152 (1997).

Mayer, Thomas, *Truth Versus Precision in Economics* (Edward Elgar 1993).

Means, Benjamin, "A Voice-Based Framework for Evaluating Claims of Minority Shareholder Oppression in the Close Corporation," 97 *Georgetown Law Journal* 1207 (2009).

Mendelson, Nina A., "A Control-Based Approach to Shareholder Liability for Corporate Torts," 102 *Columbia Law Review* 1203 (2002).

Mensch, Betty, and Alan Freeman, "Liberalism's Public–Private Split," 3 *Tikkun* 24 (1988).

Merrill, Thomas W., and Henry E. Smith, "The Property/Contract Interface," 101 *Columbia Law Review* 773 (2001).

Michaels, Jon D., "Privatization's Pretensions," 77 *University of Chicago Law Review* 717 (2010).

Michel-Kerjan, Erwann, and Paul Slovic (eds.), *The Irrational Economist: Making Decisions in a Dangerous World* (Public Affairs 2010).

Micklethwait, John, and Adrian Wooldridge, *The Company: A Short History of a Revolutionary Idea* (Modern Library 2003).

Milhaupt, Curtis J., "A Relational Theory of Japanese Corporate Governance: Contract, Culture, and the Rule of Law," 37 *Harvard International Law Journal* 3 (1996).

Milhaupt, Curtis J., "Property Rights in Firms," 84 *Virginia Law Review* 1145 (1998).

Milhaupt, Curtis J., "Privatization and Corporate Governance in a Unified Korea," 26 *Journal of Corporation Law* 199 (2001).

Milhaupt, Curtis J., "In the Shadow of Delaware? The Rise of Hostile Takeovers in Japan," 105 *Columbia Law Review* 2171 (2005).

Miller, Merton H., "Financial Innovation: The Last Twenty Years and the Next," 21 *Journal of Financial and Quantitative Analysis* 459 (1986).

Miller, Merton H.,"The Modigliani–Miller Propositions After Thirty Years," 2 *Journal of Economic Perspectives* 99 (1988).

Miller, Merton H., "Leverage," 46 *Journal of Finance* 479 (1991).

Miller, Sandra K., "Piercing the Corporate Veil Among Affiliated Companies in the European Community and in the U.S.: A Comparative Analysis of U.S., German, and U.K. Veil-Piercing Approaches," 36 *American Business Law Journal* 73 (1998).

Millon, David, "Theories of the Corporation," 1990 *Duke Law Journal* 201 (1990).

Millon, David, "Communitarians, Contractarians, and the Crisis in Corporate Law," 50 *Washington and Lee Law Review* 1373 (1993).

Millon, David, "Default Rules, Wealth Distribution, and Corporate Law Reform: Employment at Will Versus Job Security," 146 *University of Pennsylvania Law Review* 975 (1998).

Millon, David, "Piercing the Corporate Veil, Financial Responsibility, and the Limits of Limited Liability," 56 *Emory Law Journal* 1305 (2007).

Millon, David, "The Still-Elusive Quest to Make Sense of Veil-Piercing," 89 *Texas Law Review* 15 (2010).

Minow, Martha, "Outsourcing Power: How Privatizing Military Efforts Challenges Accountability, Professionalism, and Democracy," 46 *Boston College Law Review* 989 (2005).

Minsky, Hyman P., "Capitalist Financial Processes and the Instability of Capitalism," 14 *Journal of Economic Issues* 505 (1980).

Minsky, Hyman P., "The Evolution of Financial Institutions and the Performance of the Economy," 20 *Journal of Economic Issues* 345 (1986).

Mitchell, Lawrence E., "A Theoretical and Practical Framework for Enforcing Corporate Constituency Statutes," 70 *Texas Law Review* 579 (1992).

Mitchell, Lawrence E., "Trust. Contract. Process," in *Progressive Corporate Law* (Lawrence E. Mitchell ed.) (Westview Press 1995).

Miwa, Yoshiro, and J. Mark Ramseyer, *The Fable of the Keiretsu: Urban Legends of the Japanese Economy* (University of Chicago Press 2006).

Miyajima, Hideaki, and Fumiaki Kuroki, "The Unwinding of Cross-shareholding in Japan: Causes, Effects, and Implications," in *Corporate Governance in Japan: Institutional Change and Organizational Diversity* (Masahiko Aoki et al. eds.) (Oxford University Press 2007).

Mnookin, Robert H., and Lewis Kornhauser, "Bargaining in the Shadow of the Law: The Case of Divorce," 88 *Yale Law Journal* 950 (1979).

Modigliani, Franco, and Merton H. Miller, "The Cost of Capital, Corporation Finance and the Theory of Investment," 48 *American Economic Review* 261 (1958).

Monsma, David, and John Buckley, "Non-Financial Corporate Performance: The Material Edges of Social and Environmental Disclosure," 11 *University of Baltimore Journal of Environmental Law* 151 (2004).

Monteleone, Joseph P., and Nicholas J. Conca, "Directors and Officers Indemnification and Liability Insurance: An Overview of Legal and Practical Issues," 51 *Business Lawyer* 573 (1996).

Mooney, Charles W., Jr., "Judgment Proofing, Bankruptcy Policy, and the Dark Side of Tort Liability," 52 *Stanford Law Review* 73 (1999).

Morck, Randall K. (ed.), *A History of Corporate Governance Around the World: Family Business Groups to Professional Managers* ((University of Chicago Press 2005).

Morck, Randall, and Masao Nakamura, "Banks and Corporate Control in Japan," 54 *Journal of Finance* 319 (1999).

Morck, Randall, Daniel Wolfenzon, and Bernard Yeung, "Corporate Governance, Economic Entrenchment, and Growth," 43 *Journal of Economic Literature* 655 (2005).

Moriarty, Jeffrey, "Do CEOs Get Paid Too Much?" 15 *Business Ethics Quarterly* 257 (2005).

Morgenson, Gretchen, and Joshua Rosner, *Reckless Endangerment: How Outsized Ambition, Greed, and Corruption Led to Economic Armageddon* (Times Books 2011).

Morroni, Mario, *Knowledge, Scale, and Transactions in the Theory of the Firm* (Cambridge University Press 2006).

Mueller, Dennis C., and Elizabeth A. Reardon, "Rates of Return on Corporate Investment," 60 *Southern Economic Journal* 430 (1993).

Müller-Freienfels, Wolfram, "Law of Agency," 6 *American Journal of Comparative Law* 165 (1957).

Müller-Freienfels, Wolfram, "Legal Relations in the Law of Agency: Power of Agency and Commercial Certainty," 13 *American Journal of Comparative Law* 193 (1964).

Munzer, Stephen R., *A Theory of Property* (Cambridge University Press 1990).

Murmann, John Peter, *Knowledge and Competitive Advantage: The Coevolution of Firms, Technology, and National Institutions* (Cambridge University Press 2003).

Murphy, Liam, and Thomas Nagel, *The Myth of Ownership: Taxes and Justice* (Oxford University Press 2002).

Murray, J. Haskell, and Edward I. Hwang, "Purpose with Profit: Governance, Enforcement, Capital-Raising and Capital-Locking in Low-Profit Limited Liability Companies," 66 *University of Miami Law Review* 1 (2011).

Naffine, Ngaire, "Who are the Law's Persons? From Cheshire Cats to Responsible Subjects," 66 *Modern Law Review* 346 (2003).

Naughton, Barry, *The Chinese Economy: Transitions and Growth* (MIT Press 2007).

Neeley, Concha R., and Nancy G. Boyd, "The Influence of Executive Compensation on Employee Behaviors Through Precipitating Events," 22 *Journal of Managerial Issues* 546 (2010).

Nelson, Richard R., *Technology, Institutions, and Economic Growth* (Harvard University Press 2005).

Nicholls, Alex, "Institutionalizing Social Entrepreneurship in Regulatory Space: Reporting and Disclosure by Community Interest Companies," 35 *Accounting, Organizations, and Society* 394 (2010).

Nonaka, Ikujiro, Ryoko Tayama, and Toru Hirata, *Managing Flow: A Process Theory of the Knowledge-Based Firm* (Palgrave Macmillan 2008).

Nonet, Philippe, and Philip Selznick, *Law and Society in Transition: Toward Responsive Law* (Harper and Row 1978).

Note, "Constitutional Rights of the Corporate Person," 91 *Yale Law Journal* 1641 (1982).

Note, "Developments in the Law—Corporate Crime: Regulating Corporate Behavior through Criminal Sanctions," 92 *Harvard Law Review* 1227 (1979).

Note, "The Expanding Scope of Enterprise Liability," 69 *Columbia Law Review* 1084 (1969).

Note, "Investor Liability: Financial Innovations in the Regulatory State and the Coming Revolution in Corporate Law," 107 *Harvard Law Review* 1941 (1994).

Note, "Liability of a Corporation for Acts of a Subsidiary or Affiliate," 71 *Harvard Law Review* 1122 (1958).

Note, "The Price of Everything, the Value of Nothing: Reframing the Commodification Debate," 117 *Harvard Law Review* 689 (2003).

Note, "Should Shareholders Be Personally Liable for the Torts of Their Corporations?" 76 *Yale Law Journal* 1190 (1967).

Note, "What We Talk About When We Talk About Persons: The Language of a Legal Fiction," 114 *Harvard Law Review* 1745 (2001).

Novemsky, Nathan, and Daniel Kahneman, "The Boundaries of Loss Aversion," 42 *Journal of Marketing Research* 119 (2005).

Oesterle, Dale A., "Limits on a Corporation's Protection of Its Directors and Officers from Personal Liability," 1983 *Wisconsin Law Review* 513 (1983).

Oesterle, Dale A., "The Collapse of Fannie Mae and Freddie Mac: Victims or Villains?" 5 *Entrepreneurial Business Law Journal* 733 (2010).

Oh, Peter B., "Veil-Piercing," 89 *Texas Law Review* 81 (2010).

Oi, Jean C., *Rural China Takes Off: Institutional Foundations of Economic Reform* (University of California Press 1999).

Olsen, Frances, "Constitutional Law: Feminist Critiques of the Public/Private Distinction," 10 *Constitutional Commentary* 319 (1993).

Olson, John F., et al., *Director and Officer Liability: Indemnification and Insurance* (Clark Boardman Callaghan 2010).

Orts, Eric W., "Beyond Shareholders: Interpreting Corporate Constituency Statutes," 61 *George Washington Law Review* 14 (1992).

Orts, Eric W., "The Complexity and Legitimacy of Corporate Law," 50 *Washington and Lee Law Review* 1565 (1993).

Orts, Eric W., "The Legitimacy of Multinational Corporations," in *Progressive Corporate Law* (Lawrence E. Mitchell ed.) (Westview Press 1995).

Orts, Eric W., "Reflexive Environmental Law," 89 *Northwestern University Law Review* 1227 (1995).

Orts, Eric W., "Shirking and Sharking: A Legal Theory of the Firm," 16 *Yale Law and Policy Review* 265 (1998).

Orts, Eric W., "The Future of Enterprise Organization," 96 *Michigan Law Review* 1947 (2001) (book review).

Orts, Eric W., "War and the Business Corporation," 35 *Vanderbilt Journal of Transnational Law* 549 (2002).

Orts, Eric W., "From Corporate Social Responsibility to Global Citizenship," in *The INSEAD-Wharton Alliance on Globalizing: Strategies for Building Successful Global Businesses* (Hubert Gatignon and John Kimberly eds.) (Cambridge University Press 2004).

Orts, Eric W., "Ethics, Risk, Environmental Management, and Corporate Social Responsibility," in *Environmental Protection and the Social Responsibility of Firms: Perspectives from Law, Economics, and Business* (Bruce L. Hay, Robert N. Stavins, and Richard H.K. Vietor eds.) (Resources for the Future Press 2005).

Orts, Eric W., and Alan Strudler, "The Ethical and Environmental Limits of Stakeholder Theory," 12 *Business Ethics Quarterly* 215 (2002).

Orts, Eric W., and Alan Strudler, "Putting a Stake in Stakeholder Theory," 88 *Journal of Business Ethics* 605 (2009).

Paine, Lynn Sharp, *Value Shift: Why Companies Must Merge Social and Financial Imperatives to Achieve Superior Performance* (McGraw-Hill 2003).

Paredes, Troy A., "The Firm and the Nature of Control: Toward a Theory of Takeover Law," 29 *Journal of Corporation Law* 103 (2003).

Parfit, Derek, *On What Matters*, vol. 1 (Oxford University Press 2011).

Pargendler, Mariana, "State Ownership and Corporate Governance," 80 *Fordham Law Review* 2917 (2012).

Park, Jun Sun, "A Comparative Study of D&O Liability Insurance in the U.S. and South Korea: Protecting Directors and Officers from Securities Litigation," 10 *Chicago-Kent Journal of International and Comparative Law* 1 (2010).

Parkinson, J.E., *Corporate Power and Responsibility: Issues in the Theory of Company Law* (Oxford University Press 1993).

Partnoy, Frank, "Financial Innovation in Corporate Law," 31 *Journal of Corporate Law* 799 (2006).

Partnoy, Frank, "Shapeshifting Corporations," 76 *University of Chicago Law Review* 261 (2009).

Peattie, Ken, and Adrian Morley, "Eight Paradoxes of the Social Enterprise Research Agenda," 4 *Social Enterprise Journal* 91 (2008).

Penrose, Edith, *The Theory of the Growth of the Firm* (Oxford University Press, 3rd ed., 1995).

Perotti, Enrico, "Cross-Ownership as a Hostage Exchange to Support Collaboration," 13 *Managerial and Decision Economics* 45 (1992).

Perrow, Charles, *Complex Organizations: A Critical Essay* (Random House, 3rd ed., 1986).

Perry, James L., and Hal G. Rainey, "The Public–Private Distinction in Organization Theory: A Critique and Research Strategy," 13 *Academy of Management Review* 182 (1988).

Pettit, Philip, "Responsibility Incorporated," 117 *Ethics* 171 (2007).

Pettit, Philip, *Made with Words: Hobbes on Language, Mind, and Politics* (Princeton University Press 2008).

Phillips, Michael J., "Reappraising the Real Entity Theory of the Corporation," 21 *Florida State University Law Review* 1061 (1994).

Phillips-Fein, Kim, *Invisible Hands: The Businessmen's Crusade Against the New Deal* (W.W. Norton 2009).

Pierson, Paul, "Increasing Returns, Path Dependence, and the Study of Politics," 94 *American Political Science Review* 251 (2000).

Pierson, Paul, and Theda Skocpol, "Historical Institutionalism in Contemporary Political Science," in *Political Science: The State of the Discipline* (Ira Katznelson and Helen Milner eds.) (W.W. Norton 2004).

Polanyi, Karl, *The Great Transformation: The Political and Economic Origins of Our Times* (Beacon Press 1944).

Popper, Karl R., "What Is Dialectic?" 49 *Mind* 403 (1940).

Poser, Norman S., and James A. Fanto, *Broker–Dealer Law and Regulation* (Aspen, 4th ed., 2011).

Posner, Richard A., "The Rights of Creditors of Affiliated Corporations," 43 *University of Chicago Law Review* 499 (1976).

Posner, Richard A., *Economic Analysis of Law* (Aspen, 7th ed., 2007).

Posner, Richard A., *A Failure of Capitalism: The Crisis of '08 and the Descent into Depression* (Harvard University Press 2009).

Posner, Richard A., *The Crisis of Capitalist Democracy* (Harvard University Press 2010).

Powell, Walter W., and Paul J. DiMaggio (eds.), *The New Institutionalism in Organizational Analysis* (University of Chicago Press 1991).

Presser, Stephen B., *Piercing the Corporate Veil* (Clark, Boardman, Callaghan 1992).

Presser, Stephen B., "The Bogalusa Explosion, 'Single Business Enterprise,' 'Alter Ego,' and Other Errors: Academics, Economics, Democracy, and Shareholder Limited Liability," 100 *Northwestern University Law Review* 405 (2006).

Priest, George L., "The Invention of Enterprise Liability: A Critical History of the Intellectual Foundations of Modern Tort Law," 14 *Journal of Legal Studies* 461 (1985).

Prowse, Stephen D., "The Structure of Corporate Ownership in Japan," 47 *Journal of Finance* 1121 (1992).

Przeworski, Adam, and Fernando Limongi, "Political Regimes and Economic Growth," 7 *Journal of Economic Perspectives* 51 (1993).

Puchniak, Dan W., "The Efficiency of Friendliness: Japanese Corporate Governance Succeeds Again Without Hostile Takeovers," 5 *Berkeley Business Law Journal* 195 (2008).

Quine, W.V., *Ontological Relativity and Other Essays* (Columbia University Press 1969).

Racette, George A., "Earnings Retention, New Capital and the Growth of the Firm: A Comment," 55 *Review of Economics and Statistics* 127 (1973).

Radin, Max, "The Endless Problem of Corporate Personality," 32 *Columbia Law Review* 643 (1932).

Radin, Tara J., and Patricia H. Werhane, "The Public/Private Distinction and the Political Status of Employment," 34 *American Business Law Journal* 245 (1996).

Rainey, Hal G., and Barry Bozeman, "Comparing Public and Private Organizations: Empirical Research and the Power of the A Priori," 10 *Journal of Public Administration Research and Theory* 447 (2000).

Rajan, Raghuram G., and Luigi Zingales, "Power in a Theory of the Firm," 113 *Quarterly Journal of Economics* 387 (1998).

Rajan, Raghuram G., and Luigi Zingales, "The Influence of the Financial Revolution on the Nature of Firms," 91 *American Economic Review* 206 (2001).

Rajan, Raghuram G., and Luigi Zingales, "The Firm as a Dedicated Hierarchy: A Theory of the Origins and Growth of Firms," 116 *Quarterly Journal of Economics* 805 (2001).

Rao, Vithala R., Manoj K. Agarwaland, and Denise Dahlhoff, "How Is Manifest Branding Strategy Related to the Intangible Value of a Corporation?" 68 *Journal of Marketing* 126 (2004).

Raz, Keren G., "Toward an Improved Legal Form for Social Enterprise," 36 *New York University Review of Law & Social Change* 283 (2012).

Redding, Stephen, "Path Dependence, Endogenous Innovation, and Growth," 43 *International Economic Review* 1215 (2002).

Reich, Robert B., *The Work of Nations: Preparing Ourselves for 21st Century Capitalism* (Alfred A. Knopf 1991).

Reiser, Dana Brakman, "For-Profit Philanthropy," 77 *Fordham Law Review* 2437 (2009).

Reiser, Dana Brakman, "Governing and Financing Blended Enterprise," 85 *Chicago-Kent Law Review* 619 (2010).

Reiser, Dana Brakman, "Benefit Corporations—A Sustainable Form of Organization?" 46 *Wake Forest Law Review* 591 (2011).

Reiser, Dana Brakman, "Charity Law's Essentials," 86 *Notre Dame Law Review* 1 (2011).

Reiss, David, "Fannie Mae and Freddie Mac and the Future of Federal Housing Finance Policy: A Study of Regulatory Privilege," 61 *Alabama Law Review* 907 (2010).

Rhee, Robert J., "Bonding Limited Liability," 51 *William and Mary Law Review* 1417 (2010).

Ribstein, Larry E., "The Constitutional Conception of the Corporation," 4 *Supreme Court Economic Review* 95 (1995).

Ribstein, Larry E., "Why Corporations?" 1 *Berkeley Business Law Journal* 183 (2004).

Ribstein, Larry E., "Reverse Limited Liability and the Design of Business Associations," 30 *Delaware Journal of Corporate Law* 199 (2005).

Ripken, Susanna Kim, "Corporate First Amendment Rights After *Citizens United*: An Analysis of the Popular Movement to End the Constitutional Personhood of Corporations," 14 *University of Pennsylvania Journal of Business Law* 20 (2011).

Robé, Jean-Phillipe, "The Legal Structure of the Firm," 1 *Accounting, Economics, and Law: A Convivium* (2011) (article 5).

Roberts, John, *The Modern Firm: Organizational Design for Performance and Growth* (Oxford University Press 2004).

Robertson, D.H., *The Control of Industry* (Nisbet and Co. 1923).

Rock, Edward B., "Corporate Law through an Antitrust Lens," 92 *Columbia Law Review* 497 (1992).

Rock, Edward B., and Michael L. Wachter "Islands of Conscious Power: Law, Norms, and the Self-Governing Corporation," 149 *University of Pennsylvania Law Review* 1619 (2001).

Rodrigues, Usha, "Entity and Identity," 60 *Emory Law Journal* 1257 (2011).

Rodrik, Dani, *One Economics, Many Recipes: Globalization, Institutions, and Economic Growth* (Princeton University Press 2007).

Roe, Mark J., "A Political Theory of American Corporate Finance," 91 *Columbia Law Review* 10 (1991).

Roe, Mark J., "Some Differences in Corporate Structure in Germany, Japan, and the United States," 102 *Yale Law Journal* 1927 (1993).

Roe, Mark J., "Political Preconditions to Separating Ownership from Corporate Control," 53 *Stanford Law Review* 539 (2000).

Roe, Mark J., "The Shareholder Wealth Maximization Norm and Industrial Organization," 149 *University of Pennsylvania Law Review* 2063 (2001).

Romano, Roberta, "Metapolitics and Corporate Law Reform," 36 *Stanford Law Review* 923 (1984).

Romano, Roberta, "The Political Economy of Takeover Statutes," 73 *Virginia Law Review* 111 (1987).

Romano, Roberta, "Answering the Wrong Question: The Tenuous Case for Mandatory Corporate Laws," 89 *Columbia Law Review* 1599 (1989).

Romano, Roberta, *The Genius of American Corporate Law* (AEI Press 1993).

Ross, Stephen A., "The Economic Theory of Agency: The Principal's Problem," 63 *American Economic Review* 134 (1973).

Roubini, Nouriel, and Stephen Mihm, *Crisis Economics: A Crash Course in the Future of Finance* (Penguin Press 2010).

Royce, Josiah, *The Philosophy of Loyalty* (Vanderbilt University Press 1995) (1908).

Ruskola, Teemu, "Conceptualizing Corporations and Kinship: Comparative Law and Development Theory in a Chinese Perspective," 52 *Stanford Law Review* 1599 (2000).

Rutledge, Thomas E., and Ellisa O. Habbart, "The Uniform Statutory Trust Entity Act: A Review," 65 *Business Lawyer* 1055 (2010).

Sachs, Benjamin I., "Unions, Corporations, and Political Opt-Out Rights after *Citizens United*," 112 *Columbia Law Review* 800 (2012).

Saleh, Nabil, "Arab International Corporations: The Impact of the Shari'a," 8 *Arab Law Quarterly* 179 (1993).

Sandel, Michael J., *What Money Can't Buy: The Moral Limits of Markets* (Farrar, Straus and Giroux 2012).

Satz, Debra, *Why Some Things Should Not Be for Sale* (Oxford University Press 2010).

Saveland, Todd D., Note, "FedEx's New 'Employees': Their Disgruntled Independent Contractors," 36 *Transportation Law Journal* 95 (2009).

Scanlon, T.M., "Promises and Contracts," in *The Theory of Contract Law: New Essays* (Peter Benson ed.) (Cambridge University Press 2001).

Schane, Sanford A., "The Corporation Is a Person: The Language of Legal Fiction," 61 *Tulane Law Review* 563 (1987).

Schauer, Frederick, *Playing By the Rules: A Philosophical Examination of Rule-Based Decision-Making in Law and in Life* (Oxford University Press 1993).

Schauer, Frederick, *Thinking Like a Lawyer: A New Introduction to Legal Reasoning* (Harvard University Press 2009).

Scheppele, Kim Lane, "'It's Just Not Right': The Ethics of Insider Trading," 56 *Law and Contemporary Problems* 123 (1993).

Schlunk, Herwig J., "The Zen of Corporate Capital Structure Neutrality," 99 *Michigan Law Review* 410 (2000).

Schmidt, Elizabeth, "Vermont's Social Hybrid Pioneers: Early Observations and Questions To Ponder," 35 *Vermont Law Review* 163 (2010).

Schoenhard, Paul M., "A Three-Dimensional Approach to the Public–Private Distinction," 2008 *Utah Law Review* 635 (2008).

Schumacher, E.F., *Small Is Beautiful: Economics as if People Mattered* (Harley and Marks 2000) (1975).

Schumpeter, Joseph A., "The Creative Response in Economic History," 7 *Journal of Economic History* 149 (1947).

Schwarcz, Stephen L., "The Inherent Irrationality of Judgment Proofing," 52 *Stanford Law Review* 1 (1999).

Schwartz, Gary T., "The Hidden and Fundamental Issue of Employer Vicarious Liability," 69 *Southern California Law Review* 1739 (1996).

Schwartz, Nancy L., "Distinction Between Public and Private Life: Marx on the Zoōn Politicon," 7 *Political Theory* 245 (1979).

Scott, James C., *Seeing Like a State: How Certain Schemes to Improve the Human Condition Have Failed* (Yale University Press 1998).

Scott, W. Richard, *Institutions and Organizations* (Sage, 2nd ed., 2001).

Scruton, Roger, and John Finnis, "Corporate Persons," 63 *Proceedings of the Aristotelian Society, Supplementary Volumes* 239 (1989).

Searle, John R., *The Construction of Social Reality* (Free Press 1995).

Seavoy, Ronald E., "The Public Service Origins of the American Business Corporation," 52 *Business History Review* 30 (1978).

Seidman, Louis Michael, "Critical Constitutionalism Now," 75 *Fordham Law Review* 575 (2006).

Selznick, Philip, *Leadership in Administration: A Sociological Interpretation* (University of California Press 1958).

Sen, Amartya, *Development as Freedom* (Knopf 1999).

Sepe, Simone M., "Directors' Duty to Creditors and the Debt Contract," 1 *Journal of Business and Technology Law* 553 (2007).

Sepinwall, Amy J., "*Citizens United* and the Ineluctable Question of Corporate Citizenship," 44 *Connecticut Law Review* 575 (2012).

Sertial, Heather, Note, "Hybrid Entities: Distributing Profits with a Purpose," 17 *Fordham Journal of Corporate & Financial Law* 261 (2012).

Shahabian, Matthew R., Note, "The Government as Shareholder and Political Risk: Procedural Protections in the Bailout," 86 *New York University Law Review* 351 (2011).

Shell, G. Richard, *Make the Rules or Your Rivals Will* (Crown Business 2004).

Shelledy, David, "Autonomy, Debate, and Corporate Speech," 18 *Hastings Constitutional Law Quarterly* 541 (1991).

Siegel, Jeremy J., *Stocks for the Long Run* (McGraw-Hill, 4th ed., 2007).

Siegel, Jeremy J., and Richard H. Thaler, "Anomalies: The Equity Premium Puzzle," 11 *Journal of Economic Perspectives* 191 (1997).

Simon, William H., "Whom (Or What) Does the Organization's Lawyer Represent? An Anatomy of Intraclient Conflict," 91 *California Law Review* 57 (2003).

Skeel, David A., "Shaming in Corporate Law," 149 *University of Pennsylvania Law Review* 1811 (2001).

Skeel, David A., *Icarus in the Boardroom: The Fundamental Flaws in Corporate America and Where They Came From* (Oxford University Press 2005).

Skeel, David A., *The New Financial Deal: Understanding the Dodd–Frank Act and Its (Unintended) Consequences* (Wiley 2011).

Smart, Bruce, *Beyond Compliance: A New Industry View of the Environment* (World Resources Institute 1992).

Smith, Bryant, "Legal Personality," 37 *Yale Law Journal* 283 (1928).

Smith, D. Gordon, "The Shareholder Primacy Norm," 23 *Journal of Corporation Law* 277 (1998).

Smith, Stephen A., *Contract Theory* (Oxford University Press 2004).

Smith, Thomas A., "The Efficient Norm for Corporate Law: A Neotraditional Interpretation of Fiduciary Duty," 98 *Michigan Law Review* 214 (1999).

Smith, Young B., "Frolic and Detour," 23 *Columbia Law Review* 444 (1923).

Soifer, Aviam, "Reviewing Legal Fictions," 20 *Georgia Law Review* 871 (1986).

Solomon, Lewis D., and Melissa B. Kirgis, "Business Cooperatives: A Primer," 6 *DePaul Business Law Journal* 233 (1994).

Solove, Daniel J., "Conceptualizing Privacy," 90 *California Law Review* 1087 (2002).

Soltow, James H., "The Entrepreneur in Economic History," 58 *American Economic Review* 84 (1968).

Sombart, Werner, "Medieval and Modern Commercial Enterprise," in *Enterprise and Secular Change: Readings in Economic History* (Frederic C. Lane, ed.) (Richard D. Irwin, Inc., 1953).

Speth, James Gustave, *The Bridge at the End of the World: Capitalism, the Environment, and Crossing from Crisis to Sustainability* (Yale University Press 2008).

Squire, Richard, "Strategic Liability in the Corporate Group," 78 *University of Chicago Law Review* 605 (2011).

Starr, Paul, "The Meaning of Privatization," 6 *Yale Law and Policy Review* 6 (1988).

Starr, Paul, *Freedom's Power: The True Force of Liberalism* (Basic Books 2007).

Statman, Meir, and Denys Glushkov, "The Wages of Social Responsibility," 65 *Financial Analysts Journal* 33 (2009).

Stauss, Karl E., Note, "Indemnification in Delaware: Balancing Policy Goals and Liabilities," 29 *Delaware Journal of Corporate Law* 143 (2004).

Steinfeld, Edward S., *Forging Reform in China: The Fate of State-Owned Industry* (Cambridge University Press 1998).

Stinchcombe, Arthur L., "On the Virtues of the Old Institutionalism," 23 *Annual Review of Sociology* 1 (1997).

Stinchcombe, Arthur L., *When Formality Works: Authority and Abstraction in Law and Organizations* (University of Chicago Press 2001).

Stone, Christopher D., "The Place of Enterprise Liability in the Control of Corporate Conduct," 90 *Yale Law Journal* 1 (1980).

Stone, Christopher D., "Corporate Vices and Corporate Virtues: Do Public/Private Distinctions Matter?" 130 *University of Pennsylvania Law Review* 1441 (1982).

Stout, Lynn A., "Bad and Not-So-Bad Arguments for Shareholder Primacy," 75 *Southern California Law Review* 1189 (2002).

Stout, Lynn A., "Why We Should Stop Teaching *Dodge v. Ford*," 3 *Virginia Law and Business Review* 163 (2008).

Stout, Lynn A., *The Shareholder Value Myth: How Putting Shareholders First Harms Investors, Corporations, and the Public* (Berrett-Koehler Publishers 2012).

Strudler, Alan, "Confucian Skepticism about Workplace Rights," 18 *Business Ethics Quarterly* 67 (2008).

Strudler, Alan, and Eric W. Orts, "Moral Principle in the Law of Insider Trading," 78 *Texas Law Review* 375 (1999).

Sturm, Susan, "Second Generation Employment Discrimination: A Structural Approach," 101 *Columbia Law Review* 458 (2001).

Sugarman, David, and Gunther Teubner (eds.), *Regulating Corporate Groups in Europe* (Nomos 1990).

Sullivan, Scott M., "Private Force/Public Goods," 42 *Connecticut Law Review* 853 (2010).

Summers, Robert S., *Form and Function in a Legal System: A General Study* (Cambridge University Press 2005).

Sweeney, Matthew, Note, "Foreign Direct Investment in India and China: The Creation of a Balanced Regime in a Globalized Economy," 43 *Cornell International Law Journal* 207 (2010).

Sykes, Alan O., "The Economics of Vicarious Liability," 93 *Yale Law Journal* 1231 (1984).

Symposium, "LLCs, LLPs and the Evolving Corporate Form," 66 *University of Colorado Law Review* 855 (1995).

Syverud, Kent D., "On the Demand for Liability Insurance," 72 *Texas Law Review* 1629 (1994).

Teles, Steven M., *The Rise of the Conservative Legal Movement: The Battle for Control of the Law* (Princeton University Press 2008).

Templin, Benjamin A., "The Government Shareholder: Regulating Public Ownership of Private Enterprise," 62 *Administrative Law Review* 1127 (2010).

Teubner, Gunther, "Substantive and Reflexive Elements in Modern Law," 17 *Law and Society Review* 239 (1983).

Teubner, Gunther, "Enterprise Corporatism: New Industrial Policy and the 'Essence' of the Legal Person," 36 *American Journal of Comparative Law* 130 (1988).

Teubner, Gunther, "'And God Laughed . . .' Indeterminacy, Self-Reference and Paradox in Law," 12 *German Law Journal* 376 (2011).

Thaler, Richard H., and Cass R. Sunstein, *Nudge: Improving Decisions about Health, Wealth, and Happiness* (Yale University Press 2008).

Thomas, Randall S., Stewart J. Schwab, and Robert G. Hansen, "Megafirms," 80 *North Carolina Law Review* 115 (2001).

Thomas, Randall S., and Harwell Wells, "Executive Compensation in the Courts: Board Capture, Optimal Contracting, and Officers' Fiduciary Duties," 95 *Minnesota Law Review* 846 (2011).

Thompson, Dennis F., *Restoring Responsibility: Ethics in Government, Business, and Healthcare* (Cambridge University Press 2005).

Thompson, Robert B., "Piercing the Corporate Veil: An Empirical Study," 76 *Cornell Law Review* 1036 (1991).

Thompson, Robert B., "Unpacking Limited Liability: Direct and Vicarious Liability of Corporate Participants for Torts of the Enterprise," 47 *Vanderbilt Law Review* 1 (1994).

Thompson, Robert B., "Piercing the Veil Within Corporate Groups: Corporate Shareholders as Mere Investors," 13 *Connecticut Journal of International Law* 379 (1999).

Thompson, Robert B., "Agency Law and Asset Partitioning," 71 *University of Cincinnati Law Review* 1321 (2003).

Tillman, Rick, *Thorstein Veblen and His Critics, 1891–1963: Conservative, Liberal, and Radical Perspectives* (Princeton University Press 1992).

Toninelli, Pier Angelo (ed.), *The Rise and Fall of the State-Owned Enterprise in the Western World* (Cambridge University Press 2000).

Trebilcock, Michael J., *The Limits of Freedom of Contract* (Harvard University Press 1993).

Triantis, George G., and Ronald J. Daniels, "The Role of Debt in Interactive Corporate Governance," 83 *California Law Review* 1073 (1995).

Tribe, Laurence H., *American Constitutional Law* (Foundation Press, 2nd ed., 1988).

Tribe, Laurence H., "The Curvature of Constitutional Space: What Lawyers Can Learn From Modern Physics," 103 *Harvard Law Review* 1 (1989).

Tribe, Laurence H., *American Constitutional Law*, vol. 1 (Foundation Press, 3rd ed., 1999).

Tsai, Kellee S., *Capitalism without Democracy: The Private Sector in Contemporary China* (Cornell University Press 2007).

Tung, Frederick, "The New Death of Contract: Creeping Corporate Fiduciary Duties for Creditors," 57 *Emory Law Journal* 809 (2008).

Tuomela, Raimo, *The Importance of Us: A Philosophical Study of Basic Social Notions* (Stanford University Press 1995).

Turkel, Gerald, "The Public/Private Distinction: Approaches to a Critique of Legal Ideology," 22 *Law and Society Review* 801 (1988).

Udehn, Lars, *Methodological Individualism: Background, History and Meaning* (Routledge 2001).

Useem, Michael, "Business Restructuring, Management Control, and Corporate Organization," 19 *Theory and Society* 681 (1990).

Useem, Michael, *Investor Capitalism: How Money Managers Are Changing the Face of Corporate America* (Basic Books 1999).

Useem, Michael, *Leading Up: How to Lead Your Boss So You Both Win* (Crown Business 2003).

Vagts, Detlev, "Challenges to Executive Compensation: For the Market or the Courts?" 8 *Journal of Corporation Law* 231 (1983).

Vagts, Detlev, "The Governance of the Multinational," 23 *Wisconsin International Law Journal* 525 (2005).

Vagts, Detlev, "The Financial Meltdown and its International Implications," 103 *American Journal of International Law* 684 (2009).

Vandekerckhove, Karen, *Piercing the Corporate Veil* (Kluwer Law International 2007).

Vandenbergh, Michael P., "The Private Life of Public Law," 105 *Columbia Law Review* 2029 (2005).

Veasey, E. Norman, and Christine T. Di Guglielmo, "The Tensions, Stresses, and Professional Responsibilities of the Lawyer for the Corporation," 62 *Business Lawyer* 1 (2006).

Veblen, Thorstein, *The Theory of the Business Enterprise* (Mentor 1932) (1904).

Veblen, Thorstein, *Absentee Ownership: Business Enterprise in Recent Times: The Case of America* (Transaction Publishers 1997) (1923).

Verret, J.W., "Treasury Inc.: How the Bailout Reshapes Corporate Theory and Practice," 27 *Yale Journal on Regulation* 283 (2010).

Vincens, John R., "On the Demise of Double Liability of Bank Shareholders," 75 *Banking Law Journal* 213 (1958).

Vincent, Andrew, "Can Groups Be Persons?" 42 *Review of Metaphysics* 687 (1989).

Vining, Joseph, *Legal Identity: The Coming of Age of Public Law* (Yale University Press 1978).

Vining, Joseph, *From Newton's Sleep* (Princeton University Press 1995).

Vinogradoff, Paul, "Juridical Persons," 24 *Columbia Law Review* 594 (1924).

Waldron, Jeremy, *The Right to Private Property* (Oxford University Press 1988).

Walker, Richard, "A Requiem for Corporate Geography: New Directions in Industrial Organization, the Production of Place and the Uneven Development," 71 *Geografiska Annaler: Series B, Human Geography* 43 (1989).

Wallace, David Foster, *The Pale King: An Unfinished Novel* (Back Bay Books 2012).

Waller, Spencer Webb, "The Law and Economics Virus," 31 *Cardozo Law Review* 367 (2009).

Wallis, John Joseph, "Constitutions, Corporations, and Corruption: American States and Constitutional Change, 1842 to 1852," 65 *Journal of Economic History* 211 (2005).

Walzer, Michael, *Spheres of Justice: A Defense of Pluralism and Equality* (Basic Books 1992).

Walzer, Michael, *Just and Unjust Wars: A Moral Argument with Historical Illustrations* (Basic Books, 4th ed., 2006).

Weber, Max, *Economy and Society* (Guenther Roth and Claus Wittich eds.) (University of California Press 1978) (two volumes).

Wells, Harwell, "The Cycles of Corporate Social Responsibility: An Historical Retrospective for the Twenty-First Century," 51 *University of Kansas Law Review* 77 (2002).

Wells, Harwell, "'No Man Can Be Worth $1,000,000 A Year': The Fight Over Executive Compensation in 1930s America," 44 *University of Richmond Law Review* 689 (2010).

Wells, Harwell, "The Birth of Corporate Governance," 33 *Seattle University Law Review* 1247 (2010).

White, James Boyd, "How Should We Talk About Corporations? The Languages of Economics and of Citizenship," 94 *Yale Law Journal* 1416 (1985).

White, James J., "Corporate Judgment Proofing: A Response to Lynn LoPucki's The Death of Liability," 107 *Yale Law Journal* 1363 (1998).

Whittington, Geoffrey, "The Profitability of Retained Earnings," 54 *Review of Economics and Statistics* 152 (1972).

Whittington, Geoffrey, "The Profitability of Alternative Sources of Finance—Some Further Evidence," 60 *Review of Economics and Statistics* 632 (1978).

Widen, William H., "Corporate Form and Substantive Consolidation," 75 *George Washington Law Review* 237 (2007).

Wilkins, Mira, "The Neglected Intangible Asset: The Influence of the Trade Mark on the Rise of the Modern Corporation," 34 *Business History* 66 (1992).

Williams, Cynthia A., "The Securities and Exchange Commission and Corporate Social Transparency," 112 *Harvard Law Review* 1197 (1999).

Williams, Glanville, "Vicarious Liability and the Master's Indemnity," 20 *Modern Law Review* 220, 437 (1957) (two articles).

Williamson, Oliver E., *The Economic Institutions of Capitalism: Firms, Markets, Relational Contracting* (Free Press 1998).

Williamson, Oliver E., "Transaction Cost Economics: The Natural Progression," 100 *American Economic Review* 673 (2010).

Williamson, Oliver E., and Scott E. Masten (eds.), *The Economics of Transaction Costs* (Edward Elgar 1999).

Williston, Samuel, "History of the Law of Business Corporations Before 1800," 2 *Harvard Law Review* 105 (1888).

Winter, Sidney G., "On Coase, Competence, and the Corporation," in *The Nature of the Firm: Origins, Evolution, and Development* (Oliver E. Williamson and Sidney G. Winter eds.) (Oxford University Press 1991).

Wittengenstein, Ludwig, *Philosophical Investigations* (G.E.M. Anscombe trans.) (Blackwell Publishing, 3rd ed., 2001).

Woolhandler, Ann, "Public Rights, Private Rights, and Statutory Retroactivity," 94 *Georgetown Law Journal* 1015 (2006).

Wormser, I. Maurice, "Piercing the Veil of Corporate Entity," 12 *Columbia Law Review* 496 (1912).

Wormser, I. Maurice, *Frankenstein, Incorporated* (McGraw-Hill 1931).

Wright, R. George, "The Illusion of Simplicity: An Explanation for Why the Law Can't Just Be Less Complex," 27 *Florida State University Law Review* 715 (2000).

Zahraa, Mahdi, "Legal Personality in Islamic Law," 10 *Arab Law Quarterly* 193 (1995).

Zaring, David, "The Post-Crisis and Its Critics," 12 *University of Pennsylvania Journal of Business Law* 1169 (2010).

Zaring, David, and Steven M. Davidoff, "Regulation by Deal: The Government's Response to the Financial Crisis," 61 *Administrative Law Review* 463 (2009).

Zheng, Yongnian, *Globalization and State Transformation in China* (Cambridge University Press 2004).

Zingales, Luigi, "Corporate Governance," reprinted in *The Economic Nature of the Firm: A Reader* (Randall S. Kroszner and Louis Putterman eds.) (Cambridge University Press, 3rd ed., 2009).

Zunz, Olivier, *Philanthropy in America: A History* (Princeton University Press 2012).

Index

Page numbers suffixed with *fig* or *tab* refer to information in figures and tables respectively.

Index

Printed and bound by CPI Group (UK) Ltd, Croydon, CR0 4YY